SACRED AUSTRALIA

Essays by:

Bill Ashcroft
Deborah Bird Rose
Peter Boyle
John Bradley
Mark Brett
Frances Devlin-Glass
John Docker
Geoff Cheong
Dennis Haskell
Sudhir Kumar
Anne Marsh
Freya Mathews
Peter Murphy
Makarand R. Paranjape
Graham Seal
David Tacey
Claudia Terstappen

Sacred Australia

Post-Secular Considerations

EDITED BY

MAKARAND R. PARANJAPE

ADITYA PRAKASHAN
NEW DELHI

This publication is made possible by a grant from The Krishna Somers Foundation, Murdoch University.

First Published in 2009 by Clouds of Magellan, Melbourne.

ISBN 978-81-7742-098-2

Published by Aditya Prakashan, 2/18, Ansari Road, New Delhi – 110 002,
in association with Samvad India Foundation, New Delhi
Press: D.K Fine Arts Press, Delhi – 110 054.

To

Vin D'Cruz (1933-2008)

co-author (with Richard Steele) of *Australia's Ambivalence Towards Asia: Politics, Neo/Post-colonialism, and Fact/Fiction*
and

Vijay C. Mishra
co-author (with Bob Hodge) of *Dark Side of the Dream: Australian Literature and the Postcolonial Mind*

two outstanding scholars of Indian origin
who have loved, lived in, and contributed immensely to an understanding of Australia

CONTENTS

Foreword

The principle of sacred/non-sacred determines the propriety, ethics, and desirability of all thoughts, actions and experiences of most human beings. The "sacred," especially in the postcolonial context, offers a way of viewing "reality" in new ways and from fresh perspectives, even as it sometimes compels us to grapple with issues of tradition and tolerance. It is thereby able to end the secular-sacred dichotomy in much of Australian studies that hitherto led to the impression that the "sacred" in Australia was hard to encounter except in the "pagan" world-view of the aboriginal people. In fact, on closer examination, we find multiple and divergent perspectives from which to view the "sacred" in the Australian context. This is evident in the present volume, an excellent collection of essays on the subject, edited by Makarand R. Paranjape. The book further fosters the realisation of the continuities and connections between ancient civilizations such as India and Australia, particularly in contemporary "post-secular" Australia which has begun to see itself as part of Asia.

Sacred Australia emerges from sustained research and discussion as well as determination and persuasion that began with Makarand's AIC Fellowship in 2005. He ventured on his own even when support was not forthcoming to make the project successful. I consider his decision to experience the sacredness of Uluru/Ayer's Rock as crucial to the understanding of the sacred in Australia. As the editor points out in his Preface the task was uphill on several counts, including that of finding a publisher in Australia. It reminds one of the problems Xavier Herbert had encountered in trying to publish *Capricornia*. In that sense, Makarand is in good company.

The book is valuable because it opens up new, innovative ways of understanding the "sacred" in Australia and expands its scope to include not only well known iconic sites such as Sydney's Opera House, but also new readings of canonical Australian writers such as Les Murray and Patrick White, or in the discussion of race issues and ecological principles found in Herbert's *Poor Fellow My Country*. The secular too can be sacrilised as the 'War Precautions Act' did in forbidding the use of ANZAC as name or part-name. Then of course we are all familiar with Australia's love of sport, not to mention cricket in particular, an obsession that has the quality of the sacred about it.

Sacred Australia is a pioneering work that brings together creative writers and scholars from diverse fields of aboriginal studies, postcolonial and literary studies, theology, philosophy, psychology, folk studies, anthropology, and more, to expose us to the fresh and creative understandings of the "sacred" in Australia. It is a contribution to Australian studies that will engage not only Australian scholars and academics but all those, including us in India, who have developed an interest in Australian studies, sometimes greater than that in the country of its origin.

Sacred Australia through its seventeen contributors is an absorbing and varied introduction which I am sure will set the path for scholars who wish to further explore and discover the potentials of study and research in the area. I consider it an exciting new contribution to the growing Indo-Australian academic cooperation and collaboration and I recommend it strongly to all scholars of Australian Studies.

Santosh K. Sareen,
Professor of English, Jawaharlal Nehru University
President, Indian Association for the Study of Australia (IASA)

Preface

Makarand R. Paranjape

1

This edited, inter-disciplinary and cross-cultural collection is probably the first volume of its kind to explore the idea of sacred Australia. It has seventeen chapters written by some of the best-known academics in this field, drawn from diverse disciplines such as literary and post-colonial studies, aboriginal studies, theology, philosophy, psychology, anthropology, folk studies, media and communications, architecture, and so on. The topics covered included ways of theorizing sacred Australia, an overview of Australian spirituality, aboriginal issues and sacred geography, the sacred in Australian poetry and fiction, Anzac, performance art, public ritual and architecture. The book contains path-breaking re-readings of seminal authors such as Les Murray and Patrick White, besides new ways of understanding one of Australia's best known buildings, the Opera House in Sydney. Most of the contributors are, of course, Australian, but some also come from the US, UK, and India. They belong to diverse persuasions including Aboriginal, Christian, Jewish, Hindu, secular, and post-secular traditions. Among the contributors are Bill Ashcroft, a major critic and post-colonial theorist; David Tacey, one of Australia's foremost commentators on spirituality; Debbie Bird Rose, renowned for her sensitive writing on aboriginal matters; Mark G. Brett, a leading Australian theologian; Dennis Haskell, a prolific poet and literary critic; Peter Boyle, one of Australia's most respected living poets; and Freya Mathews, an innovative practitioner and philosopher of the sacred.

This book may best be considered as an intervention in an already existing, but as yet nascent area of study. To that extent, it might even be considered pioneering in that it tries to clarify, broaden, and deepen our understanding in a manner which has not been attempted in one volume before. It is also multi-disciplinary and therefore offers multiple perspectives from which to view the sacred, especially in the Australian context. Having tried to describe what the book is, I should also clarify what this book is not. Needless to say, it is neither the first—nor the last word on the issue. Indeed, to my understanding, the sacred resists such clear-cut beginnings and closures. Its boundaries are not precise or definable. It is essentially an open and fluid field of inquiry. But more than subject to analysis, it is primarily an area of experience, as much to do with feeling and being, as with thinking and doing.

Not surprisingly, the post-colonial sacred is one of the least explored topics in the extensive and still growing literature on post-colonialism. That is because the post-colonial has been constituted almost normatively as a 'secular' site of inquiry. The 'repression' of the sacred in post-colonial studies, however, has led not just to serious gaps in understanding, but a certain distortion of what is one of the fundamental shaping forces of our times. In fact, one might go so far as to argue that the recent upsurge in 'terrorist' violence all over the world is caused, in part, by precisely such a lack of understanding of, and inattention to, the sacred. Australia, a major post-colonial country, has a rich scope for both an alternative post-colonialiality and an alternate notion of the sacred.

That is why the fundamental premise of our endeavour has been that this is an area that deserves to be taken seriously. In addition, the shift in emphasis from the traditional to the innovative understanding of the sacred is suggested by the subtitle, "post-secular." Secularism, which is still the dominant ideology and controlling viewpoint in academic discourse, is not without its pitfalls and limitations. By becoming a sort of master narrative in its heyday, it disallowed certain kinds of questions and debates. To that extent, it served as a thought-policeman even when it professed to keep the intellectual discourse free from authoritarian constraints and impositions. By declaring that nothing was sacred it, paradoxically, turned its own premises into a new orthodoxy. The secular itself become beyond question and thus excluded itself from scrutiny and interrogation. As many of our contributors observe, the return of the sacred, almost as the repressed Other of the secular, is not just inevitable, but long overdue. The post-secular world allows us not just to return to older pieties but, more importantly, actually challenges us to rethink both the secular and the sacred not as opposites or antagonists, but as two versions or self-imagings of our times.

But what do we mean by the sacred? The word has two primary meanings, which suggest different facets. First of all, the sacred means the holy, the venerable, that which is worthy of respect, adoration, worship, devoted or dedicated to a deity or God, that which is revered and associated with religious or spiritual practices.[1] This is the more common or usual meaning of the word.

The other meaning, which is also important, especially to our discursive rethinking, is the sense of the sacred as that which is secured against violation or interference, therefore off-limits or exclusive. This makes the sacred something that is clearly demarcated from the ordinary and the mundane, its boundaries defined such that it calls for special treatment. An extreme form of such a cordoning off renders the sacred as the "unspeakable," in effect, that which is tabooed. By such a definition, the sacred is beyond discourse or analysis. It is outside speech or conversation. Silence or symbolic language alone will suggest it. It is the ineffable or the noetic. Even naming it thus is a self-contradictory and self-defeating act. The unnameable is, after all, just another name. We would like to retain some of this transcendental quality in our discussion of the sacred, reminding ourselves often that what we speak of cannot fully be captured in words.

While this sense of the sacred aligns it with the mystical, there is another connotation, more religious and theological, that seems more dangerous. The prohibitive aspect of the sacred comes from seeing it as belonging to the domain of faith, and by extension, of dogma. The sacred by such a reckoning is beyond question or scrutiny not because it is ineffable or mystical, but because it occupies an area outside reason or discussion, prohibited from profane analysis or inquiry. Sometimes, it is believed that this area is the sole preserve of the few, the elect, the priests or theologians. In book-centric cultures, only the clergy are empowered to adjudicate in matters pertaining to the sacred. Such a view harks back to the troubled history of the fight between the sacred and the profane, between religion and science, between faith and reason. Closed to outside meddling, the sacred can become, as it has in the past, the monopoly of the few, who exercise their exclusive power over it. In

---

[1]See, for instance, 'sacred in *Dictionary.com Unabridged (v 1.1)*. Random House, Inc. 21 May 2008. <Dictionary.com http://dictionary.reference.com/browse/sacred>.

the name of the sacred, a regime of oppression and control is set up This aspect of the sacred is certainly dangerous because it pits the sacred against much that we, as modern people, hold dear, including the right to freedom of speech and thought. Such a notion of the sacred, still seen in theocratic societies, aligns it with forces of totalitarian and repression. In this book, we have tried to refrain from and resist such a notion. While we are conscious that in aboriginal society the sacred is also the secret, closed to outsiders or those without prerequisites, we consider such beliefs as self-protective rather than oppressive. So while we respect aboriginal precautions concerning it as well as see the right of groups to self-determination when it comes to their ideas of what is sacred, our idea of the sacred is not exclusive or excluding. The sacred for us is not only open, but also inviting. It draws us into its embrace. As it unfolds, it also enfolds. On proof that this is what we have tried to achieve is the plurality of both subject and approach, form and content, evident in this collection. No one point is enforced over others, as if by a fiat.

This issue of whether the sacred is open to inquiry or off-limits to all but a few becomes rather complicated when it comes to the indigenous view of what is revered and sacrosanct. Unless permitted by the original owners of the land, we are not supposed to trespass onto sacred grounds. The white settlers cannot be said to have received such permission. To that extent they are trespassers, as are their houses, buildings, institutions, including the very universities in which some of our own authors in this volume work. Post-facto permissions cannot justify earlier violence and occupation. To that extent, all that is post-aboriginal and modern is therefore an encroachment and infringement. It's legitimacy, even from a post-colonial point of view, is questionable. Yet, white Australia is a reality today, which can neither be denied nor wished away. Moreover, many in this land recognize the historical wrongs meted out to the original inhabitants of this land. They have a genuine desire to reach out to their indigenous country men and women, even if they cannot rectify the ills of a history for which they cannot be held responsible. No doubt, many aspects of the aboriginal sacred will thus remain closed to most of us, yet, in our own ways, through books, research, field trips, conversations, and insight, we will continue to try to understand that world, while respecting how we may not enter into it fully until permitted to do so. The aboriginal prohibition against interference, at least to me, is not merely the expression of a traditional insistence on the prerequisites and fitness of recipients or even an attempt to guard and perpetuate privileges, but also a defence against further spoilage and a resistance to the invasion of outsiders into the mysteries of a tribe. Therefore, such prohibitions must be distinguished from fanatical or dogmatic closures associated with more modern faith systems, where there is inadequate separation between church and state.

While trying to understand the sacred, a question that often crops up is whether something is intrinsically sacred or does our approach to it make it so? This is an old and difficult question, with ontological and epistemological implications. In this collection, we accept both the views that some things are intrinsically sacred and others may be considered sacred by the point of view of the observer. Thus, on the one hand, several essays look at what is considered sacred, either in the tradition or in the common imagination. But several other essays also consider what is not ordinarily understood as sacred and attempt to show how it may be so. Thus, we might consider the sacred from secular perspectives or examine the secular from a sacred viewpoints; such methodological plurality allows us to explore both the secular dimensions of the sacred and the sacred dimensions of the secular.

Studying the sacred, oftentimes, involves a radical shift in the subject position of the perceiver. Cut off from or shut out of the sacred, the researcher or academic finds that his or her own perspective needs correction or alteration before the object of study is clearly understood. Else, there is the danger of epistemic violence such as the earlier, intolerant secularism imposed, thereby reducing everything to itself and its own profanity. That is why, the study of the sacred often implies a reenchantment of not just the object of study but of the larger universe in which it is carried out. Having said this, it must be acknowledged that the terrain of the sacred is ambiguous and difficult. It is a heterogeneous rather than homogeneous territory. We have tried to retain this complexity and plurality, rather than reducing and flattening it either by secular bigotry or by evangelist enthusiasm.

Especially, with regards to Australia, as many of the essays show, the sacred is riven and fissured, largely in terms of two antagonistic world views, the aboriginal and the white Australian. This fissure also encompasses binaries such as traditional and modern, colonized and colonized, subaltern and dominant, dream and reality, timelessness and time, magic and reason, and so on. While greater mutual understanding, respect, even reconciliation between the two are possible, a full integration may perhaps be too difficult to effect. When it comes to Australia, the sacred remains internally fragmented, disturbingly contradicted, and painfully wounded. This impacts the overall psyche or mentality of the nation and calls for urgent attention, healing. This book attempts to contribute, howsoever modestly, to that process. It is only through greater understanding and compassion that such an ideal can be served, not through hostility and suspicion.

2

Perhaps, what makes this book special is that this is the first to openly and directly proclaim the sacredness of Australia. Though the title has several connotations, I think it boldly asserts something that many have but dimly recognized so far, though it is so deep in the consciousness of the original people of the land. By asserting the sacredness of Australia from a secular, post-colonial, contemporary and cosmopolitan space, the book recuperates and reinforces its connection with the indigenous past of the country and with the people who owned this land for over forty thousand years. On the occasion of a new edition of this book in India appears, I offer tribute to them.

Like the indigenous people who have lived in Australia for these forty centuries or more, I believe that ancestral spirits still roam this land. Those few of us who are privileged to feel, hear, and even see them cannot but acknowledge this truth. They are everywhere; they move, whisper, caution, guide, and protect us—if only we care to listen and respect them. They shaped this country and inhabited it from the earliest times. They created this world from the basic raw materials, moulding it according to their fancy and pleasure. They filled it with myriad plants, animals, minerals, rivers, and mountains.

They gave us dreaming, which is really nothing but the law. It is the ancient decree of how to be and live correctly, in harmony with our surroundings and fellow human beings. Dreaming is non-dual; it fuses subject and object, spirit and matter, man and nature, nature and culture, the inner and the outer, earth and the heavens. Guided by dreaming, the indigenous people of this land lived a remarkably sustainable life for over forty thousand years. They had no kings, no presidents, no bureaucracies, no armies, no police, no jails, no psychiatric hospitals, no alcoholism, no delinquency. They did not colonize other lands, enslave people, or build empires. It is not that they knew nothing; in fact, they were wise and cultivated. Among them were men and women of high order, wizards and wise mothers, who taught the coming generations the abiding mysteries and verities of life. They had poetry, art, painting, song, and dance. They lived well, that is why when they died, there was unspeakable sorrow and loss. I salute them most respectfully and offer my gratitude for their hospitality, kindness, and encouragement. The idea of Sacred Australia comes from and thus flows back to them.

I also offer my thanks and gratitude to the present custodians of this continent, the descendents of the settlers, some of whom came in chains, and those that followed in their wake over two hundred years to build this multicultural and diverse country.

These two Australias, the old and the new, are thus, in some sense, the subject of our book. We believe that it is only in the sacred that they can come together meaningfully. The division and schizophrenia of this culture can be healed by submersion to the perennial current of the sacred.

But what is the sacred after all? I have already devoted a section of this Preface to this issue. Let me reiterate here that to me it is simply a dimension of our own selves, not something alien to us that must be imported from somewhere else. We *are* the sacred, the sacred is a part of us. When we recognize this, our differences cease to trouble us. We can, in fact, embrace them as beautiful expressions of the inexhaustible creative energies of our planetary consciousness. Our diversity, our uniqueness, are causes for celebration, not anxiety. This book, then, is ultimately about connections and combinations, about confluences and reconciliations. It is about hope and the power to change. It is, above all, about love that can inspirit us to relate to one another, to our pasts and presents, to other forms or life, and beyond, to the very material manifestations that support our existence.

Yet this book is not a political tract or a sermon. It is only meant to explore, describe, and invite a wider participation in an essential aspect of what it means to be Australian. And it is an *academic* book, not some New Age, feel-good, inspirational tome. It represents a rigorous intellectual enterprise, a far-reaching intervention in current debates on Australianness. We hope it is recognized as a valuable, even essential contribution to Australian Studies.

In its own way, this book, at least implicitly, applauds and honours the spirit of Australia, the warmth and generosity of its people, the courage and glory of its ancestors, the toil and commitment of its contemporary citizens, the hope and aspiration of its future generations. Fair play, egalitarianism, decency, sportsmanship—these are the common clichÈs by which this society is known. But to me all these in combination with space of a large continent, the sparsity of population, the admixture of peoples, the ancient heritage and a vibrant present afford this land greater potencies and possibilities; its agenda is not finished. I believe that Australia, along with a few other countries, is the key to the creation of alternative futures and a new world order.

I say all this knowing that I am not Australian. I am conscious of being a foreigner here, an outsider. I say this not as a complaint or even as an expression of alienation. On the contrary, I feel at home, quite comfortable. And yet I know that I belong to a different culture, a different tradition, a different people, a different nation. I can appreciate and partake of the spirit of Australia without necessarily needing to *become* Australian. But because I am an outsider, I think I see Australia differently, perhaps more clearly than some of its natives might. I see what makes it special, unique, even great. Perhaps, that is why, only an outsider could have ventured to produce such a book.

I first visited here in July 2001, coming principally for the triennial ACLALS conference in Canberra. I was fortunate to have a round-the-world ticket then—very useful those things can be. So I started in Perth, and made my way across the continent through Adelaide, Melbourne, and Canberra, before finally departing for San Francisco from Sydney.

Much has changed since then. I flew on an airline called Ansett which no longer exists. You could get a decent dinner including a drink for about ten bucks. Now Australians seem less laid back, more like the Americans, more competitive, with less leisure. The economy is also hurting, though the welfare state seems to be holding up well.

That was a memorable trip, but I had no idea that I would come again and again, let alone do a book on "Sacred Australia." Yet some force drew me back. In these nine years, I have come here eight times and, what is more, each visit has brought me to Melbourne. In this continent, I have no doubt that it is this city that means the most to me and to which I belong so clearly. It was no surprise, therefore, that it is in Melbourne that I found my Australian publisher, Gordon Thompson. When I went to Melbourne for its launch in May 2009, once again I found myself staying in Parkville, on Royal Parade, at Whitley College, next to International House.

During my very first visit in 2001, I had discovered ProfessorVin D'Cruz, who also lived in Parkville. He died last year of cancer. This book is dedicated to him. He was one of the most knowledgeable people on Melbourne, having lived and taught here for nearly fifty years. He was a great authority on its oral history, its pattern of migrations, its neighbourhoods and inhabitants, its politics and culture. I owe a great deal to Vin. Though he did not directly contribute an essay to this book, he was one reason I kept coming back to Melbourne.

Another Australian friend of Fiji-Indian origin is Vijay C. Mishra, Professor of English at Murdoch, and one of Australia's leading scholars in English studies. I had met Vijay in India in 1988 at a conference on post-colonialism in Shimla, in the erstwhile imperial summer capital of India, in the Himalayan foothills. Later, in 2001, I renewed my acquaintance with him again in Perth. Since then, he has been a friend, philosopher, and like family elder. This book is also dedicated to him.

3

This book began as a part of my proposal for an AIC Fellowship. But the fellowship finished quickly and then the book seemed to become an uphill task. Though I have written or edited dozens of books, none felt less certain or more difficult to attempt. "Sacred Australia" seemed, from the first, not just a chancy, but dangerous enterprise. I felt uncertain, out of my depths, foolhardy, even unreasonable in aiming to do such a book. To tell you the truth, every now and then, I lost both my nerve and my faith in my ability to bring it to fruition.

I sought and obtained an Australian co-editor, thinking that would put me on more sure footing. I thank her for her initial support and enthusiasm. But after a couple of years passed, she got busy with other things and excused herself. She also hinted that it was a doomed project. I was left on my own.

Somehow, I soldiered on, with the support and kindness of several of my contributors. Luckily, they didn't give up on me or on "Sacred Australia." One of them, perhaps the foremost authority on the subject, David Tacey, was kind enough to share with me his own, not always pleasant experiences of researching on this area in Australia. We took a walk together around the oval in Royal Park. I discovered that he was Irish and quite dogged. He has kept publishing in this area, even though it has brought him few rewards and certainly not commensurate with his contribution.

I met several other wonderful people, some of whom became my contributors. I met Debbie Bird Rose, an American anthropologist who works at the Australian National University and lives in the bush with her Australian partner. She is one of the most eloquent and moving writers on indigenous Australia. She presented me with a hand-made native bead pouch made by an endangered tribe of aborigines in Taiwan. Like Debbie, John Bradley is an authority on aboriginal culture, especially the Yanyuwa language, being one of the dozen or so people in the world outside to know it. Bill Ashcroft, one of Australia's leading post-colonialists agreed to give me a paper. Peter Boyle, a respected poet, introduced by Debbie, also agreed to contribute. Dennis Haskell from UWA and Graham Seale from Curtin also promised—and delivered—papers. Frances Devlin-Glass, who introduced me to Gordon, and John Docker of ANC wrote moving pieces on major literary texts. Mark Brett and Peter Murphy soon joined. In 2008, I met Geoff Cheong, an Anglican minister and sports enthusiast; he agreed to do a paper on sport as a sacred obsession in Australia. Later, thanks to Gordon, Claudia, Anne, and Freya also offered substantial papers. In addition, I secured a paper from Mark Brett, a respected theologian at Whitley College. From the start, I had a very interesting Indian take on Les Murrey by my friend Sudhir Kumar, which nicely balanced a re-reading of Patrick White by John Docker. We now had a substantial collection of papers on theoretical issues, indigenous matters, art and literature, poetry and architecture, and finally myth, media, and sports. The book was finally taking some sort of publishable shape. The process of putting it together turned out as memorable as the final product.

I began to approach various publishers. I found that academic publishing in Australia was a terribly disheartening business. Publishers had small budgets, smaller lists, and even smaller minds. They were reluctant to take risks, remained far too conventional in their approach, and were not the most efficient when it came to writing back. It seemed as to them authors were dime a dozen while publishers were few and far between. They would sit on a proposal for months or not even reply. It was impossible to meet any of them. It was almost as if their thought it their duty to discourage authors, not to invite new proposals.

Though I was doing another book with a leading University press in Australia, when it came to "Sacred Australia," the going was very difficult. No one said they were *not* interested in the project. A leading Australian academic press of impeccable British lineage even agreed to read the ms., but just sat on it for months on end, after showing initial enthusiasm. Funnily enough, their final regret letter came just as I was setting off for Australia on a trip actually to launch the Australian edition. They had taken almost two years simply to tell me that they could not do the book!

I was about to lost hope. Then Gordon Thompson showed up. He came to see me when I staying at the International House in 2008, during a visit to give the keynote address in a conference on Jean Gebser. Gordon almost did not find me, wandering all over Royal Parade, though I thought my address was pretty straightforward. I had to walk him towards my apartment on the Avenue over the phone. He came in, had a cup of tea, we chatted for an hour, and, suddenly, so many possibilities seemed to emerge. I told him straightaway that he could take his time to tell me whether he was going to publish this book, but on my part, I was ready to go with Clouds of Magellan simply because it was just the kind of Aussie venture that I really wanted to support. Before a week went by, Gordon was back with a positive offer.

4

The launch of the Australian edition in May 2009 in the Whitley College library on Royal Parade had a good atmosphere. There were about thirty-five people, from the quite senior to one little boy who was probably two. The library, with its numerous rows of books was, as I was told, a nice place in which to play hide and seek. Freya Mathews, who was the main speaker, showed how post-secular spirituality was really a great opportunity of renewal and re-connection. Neither science nor globalization really could shut off the possibilities of the numinous; that was because the phenomenal world was just that—the appearance of things.

David, so generous, said that this book would encourage younger teachers and students to come out openly with their interest rather than being afraid of ridicule. Mark said that the papers were excellent and that if surrendered the domain of the "religious" to the terrorists and fundamentalists, we would all be goners; so it was good to be spiritual in an open, critical, and compassionate fashion than to be in denial. Several people, including some personal friends of mine, bought multiple copies. I think Gordon looked quite happy at the end. I signed copies for those who attended and also for their friends and relatives. I also got a copy signed by all the contributors present.

After the launch, Geoff, who is a member, took me to one of Australia's most hallowed precincts, the Melbourne Cricket Ground or MCG. It is a grand sports arena which can seat nearly 100,000 spectators. The game in progress was between the Richmond Lions and the Brisbane Tigers. It was Australian style football, very popular traditionally in the South, especially Melbourne. The Brisbane tigers used to be a local team which was bought over by Brisbane. So they still had support here. There were several fans with wearing their colours of black and yellow. The Lions were in blue and red. It was literally a tigers vs. lions match.

When we walked in, the game was neck and neck, but in the end the Lions raced ahead to a nearly thirty point lead. The stadium was electrified with energy when we had entered, though towards the end, the Tigers' fans had had enough and were leaving. Geoff had intended to take me to the Long Room, to get into which you need a jacket, tie, and dress shoes. Who said that the Australians were a completely informal nation! Here you could watch the game with a mug of beer or a glass of wine, seated on fine leather sofa, behind a glass enclosure separated from the hoi polloi. The cafÈ had South Asian waiters and one of the highest wicket takers on this ground was Sarfaraz Nawaz. Cricket was a part of an older, colonial cosmopolitanism.

When we walked out, we saw several fathers with their sons (some with daughters too), kicking and catching the oblong ball—the new generation was been initiated into their ancestral traditions. Like religion, you were also born with a football team affiliation. The weather, which had been very pleasant, was suddenly turning a bit cold. Hordes of people lined up the station near the MCG, crowding into trains to go home. There were special cops to monitor the traffic. I realized that I had been initiated into a peculiarly Australian rite this evening.

On the way back, Geoff told me about a Melbourne mystic and healer called Elinor; he also told me of his Friday morning fellowship with a German Buddhist. Geoff is an Anglican Chaplain with some Chinese blood in him. He is both sports-lover and spiritual counsellor. He asked me what being spiritual meant to me as a Hindu. I said, "To try to do one's utmost regardless of the situation in which one is placed in; this is the *karma-yoga* of the Bhagawad Gita that leads both to righteousness in the world and liberation from it." Our conversation confirmed the possibilities of sacred Australia that this book tried to explore.

The following evening, on the eve of my departure, I realized once again, how special this part of the city, Royal Parade and Parkville, make me fell. Though it was raining, when I walked towards the University of Melbourne, my heart soared. I had to meet a friend at the old Law Quad. I turned left after Trinity College onto Tin Lane, crossed through the Students Union, and found my friend's office. Everything was so familiar.

Later we had dinner at a vegetarian restaurant near Lygon Street in Carleton, which despite its Sanskrit name, really serves no Indian dishes. It has two wonderful Picchavai tapestries from Rajasthan in the Nathadwara style. On entering the restaurant, I saw a painting of Swami Ramdas, the guru of the 17th century Maratha king, Shivaji. All this was most uncanny—familiar, but strange at the same time.

The dinner was excellent and the meal rather boisterous; it was Friday night after all. The dessert—an scrumptious apple crumble—came in a casserole straight out of the oven it would seem because when I touched the dish, it was so hot that I almost dropped it. My friend, a professor of Philosophy gently but firmly chastised the waitress, saying that if this was California, they would have been sued for burning my fingers. I held on to the glass of cold water while the waitress apologised profusely, over and over again. Later, they took that dish off our bill. Here was a law-abiding society where moral ambiguity did not have much scope; if you were wrong you had to say sorry or face the consequences. You couldn't rewrite the rules every time to suit your convenience.

Though there were parts of my life which were jagged and painful, I was conscious of the great flow of grace that had touched me, once again, in Australia this evening. When I had embarked upon this book, I had had a more spectacular vision of the great Rainbow Serpent at Uluru, about which I had written in my Introduction to the book. Now, this was a quieter, but no less certain touch of the loveliness of the universe. As my great teacher Yogi Ramsuratkumar had once said, "There is an unbroken shower of grace, flowing like a continuous current; only we are at times too blinded to perceive/receive it."

5

Broadly speaking, the essays collected here fall into four categories. First, are theoretical considerations and broader overviews. Then there are reflections on aboriginal concerns, followed by literary considerations. Finally, there are interdisciplinary analyses. It has been a unique privilege to work with the contributors over a two year period. I thank them from the bottom of my heart for their patience and continued faith in this project, through periods of doubt, uncertainty, inactivity, and through the many setbacks that we faced.

I am grateful to the Australia-India Council (AIC) for a fellowship that I competed for and was awarded in 2005. This enabled travel to Australia, the use of library resources, and, above all, meeting academics and contributors. I should like to thank my colleagues at JNU, especially Santosh Sareen, our leading Australianist, who has also been kind enough to write a Foreword for the Indian Edition of this book, for his encouragement and support, as also been the current president of Indian Association for the Study of Australia, Darvesh Gopal. From the AIC, I am especially grateful to Asha Das and

Aparna Gupta in India, and to Richard Nile and Carol Robertson in Australia. Special thanks to Vijay C. Mishra, Bruce Bennett, Vin D'Cruz, Andrew Hassam, Shalmalee Palekar, Mira and Garry Cummins, Sunil Govannage, Satendra Nandan, and all those who offered help and hospitality during the project. I shall always treasure their warmth, friendliness, and generosity of spirit. I would also like to acknowledge the assistance from my Project Fellows and students at various stages of the work. My special thanks to Gareth Griffths and Paul Sharrad for their comments on the ms. Gordon Thompson, the founder-publisher of Clouds of Magellan has played a crucial role in shaping this volume. I am grateful to him for the many hours and hundreds of emails in which we discussed this project. He has taken a personal interest in the quality both of the contents and the production of the book. I am convinced that committed independent publishers like him make a great difference to academic discourse. Likewise, I would like to thank my Indian publisher, Aditya Goel, for his faith in this project. As a consequence of all this cooperation, the ensuing circulation of ideas has been trans-national and cross-cultural.

In sum, a great many folks—not all of whom I have been able to name—in Australia, India, and elsewhere have played a vital role in this venture. In addition, I hope a greater number will actually go on to read, study, criticize, enjoy, and engage with this book. If I have vindicated, in small measure, the trust of the former, and the interest of the latter in this project, then I shall consider this book as having accomplished its aim.

Makarand R. Paranjape

24th December 2009

SACRED AUSTRALIA

A PASSAGE TO ULURU: RETHINKING SACRED AUSTRALIA

Makarand R. Paranjape

APPROACHING ULURU

In *Radiance of Being,* an extraordinary and widely appreciated account of the evolution of consciousness, Allan Combs offers a useful taxonomy of wisdom traditions. He founds his model on a system of coordinates with four axes:

- ontic/noetic
- anabolic/catabolic
- constructive/emergent, and
- introverted/extraverted.

Let us consider each of these axes by turn, starting with the ontic/noetic. According to Combs, the ontic end emphasises the transformation of the individual while the noetic end stresses the acquiring of higher knowledge. Anabolic traditions 'build up', constructing more refined structures of mind, while catabolic traditions 'break down', or deconstruct those structures which obscure understanding. Constructive traditions recommend gradual progress towards higher levels of consciousness and being, while emergent traditions suggest sudden leaps and breakthroughs. Inner traditions highlight withdrawal from the world in order to attain perfection within, while extraverted traditions call for an engagement with the world in order to attain perfection.

On deeper reflection, we realise that these coordinates are not opposites or poles, but parts of an integrated whole. What from one dimension may be seen as a scale in another dimension is a whole, like a sphere. In other words, we cannot have the ontic without the noetic, the anabolic without the catabolic, the constructive without the emergent, and the introverted without the extraverted. Each is implicated in the other; the pair is really made up of two faces of the one. It is only in the integration of these seemingly opposite emphases that a richer understanding of the sacred emerges.

If we apply Combs's framework to sacred Australia, we will see a similar need for the integration of what look like two opposites, the aboriginal sacred and the white Australian secular. Though it may not be clear at first, we will gradually come to see how these two totally different worlds of the aborigines[1] and the settlers have deeply impacted and interpenetrated one another, even if this may not be easily evident on the surface. The relationship between them is not only evolving through time, but simultaneously contains all the elements that have gone into this complex history. So we have conflict and opposition, separation and division, co-existence and tolerance, and mutuality and dialogue, all present over time and simultaneously. The association between the two subsists in an environment of both hostility and hospitality. Of course, from the very beginning to present times, the aborigines have been subordinate while the settlers dominant. This fact of unequal and asymmetrical power has forever distorted the relationship between the two, resulting in the colossal tragedy of the aborigines and an uncertain triumph of the settlers.

Undoubtedly, when it comes to the Australian sacred, these two universes, which in daily life seem so far apart as to exist almost unknown and unheeding to one another, are inevitably intertwined—the story of aboriginal dreaming has become inseparably linked to the onslaught of white Australian realism. One cannot theorise the Australian sacred without taking both into account. They are indivisible, even if they are opposed to one another or in tension with one another. Indeed, to all appearances, they seem to be a series of binaries, impossible to reconcile.

Aboriginal	Anglo-European
Black	White
Traditional	Modern
Backward	Advanced
Sacred	Secular
Dreaming	Realism

[1] There are no satisfactory terms to name the original inhabitants of the land we now call Australia. Natives, indigenous people, 'first nations', aboriginals—are all neither fully accurate nor adequate. I have used the word 'aborigines' which, as a noun, is more respectful than 'aboriginal', which is an adjective.

Colonised	Coloniser
Subordinate	Dominant
Integrated	Fragmented
Mythical	Rational
Eco-spirtual	Instrumental
Secret	Overt
Residual	Prevalent
Pre	Post[2]

We could continue to pile up such binaries without necessarily achieving greater progress or understanding. I say this because to reiterate their differences will neither erase them nor lead to greater appreciation of how Australia as a society functions. The only way forward is to bring these two worlds into closer contact and proximity. This is one of the greatest utility values of studying the Australian sacred. For it is here that we see how closely they are really linked.

Such call for integration, however, takes us on a different kind of journey in which we will have to combine skills that are contradictory, almost mutually exclusive. The way of understanding and comprehension is neither simple nor straightforward. We shall have to experience the deeper structures and yet be able to analyse the overlays that contradict these. We shall have to be at once aware of the history of colonisation, extermination, and expropriation, and the contemporary urge to be democratic, just, and multicultural. There are clear tendencies, but no answers—tensions, but no resolutions.

That is why it becomes clear to any researcher that the landscape of the Australian sacred is both uncertain and controversial. It is akin to what Michel Foucault called 'a heterotopia'. I use the topographical metaphor to approach it because every single inch of the Australian continent has been and is, quite literally, holy ground, inscribed with the sacred memory and presence that is Dreaming. The subsequent colonisation of this territory and the post-colonial remorse have only made this sacred space contentious, even litigious, but no less holy.

At the heart of the matter is the peculiar paradox that from the dominant, 'white', secular Australian point of view, the sacred is hard to find in

[2] David J Tacey in *Edge of the Sacred: Transformation in Australia* also begins with a series of such antinomies.

contemporary Australia, but from the subaltern, aboriginal and now displaced perspective, every thing about Australia was or is sacred. Similarly, from the perspective of the modern academy, 'nothing is sacred', that is barred from interrogation or inquiry. At least overtly, there can be no proscription or foreclosure of bringing to bear a historically constructed rationality on any field of study. Ostensibly, anyone from anywhere is welcome to examine or study any aspect of human experience. On the other hand, the sacred from the aboriginal point of view is literally off limits. It is also the secret into which the outsider is prohibited entry. Only the elders of the tribe can relax this interdiction to invite or initiate an outsider into their meaning universe.

As I see it, our interventions in this book mediate between such extremes. These essays attempt both to provoke debate and reconcile hostile positions. To me, neither the dictum that nothing is sacred nor the idea that all except insiders or initiates be excluded is an absolute. In fact, our involvement in this ambiguous and fraught terrain is premised on the paradoxical belief that sometimes it takes a stranger to reveal to yourself who you are. Only an outsider can disclose to us certain facets of ourselves; to that extent, only a foreigner could have attempted to put together this sort of book.

What I, as an outsider, can try to do is to mediate between two worlds, the aboriginal and the white, the sacred and the secular, the pre-historic and the contemporary, the traditional and the post-modern. In this specific instance, I do so through a personal narrative of a journey to one of Australia's most well-known sacred sites, Uluru.

Why Uluru? The choice is at once obvious and problematic. Uluru has been touted both to Australians and to foreigners as one of Australia's most prized tourist destinations. Two contradictory kinds of appeals are superimposed on it. On the one hand it is a site of natural wonder and beauty, thus appealing to post-romantic notions of the Western sublime. On the other hand, as a place sacred to the indigenous people of Australia, it has an added and exotic appeal to those who do not necessarily subscribe to aboriginal beliefs or values. Indeed, the latter allure of the rock is only supplementary to the former; tourism usually triumphs over spirituality. Yet, the dominant discourse cannot entirely subsume or erase the marginal. The spiritual as supplement radically alters the fundamental meaning of the site, even for an ordinary Western visitor. The aboriginal thus destabilises any comfortable notion of a natural beauty or touristy curiosity.

My journey revealed, once again, the fractured nature of the Australian psyche, with competing narratives and frames of reference uneasily co-existing, but unable to integrate. The rock is thus a contested site, marked by ideological conflict rather than spiritual harmony. Being one of Australia's most visible and visited tourist destinations, it has also been 'captured' by the master-narrative of global capitalism in such a way that it is virtually impossible to explore or experience it 'innocently'. Yet, on rare occasions, the natural energy of the place does break through these encrustations: rupture leads to rapture. My intervention is also a plea for a new reflection in the context of globalisation, which has produced a new, post-secular liminality in our times, and which challenges us to move beyond our present structures of consciousness into something more transformative and integral. It is a call for a new idiom, a new way of speaking to and of the sacred.

While undertaking the journey I was deeply conscious of these contradictory significations. Was I being drawn to it precisely because it was so *obviously* a symbol of the sacred? What if a small muddy pond was actually a more important sacred site to the aborigines? Would I still venture a difficult pilgrimage to such a site? The fact, as noted earlier, is that all of Australia is sacred from the aboriginal point of view. It is not simply that the present sites of dams, mines, breweries, or modern developmental projects are sacred. Every other place in Australia is sacred too. Its use and inhabitation is thus governed by the same aboriginal 'law' which is quite at variance with modern notions of ownership. Colonialism is predicated on 'rights of conquest'. From the point of view of the colonised, however, these rights are questionable. Instead, what you have is a stolen continent. That is why some critics including Ken Gelder and Jane M Jacobs have argued that the aboriginal and modern positions are incommensurable, thus making a dialogue impossible (p. 18).

I began with such dismal and depressing considerations. I admitted to myself that Uluru was as convenient an icon for my purposes as it was essential. Yet, I also felt, intuitively perhaps, that neither my journey nor its conclusion would be futile. To consider the aboriginal and the modern as totally incompatible was to me counter-productive. Instead, I thought that the imperative was to look for spaces of mediation. As I propose to show, fortunately or fortuitously, by the end of the trip my doubts were not just stilled but actually transformed into a sense of wonder and affirmation. Not just this journey, but the whole quest for sacred Australia seemed worthwhile.

That is why I consider Uluru significant. Though looking for the Australian sacred here is to look for it where it is most obvious, Uluru, at least for an outsider, serves as a convenient, and methodologically fruitful starting point. It is neither a muddy pond sacred only to the aborigines nor the Sydney opera house, a proud representative of what might be sublime to the modern, white, secular Australia. Especially, for those who wish to mediate—mediate—and integrate, Uluru, sacred to the aborigines, iconic to modern tourists and nature-lovers, then, is a much more convincing point of arrival, if not departure.

Arriving at Uluru

The politics of name reveals the tussle over the rock, one of the largest monoliths on the planet, an exceptionally beautiful brownish-red horse-shoe shaped natural formation, jutting out of the heart of the Australian continent. Named Ayers Rock by the settlers, its aboriginal name has now been restored so that it is more often known as Uluru. The name given by the white settlers, of course, persists in a sort of bi-lingual arrangement. The bi-linguality is actually symbolic of the dual signification of the monument and to two different ways of inscribing landscape. The rock thus at once means two different, often contradictory things. It is both sacred site and tourist spot, both very local and globally attractive. Similarly, the entire monument has been 'returned' to the indigenous people, even though it is run by the National Parks authority that is an arm of the modern Australian state. Two names, two ownerships, two meanings—that is Uluru/Ayers Rock today. As such, it is yet another example of what Bob Hodge and Vijay Mishra call 'double messages' that produce 'a schizoid nation' (p. xiv), exemplifying 'the double vision of Australians' (p. xv) and highlight the 'dark side of the Australian dream' (p. xvii).

I was introduced to this opposition at the heart of what Uluru signified in a rather personal and upsetting way. In 2005 I was awarded an Australia–India Research Fellowship to study Sacred Australia. On the eve of my departure, while drawing up my itinerary in Australia, I came across an unexpected problem. The authorities who administered the Fellowship objected to my plan to go to Uluru. In an email, I was informed that the Fellowship Council did not take too kindly to my desire to visit a popular tourist destination while I was supposed to be doing research and meeting scholars. I was stunned that what I considered a necessary pilgrimage to an aboriginal sacred site was regarded as tourist frivolity. Pilgrimage or spiritual tourism is deeply intrinsic to the Indian, especially Hindu ethos. As a student of the sacred I had thought that a visit to Uluru would be considered not just natural but crucial to my project. At the very least, it would constitute an auspicious beginning. Instead, I was greeted with a rebuff, calling into question my motives. Convincing the authorities was not easy. I had to assure them that I could deal with the heat of Uluru, which in November was nowhere close to the soaring summer temperatures of Delhi. In addition, I not only had to sacrifice a visit to the University of Queensland in Brisbane, but also prove that my trip to Uluru would not be more expensive than the itinerary originally planned for me. Thereafter, I was left to my own devices so to speak, having to make all the travel and accommodation arrangements on my own almost as if to teach me the price of disobedience or truancy.

At one point, my frustration was so intense that I even considered resigning from the Fellowship. I had done this once before with another grant from an Australian university, when I found that my academic freedom and liberty to research according to my own inclinations was being curtailed by too much direction and interference by both my partner investigator and the University concerned. This time, I was reminded of a poem by Dennis Kevans, 'Ah, White Man, have you any sacred sites':

> Ah, white man, I am searching for the sites, sacred to you,
> where you walk, in silent worship, and you whisper poems, too,
> where you tread, like me, in wonder, and your eyes are filled with tears,
> and you see the tracks you've travelled down your fifty thousand years.
>
> I am searching round Australia, I am searching, night and day,
> for a site, to you so sacred that you won't give it away
> for a bit of coloured paper, say a Church you're knocking down,
> or the Rocks, your nation's birthplace, by the bridge, in Sydney town.
>
> Your cathedrals I have entered, I have seen the empty aisles
> where a few knelt down in sorrow, where were all the children's smiles?
> Big cathedrals, full of beauty, opal glass, and gleaming gold,
> and an old man, in an overcoat, who had crept in from the cold.

> Your schools, I drifted through them, heard the sound of swishing canes,
> heard the yell of angry teachers crushing flowers in their brains,
> heard the bark up on the rostrum where the powers had their say,
> wouldn't children's hearts be sacred, though they're made, like mine, of clay?
>
> Where's your wonder? Where's your worship? Where's your sense of holy awe? (1985, p. 21).

Kevans had written the poem as a response to Hugh Morgan of the Western Mining Company who called the aborigines 'pagans' when they opposed the Noonkanbah mining project in 1984.[3]

Indeed, throughout my trip that year, whenever I told people that I was researching on 'Sacred Australia', I was greeted with sneers or surprise. As Kevans put it, 'Sacred ... sacred ... sacred ... gee you chuck that word about,' (ibid). A typical remark was, 'Well, you'll have to work very hard to find it,' or, 'We don't have any of it, except when it comes to Rugby.' Admittedly, most of those who reacted this way were the so-called 'ordinary' Australians, not fellow-academics. Though not ill-intentioned, these comments suggested the predominantly secularlist temperament of contemporary Australians. They also revealed a near-total lack of interest in and ignorance of aboriginal views on the subject. No one said, for instance, 'O yes, this whole land was sacred to the aborigines who believed that their ancestors, the great beings of Dreaming walked here and shaped the landscape thus.' I had to read about these things in books: even scholars and academics rarely talked about them. On the other hand, my academic friends said, 'Oh, the sacred ... are you in aboriginal studies, then?' Either group seemed determined to circumscribe me into a limited and splintered space.

Time and again, I was asked what I meant by the 'sacred'. It seemed difficult for my interlocutors to relate to what I was researching. Once more, I was reminded of Kevans' evocative lines:

> Sacred means that ... sacred ... it's a place where spirits rise, with the rainbow wings of sunset, on the edge of paradise, Sacred ... that's my

[3] http://www.nyungah.org.au/documents/AhWhiteM.html; accessed 12th May 2008.

father, that's my mother, that's my son, Sacred ... where the dreaming whispers hope for everyone. (ibid)

This sense of the sacred is, by and large, not available to modern Australians. Even the churches and monuments lack it. What they have is solemnity and grandeur, but not the intense relationship with the place as though it were a living ancestor, an intimate and uplifting presence, the source of awe and elevation. I too felt like asking, along with Kevans, 'Is there dreaming in you, man?' (ibid). The answer to the question was provided even earlier in the title of WEH Stanner's influential book *White Man Got No Dreaming: Essays 1938–1973* (1979).

Luckily, in the end, things worked out satisfactorily and I was able to go to Uluru. As I flew from Perth to Ayers Rock airport, I knew that I had embarked on an extraordinary journey. As the plane circled in the air before landing, there were the most magnificent views of Uluru and Kata Tjuta. I was alone and so entranced that for the next three days I did not want to talk to anyone. Uluru is perhaps the single largest, natural millennia-old monolith on earth. It is ten kilometres wide and about 350 metres tall. A World Heritage Protected Site, it has earned its place in the list for both natural and cultural values. The aboriginal inhabitants are Anangu who gave it the name 'Uluru'.

My interest in Uluru and in aboriginal Australia pre-dated this trip. I had read many years ago of a remark, which I have since been unable to trace, by Sri Ramana Maharshi, the great teacher of non-dualism from South India, that there was a link between the indigenous peoples of India and Australia. Linguists, anthropologists, and enthnographers too support this view with theories of migration from Africa to Australia, via India and Indonesia, going back some 40,000 years or so. In 1992, when I went up Arunachala, the sacred mountain at Tiruvannamalai, where Ramana Maharshi lived, I saw people who actually resembled the Australian aborigines. In India circumambulation of a sacred site is a common and age-old practice. I myself have walked around Arunachala several times in a clock-wise fashion.

Now, I found myself performing a similar ritual in Uluru. According to Anangu beliefs, climbing up the rock was not considered appropriate. The rock was sacred so tramping up on it would be to show disrespect to it. Besides, it could be dangerous because of the winds and the slippery slope of the rock. Several people had lost their lives trying to do so. The Anangu are saddened when this happens. The Park authorities post warnings for climbers and shut down the way up when the weather becomes unfavourable. I still saw several people climbing up the rock. The attitude of conquest not reverence is very common among visitors to the site.

Instead, like a good Hindu, I performed my circumambulation. The walk is about 11.6 kilometres in all. I also did the other recommended walk to the Valley of the Winds, which is about eight kilometres. Being all by myself, my experience was so much more concentrated. As the anonymous author of this beautiful passage puts it:

> The Australian continent is criss-crossed with the tracks of the Dreamings: walking, slithering, crawling, flying, chasing, hunting, weeping, dying, giving birth. Performing rituals, distributing the plants, making the landforms and water, establishing things in their places, making the relationships between one place and another. Leaving parts or essences of themselves. Where they travelled, where they stopped, where they lived the events of their lives, all these places are sources and sites of Law. These tracks and sites, and the Dreamings associated with them, make up the sacred geography of Australia; they are visible in paintings and engravings; they are sung in the songs, depicted in body painting – they form the basis of a major dimension of the land tenure system for most aboriginal people. To know the country is to know the story of how it came into being, and that story also carries the knowledge of how the human owners of that country came into being.[4]

Most of the walks were very early in the morning, before it got hot. So I used to get up around 4:00, then take the tour bus to the site, catch the sunrise, walk around, come back around noon, eat, then rest in the afternoon when it was the hottest, then go back in the evening to watch the sunsets, which were invariably spectacular. The rock, with its peculiar markings and crevices does seem as yet unfinished and plastic, as if some giant being had played with a large lump of clay, shaped and fashioned it to his liking, and left it like a large mud pie, after he had tired from his sport. There were areas designated as 'male' and 'female,' and still others were off limits. I remember the account of a fellow-traveller from Israel, Jani Roberts, who tells the story of the struggle for women to have their sacred spaces properly fenced and

[4] http://www.crystalinks.com/aussacredsites.html; accessed 23rd November 2005.

protected from prying tourists and inquisitive men.[5] It became clear to me that the rock was also a teaching site, where people learned not only about their past but also about the facts of life and all that was necessary for their day to day survival. Some of the caves had paintings inside them. It was impossible to date these because they had been renewed many times over by the passing generations.

On my last evening at Uluru, I was treated to the most unusual sight of the rain lashing the rock, which made it turn a slate gray from the usual red. It rains very little in that area, which is normally classified as a desert. The vegetation is stunted, small shrub and undergrowth, which can survive on very little moisture. So rain here is considered very, very extraordinary.

I was in a tour group. When it began to rain, our driver decided to drive us around the rock since it was not practical to get off. It all began while we were standing on the south side of the rock, waiting to walk to one of the many picturesque spots. Suddenly, a dust storm worked its way to the rock, where we were standing. It was fierce. I have a picture that shows a red ball coming, almost animated and embodied. Inside the tour bus, the guides began to teli us how it is unusual for there to be any rain, so not to expect it. But even as they spoke, it began to pelt down on us.

As we drove around, we saw the water pouring down from all sides of the rock. In some places, it looked like frost, in other places like a grey mantle over the mountain. Then even as we looked, mouths agape, a rainbow appeared in the sky, dipping down in an arc to embrace the mountain.

This apparition was really the moment of epiphany, appearing ever so faintly, then more and more clearly, even as the sun emerged bright and yellow from underneath the clouds just before setting finally. Those of us who were witness to this transfiguring phenomenon remembered that the rainbow is of course the great serpent spirit of the aborigines who unites the heavens with the earth and helps create whatever we see of the landscape during the dreaming.

In *Understanding Aboriginal Culture,* Cyril Havecker tries to explain the significance of Uluru in Aboriginal mythology:

> Uluru is the Intelligent Snake from the higher spirit realms of the universe who brought forth a great rainbow. From this rainbow a huge spirit snake

[5] http://inquirer.gn.apc.org/uluru.html; accessed on 23rd November 2005.

> slithered down to earth. This was Uluru, the Great Rainbow Serpent. Uluru is depicted by Aborigines as a symbol of fertility. It is shaped like a horseshoe lying on its side, the open end to the left. The lower part of the 'U' undulates and is filled with eggs. Thus the figure symbolises both male and female and is considered to be the father and mother of all forms of life. (1998)

What we had experienced, therefore, was nothing less than the *darshan* or vision of the Primal Deity of Australia. What a blessing this was. Even those who did not have the mental apparatus to recognise or comprehend it were not unaffected. For instance, with me was an unusual traveller, Sean McVain, an American, who was travelling around the world because he didn't want to do a regular job. He owned his own home and worked only to make enough money to embark on his next journey. It was as if the Deity had chosen us specially for this grand experience, each of us being prepared for it for our different circumstances and prior journeys. In the end, the sun also peeped out from behind the clouds, shining in all its glory before sinking. And, to top it all, was the rainbow, curving from the heavens to Uluru.

For me, this was an unforgettable and uniquely Australian experience. Uluru, a place of natural grandeur and spirituality, put me in touch not only with what Australia must have been like before colonisation, but a time when human beings and natural objects co-existed in close kinship. Sometimes from the depths of our hearts a huge sound comes roaring out. It is our cry to know the Reason for Everything—RoE. The Physicists have their equivalent of this. They call it the quest for the Theory of Everything (ToE). Only, their work is painstaking, accumulating, mathematical, punctuated, no doubt, by stabs of doubt and flights of inspiration. For the rest of us, it is something simpler, more primal. Just coming in contact with our own vastness, consciousness expanding, stretching out to touch the sky. That is what Uluru and Kata Tjuta had been for me.

As I took off from the Ayers Rock airport, I had yet another insight into the importance of the landscape. I realised that many of the aboriginal paintings that I had seen were actually a fairly accurate depiction of how the landscape looks, especially from an aerial view, when the actual undulations and physical features begin to resemble geometric markings and rhythmic patterns in ochre, red, and green. What the paintings depict, then, is an abstraction of the actual landscape that the aborigines hold sacred. I understood how for the aboriginal people there is no one God, but many ancestral spirits, who shaped the territories and gave the religious, moral, and ceremonial laws to each tribe. Each sacred site is imbued with spiritual energy, which then becomes the source of the transmission of grace. As Tony Swain puts it, aboriginal spirituality is 'geosophical' (quoted in Charlesworth, p. xix-xx).

Some might question my experience, saying that it was typically 'Hindu', thus not 'true' either to indigenous nor non-indigenous Australians. But, as I have tried to suggest earlier, it is precisely by mediations of this sort, in which notions of the sacred can be problematised, that we can hope to understand and dialogue with one another. The sacred responds to and is responded to by our unique subjectivities, which we need not deny or hide. Yet, to be locked into these subjectivities, being unable to reach out or be open to other perspectives, would also be counter-productive. Once again, we see that neither repudiation nor imprisonment in our inner worlds is the answer. The sacred invites us to be ourselves, but to expand our notions of who we are so that we are alive and available to what is more than us.

After Uluru

In his fine Introduction to *Religious Business: Essays on Australian Aboriginal Spirituality*, Max Charlesworth tells the long, painful, and slow story of western attempts at understanding aboriginal spirituality. In the late 19th century, with the evolutionary paradigm dominating, it was thought that aboriginal religion was non-rational or pre-logical, akin to magic, whereas classical religions, such as Judaism or Christianity believed in and appealed to a higher power called God (p. xiv). The aborigines were thus thought to be primitive, representing what the West might have once been before it advanced, by the application of reason, to its present state. Charles Frazer who wrote *The Golden Bough* may be considered as a major representative of this view.

Then came Durkheim, whose influential book *The Elementary forms of Religious Life: The Totemic System in Australia* (1912), argued that aboriginal beliefs were anything but elementary or rudimentary when compared to other religions. Yet, most anthropologists believed that religion was inferior to science (p. xv). It has taken long to change this attitude.

The next problem was the christian missionaries who, apart from academics, were the other main group interested in the aborigines. As Max

Charlesworth puts it, 'It was an unquestioned assumption among the early nineteenth-century christian missionaries that civilisation and Christianity were inextricably linked ... conversion to Christianity would result in the civilising of native peoples' (p. xvi). Most missionaries suffered from the belief that monotheism was the highest form of religion, therefore aboriginal beliefs were in need of reform. In an important book that challenged this thesis, David H Turner argued that aboriginal people made a 'quasi-deliberate' choice to reject monism and monotheism to escape from 'monarchy and hierarchy, tribalism/nationalism, exclusivism, the centralisation of power and authority, and violence' (p. xvii). Aborigines, thus, had a much more egalitarian and open culture than the so-called advanced countries of Europe.

Among the other problems that Charlesworth lists was the assumption that aboriginal beliefs or culture were unitary. When Cook arrived, the total aboriginal population was 750,000, divided in 500 groups, with 200 languages. Neither the aborigines, nor the white settlers are homogenous. The latter also come from different parts of Europe, although the Anglo-Celtic strain is dominant. However, vis-à-vis the aborigines, the different white groups functioned in a broadly similar fashion. Similarly, over time the different aboriginal groups were more often than not seen as similar and were constituted into a new collective identity. When it comes to notions of the sacred, we do see several common features, including the role of ancestor spirits, concept of dreaming, sacredness of the land, and the myth of the rainbow snake (p. xviii).

The other fallacy was that aboriginal religion was unchanging or frozen in time. The fact is that like all cultures, theirs is also constantly changing, adapting, and reforming. Another assumption that needs to be challenged is that aboriginal religions are male dominated. This is not strictly true because women had their own rights and rites where men were forbidden from entering.

This history of misunderstanding, I believe, was responsible for the terrible atrocities meted out by white Australians on the aborigines. Towards the end of his Introduction, Charlesworth observes:

> One is left with the dispiriting impression that most white Australians—both political leaders and the general populace—seem to be ignorant of the true reality of the white occupation of Australia and what CD Rowley has called 'the destruction of Aboriginal society'. A similar destruction

took place in many parts of the world, including Africa, South America, and Asia. (p. xxiii)

He goes on to recount the true extent of this historical tragedy:

Generally Aborigines were treated by pastoralists as chattels and kept in a position of virtual slavery where their wives and daughters were often sexually exploited; again, they were subjected to spasmodic massacres and arbitrary detention, while their children were often removed 'for their own good' ... this pattern of cruel repression resulted in the near extinction of many Aboriginal groups and the disappearance of their languages, kinship systems, and above all their rich and complex religions. (p. xiv)

If we go by the UN Convention on the Prevention and Punishment of Genocide (1948), there are five defining marks of genocide: 1. killing members of the group; 2. causing serious bodily or mental harm; 3. deliberately inflicting on the group conditions of life calculated to bring about its physical destruction; 4. imposing measures intended to prevent birth within the group; 5. forcibly transferring children to another group (cited on p. xxxvi). By these yardsticks, the white settlers did carry out a genocide against the aborigines during the first 100 or more years of their occupation. The foundational accounts of this terrible annihilation can be found in the series of books that CD Rowley wrote in the 1970s starting with *The Destruction of Aboriginal Society*.

The traces of this colossal misunderstanding and neglect are still visible everywhere in Australia. At the Ayers Rock-Uluru Resort, where I was staying, the bar was haunted by a few aboriginal men, who were drunk from 10 o' clock in the morning. I felt a stab of pain as I saw one of them, an elderly man, staggering about, trousers half undone, with a dopey grin on his face. Earlier, in the fashionable Northbridge suburb of Perth, known for its pubs and nightlife, I had encountered what was perhaps the saddest human being I had ever seen. An extremely emaciated woman, half aboriginal, half white, barely able to stand, looking utterly lost and devastated, supported by some friends who walked her up and down James Street, trying to keep her from falling down. She did not look benumbed but in acute pain, as if living itself were a torture. The alcohol and drugs that she had consumed were of no help. She looked cut off from all sources of inner nourishment.

Indigenous communities are endangered and beleaguered all over the world, but the high levels of dysfunctionality in such communities in Australia were all too evident. I began to think of how well-being might be restored in such societies even under adverse circumstances? One way was to understand and confront the whole history of colonisation, violence, oppression and through such an understanding to attempt a recovery. This would be the secular way. But wellness is also restorable if we find a way of recuperating spiritual knowledge and practices. What I realised was that wellness is not just economic and social, ecological and medical, but also emotional, cultural and spiritual. In fact, the interrelatedness of all these forms of well-being makes current, contractual approaches of state bureaucracies ineffective because they focus primarily on the economic, education, or the civic aspects. Most attempts to 'convert' indigenous people into model citizens of modernity have likewise failed. But several traditional spiritual practices, including rites and rituals may have been rendered very difficult or virtually impossible to perform in today's world. Consider, for instance, the disruption of the totemic relationships between land, community, and bird or animal species. How is it possible to restore or rejuvenate some of these practices in the present day? Even when we do see them performed, they seem staged and exotic, as if catering to the Western gaze. Is it possible for other practices, such as story telling or art and craft to substitute or partially compensate for their loss?

It seemed as if the great tragedy of the aborigines was that they had been woken from the dreaming into a never-ending nightmare that was modernity. Denied dreaming, or cut off from their nourishing terrains, both material and spiritual, they seemed to be condemned to insomnia or insanity. What survives? What can be reinvented? What can substitute the loss as far as both individual and community well-being are concerned? Some of these questions troubled me after Uluru.

Tacey has argued that the recovery of the sacred is imperative, both for aboriginal and white Australia: 'White Australians *deny* the sacred, and many black Australians *have been denied* the sacred' (1995, p. 9). He believes that *unconscious compulsion toward sacrifice*' (pp. 4–5) in the white Australian psyche can help steer a middle course between an overassertive ego and a disintegrated ego (p. 5): 'Australian society is notorious for its brute masculinity, its tough machismo, its laconic shyness, its disregard for the interior world and its disrespect for the nonrational.' (p. 5) He calls these strong defences' of a masculine psyche against the unconscious. He wants

Australians to shed this psychological armour, to soften and open themselves to the numinous. In such a regeneration, landscape can make a crucial impact on the psyche (pp. 6–7) because it is vital to both the aboriginal and white imaginary. He calls for a transformation of the degraded sacred in both aboriginal and white society (pp. 8–9) through the rites of ecstasy, which literally means to stand outside oneself (ex-stasis). According to him, resacralising is a social and political necessity (pp. 10–11): what is needed is nothing less than a 'New Dreaming' (p. 148–176).

I think it is in this spirit that Australia's current Prime Minister Kevin Rudd issued a remarkable apology to the aborigines on 13th February 2008. Not only is this a clear and unambiguous expression of atonement over past wrongs, but a commitment to reconciliation:

> We apologise for the laws and policies of successive parliaments and governments that have inflicted profound grief, suffering and loss on these our fellow Australians.

The Prime Minister promises to end this chapter of shame and to begin working for a new future:

> A future based on mutual respect, mutual resolve and mutual responsibility. A future where all Australians, whatever their origins, are truly equal partners, with equal opportunities and with an equal stake in shaping the next chapter in the history of this great country, Australia.

This moving document, by a head of state, is a powerful testimony to the possibility of healing and the hope for future recovery. It redresses the concern voiced so eloquently by Hodge and Mishra that regards the 'Australians' attempts to construct a national identity … as the unjust act of an imperial power whose direct beneficiaries have still not acknowledged that injustice nor succeeded in constructing a viable alternative basis for their legitimacy' (p. x).

Yet, a note of caution is needed here. It is instructive to compare Rudd's statement with a similar apology made by Canadian Prime Minister Stephen Harper on 11th June 2008. This statement, also made in the Parliament, was more specific, apologising for the abuse of children in residential schools specially created for Canadian 'Indian' or first nation children:

> Two primary objectives of the residential schools system were to remove and isolate children from the influence of their homes, families, traditions and cultures, and to assimilate them into the dominant culture. These objectives were based on the assumption aboriginal cultures and spiritual beliefs were inferior and unequal. Indeed, some sought, as it was infamously said, 'to kill the Indian in the child.' Today, we recognise that this policy of assimilation was wrong, has caused great harm, and has no place in our country. (Prime Minister Stephen Harper's statement of apology)

The Canadian apology comes after months of hard work to reach an understanding and settlement between the state, which instituted the system, and its survivors. The cornerstone of the settlement is the setting up of the Indian Residential Schools Truth and Reconciliation Commission (ibid). But the key difference is that this apology is a part of a substantial initiative involving a settlement of $1.9 billion to redress the wrongs meted out to native Canadians ('Canada to apologise to Native students'). Such promise of compensation and restitution has been ruled out by Rudd. An apology empty of action will produce only a false reconciliation, even adding to white self-congratulation without producing a genuine recognition of the felt experience of aboriginal alienation.

Ultimately, the whole tussle over the sacred in Australia boils down to one thing, *land*. How to relate to the land? In the case of Australia, all the land is, in a sense pre-coded with the idea of the primal sacred. This is totally opposed to the notion of Australia as *terra nullius*, empty land. With the ongoing deindustrialisation of Australia, the main source of wealth is the land, or rather what lies beneath it, the minerals and the natural resources. Uluru is a part of the iconography of the settler sublime precisely because it has no 'practical' value; imagination can thus take over reason. But the sublime is also marketable, especially to never-satisfied tourists, looking for newer and newer destinations to satisfy their craving for wonder. The ancient sacred of the aborigines also finds unexpected allies in post-modern discourses such as deep ecology and eco-feminism. All told, for the reconciliation to be effective the land that is Australia needs to be re-coded in a fashion that makes it intelligible both to the original owners of the land and to the settlers who rule it now.

In an example of innovative and ground-breaking scholarship, Peter Read shows that white Australians also have a very powerful sense of belonging to the land. At the end of his journey to understand how non-indigenous Australians relate to the land, he concludes:

> I have no right to claim on behalf of non-Aboriginal Australia that all the non-Indigenous are now part of Australia's deep past, nor do I wish to. Belonging ultimately is personal. There are as many routes to belonging as there are non-Aboriginal Australians to find them. My sense of the native-born has come—is coming. It comes through listening but with discernment; through thinking but not asserting; through good times with my Aboriginal friends but not through wanting to be the same as them; through understanding our history but being enriched by the sites of past evil as well as good. It comes from a belonging that means sharing and that sharing demands equal partnership. (2000, p. 223)

This evocative and tempered statement suggests the many shared ways in which indigenous and non-indigenous Australians can both relate to and have reverence for the land.

There is also another group who though somewhat tangential to this issue may actually have a valuable role to play. Almost all the secondary literature so far has concentrated only on aboriginal and white Australia when it comes to a discussion of the sacred. But there is a third, more recent immigrant intervention that needs to be considered more seriously. The arrival in Australia of non-white settlers, mostly from Asian countries, may impact this question of sacred Australia. Though some of these Asians, such as the so-called 'Afghans' have a history of nearly 150 years in this continent, most of them are much more recent. These new immigrants may present a third way. Coupled with the internationalisation of Eastern spirituality in the last thirty years, we have today in Australia other expressions of spirituality than aboriginal or white Australian. Buddhism, Transcendental Meditation, Yoga, Hare Krishna, or Sufism are just a few of these. When the proliferation of various New Age philosophies and practices is also taken into account, sacred Australia becomes a very complex area of exploration.

Imagine what would happen if the best of the oldest and newest civilisations of the world were to combine in Australia. Imagine what that would do not just for Australia, but for the rest of the world. To me, an outsider and student of the sacred, this sounds like a dream whose time may have come.

WORKS CITED

'Canada to apologize to Native students on Wednesday, Tuesday, June 10, 2008.' http://www.indianz.com/News/2008/009200.asp. Accessed on 15 June 2008.

Charlesworth, Max, ed., *Religious Business: Essays on Australian Aboriginal Spirituality.* Cambridge, CUP, 1998.

Combs, Allan, *Radiance of Being.* 1995. 2nd ed. St Paul, Minn., Paragon House, 2002.

Foucault, Michel, 'Of Other Spaces'. *Diacritics* vol. 16, no.1, pp. 22–27, 1986.

Gelder, Ken and Jane M Jacobs, *Uncanny Australia: Sacredness and Identity in a Postcolonial Nation.* Melbourne, Melbourne University Press, 1998.

Havecker, Cyril, *Understanding Aboriginal Culture.* Sydney, Cosmos Periodicals, 1988.

Hodge, Bob and Vijay Mishra, *Dark Side of the Dream.* Sydney, Allen and Unwin, 1991.

Kevans, Dennis, *Ah, white man have you any sacred sites.* Sydney, n.p., 1985.

'Prime Minister Stephen Harper's statement of apology.' http://www.cbc.ca/canada/story/2008/06/11/pm-statement.html. Accessed 15 June 2008.

Read, Peter, *Belonging: Australians, Place and Aboriginal Ownership.* Cambridge, CUP, 2000.

Rowley, C D, *The Destruction of Aboriginal Society.* Canberra, ANU Press, 1970.

—— *Outcasts in White Australia.* Canberra, ANU Press, 1972.

—— *The Remote Aborigines.* Canberra, ANU Press, 1972.

Rudd, Kevin, 'Text of Australian Prime Minister Kevin Rudd's apology to Aborigines.' http://www.hindu.com/nic/auspmapology.htm, accessed on 13th May 2008.

Stanner, WEH, *White Man Got No Dreaming: Essays 1938–1973.* Canberra, ANU Press, 1979.

Tacey, David J, *Edge of the Sacred: Transformation in Australia.* Blackburn, Victoria, HarperCollins, 1995.

Turner, David H, *Life Before Genesis, A Conclusion: An Understanding of the Significance of Australian Aboriginal Culture.* New York, Peter Lang, 1985.

THE SACRED IN AUSTRALIAN CULTURE

Bill Ashcroft

During the 1990s debates concerning the traditional and sacred beliefs of colonised, indigenous, and marginalised peoples increased greatly in importance to post-colonial studies. This amounted to something of a paradigm shift in western thinking because since the Enlightenment any mention of the sacred had been considered a sign of the worst kind of intellectual bad taste. Secularity, economic rationalism and progressivism have dominated in Modernity, while 'the sacred' has so often been relegated to primitivism and the archaic (Chakıabarty 2000; Scott & Simpson-Housley 2001).[1]

At the end of the twentieth century, this situation began to change. Debates about the sacred became more urgent as issues such as land rights and rights to sacred beliefs and practices began to intensify. But most urgent, of course, was the changing nature of global power relations after the fall of the Berlin wall and eventually the Soviet government. The US Hypernation, self-elected as the world's policeman, began to conduct itself more and more within the rhetorical language of the religious right. The invasion of Iraq was provocatively referred to as a 'crusade' and soon the insurgents regularly referred to their war against the 'crusaders'. With surprising speed the post-Cold war power relations reverted to the polarities of the Middle Ages, with about the same level of misunderstanding, Othering and demonisation.

But alongside this use of religious rhetoric for political purposes, a shift has been occurring in the area of the sacred, particularly in post-colonial theory, occasioned by the complex, hybrid and rapidly changing cultural

[1] It is interesting to observe the regularity with which issues surrounding the sacred, religion, morality are relegated to the past. They are either medieval, 'Victorian' or even a feature of the conservative 1950s. While Time is a prominent feature of Modernity it is always valued in the context of future change, of further 'modernising'.

formations of marginalised and fourth-world peoples, as well as the greatly increased visibility of Islam. The sacred has followed the trajectory of other 'denied knowledges', as Bhabha puts it, entering the dominant discourse and estranging 'the basis of its authority—its rules of recognition' (Bhabha 1994, p. 114). This is why Australia, a former colony—marked by the tensions, conflicts and ambivalences of imperial influence, increasingly transformed by the cultural practices of diasporic groups—finds itself in a climate in which ideas of the sacred and practices surrounding faith and belief are of growing concern. The sacred has been an empowering feature of post-colonial experience in two ways: on one hand indigenous concepts of the sacred have been able to interpolate dominant conceptions of cultural identity; and on the other western forms of the sacred have often been appropriated and transformed as a means of local empowerment. In a complex and intensely mediated way both these features have been true of Australian experience. The sacred occupies the region of the repressed in Australian cultural life and moments of cultural trauma demonstrate a return of the repressed, sometimes, as in the case of the Lindy Chamberlain affair, in quite violent ways. Complicated by an intense fascination with indigenous mythologies, with its battle to localise received European and imperial forms of religious observance, and with its reliance on the literary imagination to tap into this repressed energy, Australian culture has, like many other post-colonial societies, begun to encounter the sacred as a region of difference, transformation and empowerment.

In the middle of the twentieth century new forms of Australian sacredness were brought to birth in the hard-won and original idioms of writers such as Patrick White, Francis Webb and Judith Wright. These contemporary forms of sacredness, emerging differently from the individual writers, share common strands which have informed the work of writers who followed them: this is the sacred imagined as earthed, embodied, humbled, local, demotic, ordinary and proximate. It is also the sacred of interrelationship—an ethics which is open not just to the agency of human ego but also to the other, to the land, and to that which is not human. A new literature had to be created to reach towards this sacredness, in tension with but different from those inherited forms of the European masters.

It is a cliché to say that a conventional sense of the sacred, particularly as religious observance, has never occupied a prominent place in Australia's myth of national identity. Rather, the 'sacred' became captured by national mythology in the popular imagination, most spectacularly in the ANZAC myth—which has developed all the rituals, memorialisation and sanctity of religious observance—but also in the form of sporting idols and fantasies of national character.[2] The sacred as a sense of numinous and inexplicable otherness failed to take hold in the national consciousness because, from quite early in white history, it began to take a different, post-colonial path in the aesthetic imagination. A radical transformation of the sacred began to occur in Australian art and writing of the nineteenth century in a development that remains one of the most fascinating aspects of Australian artistic culture. It originated squarely in the colonial encounter with a new and threatening land, and the post-colonial transformation of that encounter. This encounter seemed to operate from one of the poles of Australian ambivalence: while national mythology produced the self confident notion of Australian identity, the literature arose from that dimension of Australian life best described by the terms 'exile', 'displacement', *unheimlichkeit*—a dimension of awe and uncertainty, of question and discovery.

The numinous, the unpresentable, the awesome—those features of the sacred most implicated in what Hegel calls 'the infinite Subject'—became projected in the Australian literary and artistic imagination onto the incomprehensible vastness of Australian space. The sacred offered a language in which to consider that vastness and that difference. This is the language of the sublime. What follows is an explanation of the way in which the sublime became transformed in the Australian imagination from its vertical and temporal conception in European Romanticism to the horizonal and spatial. This change is most noticeable in painting but it is a characteristic also of the attempt by nineteenth century writers to produce an aesthetic that could fully apprehend the way in which Space had overwhelmed History in the Australian imagination.

What was at stake here was the capacity of literature to conceive of a sense of the sacred that was fully 're-placed' into an Australian consciousness. It is perhaps obvious that an Australian theology would be one that started with the presuppositions, the experiences and the sense of difference developed in Australia, putting its European heritage behind it. But the struggle with that

[2] The plan by the Australian Cricket Board to replace the 'baggy green' cricket cap of the Australian team with an American style baseball cap prompted a headline in the *Daily Telegraph* urging 'Keep the Baggy Green Sacred'.

heritage has been more or less continuous for two centuries, perhaps nowhere more so than in the realm of religious experience. Australian novelist, Tim Winton, once suggested that due to our mostly European rational heritage, we have a 'limited capacity to discover spirituality in the land, to dream visions, to see the numinous in the midst of the ordinary' (Batstone 1992, p. 21). But art and literature (Winton's included) have been the cultural discourses most successful in shedding the European yoke, conceiving a sacred appropriate to, and emerging from Australian place. The first example of this occurs with a peculiarly Australian connection of sacred and sublime.

I concentrate on Patrick White and Francis Webb in discussing this twentieth century transformation, because they, more than any other writers, exemplified the struggle to move from a conception of the sublime sacred in distance to one located in the proximate reality of things. In their different ways White and Webb identified a renewed concern with the sacred in the post-colonial Australian literary consciousness, a consciousness struggling with received religious institutions—institutions that were seen by both writers to be those of an imperial political and cultural influence. This post-colonial sensibility may seem surprising in a novelist who appeared to many to be English in temperament and patrician in attitude, and a poet whose intense and almost impenetrable Catholicism seemed to make little room for the political. But in their conception of the sacred, and particularly that peculiarly Australian perception of the sacred in place, they signalled a dialogue that was to recur in the Australian imagination over and over again.

Curiously, this process, this continual and repetitive oscillation between Otherness and intimacy, is one that we can find to be most characteristic of the immigrant. But here it is a diasporic displacement with a difference. Diasporic literature finds its utopia in a myth of return, a past that runs the risk of becoming a nostalgic paradise, but more often becomes a prophetic intervention of memory into the locatedness of the present. But the Australian discourse of arrival, of dis-placement, becomes very quickly a concern, even obsession with place. For it is in the immensity of Australian space, an immensity that maintains a curious hold on this most urbanised of countries, in which both the sublime and the sacred, the utopian and the dystopian seem to be contained. Time is overwhelmed by space in the Australian psyche. History—the 'wasted decadent packhorse' of European pretension that Francis Webb describes in *Eyre All Alone*—stumbles into and becomes lost in the unremitting Australian horizon.

TRANSFORMING THE SUBLIME

The first gesture towards an aesthetically conceived sacred in Australia occurred in a transformation of the sublime. The sublime emerges in the writing of Longinus but its reformulation in the work of Addison, Burke and Kant in the eighteenth century was to affect European and colonial art for a long time after. Burke remarks in his *A Philosophical Enquiry into our Ideas of the Beautiful and the Sublime* that 'Whatever ... is in any sort terrible, or is conversant about terrible objects, or operates in a manner analogous to terror, is a source of the sublime' (Burke 1757, p. 39). Anything that can occasion pain or terror is a source of the feeling of the sublime because the emotions stimulated by such experiences '... are capable of producing delight; not pleasure, but a sort of delightful horror, a sort of tranquillity tinged with terror' (Burke, p. 136).

The strange combination of enjoyment and horror underpins Kant's notion of the sublime as well: mountains with peaks above the clouds, descriptions of raging storms, Milton's portrayal of hell. For Kant, 'In order that the 'enjoyment with horror' occurs to us, we must have a *feeling of the sublime*, and, in order to enjoy the beautiful [which gives us a 'joyous, smiling, sensation'] we must have, a *feeling of the beautiful*' (Kant 1784, p. 46). Indeed the usual source of sublime affect was the sight of high mountains, deep gorges—the landscape that produced terror and which many colonial painters sought to reproduce. But in all representations of the sublime the sacred figures centrally, not only as an example but as the example *par excellence* of sublimity.

In Greek, the root of the term *hupsos* means 'height', 'grandeur' or 'sublimity' (Longinus, xlvi) and *Ho Hupsos*—the Most-High—has been the term for the God of the Bible since the first diaspora into Greek territory. This convergence of sublime and sacred continues into the eighteenth century. In *The Spectator* of 1712 Joseph Addison asserts the sacred *purpose* of the sublime lies in the delight of what is great and unlimited, giving our souls 'just relish' in the contemplation of God's being (Ashfield & Bolla 1996, p. 66).

A century later the link between the sublime and sacred became ontotheological in Hegel's contention that 'Sublimity is the relation of God to the natural world ... ':

> We cannot call the infinite Subject sublime: for it is absolute in and for itself; it is holy. The idea of sublimity first comes in connection with the

> manifestation and relation of this infinite Subject to the world, when the world is thought of as a manifestation of the Subject ... Sublimity is therefore this particular appearing and manifestation of God in the world. (Cited in Lacoue-Labarthe 1991, Part 1, p. 22).

The question 'What is the sublime?' therefore, cannot be separated from 'What is the sacred?' in eighteenth century philosophy. The sacred and the sublime were linked by what Kant calls the 'sacred thrill' in the observation of 'massive mountains climbing skyward, deep gorges with raging streams in them' (Kant 1790, p. 129).

The interesting thing about the European sublime is the very different perception of space it entailed, compared to the Australian experience. For Addison a 'spacious horizon' instils a sense of self-transcendence, a release from confinement (Addison 1890, p. 398). Contrary to the sublime view of mountains and gorges, 'a spacious horizon is an image of liberty, where the eye has room to expatiate at large on the immensity of its views' (Addison, pp. 397–8). Addison's horizon focuses on the utopian possibility of space. It is a humanised, inhabited horizon, more amenable to the picturesque than to the terror of displacement, or worse, of 'placelessness'. But in Australia it is precisely the excess of space that engenders the dystopian terror of an absolute displacement intimated by the 'psychic line' of the Australian horizon in so much colonial art and literature. The Australian horizon was potentially liberating but terrifying at the same time because it projected the soul utterly beyond the civilised limits of place.

In nineteenth century Australia the unpresentable sacred Subject quickly became the sublime intimation of this excess of space. While the sublime in Australian painting continues to be perpetuated in its Romantic form in the depiction of mountains and gorges, there is a movement in the Australian art and writing around the middle of the nineteenth century toward a conception of the infinite in the representation of place that deepens the sense of the uncanny, the displaced, the *unheimlich*. The horizonal sublime enters the Australian imagination through painting in the 1840s and in the journals of explorers such as Leichhardt, Sturt and Eyre in the 30s and 40s. It gains currency as those journals become more widely disseminated in the 1850s and 1860s and becomes more elaborated in the writing of the 1890s as Australian literature matures. This is not a simple process but an overlapping and many faceted post-colonial struggle over representation. We still see the Romantic sublime in Harpur's 'Creek of the Four Graves' where the explorers are faced with a barrier 'of unknown mountains, that like ramparts towered / Full in front'. (Perkins 1984, p. 162) The vision of place is a continual struggle between the Arcadian and the dystopian, the picturesque and the sublime, between a vision of placelessness and a vision of 'no-place' (u-topia).

While there is a rich array of texts to examine the emergence of the horizonal sublime in colonial Australia, the phenomenon is most clearly indicated in painting. The tradition of the Romantic sublime is still present in paintings such as Nicholas Chevalier's *Mt Arapiles and the Mitre Rock* (1863).[3]

But three paintings of the 1840s demonstrate the way in which the vastness of Australian space came to dominate the imagination: EC Frome's *First view of Salt Desert, called Lake Torrens* (1843)[4] captures the moment in which the explorer, about to set off into the vastness of the desert, considers the overwhelming prospect of the horizon; George French Angas's *Emus in a Plain* (1844–45)[5] places the unique birds as signifiers of an *unheimlich,* sun-scorched wilderness of space beyond human amenity; ST Gill's *Invalid's Tent, Salt Lake* (1846)[6] demonstrates the isolation and physical vulnerability of the human at the mercy of the vastness of Australian space.

Whether as visual plenitude, *unheimlich* location or antagonistic environment, each painting depicts the 'psychic line' of the imagination of place in Australia, the horizon that intimated the distance and 'placelessness' that overwhelmed the colonial imagination. This horizonal sense of the infinity of visual space becomes domesticated in many works of painting and writing later in the century (for example, Eugene von Guérard's *Lake Gnotuk* (1857)[7], and *Yall-y-poora Homestead* (1864)[8], where the purely dystopian becomes more sublime as human habitation is placed in the context of the horizon), but its sublime implications remain a powerful substratum of Australian representations of place.

---

[3]http://nga.gov.au/Exhibition/Turnertomonet/Detail.cfm?IRN=62487&ViewID=2&MnuID=1.

[4] http://www.artgallery.sa.gov.au/TLF/709hp15/

[5]http://collection.artgallery.sa.gov.au/agsa/home/CollectionOnline/detail.jsp?ecatKey=13

[6]http://collection.artgallery.sa.gov.au/agsa/home/CollectionOnline/detail.jsp?ecatKey=1303

[7] http://www.gnotuk.com/media_guerard.shtml

[8]http://ngvartbeat.org.au/collection/pub/zoomObject?artworkID=59650&height=625&width=600

PRESENCE

Unpresentability has long been a key feature of the 'presence' of the sacred. To Longinus the mystery of the sublime, and its capacity to draw the reader to new heights, lay in its capacity to defeat every effort of sense and imagination to picture it. Its presence reduces all else to nothingness. For Kant, statements of the highest sublimity are statements of unpresentability (*Critique of Judgement*, cited in Lacoue-Labarthe Part 1, 6). Arguing that the sacred is analogous to the sublime rather than the beautiful, Mark C Taylor in 'Denegating God' asserts that the offering, or sacrifice of the sacred *itself* is sublime:

> The sublimity of the sacred is its informality and unpresentability ... the sublime offering is the unpresentable presentation of presentation, which takes place without taking (a) place ... sublime excess astonishes by tracing the edge of all form where *no-thing appears*. The void of nothing is not the abyss of nihilism but a clearing that creates the space for a yes-saying so radical that it can even joyfully embrace no. To say yes to no is to follow the sacred by denegating God (1994, p. 607–8, original emphasis).

Taylor's intervention is important because it links the two major features of the sacred-sublime—sacrifice, or offering, and unpresentability—'sublime excess astonishes by tracing the edge of all form where *no-thing* appears.' More challenging, perhaps, is the idea that the sublime presentation of the sacred 'takes place without taking (a) place'. This disrupts the Romantic tradition of the sublime, with its focus on wild natural places, but it opens the way to a perception of the sacred in the *excess* of place that characterises the horizonal Australian experience. The uncanniness of that experience, its 'not-at-home-ness', is a direct consequence of sublime plenitude of place rather than its 'form' or location. The horizon traces the 'edge' where *no-thing*—the unpresentable Subject—appears.

The problem was that even with the horizonal transformation of the sublime, Australian conceptions of the sacred were caught in structures of meaning that privileged the European heritage by default. The second remarkable shift in Australian literature occurred around the middle of the twentieth century, when writers began to conceive of a sense of the sacred, still in some ways gesturing towards a sublime otherness, but now imagined outside structures of meaning themselves—a sense of the sacred that we can call 'presence'. The concept of presence emerges in Jean Luc Nancy (1993), Maurice Blanchot (1992), Hans Ulrich Gumbrecht (2004) and others as a radical departure from the hermeneutic orientation of the humanities. 'Presence' suggests the apprehension of the world outside 'structures of meaning' that are fundamental to Western ways of thinking. I use this term as one of the descriptions of those moments in which the sacred is apprehended in art and literature, moments of sacredness outside the hermeneutic of received religion or systematic theology. This distinguishes the *sacred*, which may be glimpsed in an (aesthetic) moment 'beyond meaning', from *theology*, which may be regarded as a systematic conceptualisation of *theos,* God, ironically, but necessarily, located within the kind of interpretative framework that has characterised humanistic discourse since the Enlightenment.

The nineteenth-century perception of the horizonal sublime continues into the twentieth century, most significantly, in the middle of the century, by poets and novelists such as Francis Webb, Patrick White and Randolf Stow and artists such as Sidney Nolan and Russell Drysdale. Each of these writers and artists approaches the horizonality of Australian space as a location of sublime otherness, but in White, Webb and Stow, writing after World War II, a major shift occurs. There is a pulling back, a quite deliberate and concerted retreat from the structures of meaning in which conceptions of the sublime sacred had been located. For these writers 'unpresentability' occurs not so much in the expanse of Australian space, which for White's Voss and Webb's Leichhardt becomes the stage of historical exaltation, but in the proximate details of everyday life—objects observed beyond the possible entrapment of language, which resist interpretation, objects whose luminosity defies explanation, whose material being bodies forth a presence that lies outside structures of religious meaning.

It might be truer to say that White and Webb initiate an aesthetic dance in Australian Literature, a dance that swirls continually between the perception of the sacred sublime, the 'presentation of the unpresentable' in distance—the horizonal openness of Australian space (neither of them fully relinquishes the fascination with space)—and in the intimate and proximate presence of material things, which in their own way *intimate* the unpresentable in their very presence. This is the force of Himmelfarb's statement to his wife in *Riders in the Chariot* when she asks what ordinary people like her can hold in their minds to receive revelation:

> 'This table,' he replied, touching it gently.
> 'Oh, Mordecai,' she whispered, 'I am afraid. Tables and chairs will not stand up and save us.'
> 'God will,' he answered. 'God is in this table.' (pp. 141–2)

This is an extraordinary moment because Himmelfarb had chosen the path of the intellect to gain access to spiritual enlightenment. The mystical works of the Kabbala have been able to bring him at least to a revelation of his face in the Chariot. But ultimately words, intellect, religion, reduce to the simple corporeality of material being—God is in this table. But the crucial fact for the perception of an Australian sacred, perhaps, is that it is *this* table, not any table, not the Platonic idea of table, but the present 'thisness' of material being. It is this revelation in which White attempts to translate the universal abstractions of religion into the material locality of a *particular* sacred. It is this proximity, this particularity that matters rather than any national transformation of religious experience. But this particularity is socially as well as materially situated and it is White's capacity to see the way in which the social and the material interact that provides his particular view of a located sacred. Ironically, this epiphany cannot really escape the meaning structures of language through which Himmelfarb communicates it to his wife, structures in which 'God' 'in' and 'table' continue to operate as signs. This is the paradox of language with which White and Webb continually wrestle. Once it enters language the unpresentable moment becomes an *interpretation.*

The most remarkable thing about this perception of the proximate, embodied sacred hovering at the edges of language is that it also, just as surely as the sacred thrill of distance, *intimates the sublime,* because the presence of things continues to 'present the unpresentable'. This comes sometimes in the encounter of the perfection of the ordinary, as when Miss Hare is observed in *Riders in the Chariot*—'In all that dreamy landscape it seemed that each particle, not least Miss Hare herself, contributed toward some perfection. Nothing could be added to improve the whole' (p. 8). It emerges in Francis Webb's poem 'Five Days Old' when he observes that 'The tiny not the immense / Will teach our groping eyes' (p. 150). There is a sense of awe perhaps, though not of terror, so it is not the Romantic sublime, but at least in these two writers, we might refer to it as a 'Modernist' sublime because for both it would appear that the sacred is accessible in the proximate most surely through a process of abstraction. The climax of this is Alf Dubbo's painting of Himmelfarb's crucifixion and deposition, discussed below.

PRODUCTION OF PRESENCE

The term around which this movement of a reconfigured sublime circulates is the word 'presence'. In using this term I am prompted by its importance in Hans Ulrich Gumbrecht's *Production of Presence* (2004), which challenges 'a broadly institutionalised tradition according to which interpretation, that is, the identification and/or attribution of meaning, is the core practice, the exclusive core practice indeed, of the humanities' (p. 3). Interpretation is so institutionalised in the humanities that it is unlikely many would see anything wrong with it. But Gumbrecht's dissatisfaction arose from a sense that 'materialities of communication' were completely ignored in the humanities. The term 'materialities of communication' refers to the idea that different media affect the meaning they carried. The 'production of presence' implies that the tangible effects of the particular communication media (sound, print and computer screen, for instance) will affect the meaning, and this production of presence will occur in any form of communication, in which its material elements will 'touch' the bodies of the persons communicating (p. 17). Poetry is one of the most obvious examples of this, producing a simultaneity of presence effects and meaning effects, 'for even the most overpowering institutional dominance of the hermeneutic dimension could never fully repress the presence effects of rhyme and alliteration, of verse and stanza' (p. 18). This is clearly apparent when we read the printed lyrics of a song, for example, compared to hearing it performed. Such a resonance between the 'presence effects' and the 'meaning effects' of the communication, particularly if it is a work of art, appears fairly obvious, even trivial once we begin to think about it. But it seems to have been completely forgotten 'ever since the Cartesian cogito made the ontology of human existence depend exclusively on the movements of the human mind' (p. 17).

Where the production of presence becomes useful for understanding the literary exploration of the sacred in Australia is in its suggestion that there are ways of experiencing, responding to, of 'understanding', the world apart from structures of meaning: that is, apart from the kind of interpretation that can be fixed in language. 'Everything except language / Knows the meaning of existence' says Les Murray, perhaps because it simply *is*. The fact that these moments can be suggested in art, especially literature, is an important feature, for the concept of presence privileges the aesthetic moment. Writers such as Patrick White and Francis Webb, Judith Wright, Tim Winton, Kim Mahood, David Malouf, and Les Murray are constantly deferring to music and art, which seem to produce effects beyond meaning, beyond language itself, even though their own use of aesthetic language is often superb. This takes the form in their work of moments of luminous comprehension—what we could call 'revelation'—emerging out of and sinking back into lives of general incomprehension. But their works always resolve into particular moments of epiphany drawn out of the material world. It is in such moments, which appear to be comprehensively *aesthetic* moments, that the presentation of the unpresentable sacred occurs.

Why it should be the task of art and literature to locate the sacred goes to the heart of the way art works in human society. In so many ways the artist and writer expose truths that they may not even personally experience, truths they are grasping for, that may only be intimated in the horizons of imaginative language. But it is also in the nature of presence to be accessible beyond the constricted languages in which human experience and endeavour are often contained. This is why, ironically, the 'aesthetic' nature of presence goes beyond the language of aesthetics. The sacred may often lie in the very silence towards which all imaginative language strives.

What we are looking at, then, in these writers, are moments of aesthetic presence in which the sacred is glimpsed outside structures of interpretation. The origin of the dominance of interpretation, according to Gumbrecht, occurs at the beginning of the Enlightenment when man is no longer seen as part of and surrounded by a God-ordained world but becomes eccentric to the world and 'this human figure in its eccentricity vis-à-vis the world is a purely intellectual, disembodied entity' (p. 24). This can be represented schematically by a horizontal axis in which humans exist in an embodied relation to the world, and a vertical axis, which 'stands for the act of world-interpretation through which the subject penetrates the surface of the world in order to extract knowledge and truth as its underlying meanings' (pp. 27–8). Gumbrecht calls this the 'hermeneutic field'. A good example of the distinction occurs in the Eucharist. The words 'this is my body' referring to transubstantiation—the transformation of the substance of bread into the substance of Christ's body—were perfectly plausible to medieval culture. There was no problem with bread being the 'form' that made the 'substantial presence' of Christ's body perceptible.

> But it was precisely the presence of Christ's body and of Christ's blood as substances that became problematic in Protestant (that is, early modern) theology. Through intense theological discussions that lasted several decades, Protestant theology redefined the presence of Christ's body and blood into an evocation of Christ's body and blood as 'meanings'. Increasingly, therefore, the 'is' in the sentence '... this is my body' must have been understood as 'this signifies' or 'this stands for' my body' (p. 29).

We might say therefore that systematic theology, *both* Catholic and Protestant, is a consequence of this early modern move towards an interpretation of the world and man's place in it. Modern theology is launched by the need in humanistic discourse to understand the world by means of structures of meaning—by interpretation. This, ironically, depends upon a separation of God and man that had not existed before, for the separation is that which calls forth the need for meaning.

In Patrick White's *The Tree of Man* we begin to see how radical this shift towards presence is in the literature, because it is something like a shift towards a totally different way of seeing. When Stan Parker takes communion we get a sense of a man hovering on the edge of two worlds in the Eucharist as he tries to respond to its meaning. Stan spends his life struggling within the structures of meaning by which he is supposed to understand God—toying with the possibilities of prayer, drawn again and again to the unsatisfactory rituals of religious worship, trying to formulate a conception of God's presence but continually betrayed by the inadequacy of language. Taking Communion, Stan Parker 'was in every way correct, but dry' (p. 431).

> Why have I come here ... Lord? He asked
> That word which he had slipped in last did not come naturally to him, though he could feel it. He knew it. (p. 431)

Receiving the communion cup, he continues to wait when it is over, why he did not know. But as a fly crawls over his hand, 'It is not possible, he considered, that I shall not eventually receive a glimpse. Which made him smile luminously' (p. 432). A fly, rather than the beauties of the ritual introduces him to a deeper communion—with place, and with simple, proximate, even abject things, which simply *are*. This is intimated rather than clearly glimpsed, just as the term 'Lord' is *felt* rather than understood by Stan. But one function of literature in this scheme of things is to point the way to the sacred as continual and imminent possibility of experience in the ordinary.

In the work of Francis Webb this same intense reflection on the *thisness* of things is related to his pre-Enlightenment theological antecedents. In particular his work resonates with the 'Natural Theology' of Thomas Aquinas, which held that the world of corporeal experience provided the clear expression of God's Being. The 'essence presence and power' of God in all things remains the essence of Thomist theology. Equally Webb responds to the concept of the *centrality* of God in all things in Augustine's philosophy: 'For all things find in you their origin, their impulse, the centre of their being' (1970, p. 22). The consequence in Webb is the recognition of corporeal creation as an avenue to God, but rather through an appearance in the aesthetic moment than by the systematic movement of the intellect—an intuitive and poetic 'openness' to the world.

TOWARDS A PRESENCE CULTURE

The cultural implications of this turn away from interpretation in Australian art are profound, for the writers' approach to the sacred seems to strike a deep resonance with Aboriginal culture. While Judith Wright forges her new poetic vision in relation to indigenous Australia, to say that White or Webb were influenced in any way by Aboriginal conceptions of the sacred would be quite wrong. It is only later in the century, after a succession of political victories over land rights, the growth of Aboriginal writing and proliferation of indigenous theory, that the relationship between the two cultures—and particularly the influence of Aboriginal culture on the white—begins to develop. Wright of course was deeply involved as an activist in these movements, particularly through her close friendship with Aboriginal poet Oodgeroo Noonuccal. There does, however, appear to be a fascinating parallelism between the work of these white writers and Aboriginal experiences of the sacred, which suggests that something quite revolutionary is beginning to occur in Australian writing around the middle of the century. This parallelism continues in a more conscious, but no less striking (or controversial) way in the poetry of Les Murray. At least in certain respects the writers appear to be moving away from the 'meaning culture' of white Australia to the 'presence culture' of those already occupying the continent. By the 1990s the 'presence' of the Aboriginal sacred is ubiquitous in Australian writing as a locus of the 'supervital'.

The idea of a 'presence culture' helps to define the nature of the distinction between 'presence' and 'meaning'. Gumbrecht's explanation of the characteristics of a presence culture and a meaning culture strikes some very resounding chords in our observation of the writers.

> If the body is the dominant self-reference in a presence culture, then ... space, that is, that dimension that constitutes itself around bodies, must be the primordial dimension in which the relationship between different humans and the relationship between humans and the things of the world are being negotiated. Time, in contrast, is the primordial dimension for any meaning culture, because there seems to be an unavoidable association between consciousness and temporality (think of Husserl's concept of the 'stream of consciousness'). Above all, however, time is the primordial dimension of any meaning culture, because it takes time to carry out those transformative actions through which meaning cultures define the relationship between humans and the world (p. 83).

The clear movement of Australian literature at the middle of the century is away from Time—and its correlates, such as History and rationality—to Space which overwhelms it, and to the bodies and the proximate material world, and their stories, around which space is constituted. The conclusion to be made from this is that the literary engagement with place during this period, veering away from the horizonal sublime towards the sense of the sacred in the proximate, ordinary and material world, undertakes an *unconscious* movement towards Aboriginal experience, towards place as an embodied presence—beyond meaning and beyond language—characteristic of Aboriginal culture. Not only does the sacred become a function of place in terms of its meaning in totally different cultures, but the white writers, in their attempt to conceive of a post-colonial Australian place, move towards a conception of place that is characteristic of a presence culture. The transformation that occurs in these writers, sometimes within a single poem—from a horizonal sublime located in the immensity of space towards a conception of the sacredness of the ordinary—occurs within Australian literature again and again over the course of the twentieth century. With these comes a problematising of seeing, a reconciliation of space and time and a phenomenological acceptance of the grounded and embodied indigenous sacred.

'BEING COMPOSED'

This is a move in the literature that looks very much like a refusal of the doctrine of man as a purely cognitive subject, towards a sense of being as 'being in the world'. In what might be called a reformulation of 'unpresentability' we move, philosophically, from Hegel to Heidegger, from the infinite Subject to 'Being'.[9] Heidegger's concept of Being is important because Being is always in relation to the world. The decisive conceptual move in Heidegger's *Being and Time* is 'the characterisation of human existence as 'being-in-the-world', that is, as an existence that is always already in a substantial and therefore in a spatial contact with the things of the world' (p. 66).

Being has often been embraced in continental theology where it shares with human being the capacity to approach divine immanence. We don't need to go down this path, but Heidegger's manner of presenting Being, the fact that it stands so far outside the Cartesian oriented structures of meaning of the humanities, and the way in which he aligns it with truth, make its connection with a non-rational experience of the sacred irresistible. For Heidegger Being takes over the place of truth occupied since Plato by 'ideas'. This is not conceptual, for truth is something that 'happens'. But the role of human existence—*Dasein*—in the 'unconcealment' of Being is extremely important for our purposes, because it is a state best translated as 'composure' (*Gelassenheit*), the capacity of *letting things be*. 'Clearly, *Dasein* is not supposed to occupy a position that can be associated with manipulating, transforming, or interpreting the world' (Gumbrecht 2004, p. 71).

[9] Gumbrecht mischievously points out that to use concepts such as 'substance', 'presence' and perhaps even 'reality' and 'Being' has long been a symptom of despicably bad intellectual taste in the humanities. He draws on affinities with several thinkers: Jean-Luc Nancy, Karl Heinz Bohrer, George Steiner, Judith Butler, Michael Taussig to do so. But it is to Heidegger and particularly his concept of Being to which the discussion of presence is irresistibly drawn. Being has been the one concept, according to Gumbrecht, that can never avoid falling under the anathema of 'intellectual poor taste' in contemporary mainstream thinking (p. 66).

The striking thing about Webb and White is that the apprehension of the sacred presence of proximate things—their embodiment—comes about when the struggle to 'manipulate, transform or interpret' the world, both for them and their characters, has been abandoned. 'Letting things be' means being open to Being. It doesn't refer to passivity, and certainly not to turning one's back on the world. It means being attentive to the world, allowing the inexplicable, sublime beauty of the ordinary to emerge outside structures of meaning, particularly those that may be best described as 'structures of belief'. The immediate question is: how does the very intense and energetic transformation required to produce the literary work, the simple *craft* of writing, manage to 'let things be'? This is perhaps much easier to see in music, sculpture or painting but it can also be applied to some extent to the literary work, which is more obviously compelled to produce meaning. Heidegger gives a special role to the unconcealment of truth in the work of art. His statement that the 'opening of the Open' only occurs 'as the openness is projected', implies that the simple object—the silver nutmeg grater, or the gob of spittle in *Tree of Man*, the tools that Judd reveres in *Voss*, the sense of God in the table perceived by Laura in *Voss* and Himmelfarb in *Riders in the Chariot*—becomes the unconcealment of truth as it is projected in the work of art.

But what might composure, *Gelassenheit*, look like in the literary work? Clearly, it cannot be the 'presence' of such composure but the *presentation* of those moments in which the sacred, the unpresentable, Being itself, reveal themselves. How does the literary work do this? I will explore this question in four examples, three from White and one from Webb. The first is a moment in *The Tree of Man* when we see how the sublime and proximate aspects of colonial place are not so much in a binary opposition as interpenetrating one another. We discover a 'space' that becomes 'place' not only by the constant inscription and re-inscription of a settler society (Carter 1988), but by a vision of the actual limitlessness of the present moment.

> Now that they stood at the window, their arms touching, present and absent, she did not deny the goodness of their common life. He could feel it in his whole being, through the early morning weariness, and also the achievement ... That he saw with his eyes and felt with his bones. But as he did not know how to say such things, he stood pinching up the skin of her hand. And it was not necessary, perhaps, to speak, he began to feel in

> the skin of her hand. She had begun to see the shapes of the trees, the white columns, and the humbler, shaggy ones stirring and inclining towards them in the morning light. The sky was moving in an extravagance of recovered blue, so that the man and woman arrested at their window seemed also to move for a moment, to sway on the stems of their bodies, as their souls stirred and recognised familiar countries. For that moment they were limitless (p. 97).

This hymn to the ordinary life comes out of the momentary perception of its limitlessness. It is only momentary, but it is in such moments of simultaneous presence and withdrawal that the limitless is intimated. The most moving aspect of this moment is that Stan puts aside his difficulty with language. He doesn't know how to express what he feels, but the experience of what Heidegger calls 'truth', what we might call the sacred, requires the kind of composure that puts language aside—'it was not necessary, perhaps, to speak.' In this moment 'truth' *happens* to him. We get the sense that the author's struggle with the inability of language to fully convey the meaning of such moments is displaced onto his protagonist. In letting things be Stan Parker begins to open himself to the sacred dimensions of the experience. Ironically, neither he, nor White the author, stay in that moment. The searcher must set out for that horizon of language before the sacred is found, yet again, in the present moment, the innocent object, in the overlooked simplicity of life. In the end, it is always—whether in distance or proximity, or both in strange collusion—*place* that remains the path to the sacred.

The second is a moment in *Voss* when Le Mesurier, a prototype of the writer, makes a speech that, although it has nothing to do with religion, suggests why for White, and also perhaps for Webb, the certainties of doctrine, the structures of meaning in which religion confines the sacred, must be overcome.

> In the beginning I used to imagine that if I were to succeed in describing with any accuracy some thing, this little cone of light with the blurry edges, for instance, or this common pannikin, I would be describing all truth. But I could not. My whole life has been a failure, lived at a most humiliating level, always purposeless, frequently degrading. Until I became aware of my power. The mystery of life is not solved by success,

> which is an end in itself, but in failure, in perpetual struggle in becoming (p. 271).

We sense here the *horizonality* of the simplest objects, and consequently their resistance to the kind of interpretation that might lead to a perfectly accurate description by the artist. Le Mesurier recognises the way these simple material objects adumbrate 'all truth'. But they continue to resist perfect comprehension. Hence the need for continual becoming, a reason both for 'letting things be' and for the need in many Australian writers to engage the journey towards the sacred again and again. It is in the writing that the utopian potentiality of the imagination is most fully realised. But it is also in writing that the journey towards potentiality can never be finally completed. 'Becoming' as Le Mesurier discovers, is the ultimate composure of *Dasein*.

The third is the climax of *Riders in the Chariot* when Alf Dubbo paints the masterpieces that will never be seen. Watching Himmelfarb's crucifixion he was 'Neither an actor, nor a spectator, he was that most miserable of human beings, the artist' (p. 407). Dubbo works on the picture, pouring himself into it, while 'all the emotional whirlpools were waiting to swallow him down, in whorls of blue and crimson, through the long funnel of his most corrosive green, but he clung tenaciously to the structure of his picture, and in that way was saved from disaster' (pp. 453–6). At last he is ready to paint the Chariot itself.

> Just as he had not dared completely realize the body of the Christ, here the Chariot was shyly offered. But its tentative nature became, if anything, its glory, causing it to blaze across the sky, or into the soul of the beholder.
>
> The Four Living Creatures were a different proposition, of course. He could not shirk those. So, set to work painfully to carve their semblance out of the solid paint. One figure might have been done in marble, massive, white, inviolable. A second was conceived in wire, with a star inside the cage, and a crown of barbed wire. The wind was ruffling the harsh, fox-coloured coat of the third, flattening the pig's snout, while the human eye reflected all that was ever likely to happen. The fourth was constructed of bleeding twigs and spattered leaves, but the head could have been a whirling spectrum. As they sat facing one another, the souls of the four living creatures were illuminating their bodies, in various colours.

> Their hands, which he painted open, had surrendered their offerings, but not yet received beatitude. So they were carried on, along the oblique trajectory, towards the top left corner. And the painter signed his name, as Mrs Pask had taught him: A Dubbo. (pp. 458–59)

There is a marriage here between the suggestive power of words and that of paint. We can see why Dubbo's painting is the proper medium of revelation, because it does not enclose meaning, rather it opens up the meaning of the scene, as it does the meaning of the sacred, to a richness of possibility that can only be experienced, paradoxically, in the richness and ordinariness of the proximate moment. The moment hardly describes a state of composure, indeed, this is artistic labour at its most intense and scarifying. But truth *happens* to him as well—he doesn't *make* it happen. Curiously, it is the modernist abstraction of his painting that resists definition, perhaps discards meaning—reproducing the presence, and the expression, of the sacred in the *illuminati*.

The fourth example occurs as Francis Webb sits at a window in Ward Two of Plenty Hospital in Melbourne. In the poem 'Wild Honey' the poet watches a girl sitting on a rock in the hospital grounds combing her hair and this stands for him as the epitome of the absolute beauty of moments of ordinary life. Such moments are so beautiful, so redolent, that they demonstrate a sacred that has finally even escaped the province of Webb's own theological vision.

> Under the rain, in atrophy, dare I watch this girl
> Combing her hair before the grey broken mirror,
> The golden sweetness trickling. Her eyes show
> Awareness of my grey stare beyond the swirl
> Of golden fronds: it is her due. And terror,
> Rainlike, is all involved in the golden glow
> Playing diminuendo its dwarfish role
> Between self-conscious fingers of the naked soul.
>
> Down with the mind a moment, and let Eden
> Be fullness without the prompted unnatural hunger,
> Without the doomed shapely ersatz thought: see faith
> As all such essential gestures, unforbidden,

Persisting through Fall and landslip; and see, stranger,
The overcoated concierge of death
As a toy for her gesture. See her hands like bees
Store golden combs among certified hollow trees.

Have the gates of death scrape open. Shall we meet
(Beyond the platoons of rainfall) a loftier hill
Hung with such delicate husbandries? Shall ascent
Be a travelling homeward, past the blue frosty feet
Of winter, past childhood, past the grey snake, the will?
Are gestures stars in sacred dishevelment,
The tiny, the pitiable, meaningless and rare
As a girl beleaguered by rain, and her yellow hair? (p. 232)

In the face of rain, of incarceration, of the mind and its ersatz thought, in face of 'the overcoated concierge, death', beyond the will, beyond suffering, lies the moment of transcendence in the ordinary—above all a *meaningless* and rare moment of pure presence. In the final question of the poem lies a re-affirmation of the importance of the simple and proximate aspects of experience. Shall ascent be, finally, an immersion in such moments as this: 'the tiny pitiable, meaningless and rare / As a girl beleaguered by rain, and her yellow hair?' Human consciousness, in its constant battle between the yearning for a focus of order and its awareness of an ever-present indeterminacy seems caught in the terrifying struggle of constant change. Our ascent 'beyond the grey snake, the will' is an ascent into 'Being-open', where we discover that the simple *is* the vast, the 'centre' lies on the margins, the 'essence' is in the act.

By the end of the twentieth century, the same struggle between horizonality and presence, between exploration and composure, had been well established. By this time the interrelation of indigenous and white engagements with place, with the supervital, with what deep ecologists have also called the 'Plenum', had begun to feature, if not entirely characterise the presence of the sacred in literature. But the sublime horizon of Australian distance still has its pull on Australian writers, as, indeed, it had its pull on artists, musicians and film-makers. But time and again, in writer after writer, the apprehension of presence, of the inexplicable, unpresentable moment of sacred experience, located in the proximate, earthed and embodied experience beyond language, is brought into writing in different ways. Literary writing comes to identify an Australian sacred beyond nationality. The writer must set out for that horizon of language before the sacred is found, yet again, in the present moment, the innocent object, in the overlooked simplicity of the ordinary. In the end, it is always—whether in distance or proximity, or both in strange collusion—*place* that remains the path to the sacred.

WORKS CITED

Addison, Joseph (1890), *Collected Works iii* ed. H Bohn London: Bell & Sons.

Ashcroft, Bill (2001), *Post-Colonial Transformation* London: Routledge.

Ashfield, Andrew and Peter de Bolla eds. (1996) *The Sublime: A Reader In British Eighteenth-Century Aesthetic Theory*, Cambridge: Cambridge University Press.

Augustine, St (1970), *Confessions* Harmondsworth: Penguin.

Batstone, David (1992), 'Spinning Stories and Visions: An interview with Tim Winton' *Sojourners* (Oct 1992): 20–21.

Bhabha, Homi (1994), *The Location of Culture* London: Routledge.

Blanchot, Maurice (1992), *The Infinite Conversation* trans. And foreword Susan Hanson, Minneapolis: University of Minnesota Press.

Blanchot, Maurice (1995), 'The 'Sacred' Speech of Hölderlin', in *The Work of Fire*, trans. Charlotte Mandell, Stanford, California: Stanford University Press.

Burke, Edmund (1757), *A Philosophical Inquiry into the Origins of Our Ideas of the Sublime and the Beautiful* ed. John Bolton, London: Routledge and Kegan Paul (1958).

Carter, Paul (1988), *The Road to Botany Bay* London: Faber.

Chakrabarty, Dipesh (2000), *Provincializing Europe: Postcolonial Thought and Historical Difference* Princeton, NJ: Princeton University Press.

Guerlac, Suzanne (1985), 'Longinus and the Subject of the Sublime', *New Literary History*, vol. 16, no. 2 (Winter, 1985): 275–289.

Gumbrecht, Hans Ulrich (2004), *Production of Presence: What Meaning Cannot Convey* Stanford: Stanford UP.

Heidegger, Martin (1971), '... Poetically Man Dwells ...' in *Poetry, Language, Thought*, trans. Albert Hofstadter, New York: Perennial.

Hitt, Christopher (1992), 'Sublimity and the Ends of Art' in Timothy J Reiss, *The Meaning of Literature* Ithaca and London: Cornell University Press.

Hitt, Christopher (1999), 'Towards an Ecological Sublime', *New Literary History*, 30.3 (1999): 603–23.

Kant, Immanuel (1790)), *Critique of Judgement*, trans. Werner S Pluhar, 1987.

Indianapolis and Cambridge: Hackett Publishing Company.

Kant Immanuel (1784), *Observations On The Feeling Of The Beautiful And Sublime* trans. John T Goldthwait. Berkeley: University of California Press, 1981, c1960.

Lacoue-Labarthe, Philippe (1991), 'Sublime Truth', trans David Kuchta, Part 1 *Cultural Critique*, no. 18 (Spring 1991), 5–31; Part 2, *Cultural Critique*, no. 20 (Winter, 1991–2): 207–229.

Longinus (100), *On the Sublime* (*Peri Hupsos*) translated by Boileau 1674, in *Classical Literary Criticism*, trans. Penelope Murray and TS Dorsch, Harmondsworth: Penguin, 2000.

Nancy, Jean-Luc (1991), 'The Unsacrificeable', trans. Richard Livingston, *Yale French Studies*, no. 79: 20–38.

Nancy, Jean-Luc (1993), *The Birth to Presence* trans. Brian Holmes & others, Stanford: Stanford UP.

Pease, Donald E (1984), 'Sublime Politics', *boundary 2*, vol. 12, no. 3 (Spring–Autumn, 1984): 259–279.

Perkins, Elizabeth ed. (1984), *The Poetical Works of Charles Harpur*: Edited with Introduction and Bibliography by Elizabeth Perkins. Cambridge: Chadwyck-Healey, 2000.

Poland, Lynn (1992), 'The Idea of the Holy and the Sublime', *The Journal of Religion*, vol. 72, no. 2 (Apr., 1992): 175–197.

Scott, Jamie S and Paul Simpson Housley (eds), *Mapping the Sacred: Religion, Geography and Post-Colonial Literatures* Amsterdam and Atlanta: Rodopi 2001.

Taylor, Mark C (1994), 'Denegating God', *Critical Inquiry*, vol. 20, no. 4 (Summer, 1994): 592–610.

Webb, Frances (1969), *Collected Poems* Sydney: Angus and Robertson.

White, Patrick (1956), *The Tree of Man* London: Eyre and Spottiswoode.

White, Patrick (1957), *Voss* Harmondsworth: Penguin,1979.

White, Patrick (1961), *Riders in the Chariot* London: Penguin Books, 1964.

Winton, Tim (1991), *Cloudstreet,* Harmondsworth: Penguin.

SPIRITUALITY IN AUSTRALIA TODAY

David Tacey

THE PUZZLE OF AUSTRALIAN SPIRITUALITY

'Australian spirituality' is a puzzling creature, perhaps a bit like the Bunyip at the swamp. Sometimes we catch a glimpse of this creature, and at other times we think, in a more sober mood, that it never really did exist. We were only 'imagining things' or 'making it up'. But there have been many reported sightings of Australian spirituality, especially in the arts and literature, and so we had better take these sightings seriously.

I sometimes think that 'Australian spirituality' might be the wrong term. It suggests something already fully grown, identifiable and complete. Perhaps 'spirituality in Australia' would be a better term; it is less grandiose, more humble and truer to the facts of our experience. But with regard to this subject, however it is defined, we have to do with the problem of reading our national experience. A colleague of mine once suggested that 'Australian spirituality' is a contradiction in terms, an oxymoron, since Australia stands for what is rational and practical, what is modern and commonsensical.

But this does not preclude Australians from having a spirituality, since there is nothing more practical and realistic than developing a personal relationship with the deeper foundations of one's own life. In many ways it seems irrational and impractical *not* to attempt such a relationship, given the flow-on effects, the sense of wellbeing and security that can arise from a healthy and vibrant spirituality. Part of the problem stems from this word 'spirituality', which to some ears sounds spooky and superstitious, referring to things that are otherworldly and abstract, having no practical consequence.

Those who are unfamiliar with how this word is being used in the modern world, often associate it with ghosts, spirits of the dead, séances, channelling and widgie boards. They are confusing 'spirituality' with a more narrow area called 'spiritualism'. Defined broadly, as a search for ultimate meaning in one's life, as a quest for the integration of body, mind and spirit, spirituality can readily co-exist with practical and down-to-earth attitudes, such as we find in Australia. As theologian Sandra Schneiders has said:

> I define spirituality as the experience of conscious involvement in the project of life integration through self-transcendence toward the ultimate value one perceives. It is an effort to bring all of life together in an integrated synthesis of ongoing growth and development. (Schneiders 2000, p. 4-5)

She observes that although this term has a background in religion and mysticism, it has been extracted from that context today to refer to the search for meaning:

> The term 'spirituality' no longer refers exclusively or even primarily to prayer and spiritual exercises, much less to an elite state or superior practice of Christianity. Rather, from its original reference to the 'interior life' of the person, usually a cleric or religious, who was 'striving for perfection', for a life of prayer and virtue that exceeded in scope and intensity that of the 'ordinary' believer, the term has broadened to connote the whole of the life of faith and even the life of the person as a whole, including its bodily, psychological, social, and political dimensions. (Schneiders 1989, p. 679)

The dramatic changes in the use of this term took place, sociologists have noted, during the 1960s and 70s, but some people have been unaware of the altered meanings of the word (Heelas & Woodhead 2004). In advocating 'spirituality', contemporary people are not saying they want to become angelic, perfect, holy or devout. Far from it. If they have 'wholeness' in mind, they realise that this must include the instincts and the drives, the baser elements of the whole self. But in using the word 'spirituality', they are suggesting that some (not all) elements of human nature may actually have a transcendent dimension, and be related to a mystery that we can only partially comprehend.

PERSONAL AND PUBLIC DOMAINS

One could be excused for having double vision with regard to spirituality in Australia. Through one lens, it looks as if a great many Australians are interested in spiritual questions, from the way people talk about their 'spirituality' in conversations and group discussions, and from the sorts of books that sell in our major stores. But through another lens, the issue of spirituality is almost invisible and is not even on the public agenda. Many students at my university profess an interest in spirituality, but educational institutions and governments do not share this interest, and give students almost no room to express their interests.

There seems to be a fault line in the national psyche, a division between the public and the private. I meet people all the time who have private interests in spirituality, but never or rarely declare these in public, lest they be regarded as strange, weird or unAustralian. It is as if a taboo operates in the public sphere that does not operate in the private domain. When we walk across the line separating the personal from the public, we enter a different world.

This is a legacy of our secular society, in which matters of spirit and meaning are removed from the public arena and confined to personal experience. In Australia, we have no national church, faith is a matter of personal choice, and it does not rank as a matter of 'national interest'. At the time of our federation, governments were meant to look after our economic and social interests, and churches were deemed to be responsible for our spiritual wellbeing. This separation between church and state worked in the past, when society was stable and the churches could meet our 'spiritual' needs.

But increasingly, as I will show, the spiritual and the religious are separating categories of Australian experience. This has left a gap in society, where 'spirituality' has no social support or institutional belonging. This has become a major problem in modern Australia, where formal religious affiliation and membership is decreasing, but where spiritual interest and discovery is increasing. The new wine of the spirit, apparently, cannot be poured into the old wineskins of traditional religion.

THE HABIT OF IRONY

It seems to be a typical Australian habit to denounce and refuse a religious identity, and to go on to demonstrate, in one's values, actions and behaviour that one is broadly speaking 'spiritual' after all. This is the impression the average Australian receives, for instance, if tuned into the national broadcaster, the ABC.

I have in mind two prominent radio presenters, Phillip Adams and Helen Razer. In opening a meeting on religion in Australia, Phillip Adams announced that he had 'the spirituality of a house brick'. This raised laughter in the audience, but as the discussion deepened, it was clear that Adams has a very strong spirituality in his life, a fierce commitment to social justice, to community, and a life-long preoccupation with the idea of eternity and God. The fact that these interests go on beneath his self-description as an 'atheist' should not fool us too much. Adams is the kind of atheist who quarrels with God every day; that is, he is very close to God.

On a Christmas Day broadcast, Helen Razer apologised to the radio audience, saying she did not feel sufficiently religious to be doing a talkback show on an important day in the religious calendar. She described herself as having 'all the religious faith and fervour of a clothes-line'. But then she, like Adams, went on to reveal in her conversations with listeners that she cared very much about the role of spirit, hope, faith, charity and community in everyday life. The typical Australian gesture is to wipe all 'talk', all 'pretence' about religion away, and then in an ironic reversal, to demonstrate those very religious virtues and values that one has just denounced.

It is difficult for Australians, much less for visitors or observers from overseas, to understand our national habits, and to make sense of them. Americans, in particular, find us hard to comprehend, especially because the spiritual and the religious do not seem to have been so radically separated in America as they have been in Australia, for reasons I will suggest.

The habit of irony, a term borrowed from Wallace-Crabbe (1974), is central to the Australian style. Even when friends are greeted they are often subjected to verbal scorn and abuse, sworn at and called names, and all in the spirit of friendship. If you really like someone, you heap a lot of gentle abuse upon him or her, to show him or her that you care so much. If you don't like someone, you are often very polite and affable, because as yet there is no basis upon which to launch into the friendly banter of Australian irony. In Australia, a lot of things are topsy-turvy, upside down, or in Aussie language, 'arse about face'.

TRADITIONAL RELIGION AND MODERN TASTE

In relation to religion and spirituality, the ironic mode seems to accord not only with Australian taste, but also with broadly modern and 'Western' behaviour. This is because the modern mind, nurtured by science and education, brought up on secular and humanist values, does not understand religious language, which is based on pre-modern, theological and metaphysical thinking. The modern mind refuses the structures or 'master narratives' of religion, finding them difficult to believe and hard to assimilate.

This is because religion has not managed to find a new way of speaking about the world that accords with our scientific point of view. The language of supernaturalism, miracles and wonders, virgin births, heaven and hell, leaves the modern mind cold, and we would prefer a philosophy of life that was more down to earth and not premised on an otherworldly logic that we have no access to and cannot believe. This is not to say that the modern mind is not responsive to spiritual values, to themes like love, connectedness, compassion, and even to the idea of God, so long as God is interpreted in a modern, nonliteral way, as a force, an energy, a depth dimension of the world (Ward 1997).

The crisis of the modern is not so much loss of faith in the invisibles, as loss of belief in the mythological language and constructs of religion. To the modern mind, much of religion looks 'superstitious' rather than spiritual. We are suffering from a crisis of language and not of faith, a crisis of religious form and not an absence of spirit. Hence so many Australians today say 'I am spiritual but not religious'. In the websites and newspaper columns where single people search for dates and partners, the term 'SBNR' is now a recognised self-defining category. Such people feel comfortable with the idea of spirit and soul, but do not feel comfortable with the dogmas, creeds, rituals of old-style religion.

THE SOCIAL AND HISTORICAL CONTEXT

In Australian culture, we often meet a distinctly anti-religious temper, but a deeply spiritual interest in art, life, relationships, community, nature and Aboriginal religion. This is a puzzling scenario, and critics of our culture have had difficulty trying to decide whether the Australian ethos is debunking, atheist and irreverent, or whether it is mystical, reflective and spiritual. The fact is that Australian culture is both at the same time.

Australia has defined itself in terms of reason, rationality and practicality, and the more subtle features of human nature have been suppressed or ignored. Unlike the United States, Australia did not begin its colonial history as a quest for a religious utopia. Rather, Australia began less gloriously as a dumping ground for the over-crowded prisons of Britain and Ireland. American historical foundations lie in the seventeenth century, an age which was hotly metaphysical, but Australian society was founded in the last days of George III, and discovered its identity in the midst of nineteenth century utilitarianism. AG Stephens wrote in 1904:

> Our fathers brought with them the religious habit as they brought other habits of elder nations in older lands. And upon religion, as upon everything else, the spirit of Australia has seized; modifying, altering, increasing, or altogether destroying. In the case of religious belief the tendency is clearly to destruction—partly, no doubt, because with the spread of mental enlightenment the tendency is everywhere to decay in faith in outworn creeds; but partly also, it seems, because there is in the developing Australian character a sceptical and utilitarian spirit that values the present hour and refuses to sacrifice the present for any visionary future lacking a rational guarantee. (quoted in Turner 1968, p. x)

What Stephens says is true. Australia is not 'religious', and church attendance has dropped to about 7% of the population. To some extent any remaining 'religiousness' is constructed as a colonial hangover from traditions imported from 'older lands'. Our temperament is rational and pragmatic, our spirit democratic and egalitarian. We are more like secular France than religious America. Australians adopt an ambivalent relationship to churches, which are viewed not as sacred traditions ordained by God, but as fallible social institutions created by human beings. Our outlook is sceptical and disbelieving, our spirit closer to existentialism than to Christianity. We hover at the edges of nihilism, refusing to take comfort from talk about other worlds, an after life, or heaven and hell. To many Australians, these ideas are outdated myths of the past, myths that have been seen through and exposed by education and reason.

This is the 'official' character of Australia, a character enshrined in the literary works of Henry Lawson and Banjo Paterson, Joseph Furphy and Thomas Keneally, and found in the 'Anzac' tradition, in our sporting culture, in myths of mateship and spirit of place. However, beneath this official character is another dimension. This deeper dimension is not 'religious' in the traditional sense, but it is spiritual and mystical. This unofficial Australia is enquiring, searching, and anxiously in search of truth. It is found in the novels of Patrick White and Tim Winton, in the poetry of Judith Wright and Les Murray, in the paintings of Arthur Boyd and Sidney Nolan, in the music of Peter Sculthorpe and Ross Edwards, in the cartoons of Michael Leunig. Some of these artists are negative about organised religion, but not about the human pursuit for spiritual truth.

Thus we have two Australias, one non-religious, anti-metaphysical, and rational, and the other engaged in a search for truth, including the truth of the spirit and even of mysticism. These two images of the Australian character have conflicted with each other, causing social tension, misunderstanding and 'culture wars' between competing parties. My own view is that both of them are true, and they reflect different phases of national identity. The debunking, rational and practical style is mainly from our colonial heritage, and the mystical, reflective, sensitive style is characteristic of our post-colonial experience.

One will notice that the exponents of the 'official' Australia—Lawson, Paterson, Gordon, Furphy—are 'muscular' and nationalistic writers of the nineteenth century, whereas the mystical and reflective Australia of White, Wright, Boyd, Nolan, Sculthorpe, is a product of twentieth century tastes, and derives mostly from an antiheroic spirit that arose after the Second World War. In spiritual terms, it is as if Australia cast off the old religiosity it had imported from Europe, and then found, in its new-found nakedness and near-nihilism, that it had to go in search of spiritual values again. By the 1960s, Australian culture had come full circle; it had been through its atheist phase, its heroic and colonial pragmatism, and now it was searching for a relationship with the invisibles again.

But as Patrick White said in 1973, after he was awarded the Nobel Prize for his 'religious' novels, 'my faith has nothing to do with the churches'. The post-1960s spirituality of Australia is heretical rather than orthodox; its central symbolic figure is the prophet, not the priest.

SPIRITUALITY WITHOUT CREED, GOD WITHOUT CHURCH

An invaluable source for exploring the basis of Australian spirituality is Manning Clark's 6-volume classic, *A History of Australia* (1963–87). In this work, Clark tells a strange national story of gradual religious disaffection and declining 'churchiness', countered by the unexpected presence of heightened spiritual interest, especially in the arts, music and culture. Manning Clark argues that Australians are less inclined than more traditional peoples to support a strong identity between God and the institutions of faith. They are more likely to want to separate God and church, and to argue that they can follow God and not the institution. He argues that Australians are against systems of authority, an attitude that goes back to our convict origins, and Australians are as suspicious of religious authorities as they are of political, legal, educational, or industrial authorities. Clark argues that the secular, and not the religious, is the largest domain of Australian spiritual experience—a view which caused a storm in academic circles.

Clark acknowledges that Australians have to accept the consequences of this view, which is that 'spirituality' separated from public institutions can often lead to loneliness and isolation, rather than to community and fellowship. But many Australians seem prepared to accept spiritual isolation, if the alternative is conformity to institutions that are disliked and reviled, or viewed as hypocritical, exploitative and manipulative. In recent times, the scandal of paedophilia and sexual abuse among the clergy has served to undermine even further any public trust that was still held in the institutions of faith.

According to Manning Clark, this 'protesting' view against the churches can be misrepresented by the religious as a 'materialistic' or 'profane' attitude to life, thus giving a false or incomplete view of the Australian character. If the churches believe they hold a monopoly on the sacred, they are not going to see anything 'spiritual' in certain typical Australian attitudes. As such, they have not been generous in their capacity to see or appreciate unconventional spirituality. The churches have ignored much Australian spirituality, because they have been unable to see it. Here the words of historian of religions Mircea Eliade are insightful:

> In this period of religious crisis one cannot anticipate the creative, and as such, probably unrecognisable, answers given to such a crisis. Moreover,

> one cannot predict the expressions of a potentially new experience of the sacred ... which might not be recognizable as such from a Judeo–Christian perspective. (Eliade 1969, pp. iii-iv)

Eliade could be writing about Australia, but he is writing about the 'postmodern' revival of the sacred in Europe, North America and the West. Eliade and Clark are saying the same thing: the search for the sacred is innate or instinctive, but we should not expect the churches to support or recognise this search if it departs from the conventional path (Forman 2004).

What is forcing change in religious institutions in Australia is the fact that Australians are finally becoming articulate about their spiritual lives. They are more prepared these days to challenge the authority of the churches, and to claim back spiritual authority for themselves. Instead of merely ignoring the churches or going on their private, inward, and silent searches, many Australians, especially young Australians, are no longer shy to announce that a search for spirituality is a major personal concern (Tacey 2003).

As mentioned, in Australia today it is fairly common for people to say 'I am not very religious, but I am interested in spirituality'. Young people, in particular, are saying this in various educational contexts, including secular state schools that are reluctant to enter a discourse of the spiritual, and religious or 'private' schools that are resistant to the exploration of spirituality outside their known boundaries. As a result, there has been enormous scepticism coming from both religious and secular quarters about the so-called 'new spirituality'. Secular authorities are embarrassed by the return of the spiritual to the lives of young students, and don't know what to do about it. Mostly, they hope it is a fad that will go away. However, I would say it is here to stay, and has been here all along, but silent and unexpressed.

On the other hand, religious authorities have developed similar resistances, and engage in a war of words, saying that 'authentic' spirituality is the form they recognise and meets conventional expectations, and 'inauthentic' spirituality is the form that young people are often practising. In this war of words, the term 'New Age' is bandied around a lot, and used as a weapon to beat people over the heads who are not moving in a conventional direction. My sense is that we should drop the term 'New Age'—it has become an insult, a way of condemning a movement of the spirit in our community that is not yet understood by religious or secular authorities.

AFTER 'THE DEATH OF GOD': THE POST-SECULAR RETURN TO MYSTERY

This resurgent spirituality, I believe, has a lot to do with the postmodern condition, a condition which is also post-secular (Caputo 2001). One of the features of postmodernity is a loss of belief in the hopes and ideas of modernity. A key modern idea was the notion that God was dead and religion was about to fade away. Modernity wanted to replace religion with science, with a new belief in the capacities of medicine, technology and politics to create a better world and a social panacea. This has not happened, and modernity has not delivered its promised utopia of science and reason. Rather, the modern era has plunged us into moral uncertainty and psychological instability. We are 'better off' in material terms, but we don't feel better at the spiritual or human level. People are abandoning the modern dreams of secular and political utopia, and looking for something that will give them stability and certainty (Berger 1999).

Many are turning to the spiritual to find this stability, and this has given rise to the idea of 'the death of the death of God', which postmodern philosophy has been studying in recent years (Ward 1997). God is back and magic is afoot. The quasi-religious expectations that had been invested in science and technology can no longer be contained or held by secular pursuits. Our projections of paradise or heaven have 'rebounded', and are, apparently, in the process of returning to their religious source and origin. The postmodern enquiry has been interested in the nature of this *return*, and Derrida has been at the forefront of this debate:

When we speak ... so ordinarily and so confusedly today about a 'return of the religious', what do we thereby name? To what do we refer? (1998, pp. 32–3)

Some believe we are 'returning' to religion in its premodern form, and this has given impetus to the rise of religious fundamentalism, which is a very obvious and public expression of this counter-modern movement (Gellner 1992). The rise of fundamentalism is not a legitimate direction for the future, but is a politically motivated misreading of the religious spirit of our time. Something new is on the cultural horizon, but it is not completely clear at this stage what it is.

The postmodern intelligentsia are opposed to religious fundamentalism, whether Christian, Muslim, Jewish, or any other kind. In dialogue with Derrida, Gadamer makes this point quite explicit:

> Clearly, 'return' cannot mean a return to metaphysics or to any sort of ecclesiastical doctrine. No matter to what extent we recognise the urgency of religion, there can be no return to the doctrines of the church. (Gadamer 1998, p. 207)

I agree with Gadamer's position, since I cannot see how we can reconcile the postmodern, scientifically educated mind with the doctrines and beliefs of premodern religion. The tendency of most religions to treat their revelations as absolute, to condemn or criticise the revelations of other religions, and to promote their own ideas at the expense of others—none of this can be condoned if we want to live in peace and harmony in a complex and plural world. The religions must accept the 'demotion' that postmodern culture is presenting, namely, that all revelations are relative, that there is no such thing as absolute truth, and that all spiritualities are of necessity conditioned by history, culture and society.

Moreover, contemporary knowledge presents an even greater challenge to the religions: their miracles, wonders and revelations are not literally true, do not necessarily record real events in history, but are stories and myths which have a symbolic significance for those who choose to believe in them. The postmodern discourse wants to return religion to its foundations in *mythos,* and regards the sacred narratives of religion as expressions of a symbolic and metaphorical consciousness that, for various reasons, was wrongly confused with rationality and logic and treated as historical. The postmodern discourse wants us to retrieve the 'truth' of mythos, rather than pretending that the things of myth are expressions of events that can be read through logos.

Postmodernism seeks to demote traditional religious claims of truth, and to promote the imagination, myth and story to a new level of cultural importance. For something to be 'true', it does not need to have happened in time and space as a literal event, but can be 'true' insofar as it tells us something about the realm of the spirit and the life of the mind. The arts, theatre, imagination, music are elevated by the postmodern to a new significance, and the spirit expresses its reality indirectly through symbol, metaphor and myth. God has 'returned', not as a being or a metaphysical object, but as a sense of mystery and wonder that pervades life, reality and world. The new God is revealed through intuitive apprehension and expressed through imagination and creativity.

Depth and Divinity: The Natural Sources of the Sacred

The new apprehension of the sacred could possibly emerge from creative or 'heretical' voices within the traditional religions. It depends largely on the ability of believers to switch from premodern to postmodern modes of awareness. If such a transition can occur, so much the better for the traditions, which will survive the onslaught of the postmodern challenge. If traditions cling to their former literalism, absolutism and metaphysics they will probably be destroyed by the onward march of knowledge and reason.

Some philosophers have speculated that a new religion is needed, a 'religion of the spirit' that accepts such positions as the relativity of truth, the nonliteral basis of sacred narrative and the elevation of mythos as a mode of knowing the world (Trias 1998). I am sceptical about this claim for a new religion. For me, it is equivalent to the expectation of Dr Zamenhof that an invented language could be developed for international use, founded on word bases common to the existing languages. Esperanto was a failure and I think any newly invented religion would meet a similar fate. Although it is true that we need a universal spirituality to express the strivings of the spirit, in reality languages of the spirit only emerge from specific cultural conditions and historical contexts. The universal, paradoxically enough, tends to emerge only from the particular, and I do not see this changing in the near future.

If I choose to indulge in predictions about the future, my sense is that the new religious vision will emerge from two major sources: firstly, thinking people in the religious traditions who manage to deconstruct their traditions to make traditional wisdom available in a new way; and secondly, leading-edge scholars in the scientific and philosophical traditions who seek to find spirit and depth in the world, and to make this accessible to public imagination and general knowledge. In other words, the new spiritual vision will be arrived at by both religious and secular pathways, giving us more choices than we have had before.

Secular knowledges appear to be journeying into an intuitive apprehension of the spirit, unaided by the revelations of religious traditions (Kovel 1991). There are many areas of scientific and artistic pursuit in which 'spirit' is being included as a dynamic element in human experience. These include the new sciences of quantum mechanics and astro-physics, the new biology, medicine and neuroscience, transpersonal and analytical psychology, postmodern philosophy, political theory, education theory, the arts, music, and ecology (Bohm 1980, Capra 1982, Crick 1994, Pearce 2002). These areas of enquiry represent important and ground-breaking developments within established and contemporary areas of knowledge.

Importantly, each of these new areas of knowledge is showing that the divine is a natural dimension within the heart of reality. We do not need to rely on metaphysics or supernatural revelations coming to us from 'above'. In fact, the whole concept of transcendence as defined by metaphysics as something 'superimposed' upon this world has disintegrated and lacks credibility. Instead, the divine is being seen as a depth dimension of the real, a dimension that has previously been hidden from our sight, and is now being revealed to all the *depth* inquiries, as in deep ecology, depth psychology, subatomic physics and molecular biology. This means that the old, persistent and damaging dualism of spirit and matter has collapsed, and no longer has to divide our world into above and below, sacred and profane, mind and body, God and nature.

Guided by science and philosophy, and not by otherworldly revelation, the modern enquiry has relocated the transcendent as a deeper dimension of the immanent world, which means that spirit can be found in phenomena, and is no longer located only in 'numina' that no-one can see or touch. We are to be guided by the natural light within nature, the *lumen naturae*, to recover the sacred at the heart of creation. This represents a scientific and postmodern recovery of what the romantic poets and philosophers already knew, namely, that if God is to be found anywhere, he or she is to be found in nature, body, and earth, in our sensual and physical experience.

This is not the same as the pagan worship of nature, for we are not saying that God is confined only to creation (pantheism), and therefore must be reduced only to the natural order. Rather, the post-secular vision argues that all things have their essential being and groundedness in God (pan-en-theism). God can still be imagined as a reality greater than creation, but creation can no longer be imagined as separate or apart from its embededness in God. We no longer need supernatural vision to see God, but we need deeper vision to discern the extraordinary at the core of the ordinary. What lies ahead for civilisation, I believe, is a turn of perception in which the sacred is revealed as the hidden, yet entirely accessible, depth dimension of the ordinary world.

MYSTICAL INTERIORITY

The new interest in God as the depth or ground of our being is found not only in a new receptivity to nature and the earth, but in a new interest in the depths of the human psyche. Many Australians are turning within, partly because they do not know where else to turn, but also because the suppressed traditions of mysticism and gnosticism have found a new outlet and expression in the religious impulses of our time.

There is a hunger for experience in the Australian psyche, a desire to find out for ourselves, and not receive things second-hand or through hearsay. We may be 'beyond belief', but we are certainly not beyond the human experience of God. This pragmatic and existential desire, when applied to religious matters, will make us a nation of mystics, because we will not be content with any standard, pat formula. We will push propositional faith and dogma away, because they feel like impositions on the soul. We will want to know for ourselves whether there is anything 'more' in reality. Mysticism and religious experience were not so important in the past, when the institutional forms of religion supplied meaning for us. But now, when spiritual hunger becomes evident, our journeys are tinged with urgency and passion.

Religious traditions worry and complain about the new interest in interiority, because they see it as egocentric and not in the service of God. Churches and synagogues condemn the rise of what they call 'New Age' spiritual interests, and frequently attempt to argue that the interior journey is an expression of egocentrism and not of religious interest. But their complaints and anxieties are not being heard by vast numbers of Australians who are turning within to discover something sacred in their lives.

The fastest growing religion in Australia is Buddhism, and this completely accords with the spirit of the time. The new man and woman are looking for the God within, for an interior reflection of an objective sacred presence. They find it impossible to concentrate on the old external God in heaven, but the new interest is in locating a sense of the divine in the interior life, the internal voice, the guiding conscience. Even if Buddhism has no concept of God *per se*, it is nevertheless catering to this hunger for the exploration of the sacred within. Esoteric versions of Christianity and Western mysticism could cater to this need, but they are not generally on offer, and have been mostly outlawed by the orthodox churches. Unable to uncover the interior traditions of the

West, Australians are turning to the East, and often finding a great richness and depth in this journey.

The desire for interior experiences of the sacred has invited us into a mystical temper, an esoteric mood. In some ways, it is strange to see so many pragmatic and secular Australians finding a sudden hunger for Tibetan and Mahayana Buddhism, Zen, Taoism, meditation, contemplation, and earth-based spirituality. But Christian churches and Jewish synagogues that do not understand this hunger are destined to decline and even to disintegrate on a grand scale and in a rapid time-frame. The sacred has come 'down to earth' and now needs to be proved and tested in the laboratory of individual experience. People no longer want to hear about a distant or faraway God, or to listen to sermons about the good life. They want to experience God for themselves, to experiment with their own lives in locating the sacred in ordinary experience.

Our traditional religious activities have been public activities, experienced in community, in the mass, in large church groups, and in work in the wider community. Attention to the interior life has been frowned on as self-indulgent, narcissistic or 'un-Christian'. But that is because the exoteric churches were not familiar with it. There has always been a strong interest in interiority in the Christian mystical tradition, but this has been confined to monasteries, mystics and monks. Today, we have entered a mystical phase in the religious life. Not only mystics want an inner life, but most people who seek a meaningful religious life demand an interior life of the spirit, and this has taken religious traditions by surprise.

AUSTRALIAN AND ABORIGINAL CONTRIBUTIONS TO THE NEW SENSE OF DIVINITY

The new religious paradigm will announce something bold and radical, which is the sacrality of the secular and the mystery of the natural. It will show that God is not confined to the places designated as holy by tradition, and God's existence does not require an act of belief in miracles and wonders. The miraculous is already inherent in creation, as its spiritual and mystical core. As Paul Tillich put it in his contemporary theology, God is no longer believable as a 'being' up in the sky, but a new world opens when we see God as Being. 'The God whom we cannot flee is the Ground of our Being' (Tillich 1949, p. 54).

I see Australia playing an important role in this new perception of God. Australians are not enthusiasts for the supernormal, nor believers in the supernatural. We are 'down to earth', and one of our major contributions will be to show that God is immanental and already present in creation. God is not only the Lord of Heaven and the Future Life, but our partner and intimate companion in this life. Our high culture, literature, and music are concerned with the sacralisation of the everyday, the enchantment of the ordinary. Whether we turn to the novels of Patrick White and David Malouf, the poetry of Les Murray and Judith Wright, the drawings of Michael Leunig, or the music of Peter Sculthorpe and Ross Edwards, we bear witness to sublime values and concerns being found in ordinary places, people and things (Tacey 1995).

The poet Les Murray puts this well, when he writes of Australian spirituality:

> What we have received
> is the ordinary mail of the otherworld, wholly common,
> not postmarked divine. (p. 193)

I would call this an expression of Australian spiritual pragmatism, which can look like atheism or materialism to an eye not trained to look in the right way for sacred resonances. For Australians, if God exists, God is to be uncovered in this world. We cannot know of heaven or the 'next' world. If there is anything sacred, let us discover it in the here and now. There is an impatience in the Australian character that derides any metaphysical position that takes our attention away from this world. If the sacred can be revealed in the depths of what we already do and say and experience, then so much the better, but sacredness apart from this world is seen as theoretical or academic, and of very little national concern.

In this sense, AG Stephens was right: Australians are concerned with the here and now, are focused on the present hour, but paradoxically this will not drive us to the materialism that Stephens advocated as part of the Australian character. For the here-and-now that we seek, the present hour, will include a spiritual dimension, since the spiritual will no longer be relegated to an other world, a life beyond the grave, or to the heavens above. The spirit will be revealed as a dimension of the present reality, and we will be called to witness to the depths that can be shown to be part of the present reality, its soulful resonance.

Here I suggest we are influenced by the indigenous traditions of spirituality, in which sacred presence is perceived as immanental and this-worldly. For Aboriginal people, everything is potentially sacred, and the vast expanses of rock, sand and desert are the 'cathedrals of stone' in which the sacred is recognised and worshipped (Charlesworth 1998). Aboriginal spirituality is chiefly a tradition of transparency, in which the numinous shines through the forms of this world. Here in Australia, ancient and post-modern perceptions of the sacred are bound to coalesce and interact with each other. This is perhaps what Max Charlesworth had in mind when he wrote:

> I have a feeling in my bones that there is a possibility of a creative religious explosion occurring early in the third millennium with the ancient land of Australia at the centre of it. (1992, p. 287)

TRACKING THE BUNYIP AT THE SWAMP

Our Australian interest in spirituality will be practical and pragmatic, not concerned with theological dispute or dogmatic statements, but rather with whether or not 'spirituality' makes a real difference to the quality of our lives. It is to be anticipated, therefore, that when spirituality finally comes out of the closet in Australia, it will be linked with practical issues, such as emotional and mental health, education, workplace culture, sexuality and lifestyle.

In recent years in this country, there has been developing interest in spiritual questions found in a number of disciplines, especially in psychiatry and psychology, counselling, social work, nursing, palliative care and psychotherapy (Lindsay 2002, Rumbold 2002). I have been following this discussion with much interest, although I am not myself in the health professions but I can see why these professions would be so concerned about spirituality. Many of the ailments that afflict Australians are complex and deep problems that involve questions of meaning and purpose. We are suffering from epidemics of depression, suicide, anxiety disorders, and mental health problems. The 'lucky country' is down on its luck, and suffering people are reporting that there is something missing in their lives, and this 'something' may have to do with spirituality (Eckersley 2004). All of this is at the earliest stages, and I would be the first to admit that we are not yet on solid scientific ground, but the intuitive indicator is pointing this way.

The standard literature on the relationship between spirituality and health has emerged from the United States, but this literature is produced by scholars with religious commitments, who assume that 'spirituality' and 'religion' are identical. A major figure in this discourse is Harold Koenig, and drawing from his American research he has attempted to apply his findings to the Australian situation (2003). A debate on this issue has emerged in the *Medical Journal of Australia*, in which Hedley Peach of the Medical School of the University of Melbourne points to the limitations of Koenig's research, and argues that 'associations between religiosity and health are not as relevant to Australians as they are to people in the US' (2003, p. 87). Peach argues that there is no simple correlation between spirituality and religiousness, and that American research methods which rely on church attendance figures to discover the spiritual 'index' of the nation are unreliable and not applicable here.

In pondering this conundrum, Peach offers this important statement:

> Although less religious than Americans, Australians may still hold spiritual beliefs. However, our understanding of Australian spirituality and its relationship to health is very limited. (Peach 2003, p. 87)

He points out that more research is needed, and this research will have considerable impact on the health disciplines in this country:

> More research is required to better understand the nature of Australian spirituality, its relationship to health and the spiritual needs of patients. (ibid., p. 88)

It is going to be difficult for the 'hard sciences' to find evidence for spirituality in Australia, if there is no correlation between spirituality and religion, and if the spirituality of the nation is found, for instance, in the arts, music and literature. In America, scholars merely look up figures on formal faith practice and draw conclusions from these about American spirituality. But in Australia we are going to have to work harder and be more creative to find the index of national spirituality. We might need to enquire into the study of consciousness itself, and ask what Australians are feeling, for instance, when we walk through the 'cathedrals' of nature, what we feel when we touch the land or sit on the beach.

The task of studying Australian spirituality is formidable, when we consider that much of it is not caught by census forms, surveys of religious beliefs or formal faith practices. It cannot be understood by 'religion', and without any hard evidence, it cannot easily be integrated by trainings in medicine or science. It would seem that the study of Australian spirituality calls for vigorous interdisciplinary research, and this is an area where the humanities and the sciences can find common ground. Medical students are not likely to study Australian literature, music, film, visual art or theatre, in which case some potted surveys of the arts and humanities may be needed to inform science students about the existence and character of spirituality in Australia. All of us will have to read outside our specialised areas, outside our professional comfort zones, to come to terms with this thing called Australian spirituality. We will need some familiarity with Aboriginal studies, anthropology, history, musicology, literary studies, health studies, religious studies, theology, philosophy, social work, psychiatry, psychology ... the net has to be cast wide because 'God' is outside religion and spirit is out of the bottle.

A medieval mystic once said that God in creation is an anomaly, since he is felt everywhere and seen nowhere. This strikes me as a valid description of Australian spirituality, which is sensed everywhere, in numerous fields of enquiry, but it is 'gathered' nowhere. There is no 'headquarters' for Australian spirituality, no shrine, no museum, no temple, no think-tank or university. It is the ultimate postmodern subject, in that it is often referred to and yet while its reality is sensed, it is merely virtual or subliminal. 'Pity the high madness that misses it continually', writes Les Murray of spiritual reality in Australia (1986, p. 236). It is difficult to pin down, is not caught by the traditional labels or categories, and yet this does not mean that it does not exist. Australian spirituality is a large entity with many contours, many features, and we have a lot of work to do to track it down and follow its lead.

WORKS CITED

Berger, Peter, 1999: *The Desecularization of the World.* Grand Rapids: Eerdmans Publishing.

Bohm, David, 1980: *Wholeness and the Implicate Order.* London: Routledge and Kegan Paul.

Capra, Fritjof, 1982: *The Turning Point: Science, Society, and the Rising Culture.* London: HarperCollins.

Caputo, John, 2001: *On Religion*. London: Routledge.

Charlesworth, Max, 1992: 'Terra Australis and the Holy Spirit'. In Helen Daniel (ed) *Millennium*. Melbourne: Penguin.

—— 1998: *Religious Business: Australian Aboriginal Spirituality*. Cambridge University Press.

Pearce, Joseph Chilton, 2002: *The biology of transcendence: A blueprint of the human spirit*. Rochester, Vermont: Park Street Press.

Clark CMH, 1963–1987: *A History of Australia*. Six Volumes. Melbourne University Press.

Crick, Francis, 1994: *The Astonishing Hypothesis: The scientific search for the soul*. New York: Simon & Schuster.

Derrida, Jacques & Vattimo, Gianni (eds.), 1998: *Religion*. Stanford University Press.

Eckersley, Richard, 2004: *Well and Good: How we feel and why it matters*. Text: Melbourne.

Eliade, Mircea, 1969: *The Quest: History and Meaning in Religion*. University of Chicago Press.

Forman, Robert, 2004: *Grassroots Spirituality*. Charlottesville, VA: Imprint Academic.

Gadamer, Hans-Georg, 1998: 'Dialogues in Capri'. In Jacques Derrida and Gianni Vattimo (eds.) *Religion*. Stanford University Press.

Gellner, Ernest, 1992: *Postmodernism, Reason, and Religion*. London: Routledge.

Heelas, Paul & Woodhead, Linda, 2004: *The Spiritual Revolution*. Oxford: Basil Blackwell.

Koenig, Harold G, 2003: 'Religion, spirituality and health: an American physician's response'. *Medical Journal of Australia*, 178: 51–52.

Kovel, Joel, 1991: *History and Spirit*. Boston: Beacon Press.

Lindsay, Rae, 2002: *Recognising Spirituality*. Perth: University of Western Australia Press.

Murray, Les A (ed.), 1986: *Anthology of Australian Religious Poetry*. Melbourne: Collins Dove.

Peach, Hedley G, 2003: 'Religion, spirituality and health: how should Australia's medical professionals respond?' *Medical Journal of Australia*, 178: 85–88.

Rumbold, Bruce ed., 2002: *Spirituality and Palliative Care: Social and Pastoral Perspectives*. Melbourne: Oxford University Press.

Schneiders, Sandra, 1989: 'Spirituality in the Academy'. In *Theological Studies*, 50 (2).

—— 2000: 'Religion and Spirituality: Strangers, Rivals, or Partners?' *The Santa Clara Lectures* (California), Vol. 6, No. 2.

Tacey, David, 1995: *Edge of the Sacred: Transformation in Australia*. Sydney: Harper Collins.

——2003: *The Spirituality Revolution: The Emergence of Contemporary Spirituality*. Sydney: Harper Collins.

Tillich, Paul, 1949: *The Shaking of the Foundations*. London: Penguin, 1963.

Trias, Eugenio, 1998: 'Religion of the Spirit'. In Jacques Derrida and Gianni Vattimo (eds.) *Religion*. Stanford University Press.

Turner, Ian (ed.), 1968: *The Australian Dream*. Melbourne: Sun Books.

Wallace-Crabbe, Chris, 1974: *Melbourne or the Bush*. Sydney: Angus and Robertson.

Ward, Graham (ed.), 1997: *The Postmodern God*. Oxford: Basil Blackwell.

NOT TO GENERALISE: THE 'SACRED' IN YANYUWA COUNTRY

John J Bradley

'*Kurdukurdu, nganjirra, warruki, wirrimalaru* and maybe *lhamarnda*, that's all the words now, that's how we talk for the sacred, and I tell you now the Law makes them work.' (Annie Karraykayny 1998)

To write this article is to position myself in some degree with a split persona, one which demands the acknowledgement of a personal journey of embodied experience and the other is to write how my own western society has lead me to see issues that surround any discussion of the Indigenous sacred in Australia.

I write also with hesitation because to undertake the writing of this paper I will have to reveal myself and the people who have mentored me over the last near three decades in the way of their Law that sometimes is equated with the sacred, and much of this journey has been one of intimacy and within the experiences of the gamut of human emotions.

I am of course by the way that I wish to write this paper having to confront what I may consider to be the sacred in Australia, or what it is that really defines the sacred. How do we know the sacred when we see it, feel it, smell it, touch it or taste it? Is it revelation, divinity, people-hood, history, memory or emotion? Maybe it is all or some of these things, and if I accept this as the case, I have created for myself a pathway by which I may then approach some notion of the sacred in Indigenous Australia, because firmly emplaced within any discussion of this must be issues of people, history, memory, emotion and place.

A summary of the meaning of the term sacred as defined in any number of dictionary entries may include the following: something that is set apart for worship or worthy of veneration, or made or declared to be holy, dedicated or devoted to a particular single use or worthy of respect. While this may seem a tedious pursuit it is important to revisit such definitions as they arise from a western way of viewing things, and yet there is ambiguity in the ideas and maybe the west has left it intentionally vague so that individuals or groups can interpret the concept in their own way. From a practical point of view perhaps it would not matter if we were talking about some vague inconsequential feelings, as the sacred may be for some people, but the reality is that for many Indigenous people, that which is labelled the sacred by the west is to talk and engage with things that define the quality of much of a peoples' way of life and that, unlike suggestions and arguments in texts created by authors such as Tacey (1995; 2000), Gelder & Jacobs (1988), cannot be reduced to a content free, unrestricted, undefined generalist agnostiscm.

There are many questions to be asked about the nature of what might be meant by the sacred before even attempting to understand where it might fit within an Indigenous context; the sacred by its very nature in the west might be described as elusive and dependant on circumstances and events that are quite often beyond our control. Is the sacred then a 'skill' that, once acquired, endures through the ups and downs of life? Or has the sacred been so overused and over studied that people have given up on it, turned off by the illusions and platitudes it evokes? For some even to talk of the sacred is now considered bad taste, New Age and worthy of little discussion; the sacred has become so coated in a veneer of intellectual complacency that it is sneered at in much the same way as we would an overly sentimental novel or film.

There are questions here that are beyond this paper that I will ask and then leave but we must ask how did this devaluation come about? Is it a reflection of artifice and neediness that is constructed by New Age texts and advertisements? Is it because it has been described so much in popular and academic circles that there is nothing more to say? It is a result of our failed attempts to really try to understand how the sacred, if it exists by that name, in other cultures lives and breathes.

My engagement with Indigenous people has taught me that if there is an Indigenous sacred, it is one that cannot be limited to a few pleasant sensations and feel-good desires, or to some intense pleasure and eruption of a fleeting sense of serenity or to a cheery 'magic' moment that catches us by surprise. Such diverse facets that are sometimes associated with an experience of the Indigenous sacred are not enough in themselves to build an accurate image of the profoundly political, familial and embodied events that characterise any notion of the Indigenous Australian sacred. My own experience of the

Indigenous sacred has led me to a deep sense of flourishing that arises from an understanding of the connections that are necessary to grasp in relation to the country-bound nature of knowledge, and that for people engaged in the serious day-to-day task of working with the sacred it is not a mere pleasurable feeling, a fleeting emotion or a mood: the issues are much more grounded, serious and pragmatic. An engagement then with this knowledge that we may label as the sacred is a profound way of interpreting a place, and while it may not appear to change the place in any real physical way, it is always possible to renew and review the way we may look at it.

Changing the way we see a place because of an added awareness or effort does not imply naïve or artificial euphoria; rather it is learning to see things in another perspective and to understand the ontological and epistemological bridges that need to be constructed and crossed to reduce the gap between what we may seek the sacred to be and what it really might imply.

I begin however with the understanding that I will make no claim to any generic understanding of the Indigenous sacred in Australia, I will only claim to the experiences that I have had and understood in a small part of Australia in the south west Gulf country of the Northern Territory. It is in this part of Australia where the homelands of the Yanyuwa people lie; their country is evidenced by the broad sweeps of the lower McArthur and Wearyan Rivers and the vast horizons of the savanna grasslands and the dazzling glare of the coastal saltpans that are edged by the emerald green of the dense mangrove forests. Then there is the sea, the shallow waters of the south western Gulf which is home to extensive sea grass meadows where sea turtles feed, rise and gasp for air and where herds of dugong move, feeding and surfacing to snort and blow as they take breath before diving again. Scattered across this area of sea are the Sir Edward Pellew Islands. It is to this country, the sea, mangroves and savannah and the Yanyuwa people who call it *wirriyarra awara*, the place of their beginnings, their place of original origins that will address my intentions.

The west has laboured under the triumph of Cartesian science (Leaf 1979), a world of constructed dualities of interest to this paper, sacred and secular, and so often cultures such as that of the Yanyuwa are relegated to the same structures because the 'west is best'; however what is rarely discussed when this happens is the life of the Indigenous is exposed through a particular set of lenses but the particular subjective and epistemological interests of the observer and writer are all too often concealed from view. As a result a vital link between culture and country is all too often missed, raising questions regarding the relevancy of these explanations for the people who they purport to describe. So often it has been the case when discussing these kinds of writings Yanyuwa men and women will sit with incredulous looks on their faces and then say, 'They've (the writers) got no idea, we don't speak like that', and this is particularly so when issues of a more sensitive kind have been written about, issues that concern the sacred for example.

The terms sacred and secular divide as do similar descriptions like restricted and unrestricted, which may be used to delineate who can access knowledge and enter places. Generally speaking the use of these terms implies that 'restricted' refers to events and places that limit an individual's participation based on gender, age and/or kinship affiliation. In contrast the term 'unrestricted' denotes performance that does not have any conditions attached on who may participate, view or enter a particular place. The Yanyuwa have a number of words to describe these terms and even though they may be equated with some English understandings they should not be seen to be synonymous. These words are *kurdukurdu, nganjirra, warruki, wirrimalaru* and *lhamarnda.*

Kurdukurdu is often equated with the terms 'secret and sacred' and 'restricted', *nganjirra* is more powerful than *kurdukurdu* and often is translated as 'forbidden', *warruki* is 'a little bit sacred' or more often more obliquely translated as 'half and half sacred', *wirrimalaru* is 'power', the 'force of the sacred' and *lhamarnda* is often translated as 'free'. As with many such words in Indigenous languages however the terms are multivocal and are open to interpretations that are dependant upon time, place, event and the gender balance at any one moment. The following example may illustrate this.

I was once asked by the school principal at Borroloola if he and his staff could come and view *Kulyukulyu* Brolga funeral rituals for a man who had had close associations with the school. I asked the senior men associated with the ceremony and one of them said, 'You tell them it is really *kurdukurdu* you know, but they can come because its *lhamarnda..*' It read like a contradiction: how can something generally translated as *kurdukurdu*, 'secret and sacred' also be *lhamarnda*, 'free'? Let me try and illustrate with one more example. During the very important a-Kunabibi rituals an old woman was berating her sons, '*Kurdukurdu a-mangaji a-yinjatha nganjirra barra kalngi*, it is 'secret and sacred' that ceremony, it is deadly, it is forbidden truly I tell you this'.

What has to be understood is that the events being described are carrying a force which is seen to be physical and will effect people, this is the *wirrimalaru*, the force or power that is given off from the event, and depending on how this 'force has to be managed' will depend on who can access the event or place. The Brolga rituals mentioned above carry much power but their management does not require too much exertion and contact with more powerful forces, while the a-Kunabibi rituals require enormous effort and control and brings forward many objects, songs and movements of enormous power.

The term *warruki* is associated with places and objects that once contained great power and force but due to the passage of time the power has diminished and is safe for people to view or experience. Another way of viewing the slippage between these words is to see them in terms of what people such as the Yanyuwa often describe as 'inside' and 'outside' (cf Keen 1994; Morphy 1991). The terms 'inside' and 'outside' allow for knowledge to be seen as a continuum and not as separate boxed entities. While 'inside' might be equated with 'restricted' and 'secret and sacred', the 'outside' as the secular mundane world, this is too simplistic because there is fluidity between them in so far as the world of human and creation ancestors reaches into the everyday world and the inside flows to the outside and vice versa, therefore there is constant interaction and interconnection between then. What is generated then is an idea of public secrecy that can be both inside and outside depending on context. An example of this is given in the quote below by a senior Yanyuwa woman, Dinah Norman Marrngawi. To the trained ear her comments are saturated with what we may call elements, important keys to the sacred but at the same time it is of the everyday; her words are an excellent example of the everyday 'livingness' of such knowledge:

> Let me tell you something, the sea, the saltwater, the waves, they are my mother, the sea is my mother, it is my mother's Ancestor. I know this, I have known this since I was small. Further I will tell you the sea has names, many names, names for the reefs, names for the sea grass beds, names for the sand bars, and the sea has boundaries, we know these boundaries, they did not come here recently. From the time of the Ancestral beings and our human ancestors they have been here. Our songs and ceremony are also in the sea, they are running through the sea, both along the bottom of the sea and they also rise and travel on the surface of the sea. White people think the sea is empty that it has no Law, but the Law and the ceremony is there in the salt water, in the fish, in the sea

birds the dugong and the turtle, it is there and we knowledgeable people are holding it.

When Dinah speaks of the sea being her mother she is not speaking in some vague, over-arching spiritual sense, she is speaking in the sense that her actual biological mother's life spirit came from the Ancestor which is the sea; as a result Dinah is *jungkayi*, guardian for the sea, for her mother, for its physical reality and for the Law and knowledge that is derived from it.

In the Yanyuwa language the sea, *antha*, is masculine, while the waves, *a-rumu*, are feminine, male and female combined, no separation. The waves are feminine because they were created by the female Sea Snake Ancestress, *a-wirininybirniny*, thus the foaming white crest of a wave is called *nanda-rayal*, her spit, the fine sea spray from wave, *nanda-minymi*, her condensation, the external arch of the wave is *nanda-wuku*, her back, and the concave interior, *nanda-wurdu*, her stomach, the Wave and the Sea Snake are one and the same, there is no separation. Today the Wave and Sea Snake are embodied both as the physical phenomena of the wave, a biological entity the sea snake and as a massive wave-shaped sand dune on the northern most tip of Vanderlin Island, the largest island in the Sir Edward Pellew Group. This sand dune is located at a place the Yanyuwa call Muluwa, and that subsequent colonial overwriting call Cape Vanderlin. The sand dune is the source of the power of the Sea Snake and Wave.

The Sea Snake is but one of many Ancestors that travelled Yanyuwa country, giving it meaning and imbuing all of the land and sea with an essence or thick substance: in Yanyuwa this is called *ngalki*. The *ngalki* is still there in the sea, on the islands, on and in the sea, on the coastal lands of the Yanyuwa and in every living and non-living thing including Yanyuwa people. There are four different types of this substance, which now equate with the four clans comprising the Yanyuwa people: Rrumburriya, Mambaliya, Wuyaliya and Wurdaliya. Each original Ancestor carried one of these distinctive essences. The Sea and the Waves are Rrumburriya; it is the clan of Dinah's mother, but her own clan and that of her siblings, the clan of her father and paternal grandfather also, is Wuyaliya and their ancestor is the large fish, *a-kuridi*, the Groper. Descent in Yanyuwa country is paternal and spouses must be found outside of one's own clan; however children have important rights of guardianship to the clan sea and lands and living things which belong to their mother. The four clans also represent other relatives, so for Dinah the Ancestral beings of her own Wuyaliya clan she calls *ja-murimuri*, my most senior paternal grandfather, the Rrumburriya clan calls *ja-yakurra,* my Ancestral mother, Wurdaliya, *ja-wukuku,* my most senior mother's mother and Mambaliya, *ja-ngabuji,* my most senior father's mother. Thus Dinah is related to all things in Yanyuwa country, she is a part of a multitude of invisible threads of connection, she stands in a matrix that sees her able to call all people and country and all animate and inanimate things in Yanyuwa country as kin; thus if they are kin there can be no non-animation, so all things, the sea included, are sentient. In the same way all other Yanyuwa men, women and children, depending on their clan, stand in similar webs of relationships.

It is common in much of Australian literature that speaks about Indigenous people to call the relationships as described above as Dreaming. The Yanyuwa people use this term also, but they also use their own word *Yijan.* Both the English word and the Yanyuwa word have nothing to do with sleep, rather it is a term that refers to the relationships between people and their country and the Law, *narnu-yuwa,* that is embedded in the country, and it is this Law which sets out the realm of Yanyuwa experience. It is the Law which embodies their beliefs, and the Law or 'business' in Aboriginal English is said to be derived from 'the Dreamtime' or 'the Dreaming'. This English term however is misleading because it carries connotations of an imaginary or unreal time. Despite its popular currency amongst both Indigenous peoples such as the Yanyuwa and non-indigenous people the term Dreaming and Dreamtime carries a series of ideological and political connotations stemming from colonial discourses of conquest and dispossession and these terms are discussed and highlighted by Wolfe (1991).

In much of the discussion that centres around this term Dreaming and Law there has, as I have mentioned above, always been the tendency in the west to construct binaries of the sacred and the secular, or non-sacred. This binary does a huge disservice to the way in which the Yanyuwa people see their place, and the place of all living and non-living things in their country. All things that belong to Yanyuwa country, including the country, have Law; Law can be their observed biological behaviour, or it can be the songs, rituals and important body designs and objects as well as the powerful places in the land and sea associated with them. Because of the images of relatedness that have been described above there can be no separate 'boxes' of sacred and secular. There exists rather the potential for all living and non-living things to carry their more normative forms and the potentiality to become something else: this potential is always present. Thus the Yanyuwa place themselves and the inhabitants of their country into a system of classification which is primarily based upon having or not having Law, and there is in this system a flexibility based on the notion of relatedness which is articulated in the terms of human and non-human, intention and non-intention, social and non-social, moral and amoral, poetic and non-poetic in particular socio-political instances and circumstances.

These distinctions, however are not the polar opposites of a dichotomy but two points where the oscillation between vitality and super vitality of species, people and things can be observed in action. This breaking down of binaries and the replacement of terms such as sacred and secular, allows for endless re-interpretations of vitality and super vitality characterising the living world as known by the Yanyuwa to a point where it is important to state that such classification of relationships not only encompass different logics or ways of reasoning, but, more importantly, they are grounded in constant social action (cf. Povinelli 1995; Tamisari & Bradley 2006).

An illustration of the above concepts can be given by seeing Yanyuwa land and sea as a whole; it is both vital and super vital. Its vitality is demonstrated by its ability to give and sustain life; its super vitality is demonstrated by the places of power that are scattered over the land and through the sea, but also importantly by the way people can interact with it on a daily basis.

I want this article in some way to express how one comes to know this way of the Law, not just the big events such as ceremony, but rather this everyday engagement with the supervital; the reality is it is something that can only be acquired through praxis, a full embodied physical and intellectual engagement with learning within another ontological and epistemological positioning, a place where the true consciousness can be perceived, not just the 'true' nature of any one reality (Husserl 1960; Mearleau-Ponty 1964; Ricour 1974).

The rest of this paper then is a narrative that speaks of a journey relating to the knowledge of one single phenomenon, the star constellation known as the Pleiades or the Seven Sisters. I have chosen them because firstly they are physically small and sometimes seemingly insignificant in the way of things that exist in the world we occupy and because they have fascinated me since my father showed me these stars long ago.

For the Yanyuwa they are an important group of stars. The Yanyuwa word for them is *li-Jakarambirri*, which literally translates as 'those ones who have come from before'. They are used to measure the progress of the cold season, and in the wet season when song cycles are sung on the initiation grounds, the track of the Pleiades through the sky is used to pace the singing of song cycles so that they can be put back into the country as close to dawn as possible.

During my first ever trip to the sea hunting dugong and sea turtle with two old men, Isaac and Pyro, we came to a place in the Crooked River where we hugged the western bank and travelled very slowly and without any talking. That evening while making a fire at Wunguntha at the mouth of the Crooked River, Pyro told me that the country where we had slowed down was called Lidalhadahla, and it was where the Seven Sisters were. It was the Law to go quietly and slowly otherwise they might 'come up and drag the boat down'. I asked Pyro what they looked like, and he told me they were stars, but they also had a 'mob of arms'.

A number of years later I was living in Darwin and I took Dinah Norman, her elder sister Ida Ninganga and a number of other old and young Yanyuwa people to the aquarium. In one of the tanks quite bare of any vegetation there lay an old beer tin with one end open, and just inside it was a small blue-ringed octopus. As we looked at it a young boy, about three years old, who had broken free from his parents came to the tank and knocked the tank; the reaction from the octopus was to light up its rings in iridescent blue. Old Ida Ninganga continued to look with a feigned nonchalance and then said quickly to Dinah, '*Marralhawa nya-mangaji, li-Jakarambirri li-jamurimuri li-ngatha li-jibiya Lidalhadalha*, that is the star, the Pleiades, my most senior paternal grandfather, they come from the country of Lidalhadalha'. I asked Ninganga if they were really the Seven Sisters, and she said they were and that if you poked them with a stick their star 'came out', just like we had just seen. She also said they were dangerous and could kill people and had many verses in the song cycles and were associated with the cold season and the important *Wambuyungu* ceremony.

I had seen the rituals of the *li-Jakarambirri* and once while talking to Jerry Brown, a senior Yanyuwa man, about the song cycle of the Pleiades, he told me they had a 'big mob of names' and he listed them: *li-Kayukayula*, *li-Malamalaya*, *li-Malyarrala* and *nalu-Wulwari*. It was Jerry's sister Nora, with the assistance of her daughter Eileen McDinny, who helped me understand a little more about these names. I knew that any animal or being in Yanyuwa Law that had many names was of some significance. The term *li-Kayukayula* was the term used when the Pleiades were seen in the sky of the wet season months: 'they had no power then' Eileen told me. The next term, *li-Malamalaya*, was when people heard the Pleiades call out. She told me that when people camped down near the sea, at the mouth of the rivers it was possible to hear them, and that as a child she heard them a lot, but she added, 'This day nothing, must be too many whitefellas in their boats'. She said they sounded like a long deep drawn out sigh. The next term *li-Malyarrala* Eileen described as 'their power', with Nora adding it was when they were really clear in the middle of the cold season, while the final term *nalu-Wulari* was the 'Law name' for their legs. Nora then continued and said, '*Li-ja barra li-Jakarambirri kalu-warrka wanika baji barra wayka na-wini awara na-lukuluku na-manangka, kalu-yabima yala jakarda barra, na-ruwaji kulu a-rndarr a-jakarda, kalu-wadaramanthaninya barra baji Lidalhadalha kulu nguthundu anthaa Lilujujulhuwa kujika jiwini baji barra nyalunga kujika*, the Pleiades they dragged fishing nets down at the place we call the Crooked River, they made all of the many creeks that are there, the saltwater creeks and their many branches, and they made for themselves wind breaks at two places, Lidalhadalha and further to the north in the sea at Lilujulhuwa, their song cycle verses are there at those places'.

Slowly my knowledge about the Pleiades increased and each in hindsight were powerful demonstrations of Law on country and the links between country, Dreamings, people and song, all of which were lessons in the vital and supervital nature of Yanyuwa cosmology and at all times could be tied to that elusive word sacred.

One weekend in the cold season, I went camping with many Yanyuwa families; that night the Milky Way blazed in the sky and the chill air made people keep their campfires burning throughout the night. In the pre-dawn, at about four o'clock the Seven Sisters were hanging with frosty-blue brightness in the eastern sky, then from a number of camps, people began to sing. I propped myself up on my elbows in my swag, there were a number of older men and women all sitting facing the east; as they sang a number of them waved their arms as if acknowledging the eastern sky. The song was lilting and haunting and like so many of the songs of the Yanyuwa it seemed to rise up from the earth itself and take hold of the moment. They sang and then one by one they stopped singing and lay down again or stoked their fires, talking quietly, and slowly the dawn of the new day appeared.

It was Annie Karrakayny some months later who told me that what I had witnessed was the singing of the song for the Pleiades. She told me that in Yanyuwa Law the *li-Jakarambirri* or Pleiades–Seven Sisters are very powerful, they 'keep all things in the country fresh and strong'. Annie continued, 'My father gave me that song, song for those stars, old people sing them early in the morning when it's cold season. Alright we sing those stars and that makes everything good, makes everything new, new grass, new tree, all the animals get strong too, everything gets strong, kids too. Old people used to get those kids and when they sang that star they would tap those kids' knees at the same time, make them strong for walking'. She went on to tell me that the heavy sea fog, *a-wumalhu*, was *rrankili-nganji*, a close kinswoman for the Seven Sisters, and when the fog was thick over the sea country it gave them power to make everything fresh and new. She then sang the song of the Pleiades as I had heard it sung down river:

> Nu-lhambanka
> Lhuwirnbirnma
> Langanya yalyarruma
> Lhulambanka
> Lhuwirnbirnma
> Kalu-yanjarri
>
> Regenerating, the Pleiades rock in the eastern sky
> Shining brightly, regenerating,
> They rock in the eastern sky,
> Rocking low in the eastern sky
> In the cold early morning
> They have been reborn.

Annie explained that in the middle of the cold season the sea became covered with the 'fat of the Seven Sisters' and that it had a special name called *nalu-wurundurndu*. She told me that once it was possible to see it 'like a carpet, it was brown all over the sea', but not any more, maybe the country was weak because too many old people had died or maybe because too many 'whitefellas' and their boats now broke it all up.

The journey of learning about country, its Law, people and inhabitants often raised emotion and passion. The Seven Sisters was also one such learning that took people into other areas of knowledge, but as people such as Annie Karrakayny and Dinah Norman kept on telling me, 'all the Law is held by the people and song and is in the country'. There was one more event where demonstration of the knowledge of the Wuyaliya clan Law and the country of the Seven Sisters–Pleiades would again bring forth a debate over their power and which the old people used as a powerful demonstration of Law and the supervital in their country.

In the year 2000 the Yanyuwa people were engaged in a land claim, under the Land Rights (NT) Act 1976, to some of their salt water country or more properly the sea grass beds that fringe the whole coastal strip of their country. The sea grass beds, *ki-maramanda*, are important places not just because of the dugong and sea turtle that feed there but many of the sea grass beds are named and known and all of the four Yanyuwa clans have song cycles and Dreamings that move over them. From an outside perspective this claim might seem to be somewhat unusual in that the 'land' under claim might be seen not to be really 'land', but for the Yanyuwa it is country; it has emotion, memory, event and Law all associated with it and, in a strict understanding of Yanyuwa views of geography, 'real' sea country begins 13 kilometres in from the coast on the country called *narnu-ruluruluwanka*, the flat saline and clay pans that have intermittent islets of vegetation and that can be flooded during spring tides, wet season floods and cyclonic surges.

The land claim hearing was heard on Kangaroo Island, a large island in the delta of the McArthur River formed by the branching off of the McArthur River into the northward flowing Carrington Channel and the north eastern continuation of McArthur River. Kangaroo Island is Wuyaliya country. There is a small community of Yanyuwa people living on Kangaroo Island, near to a lagoon called Wulkuwulku, a place where the Barracuda Dreaming had performed her rituals of *Wambuyungu*.

The Northern Land Council, the organisation empowered under the Land Rights (NT) Act 1976 to establish hearings into claims to land, erected a number of large shade cloths to serve as a 'court house' where the hearing proper would take place, and a kitchen so that the claimants for the country under question, employees of the land council and other people involved in the business of land claims could be fed.

I had been employed to act as the senior anthropologist advising the legal staff assisting the Yanyuwa claimants to their country. It had been my task to compile a land claim book which documented the Yanyuwa people's attachment to the country under claim, the genealogical information of the families involved and a large map that illustrated the land under claim. I was also assisted by another anthropologist and solicitor from the Northern Land Council and a barrister from Melbourne who had been hired by the Northern

Land Council. The Northern Territory Government of the time objected in principle to all claims, especially claims to sea grass country, and they too had a team of legal people, an anthropologist and other advisors. The hearing was headed by the then Land Commissioner, Justice Olney, and he too had staff assisting him. Into such an intense mix were 'thrown' the claimants, the Yanyuwa owners of the country where their version of the 'sacred' was on trial.

The hearing that took place on Kangaroo Island is often called the 'traditional evidence'. It is here that the Yanyuwa people were questioned and sometimes cross-examined about their relationship and roles towards the country under claim. Every genealogy was cross checked by the judge and all senior people associated with the country were asked about the Law of the country, how they had come to know about the country, the names belonging to the country, the ceremonies associated with the country and the songs associated with the country. A number of younger claimants were also questioned about what they knew about the country. Land Claims are a singularly intense experience for the Yanyuwa people and for many of them an intimidating one as well, especially since, in their own eyes, they were having to give intimate evidence about country to try and have their rights to that country recognised under Australian law, rights which they had never, in their own mind, forfeited.

A part of the 'traditional evidence' was also travelling to the country under claim with Justice Olney, the Yanyuwa claimants and other people involved in the claim. Sometimes this was done by helicopter and sometimes by boat. One day, Yanyuwa knowledge concerning the sea grass beds that run from the mouth of the McArthur River eastwards to the mouth of the Crooked River was being examined and this time the evidence was to be heard by boat. A number of large boats had been hired by the Northern Land Council so that a considerable number of Yanyuwa people could be transported in the presence of the judge and other legal personnel so that evidence could be given on country. In addition, the June cold season weather had been mild, the days warm and without wind which made sea travel comfortable for all concerned. At times the *a-Mardu*, the cold season southerly winds, can blow through the Gulf making sea travel difficult if not impossible.

We travelled down the McArthur River and senior women such as Dinah Norman, Annie Karrakayny and Roddy Harvey recalled the journey of their ancestress the Barracuda and of their young lives travelling the river by dugout canoe and also of their contemporary lives still travelling the river and hunting on the adjacent savannah lands. Younger people also spoke of their journeys through the country and of their lives and responsibilities towards the country. The journey continued out the mouth of the McArthur River and we travelled first northwards, following the McArthur River channel, and then we turned sharply eastwards. As we did so the boat dipped into a trough caused by some rough water where two currents converged, the boat rocked and ploughed down into the trough causing a large bow wave to wash over us. Dinah's immediate reaction was to call out, '*Wayi! Barratha marningarna rrinkurra-ardu barni-walimantha nda-rayal ngathangkalu*, Hey mother, I am here, your daughter, do not throw your spit over me!' I was not totally surprised by her exclamation: Dinah was the *jungkayi*, guardian for the sea, waves and saltwater, it was her mother. What always surprised me was how often the negotiation with these other ancestors took place as everyday natural occurrences. There was no artifice or rituals; rather they were seen to be normative response to the situation at that time.

We moved eastwards following the dense mangrove fringe that Yanyuwa call *na-wurndarnda*, this fringe of mangroves that runs onto the sea grass beds. As we travelled east people called the names of the country we were travelling over the top of: Liwundalhukuntha, then moving south Kuluwarra, further southwards Wuthanda and close by Nanakurla, the mouth of Dugong Creek.

Then moving south easterly over the sea grass beds where the Wuyaliya Dingo song line moves, all the time watching the depth sounder on the boat, the tide was going out, we moved over Rumalamarlarla where the song line of the Dingo was pushed back by the Jabiru Dreaming on South West Island then over Warayny. The water was becoming shallow; we moved to the north east a little and came to Limalyalarra. People were telling the judge we were right on the 'song line'. The boat began to drag on the sea grass beds; the propellers were churning through the mud leaving a thick trail of black sediment and uprooted sea grass.

Billy Miller a senior Yanyuwa man moved to the front of the boat to try and find a channel to allow the boat to move into deeper water. Many of the younger people were watching the depth sounder and reading off the depth, half a metre and less; the boat was dragging, and then the call, 'seven metres, straight down'. Looking at the depth sounder it was possible to see the near vertical walls of the hole we were now sitting above. It was Dinah who broke the awe, silence and wonder by saying a single place name, 'Lilujulhuwa'.

We were above the place where the Wuyaliya song line was put down to rest and it was also the place where the *li-Jakarambirri*, the Pleiades, Seven Sister–Blue-ringed Octopus Dreaming was said to dwell; it was not really a safe place to be, but there was also a sense of pride in that a piece of 'whitefella' technology had proved what the Yanyuwa had always known had existed. The boat moved slowly, the hole of Lilujulhuwa was about five metres across and then we found a channel a little deeper than a metre; still churning black mud and sea grass we moved slowly into the deeper channel of the Crooked River and then back upstream and relaxed in warm low westerly sunshine of a glorious cold season day.

That night in the land claim camp of tents and campfires, the finding of the deep hole, home to the Seven Sister Dreaming and 'putting down place' of the Wuyaliya *kujika,* was talked about and wonder was still being expressed at being able to view something underwater by the use of technology. I walked back to my tent under a blaze of stars and the Milky Way, called in Yanyuwa *bunbulibunbuli*, countless tiny stars or *a-yabala*, the road. I crawled into my tent and into my swag. I did not even undress, I was tired and exhausted. In the early morning I awoke, a southerly wind was raging and there were a few drops of rain that steadily increased to a continual downpour and did not let up until dawn.

This was *Murnnyi* the winter rain, also a Dreaming of the Wuyaliya clan. In the early morning light I emerged from my tent. It was cold, very cold, the wind was chill, it was wet, the sky was cloud wracked and showed signs that more rain was on the way: it was a miserable morning by any reckoning. I went back inside my tent and changed into jeans, a jumper and coat and walked over to the camp of Dinah and her family. All the fires were out, the fire wood was wet, people sat huddled together while a few people tried to rekindle their fires to gain some warmth, some of the tents had leaked: it was a dismal and forlorn beginning to the day.

I sat there with Dinah and Leonard and other members of the family saying little when Graham Friday came over. He was the younger brother of Roddy Harvey, Dinah Norman and Annie Karrakayny: he is a man I call *kardirdi,* mother's brother. He came over and standing at some distance he said, 'What are you going to do, this weather is your fault *ardiyardi,* sister's son, you took the judge too close to that place, this weather is from the Seven Sisters, we've got tangled up in their business, it's no good, they've got strong

Law, *kurdukurdu* ('secret and sacred'—having much force) those things you should know that'.

I was initially somewhat stunned, but the accusation was normal and I had heard such conversations before. Discussion of weather was also a discussion that involved moral dimensions. This was not an argument that really involved a white understanding of events at all, this was a conversation about the potential of Dreamings to manifest themselves and become active agents into the world of their kin. Graham was really stating that I called the Seven Sister *ja-yakurra*, Dreaming mother, and that I had a role as *jungkayi* or guardian to protect the country and that place against any untoward happenings. Dinah's son Leonard and I sat there, with heads bowed, and Graham continued, 'You too Leonard, you were in that boat, you're *jungkayi* too'. I then looked toward Graham and asked what we were meant to do; if country was to be handed back we had to show the judge the country and what was known about it. I also reminded him that he was in a following boat, and as a *ngimirringki* or owner of the country he never once told us not to go there. Graham responded by saying what I had said was true, but he was worried, the country had responded in a very negative way to an intrusion and 'We were', he added, 'tangled up in its business'. It was Annie Karrakayny who then spoke up and said, 'Well that's the Law of the Seven Sisters, they are strong, they are boss for cold weather and now we know about it, maybe that judge and all the 'whitefellas' will know that there is Law in that country'. Dinah affirmed this position, it was no good blaming each other, but to this she added that in the old days it would have been a situation that could easily have ended in more violent physical accusations and responses.

Yanyuwa people often use the term 'might be something' (cf. Povinelli 1993) to speak of unusual occurrences on their country. A new sand bar, the death of a tree or the sighting of an unusual phenomenon or a creature behaving strangely may often indicate the activity of Dreaming powers and their continual presence. Sometimes this 'might be something' is discarded as 'just a nothing', just weather, there is then no further case for discussion; however something that 'might be' is discussed and negotiated, sometimes over a long period of time and then it will be agreed upon what was acting in the country to bring forth the phenomena, a Dreaming, the spirits of the deceased or other spirit beings in the country.

In the case of the boat moving over the top of the hole at Lilujulhuwa there was no need for any such comment about 'it might be something'; in this instance it was something, it could be named and known, and the result of the intrusion into powerful country manifested itself in three further days of miserable weather. The event was used to highlight issues relating to country, of its nature to be able to respond to the movements of its kin, of its *wirrimalaru*, its power. It was eventually decided that people had taken the boat and the country of the Seven Sisters for granted; *jungkayi*, guardians for the country, should have called out and announced who was present and why and that they meant no harm and then perhaps the weather would not have happened. Again people reprimanded themselves about their own perceived weakness. These comments were perhaps best summed up by Dinah who said, 'It is hard work looking after country, it is hard work fighting for country through the whitefella way, sometimes it tangles us up and we forget about the Law'.

What had been demonstrated in a seemingly small and random event, to outside eyes at least, is that relationships to things like the Pleiades is a demonstration of embedded relationships to things and country, and emotional engagement with the seemingly small and insignificant. Any one event on country has the potential to arouse narratives and song and a slippage into supervital potential. One thing stimulates the recollection of another and another; there is really only ever one story however, because of this relationship they go on and on, people, country, Dreamings, song and memory, forwards and backwards the stories are told in a constant forward and returning, in a constant matrix of tensions.

The sound of birds calling for example is their Law, not just their biological conditioning, the sound of the song that describes the birds and other creatures and country is both their Law and biology just as the cold season wind and rain is Law; the sound of objects and phenomena are inseparable from the *ngalki*, the tune of their song. It is this *ngalki*, the essence and substance that marks the song cycles and creates sound that is supervital, resonating still in country; the syllables, the sound units of the songs, combine to make up the words and phrases and at one level meaning is secondary because the words and their sounds are seen as the actual building blocks of the meaning embedded in Yanyuwa country. At its most extreme meaning song cycles when sung are like the repetition of the country's, of the creatures', of the plants', of the peoples' 'DNA' strand; to sing song cycle is to bring forward the very biology, the very ecology of the country.

All of this meaning that resonated through both country and sea was demonstrated to the Land Commissioner as the Yanyuwa people led him through their coastal country. At the end of two weeks people were exhausted; the land Commissioner then moved to hear from people who objected to the claim and then he considered all of the evidence. In 2002 Justice Olney made a recommendation to the Federal Minister for Aboriginal Affairs and to the Administrator of the Northern Territory that the country of sea grass beds and reefs should be returned to the Yanyuwa people and they should be recognised as the legitimate owners under the law of the Commonwealth of Australia. The Yanyuwa people were exultant. They had demonstrated their core understandings of their country and the evidence had been accepted, they had 'lifted up their country', they had 'embraced it again'. They would be able to manage it in a way that their ancestors would want but at the same time deal with issues of over fishing, disrespectful tourists and other travelers through their country.

The Yanyuwa people waited for a Federal Minister for Aboriginal Affairs to travel to Borroloola so that they could have their title handed to them, but it never happened. In August 2006, the Chief Minister of the Northern Territory along with the Federal Minister of Aboriginal Affairs agreed to substantial changes to the Land Rights (Northern Territory) Act 1976. These changes moved through the House of Representatives and the Senate and were passed, with hardly a murmur from opposition ministers and parliamentarians and the general populace of Australia; in doing so the successful claim of the Yanyuwa people was annulled, the sea country will never be returned, their court case was in the end for nothing. Dinah Norman, Annie Karrakayny, Graham Friday, Leonard Norman and other family who had talked strongly for their country were enraged; they felt betrayed and once again their Law and their song cycles, narratives and demonstrations of relatedness were rendered worthless in the seemingly more powerful world of Australian Territory and Federal politics.

These actions too become a part of understanding Yanyuwa knowledge. Songs, narrative and the understanding of country have always been about politics, prestige and authority. Powerful acknowledgement is given to those who can sing, recite the narratives and perform the knowledge country. White politics also affects the resonance of the Law and becomes a part of the many stories that it accumulates as it travels through country. It is an offence to sing another person's song cycles and speak about their country without permission and, in the past, it would have led to feuding in both a verbal and actual physical sense. To try and claim knowledge to which an individual has no right is seen in the same light as a government who denies the rights of people such as the Yanyuwa; such denial is to deny connection, it is seen as an attack on the power and centrality of the matrix of relationships, and it is a rejection of the authority of family ties because ultimately it is the negotiation of the vital and supervital which mediates the knowledge of self in relation to all others, both human and non-human.

If the Indigenous sacred exists at all, it exists framed and held in ways that demand intense and rigorous learning, and it cannot be separated from the land and all that it contains; nor can the fact be ignored that much of the Indigenous sacred is considered dangerous, forceful and powerful and in need of specialised negotiation that is always of the 'everyday' though to varying degrees of intensity.

We unfortunately live in a country that has rarely discriminated between the 250 or more Indigenous nations that once populated this continent, and moreover in the mainstream consciousness the Indigenous occupation of Australia's coastal regions is considered a thing of the past—in the public imagination 'remnant' populations are consigned to the urban fringes and to Australia's 'dead heart', the mythical 'outback'. According to the 'two dollar view' of Aboriginality there are very few 'real' Indigenous communities left; those that remain share a simple and common cultural idiom and dwell in marginal country. As Clendinnen (1999 Boyer Lecture 4:9) notes, '... the image of the tribal nomad captivates us still', and with that image comes a projection of simplicity but also of a desire for 'noble treasure', the sacred being one of them, without any real understanding of the intricate webs that construct and hold it.

WORKS CITED

Clendinnen, I 1999 (December), 'Inside the contact zone' (Lecture 4). *Radio National: The Boyer Lectures*, <http:abc.net.au/rn/boyers/stories/s71107.htm>, pp. 1–9.

Gelder, K and Jacobs, J 1988, *Uncanny Australia: Sacredness and Identity in a Postcolonial Nation,* Melbourne: Melbourne University Press.

Husserl, E 1960, *Cartesian Meditations: an Introduction to Phenomenlogy*. Dordrecht: Martinus Nijhoff.

Keen, I 1994, *Knowledge and Secrecy in an Aboriginal religion.* Oxford: Clarendon Press.

Leaf, M 1979, *Man, Mind and Science: a History of Anthropology*. New York: Colombia University Press.

Merleau-Ponty, M 1964, 'From Mauss to Claude Levi-Strauss'. *Signs* pp. 114–125.

Morphy, H 1991, *Ancestoral connections. Art and an Aboriginal system of knowledge*. Chicago: University of Chicago Press.

Povinelli, E 1993, Might be something: the language of indeterminacy in Australian Aboriginal land use. *Man* 28, pp. 679–704.

Povinelli, E 1995, 'Do Rocks Listen? The cultural politics of apprehending Australian Aboriginal Labor'. *American Anthropologist*, 97: pp. 505–518.

Ricour, P 1974, *The Conflict in Interpretations: Essays in Hermeneutics*. Evanston: Northwestern University Press.

Tacey, D 1995, *Edge of the Sacred: transformation in Australia*. HarperCollins.

Tacey, D 2000, *Re-enchantment: the new Australian spirituality*. HarperCollins.

Tamisari, F and Bradley, J 2005, 'To Have and Give Law. Animal Names, Place and Event' in A Minelli, G Ortalli and G Sanga, *Animal Names*, Istituto Veneto di Scienze lettere ed Arti Venezia pp. 419–438.

Wolfe, P 1991, 'On Being Woken Up: The Dreamtime in Anthropology and in Australian Settler Culture', *Comparative Studies in Society and History*, 33, 2: pp. 197–224.

JOURNEY TO SACRED GROUND: ETHICS AND AESTHETICS OF COUNTRY

Deborah Bird Rose

Peter Boyle's 'Dawn Ritual of Purification' offers a poetics of remorse and supplication that speaks directly to the settler experience in Australia. Boyle reminds us that shame and remorse pour through the generations, settling into the descendants of those who participate in slaughter. 'Dawn ritual' invites us into asking how we may inscribe a moral presence for ourselves in country we have come to inhabit and cherish, knowing, as we must, that this country is saturated with the blood of wilful death and dispossession. Drawing on my experience in the work of decolonisation, I seek some responses to the final words: 'I give back / I give back / I give back'.

*

Our journey into country will bypass generalisations and go straight into a specific reality. We will encounter an Aboriginal claim to land, and will meet people and country whose stories contain both slaughter and resilience.

Imagine the great golden savannas of North Australia. Think of the mesas, the tropical rivers that flood in the wet season and shrink back to waterholes in the dry, the watersheds and ridge tops, the bronzed grasses and the dark green foliage that marks out rivers and waterholes. In this region of the Victoria River District, Northern Territory, Aboriginal homelands are organised around the rivers and watersheds, connecting with each across the high points and joining up at junctions. Every pocket and hill is a story, every waterhole a place of Dreaming action. Stones, trees, and cliff lines tell multiple stories, holding and showing the creation, history, and continuing life of country.

One such place is Jasper Gorge, the area where Jasper Creek cuts through the Stokes Range on its way to the Victoria River. In 1988 a large group convened there for a week. By night the dingoes howled up and down the Gorge. At dawn and dusk the cliffs glowed like ancient burnished copper. During the day we ran the land claim, formally known as the Kidman Springs/Jasper Gorge land claim. There were close to a hundred of us—claimants, land council people, and the judge and his party. We camped at the western edge of Jasper Gorge in a little flat at the bottom of a pocket called TK, and there the Aboriginal claimants constructed a bough shade under which the claim would be heard.

The land claim was successful and Jasper Gorge is now Aboriginal land. The road that runs south from the Victoria highway goes through the Gorge, and it is still a public thoroughfare. Every day people drive through, and every trip is another iteration of the path of the Black-headed Python, the great snake-woman who made this place. She formed the sinuous valley with her swervy action, and parts of the story can be seen along the cliffs. Over there is a large stone that is her coolamon; here the rock is split where she cut it with her hair belt, and up there where a ridge works its way along the side of hill is another part of the snake track. The Black-headed Python walked in the shape of a woman as well as in the shape of a snake. Like many Dreamings, she was a shape-shifter, and her metamorphic power extended beyond her body to impress itself into the country as well.

I got to know the Gorge in the years before the land claim when I was living in the community of Yarralin south of the Gorge. We travelled this road many times, and people explained bits and pieces of the story, not only to me but to the kids, telling the stories, pointing out the places, holding it all alive in their minds and relating the knowledge back into the place. Sometimes we stopped to fish, and usually people called out to the ancestors and Dreamings, telling them who we were, and asking them to give us food.

In Jasper Gorge the Dreaming ancestor is so very visible that even a western person like me can see the story. The hills, gorge, stones and other marks vividly express the sacred geography of creation as it is impressed and embedded in Aboriginal country. Anyone can see it, and many of the Aboriginal owners wished that more people would see it. When we asked if they had concerns about tourism, for example, they said that they hoped tourists would come, and that through being there would understand something of what they were seeing. Visitors who took the time to learn would find the proof of creation and continuing ownership to be right there, accessible to everyone.

It is not difficult to imagine tourists who might find these stories quaint, or even cute. Such a perception misses the point of poetics as dialogue, and place as an on-going story. We might recall that Ilya Prigogine, Nobel prize-winning chemist, has described science as a 'dialogue with nature'; he reminds us that nature forever produces the unpredictable (1997, pp. 57, 72). If science is one type of dialogue, poetics is another, and is equally capable of producing complex truths that matter. So, to return to the Gorge, you can see the work of creation because it is there in front of you in the track the ancestor made. But you see creation in many ephemeral forms as well, and thus you can come to understand that creation was not a one-off event in the past, but is an on-going process of life. In her coolamon the Black-headed Python carried the seeds of many plants that she distributed as she travelled. Her action in the world created botanical communities—in the hills she put the seeds for hill country plants, and out on the flats she put the seeds for those places. On the eastern side she put boab seeds and today the trees mark the southern edge of the distribution of boabs (*jamulang* in local languages). Every tree that grows, every plant put there originally by the Python, is a contemporary effervescence of the Dreaming.

Signs of Aboriginal people are everywhere too, not only in the tyre tracks veering off the road to a favourite fishing site, or a tyre suspended from a post to mark the turn-off to an outstation, but in the scatters of flaked stone. You cannot walk across the river banks or flats without seeing remnants that tell that generations upon generations of people lived here.

New people have also left their traces. A hundred years ago the Jasper Gorge road was one of the first whitefella tracks in the district and was the life-line to the stations. Supplies were brought by boat to Timber Creek and taken inland by cart. The defile winds through the cliffs, sometimes narrowing and sometimes widening, and before the road was widened and bridges built, travellers had to cross the river six or seven times. In the wet season it became difficult or impossible to get through. Where the road hugs the side of the cliff face, travellers feared that Aboriginal people would roll stones down on to them, or hurl spears from above. Indeed, in 1886 a road crew was shot at by Aboriginal people who had got hold of guns, and subsequently were driven out of the Gorge with fire.

The place where we camped for the land claim, TK, was named for the boab (*Adansonia gregorii*) on which Tom Kilfoyle, a member of the Durack clan, carved his initials in 1884. TK was an established camp site, the place where travellers stopped and regrouped before or after hastening through the Gorge. Two teamsters, Mulligan and Ligar, along with their Aboriginal workers, were camped here one night 1895 and were attacked by local Aboriginal people. Barricading themselves among the stores from the wagons, they fought out a three-day siege, at the end of which they escaped back to the north severely wounded and weak from loss of blood. The day after their escape, Mounted Constable Wilshire arrived on the scene, assessed the damage, and sent word to Victoria River Downs station. Wilshire went north following the teamsters, and the manager of Victoria River Downs, Jack Watson, rode out with a party of stockmen, trackers, and overlanders who had been en route to the Kimberley goldfields. An unofficial account reported that sixty Aborigines were shot in retaliation for this incident. Mulligan and Ligar survived their ordeal, but both died within the next few years, probably still suffering the effects of their wounds (summarised from Lewis 2004, pp. 159–191).

Humans are not the only ones whose lives have been shattered, and the damage to country reverberates into the people for the country. After relations between whites and blacks had stabilised somewhat, the track was widened by dynamiting a huge stone that rested exactly in the middle of the road, forcing people to squeeze past. Aboriginal people remember the stone as a Dreaming and increase site for turtles. During the hearing the senior woman for the country, Violet Lungan, showed the judge a stone beside the creek, explaining that it was a fragment of the original boulder. She said that people could still go to the stone and do the increase rituals for turtles, so it seemed that the fragment was still a turtle Dreaming, blasted but not destroyed. Other sites were bulldozed, and in some cases all that remained was the design for the Dreaming (called a photograph), the song, and the knowledge of the Dreaming track and site. Allan Griffith discussed these matters in relation to his ancestor—Jirrikik, the Owlet Nightjar Dreaming. His evidence was elicited by the claimants' lawyer Ross Howie:

AG: At Kangkiji [place name] they knocked one rock, Jirrikik.
RH: And what knocked it down?
AG: The bulldozer.
RH: And how did you feel when that happened?
AG: No good.
RH: Why not?

> AG: Well, that's when. As soon as we tell the old fella, Old Dan, That's when he died from the dreaming.
> RH: When you told him that that had been knocked down, you say he died?
> AG: Yes …
> RH: And why did he die?
> AG: Well, he was thinking about for the dreaming, you know.
> RH: All right, and is that Jirrikik still there?
> AG: Yes, he's still there, but he's been moved from the tree. We lift him up and put him in the tree now.
> RH: He's a stone, is he?
> AG: Yes, a stone.
> RH: And was there a tree knocked down there at VRD [Victoria River Downs station]?
> AG: Yes, one been get knocked off right in the middle, right at the airstrip. One bloodwood.
> RH: And how did you feel when that happened?
> AG: No good. We still using a photograph every year on the ceremony time, on the ring place time, tell them that the bloodwood be still gone but we can dream …
> They shouldn't touch the tree, but they done it. We still got the photograph. (Transcript of proceedings, 1988, pp. 162–164)

During the course of eight days the claimants told their stories, songs and histories, and spoke of their families. They took the Judge to many sacred sites, calling out to the Dreamings and to the ancestors as they took the group toward each site. Their calls were addressed to the old people, the *ngurramala*. The term was used in answer to questions such as 'who are the real owners of this place?' People explained: 'They're *ngurramala* when they're dead, they look after country.'

Dreaming creation is visible in its endurance, and at the same time the created world is always coming into being, and thus always in flux. At this time the Gorge is experiencing a wave of ecological change. It is undoubtedly not the first, and assuredly not the last. In recent years the vegetation has been thickening up: trees and scrub are increasing across much of North Australia. The causes are complex, and not fully understood, but it is clear that global warming is a significant factor (Lewis 2002). One of the beneficiaries of changing conditions is a palm tree (*Livistona sp.* 'Victoria River'). Known as *walmatj* in local languages, the palm tree is a handsome plant and a delicious food. From their earlier habitat along the lower edge of the escarpment the trees have started marching down the slopes, establishing themselves in gullies and washouts. Once palms were a rarity confined to the top; now they are spreading out like mad.

Trees on the move are quite visible. Less visible are the absences, like the trees no longer there. Animals, too, are experiencing devastating losses, their habitats over-run by cattle, their tucker eaten out by cattle, and the Aboriginal burning that sustained the diversity of habitats outlawed by pastoralists. The sacred site near the homestead at Kidman Spring (a government research station dedicated to improving the cattle industry) is a place where possum and native cat Dreamings were active. At this time both animals are either locally extinct or so rare as to be effectively gone. Young people have never seen them, and they are never hunted. In addition, pastoralists have been waging an active war against dingoes, the main method being broadscale aerial baiting using 1080 poison (sodium fluoroacetate). The Northern Territory has recently instituted a moratorium on dingo baiting, but that does not stop people killing them directly, and on a recent (2006) drive through this area we saw a dead dingo thrown across a fence, clearly having been killed and then strung up on the barbed wire for display.

Presence and absence, birth and death: the flux of life pervades the Gorge. Birth, the coming into being, is women's work, and the Black-headed Python is the Dreaming source. Most impressive to me is the hill that bears the impression of her body when she was in her human form. One side of this hill belongs to Ngaliwurru people, the other side to Karangpurru people. Here she stopped, said goodbye to the country behind her, and gave birth to the language, songs and people of the country before her. Their continuing coming into being has its source in this site and in her work.

Separate gendered domains are integral to country, but do not sit easily within the Anglo-Australian legal system, and while the land claim process has been expanded to allow for secret-sacred evidence, the gendering of the legal system has meant that while men have had no difficulty bringing their Law into the court, women have more often been excluded. In this land claim there were women's sites within the claim area, and the women had secret ceremony for the Dreamings. Women wanted to prove their relationship to country in the deepest way possible, and that meant doing secret business. The Land

Commissioner, a Federal Court Judge, was a man, and for the ceremonial action to count as evidence it would have to be witnessed not only by him but by the lawyers (all men) including those representing opponents to the claim. The women decided that in spite of the Law excluding men, they would make an exception. On the morning of the day of their ceremony the men all went off on site visits that did not require women, and the women all went off to the area where they had been preparing a ceremony ground. They had brought the sacred objects from the keeping place, and their plan was to spend the day preparing for ceremony which would be witnessed in the late afternoon. Not long after we had assembled all the women and their gear, the senior women told me there was a problem. They wanted me to go back to camp and convey the message that they had decided not to show the ceremony after all. They explained: 'From Dreaming right up till now no man has looked at this. We can't lose that Law.' The rest of the day was spent doing the ceremony—for the country and Dreamings, for themselves, and for the non-Aboriginal women who had been invited to the business. Their work had no evidentiary value except that I was able to note for the record that it had occurred.

There are numerous criticisms of the land claim process that can be made, and have been made (for example, Gumbert 1994; Langton 1998; Rose 1996), and gender issues are significant in these critiques. My anger at the way women's evidence was handled in the Jasper Gorge claim was rekindled when the men had the opportunity to do their ceremony for the judge, and thus to create an account of Law and responsibility that lost the balance of men's and women's work. Notwithstanding these serious issues, my experience in eighteen land claims across the Northern Territory has been more positive than the peculiarities of the process might lead one to expect (see Wright 1998). In the Jasper Gorge claim, the Aboriginal people announced on the last day that they intended to put on a 'show' for the Land Commissioner that would involve music, dance, and body art. Their purpose, as stated by women, was that they wanted to show the Land Commissioner that women and men work together in the management of knowledge. This final 'show' was a ritual inversion of the hearing, and the reversals were so marked and humorous that the intent could not be missed. It was organised for night time, it was held outside of the bough shade where the hearing had been held, and the spatial organisation was determined totally by the claimants. The judge and all other non-Aboriginal participants (lawyers, anthropologists, field assistants, etc.)

were told that we would be summoned when the claimants were ready for us, and that we could sit and wait in the meantime.

When called, we were told to stop at the bough shade to pick up our chairs and then come forward half way and sit at a particular place. After waiting half way we were told to bring our chairs forward and to arrange ourselves in a row facing the area that had been designated as a dancing ground. The claimants used the headlights of their vehicles as spotlights for the dancers, and with imaginative use of space, lighting and personnel they created a 'show' that was by turns impressive, sweet, and humorous. The children provided humour inadvertently (in part), and some of the men took up the clowning role with exuberance. The women danced; it was their first opportunity to show the judge that they had Law to back them up.

At the close of the 'show' a senior regional law woman grouped the women together to voice the calls that speak to country, and with her hands and arms she gestured with downward motions. Then she turned to the 'audience' and said: 'We opened the country up for you, and now we are closing it down again.'

*

In a land claim one can see in action Newton's inspired definition of ethics as 'recursive, contingent, and interactive dramas of encounter and recognition' (Newton 1995, p. 12). Many cruelties have taken place here and many are happening right now, and yet the place of damage inspires new stories and responsibilities. Ngaliwurru and Karangpuru people's sites, rituals, knowledge and words contained the proof of the claim—and more. Through this legal procedure we began to unmake more than one hundred years of conquest, years in which people had experienced the most appalling forms of racial and gender cruelty. Aboriginal people's remembrance was shared with others, and thereby worked into a new story that was re-structuring local, Territory and national power. Giving shape to the future, our shared work also affirmed and enhanced the resilience that enables people to salvage life from the death work of the past. The place of slaughter is exactly the place for remorse and for new action. This is the place for learning that resilience is the eruption of new life and new hope in places of ruin and despair.

The Aboriginal claimants wanted to show the truth of their lives to the Land Commissioner, and that truth was simultaneously and necessarily the truth of their country. Without country they would have had a very different truth to tell, and without its people country would not have been as it was. The decolonising work, therefore, while it purported to focus on land 'rights', actually involved a multi-sensorial intersubjective encounter with country.

We had walked on the ground of creation and birth, of bloodshed and violence, surrounded by Dreamings and ancestors and on-going creation, and our experience engaged our aesthetic imagination as well as our ethics. Aldo Leopold, the man who initiated in the west a new dialogue on land ethics, knew that aesthetics are integral to our engagements with land. His famous definition of what is good in relation to land is explicit: 'A thing is right when it tends to preserve the integrity, stability, and beauty of the biotic community. It is wrong when it tends otherwise' (Leopold 1949, pp. 224–225). Baird Callicott (1987) has analysed Leopold's writing and shows that Leopold called for an expanded reading of the land that would include science and history as well as the study of beauty. As he and many authors note, western landscape aesthetics emerge from a consideration of art, positing an observer who stands vis à vis the observed, and this distinction has carried over into much of the literature on environmental aesthetics (see for example Kemal & Gaskell 1993). There is the human observer, and there is nature.

Edward Casey (1996) has moved our understanding of engagements with place in powerful new directions, particularly as he focuses on synaesthesia (intertwined multi-sensorial experience). His deep theorising of the phenomenology of place helps us think analytically about how we understand ourselves and how to articulate our thoughts. In a similar vein, Murali and Usha (2006, pp. 169–170) invite us to consider how an aesthetic approach to nature takes us away from a subject–object split in a mode of possession, and opens a poetics of interactive engagement. But in the end, the journey into country is not only about thought, and not only sensorial, but is transformative as well. The inadequacy of subject–object, human–nature structures becomes fully evident in Aboriginal country. Country is not nature, and humans are not the only, or the necessarily privileged, participants. In Jasper Gorge, as in many claims, Aboriginal people honoured their experience of country, and sought to share it by opening up country to a poetic, ethical, aesthetic engagement. We began to sense country as a place of creation and continuity, of current action, of hopes and memories, of people long gone and people here today, of plants, and animals, some gone, some expanding, and all doing their best to engage with life as it presents itself to them. We began to come alive in our understanding that country is a sentient and glimmeringly complex subjectivity.

This sacred ground, here and all over Australia: Dreaming beings shaped it, organised it, and left traces of their creative acts. There is bloodshed, both Aboriginal and settler, there are the tracks of colonisation, visible signs and invisible absences. Scorched by sun and wind, sustained by earth and water, in communication with the ancestors and aware of all the other living beings who belong here, one wakes up to country. This precious living ground is the source for all of us, and the winds that carry the fresh smell of spinifex and sugarbag tell us that every breath is an inhalation of creation. Every breath is a gift unasked for, and an intersubjective call for us to give back: to offer loving care and respect because the life of country is the life of the world.

WORKS CITED

Callicott, JB, 1987, 'The Land Aesthetic'. In JB Callicott, ed. *Companion to A Sand Country Almanac: Interpretive and Critical Essays*. Madison: University of Wisconsin Press, pp. 157–171.

Casey, E 1996, 'How to Get from Space to Place in a Fairly Short stretch of Time: Phenomenological Prolegomena.' In S Feld and K Basso, eds. *Senses of Place*. Santa Fe: School of American Research Press, pp. 13–52.

Gumbert, M 1984, *Neither Justice Nor Reason; A Legal and Anthropological Analysis of Aboriginal Land Rights*. Saint Lucia: Queensland University Press.

Kemal, S and Gaskell, I eds 1993, *Landscape, natural beauty and the arts*. Cambridge: Cambridge University Press.

Langton, M 1998, 'Grandmothers' Law, Company Business and Succession in Changing Aboriginal Land Tenure Systems.' In W Edwards, ed. *Traditional Aboriginal Society*, second edition, Melbourne: Macmillan Education Australia Pty Ltd, pp. 109–128.

Leopold, A 1949, *A Sand County Almanac*, London: Oxford University Press.

Lewis, D 2004, *A Wild History: The Making of Victoria River Pastoral Society*. PhD Thesis, Canberra: ANU.

Lewis, D 2002, *Slower Than The Eye Can See: Environmental change in northern Australia's cattle lands*. Darwin: Tropical Savannas CRC.

Murali, S & Usha VT 2006, *Tradition and Terrain: Aesthetic Continuities*, Delhi: B. R. Publishing Corporation.

Newton, A 1995, *Narrative Ethics*. Cambridge: Harvard University Press.

Prigogine, I 1997, *The End of Certainty: Time, Chaos, and the New Laws of Nature*, New York: The Free Press.

Rose, D 1996, 'Land Rights and Deep Colonising: The Erasure of Women'. *Aboriginal Law Bulletin*, pp. 3, 85, 6–13.

Transcript of Proceedings. 1988, 'Re the Kidman Springs-Jasper Gorge Land Claim'. Commonwealth Reporting Service, Adelaide.

Wright, A, ed. 1998, *Take Power Like This Old Man Here*. Alice Springs: Jukurrpa Books.

Sovereignty and Treaty in Religious Imagination

Mark G Brett

Introduction

In his painting *And on the Eighth Day*, the Indigenous artist Lin Onus provides a visual satire on the first chapter of Genesis: British angels arrive bearing sheep, fencing wire, a gun, a Bible, and disinfectant. 'On the sixth day', the artist commented, 'God created the earth, on the seventh day he rested, and on the eighth day he stuffed it up for Aboriginal people' (Neale, p. 21). By contrast, Albert Namatjira's landscapes depicting his home country are not known for their satirical qualities, but they may nevertheless convey a more subtle form of resistance. In *The Lie of the Land*, Paul Carter has noted how the style and tone of Namatjira's landscapes are curiously similar to representations of the Holy Land contained in Lutheran mission Bibles. Carter suggests that the paintings may have 'mimicked the iconography of Bible illustrations', perhaps in mockery of the coloniser's religious self-absorption or perhaps simply to draw attention to country no less sacred (Carter, pp. 45–46).

Whatever Namatjira's intentions may have been, Carter's hypothesis intersects with a range of broader questions about the interactions between imported spiritualities and Indigenous traditions. If census figures are any guide, the majority of Indigenous people in Australia identify as Christians, and more strongly so in remote areas where the continuities of traditional law and ceremony are also most clearly evident. Any attempt to understand 'sacred Australia' would need to face these intercultural issues head on. The popular conception among some literary critics that biblical narratives are simply incompatible with Indigenous traditions represents a simplistic response that fails to address the complexities on the ground in particular contexts (see Ranger; Rainbow Spirit Elders).

When, for example, the body of Eddie Mabo was moved to his island home in 1996, after his grave on the mainland had been daubed with swastikas, the combined island choir celebrated with a hymn about Moses. 'Koiki led the people of Murray islands from the bondage of *terra nullius*', it was explained:

> Mama namarida Mose mara memegle e naose gair mara omaskir Israil le.
> You sent Moses your servant to lead the people of Israel from Egypt. (Findlay)

In the Torres Strait, it became customary to begin native title meetings with a Christian prayer. A nuanced postcolonialism would not be dismayed at this state of affairs.

While it might be possible to account for the ostensible contradictions of Aboriginal Christianity by reference to the subtleties of postmodern ecotheology, or a more traditional Ignatian spirituality that invests the natural world with sacramental qualities, it remains the case that the regular liturgical practice of Aboriginal Christianity turns on interpretation of the Bible, often in vernacular translation. Such interpretation may reflect cultural accommodation, but it may also be an instrument of resistance. To mention, briefly, an example from across the Tasman, the nineteenth century Maori prophet Te Kooti (d.1893) appropriated scriptural patterns in shaping resistance to the British rule. He identified with the Israelites in their bondage to Egypt (reinterpreted as British imperial power), the exodus and the divine covenants with the Israelite ancestors. Even the conquest texts from Joshua were turned back on the British to insist that the colonial government would be expelled from the land. A number of analogies between Moses and Te Kooti were discerned (Binney, pp. 70–72, 115, 502–3). This, among many other examples, illustrates that religious faith has a habit of problematising concepts of sovereignty.

In this chapter, I want to go beyond the polyvalence of the exodus narratives and focus precisely on the 'heart of darkness' represented by the conquest traditions in the Bible—the traditions often thought to be wholly incompatible with the postcolonial agenda (Said; Boer, pp. 88–119). We will pursue the hypothesis that there are many promised lands and chosen peoples, and that some aspects of Aboriginal Christianity belong to a long tradition of resistance that extends back into the darkest recesses of Deuteronomy itself. In reconsidering the discourse of *berit* in Deuteronomy—a Hebrew term which is often translated as 'covenant' but can also mean 'treaty'—biblical conceptions of sacred law and country will be juxtaposed with the discourse of sovereignty in Australia. The argument will also lend added weight to the suggestion that biblical faith presents a form of authority 'distinct from and higher than government' and thus provides a foothold for Indigenous rights—evidenced for example in the historic campaigns of William Cooper and Douglas Nicholls (Attwood & Markus, p. 5; Brett 2008).

I want to suggest that the theologians who produced Deuteronomy pitted themselves against the dominant imperial power of the day, the Assyrian Crown, and they asserted that Israel had its own religious law that was resistant to the claims of Assyrian sovereignty. As is well known, Deuteronomy's theology itself became an instrument of colonial discourse in the modern period. Here I want to recover its subversive impulse in order to suggest that Australia has both a political and a spiritual need to engage in a treaty process with our Indigenous peoples, a treaty process that entails a recognition of the multiplicity of sacred countries.

To begin with, the 'promised land' and 'chosen people' motifs in Deuteronomy may be compared with the assumption of Indigenous cultures that there are many 'chosen peoples' and many 'promised lands', each with their own jurisdictions (Turner 1987, p. ii; 1988, p. 479). This version of national identity provides an alternative to those nineteenth century European nationalisms that could not conceive of a land as sacred 'unless it could put forward a unique claim in the global economy of salvation' (Hobsbawm, p. 49). Deuteronomy's version of Israelite nationalism was more modest, although this has rarely been appreciated.

The tendency to over-read Deuteronomy's core assertions arguably began early. An old poem towards the end of the book apparently provoked particular anxieties amongst its ancient editors. The manuscript evidence found in the Qumran caves preserves the older Hebrew form of the verses, while the later Hebrew version has altered the tradition in order to reflect a more consistent monotheism (Sanders, pp. 154–60).

Qumran version of Deuteronomy 32:8–9 (4QDeut)

When Elyon apportioned the
nations their inheritance,
when he divided humankind,
he fixed the boundaries of the
peoples
according to the number of *sons of 'elohim*.
Yhwh's own portion was his people,
Jacob his inherited share.

Later Hebrew version of 32:8–9 (Massoretic Text)

When Elyon apportioned the
nations their inheritance,
when he divided humankind,
he fixed the boundaries of the
peoples
according the number of the *sons of Israel*.
Yhwh's own portion was his people,
Jacob his inherited share.

'Elyon' and 'El' were Indigenous names for the high god of the Indigenous Canaanite pantheon, and *'elohim* was a plural noun for ancestral deities. In the later development of Israelite monotheism these names were melded together and retained as simply alternative names for the one God 'Yhwh'—the distinctively Israelite divinity (Smith). The older version of Deuteronomy 32 provides evidence, however, that there was an earlier form of Yahwism that allowed the existence of other gods outside Israel, with Jacob/Israel being seen as the special jurisdiction of Yhwh (a pluralistic religious perspective that is also preserved in Micah 4:4–5 and Judges 11:24).

Deuterononmy 32:8–9 provides just one piece of an historical puzzle about Israelite origins. Archaeologists now generally agree that, in contrast to the Iron Age incursion of the Philistines, the formation of Israel as a people was not characterised by the imposition of a new culture; there are no distinctive material remains that distinguish an early Israelite society from the Indigenous villages and cities. Lawrence Stager has summarised the archaeological consensus succinctly: 'The evidence from language, costume, coiffure, and material remains suggest that the early Israelites were a rural subset of Canaanite culture' (Stager, p. 102). Israelite ethnicity, it seems, arose as a fissure within Palestinian culture. In the course of time, a moderately 'inclusive' Yahwism—which had accommodated El and the *'elohim* of the ancestors—became progressively more exclusive, and Israel's history was then re-interpreted accordingly (Brett 2003).

It is highly ironic, therefore, that a couple of millennia later, Deuteronomy was deployed as a paradigm text within colonial ideologies which each asserted a 'global economy of salvation', with the imperial centre of that economy variously located in Spain, Holland, or England. While there are elective affinities between the theologies that underwrote these European colonialisms, there are also distinctive features that need to be considered.

Settlement ideology in Australia

The settlement of Australia was distinguishable from many other colonial expansions of the Common Law in at least one respect. Settlers in North America, South Africa and New Zealand did not generally deny that the Indigenous peoples were the prior owners of the land, a denial that became the standard legal ideology in the Australian colonies. In the late seventeenth century, the Puritans in North America configured themselves as a 'chosen people' with a divinely given mission—a New Israel confronting the prior inhabitants of the Promised Land with an Israelite 'right of conquest'. Biblical narratives and laws, including Deuteronomy, were drawn on to demonstrate that Native Americans had been disinherited by divine decision (Niditch, pp. 3–5).

Official legal ideology in North America was never founded on biblical discourse alone; it was blended with notions of European 'civilisation'. In the nineteenth century, the legal writer James Kent was able to claim colonial legitimacy in North America 'in consequence of the superior genius of the Europeans, founded on civilisation and Christianity, and of their superiority in the means and act of war' (Kent, p. 485). The combined forces of civilisation, Christianity and rights of conquest were pitted against the Native Americans, and through a long period of conflict, numerous treaties were signed.

In contrast, the *South Australian Constitution Act* of 1834 asserted that prior to British settlement the land of the colony was 'waste and unoccupied', an expression of the *terra nullius* doctrine which was not legally overturned in Australia, astonishingly, until the Mabo native title judgment in 1992 (Reynolds, pp. 4, 12, 32). Yet the necessity of making treaties with the Australian First Nations is still often seen as unnecessary, a position that becomes more and more fragile as Australia contemplates becoming a republic.

It would have been difficult to make the Puritan rhetoric of a 'New Israel' plausible in the early penal colonies of Australia, since they were not well known for claims to righteousness. The settlers were much more likely to see themselves in *exile* rather than in a new 'promised land' (Rose, p. 205;

Beilharz, p. 97). There is no evidence to show that the early explorer diaries configure Aborigines as Canaanites; on the contrary, there are many examples where Indigenous practices are seen to be analogous with Israelite ones (Boer, pp. 63–72). The explorers often spoke of a generalised providence, but the genre of the divine underwriting could sometimes be mistaken for a curse, as when the unfamiliar land and its creatures were seen as a kind of creation in reverse—'wrong-footed' perhaps being an appropriate rendering of 'Antipodean'. The first book of poetry printed in the colonies reiterated the old theological tradition that the Antipodes somehow escaped God's original blessing, with only the kangaroo being a clue that perhaps there was a sacredness here that European eyes might yet perceive (Boer, p. 117):

> Kangaroo! Kangaroo!
> Thou spirit of Australia,
> That redeems from utter failure,
> From perfect desolation,
> And warrants the creation
> Of this fifth part of the earth;
> Which would seem an afterbirth,
> Not conceived at the beginning
> (For GOD blessed his work at first
> And saw that it was good),
> But emerged at the first sinning,
> When the ground therefore was curst:-
> And hence this barren wood!

The idea of Indigenous Australians as Canaanites seems to have made an occasional appearance in material from the mid-nineteenth century, but the theme did not have the systemic influence that it did amongst the Puritans in North America or the Boers in South Africa. An article appeared in the *Brisbane Courier* of 1864, for example, addressing sermons by a certain Charles Kingsley which referred to Aborigines as like 'Canaanites of old to be swept off the face of the earth'. But the ideas are mentioned only to be refuted (Evans, Saunders & Cronin, p. 69).

More significant for the Australian colonists was a widely spread conviction of racial superiority, given biblical sanction in mission history by an interpretation of the 'curse of Ham' in Genesis 9:20–27 which saw the text as a universal curse on black peoples, condemning them to slavery. This tradition of interpretation has a long and complex history, prior to modern versions of colonialism and including medieval Muslim justifications of black slavery, but in Australian mission history the 'curse of Ham' seems to have mutated into a claim about the inferiority of black people rather than a sanction for slavery as such (Evans; Harris 1990, pp. 657–58; Kenny, pp. 43–63).

There is overwhelming evidence, however, that Australian colonists used Aboriginal people for forced labour in the nineteenth century—and Aboriginal labour was still exploited in the early twentieth (Berndt & Berndt)—even though the language of 'slavery' was not normally used. The 'curse of Ham' tradition was strangely compatible with the idea of slavery—as was the regulation in Deuteronomy 20:10, which suggested that in the case of peoples 'distant' from the Promised Land, they may be 'subject to forced labour'. The biblical implication, perhaps, was that forced labour becomes more thinkable as the distance from sacred land increased.

Apart from the 'Curse of Ham', the major sources of racism came from the social and natural sciences of the day that served to reinforce popular prejudice and economic interest. Indigenous people were therefore caught in an ideological pincer movement. The ideology of cultural evolution and progress had long been circulating in modern Europe, and when the English sociologist Herbert Spencer coined the phrase 'survival of the fittest' in 1850, it was just the phrase he coined, not the idea. In the same year, the geologist Charles Lyell had confidently observed that 'few future events are more certain than the speedy extermination of the Indians of North America or the savages of New Holland'. The appearance of Darwin's *Origin of Species* in 1859 was a high profile scientific event, but it also served to consolidate diverse cultural themes from the previous century. And it provided an excellent means for Europeans to relieve themselves of their 'weight of charity' towards Indigenous peoples (Harris 1968, p. 97).

Darwin caused a theological controversy, but in the wider context of cultural debates, popular ideas of social evolution could now be given a biological foundation. The idea that humans were descended from apes had the crucial qualification, both in scientific and in popular opinion, that black peoples were closer to apes than whites. The social Darwinist HK Rusden was able to write in the *Melbourne Review* of 1876:

> The survival of the fittest means that might—widely used—is right. And thus we invoke and remorselessly fulfill the inexorable law of natural selection when exterminating the inferior Australian (Evans, Saunders & Cronin, pp. 81–82).

As the historian Robert Kenny has recently observed, the idea of natural selection provided 'a new version of the right of conquest' (Kenny, p. 295). There was accordingly no need to invent an 'Israelite' right of conquest derived, as had elsewhere been the case, from biblical models in the books of Deuteronomy and Joshua.

Nineteenth century humanitarian theology

The Christian missions in nineteenth century Australia often stated their intention to protect Indigenous people from the worst excesses of the settlers—especially murder and the abuse of Aboriginal women—even though in many cases the opinions of the clergy differed little from the most extreme expressions of racism. There were, however, notable champions of humanitarian causes who *resisted* the biblical prescriptions allowing slavery, on theological grounds, and took up the just cause of Aboriginal people. Indeed, Kenny has suggested that a *secular* belief in the future of Indigenous Australians is difficult to find in the mid-nineteenth century (Kenny, p. 30).

In 1845, for example, Bishop Polding expressed his view to a committee of the New South Wales Legislative Council that Aboriginal resistance

> must be attributed to the bad feeling and want of confidence naturally caused by the mode in which possession has been taken of their country—occupation by force, accompanied by murders, ill-treatment, ravishment of their women, in a word, to the conviction on their minds that the white man has come for his own advantage, without any regard to their rights. Feeling this burning injustice inflicted by the white man, it is not in the nature of things that the black man should believe the white man better than himself, or suppose the moral and religious laws, by which the white man proposes the black man to be governed, to be better than those of his own tribe (Reynolds, pp. 159–60).[1]

[1] Quoting from the *NSW Legislative Council Votes and Proceedings*, 1845, p. 9.

Polding and others had no difficulty understanding that Indigenous peoples could lay legitimate claim to their own laws and customs, and that they possess certain inalienable rights. His own Catholic tradition had for centuries been accustomed to supplementing biblical legislation with conceptions of 'natural law', which provided the foundations on which secular philosophies of human rights were built (Otto 1999a).

What has sometimes been insufficiently recognised is that the views of people like Polding echoed concerns that emanated from the Colonial Office in London in the 1830s and 1840s. A group of powerful evangelical Anglicans in the British parliament, supported by some influential Quakers, had relentlessly worked for the abolition of slavery in the early nineteenth century, and especially after the Emancipation Act of 1833, this group focused their humanitarian attention on Aboriginal people in the colonies. In the understanding of these Parliamentarians, the twin causes of Christianity and 'civilisation' (almost inevitably linked in this period) were being damaged by injustices done to Indigenous peoples in the name of the empire. Following in the footsteps of William Wilberforce in the campaign against slavery, it was especially Thomas Buxton, James Stephen and Lord Glenelg who concerned themselves with the native peoples of Southern Africa, the Carribean, Australia and New Zealand.

Buxton's lobbying resulted, for example, in Lord Glenelg's famous dispatch to Governor D'Urban of the eastern Cape in December 1835 renouncing the annexation of Queen Adelaide Province on the grounds that 'the original justice is on the side of the conquered, not the victorious party' (Reynolds, p. 98).[2] Expressing related concerns to the South Australian colonial Commission in the same month, Lord Glenelg stated:

> Before His Majesty can be advised to transfer to his subjects the Property in any part of the land of Australia, he must have at least some reasonable assurance that he is not about to sanction any act of injustice toward the Aboriginal natives of that part of the Globe. In drawing the line of demarcation for the New Province … the Commissioners therefore must not proceed any further than those limits within which they can show, by some sufficient evidence, that the land is unoccupied and that no earlier and preferable title exists (Reynolds, p. 106).

[2] Quoting from the *British Parliamentary Papers* 1836, pp. 39, 279.

It was this kind of thinking which lay behind the settlement of New Zealand and the Treaty of Waitangi in 1840, but the *South Australian Constitution Act* of 1834 had already denied the possibility of native title by declaring that the land was 'waste and unoccupied'. The ideology of *terra nullius* could thus be used to outwit the pious reformers at the centre of the empire, and the colonial administrators often simply denied that the Indigenous people 'occupied' the land in any relevant sense. Already in 1848, a Western Australian official was able to explain the tensions between the Colonial Office in London and the administrators in Australia:

> The wishes and intentions of the home government towards them [the Indigenous peoples] have been frequently frustrated, evaded, misrepresented and successfully counteracted, opposed, not openly in the face of positive instructions, but encountered by a dead weight of indisposition towards them by a covert opposition, a persevering system of obstruction, a pulling back of the wheels of Government which has proved sufficient to hinder any efforts that have been made to upraise the Aborigines (Reynolds, pp. 158–59).

During this period, the American Supreme Court made a number of decisions that could have provided an alternative model for the Australian colonies (and one which was more in line with what the London Colonial Office was demanding in the 1830s). In a series of cases between 1810 and 1835, Chief Justice John Marshall ruled that the Indian nations had legal rights to the soil based on prior possession, and that native title did not depend on any particular mode of land-use or settlement: 'their hunting grounds were as much their actual possession as the cleared fields of the whites' (Reynolds, p. 46). The American pattern at the time was characterised by negotiated treaties and compensation—although one critic asserted in 1885 that the government had failed to fulfill the obligations of a single one of them.[3]

Justice Marshall established the principle that treaties needed to be negotiated with these 'domestically dependant nations', and while his reasoning arose from conceptions of natural law and natural rights, it will be instructive to reflect on the possible analogies between his judgments and the dynamics of Deuteronomy's discourse millennia before. As we shall see in

[3] HB Whipple's preface to Helen Hunt Jackson, *A Century of Dishonour* (1885).

more detail below, the idea in Deuteronomy 32 that Elyon had provided each of the nations with their own sacred underwriting was expressed in the context of anti-imperial cultural resistance.

Deuteronomy as a Biblical Treaty

Critical scholars have long held the view that the composition of Deuteronomy (or at least the core of it) took place in the seventh century BCE and that the Deuteronomic code is clearly distinguishable from the earlier Mosaic law contained in the book of Exodus. The arguments for this hypothesis have been recently reinforced by benchmarking the dating of Deuteronomy in relation to a number of treaty texts produced by the Assyrian empire and imposed on vassal nations during the seventh century. Israelites would have had first-hand knowledge of such Assyrian texts after the conquest of the northern kingdom and the Assyrian incursion into Judah in 701 BCE. Comparisons reveal that the treaties have a generic structure similar to Deuteronomy, including characteristic features such as a narrative prologue, a law code, provision for periodic public readings of the treaty, and a list of blessings and curses that are envisaged as flowing from compliance or non-compliance with the laws.

There are a series of particularly striking similarities between Deuteronomy and the vassal treaties of the neo-Assyrian king Esarhaddon in the wording of the curses, as well as certain demands for loyalty (Steymans, pp. 119–141). In one of the most comprehensive analyses of these comparisons, Eckart Otto arrives at a quite specific dating of Deuteronomic material between 672 and 612, arguing for example that Deuteronomy 13:2–10 subversively mimics VTE §10, by adapting the Assyrian text to demand exclusive loyalty to Yhwh, rather than loyalty to the Assyrian king (Otto 1999, p. 14; 2000, pp. 59–76). The sovereignty of the Assyrian king is both mimicked and contested at the same time:

Vassal Treaty of Esarhaddon §10[4]

If you hear any evil, improper, ugly word … the mouth of his [the king's] *ally*, or from the mouth of *his brothers, his uncles, his cousins, his family, members of his father's line*, or from the mouth of *your brothers, your sons, your daughters*, or from the mouth of a *prophet, an ecstatic, an enquirer of oracles*, or from the mouth of any human being at all; you shall not conceal it but come and report it to Ashurbanipal, the great crown prince designate, son of Esarhaddon, king of Assyria.

Vassal Treaty of Esarhaddon §12

If you are able to seize them and put them to death, then you shall destroy their name and their seed from the land.

Deuteronomy 13:7-15

7If *your brother, the son of your mother, or your son, or your daughter or the wife of your bosom, or your friend who is as your own self*, entices you secretly, saying, 'Let us go and worship other gods' – whom neither you nor your fathers have known,
8some of the gods of the peoples who are round about you …–
9do not assent to him or listen to him! Let your eye not pity him, nor shall you hold back or condone him.
10You must surely kill him …
12 If you hear it said about one of the cities that the Yhwh your God is giving you to live in,
13that scoundrels from among you have gone out and led the inhabitants of the city astray, saying 'Let us go and worship other gods'…
14If the charge is established …
15you shall surely put the inhabitants of that city to the sword, banning it (*hrm*) – all who are in it and its cattle – with the edge of the sword.

The historical study of Deuteronomy might be said to illustrate a point made by Homi Bhabha in relation to an example of biblical interpretation in India some twenty-five centuries later:

> If the effect of colonial power is seen to be the *production* of hybridization rather than the noisy command of colonialist authority or the silent

[4] The translations of VTE §10 and §12 come from Simo Parpolo and Kazuko Watanabe (eds), *Neo-Assyrian Treaties and Loyalty Oaths*, Helsinki: Helsinki University Press, 1988, pp. 33, 34.

> repression of native traditions, then an important change of perspective occurs. It reveals the ambivalence at the source of traditional discourses on authority and enables a form of subversion (Bhabha, p. 65).

Clearly, however, there is a dark side to this mimicry. In comparison with the Assyrian model, Deuteronomy 13 has a greater focus on the possibility of conflict within the most intimate family relationships—not just conflict with a 'brother' but with a 'full brother' ('the son of your mother'), not just with a wife, but 'the wife of your bosom' (Levinson, pp. 238–41; Brett 2004). Deuteronomy 13 also introduces the theme of *herem*—ritual slaughter—since immediately following the portion adapted from Esarhaddon's treaty, it is said in 13:15 that even Israelites who are proven disloyal to Yhwh shall be punished by having their entire town, people and livestock, devoted to the ban (*herem*). The reference to capital punishment in Deuteronomy 13:10 provides a bridge to the *herem* regulation in 13:15.

This allusion to ritual slaughter is particularly striking since the idea of *herem* also appears in two other chapters which provide rulings on the 'Indigenous' people of Canaan:

> ... the Hittites, Girgashites, Amorites, Canaanites, Perizzites, Hivites and Jebusites, seven nations more numerous and stronger than you: when Yhwh your God has delivered them over to you and you have defeated them, then you must ban them completely (*hrm*). Make no treaty (*berit*) with them, and show them no mercy. Do not intermarry with them. (Deuteronomy 7:1–3)

> However, in the cities of these peoples Yhwh your God gives you as an inheritance, do not leave alive anything that breathes. Indeed, you will ban them completely (*hrm*). (Deuteronomy 20:16–17)

While the meaning of the *herem* regulation in ch.7 is disputed, in the case of ch.20 the intent is genocidal. It would need to be noted, however, that the genocidal content of Deuteronomy 20:16–17 was not formed according to a conventional ethnocentric logic, since this particular version of *herem* is applied not just against strangers. As Deuternonomy 13 reveals, it is envisaged as cutting across the most intimate family relationships within Israel.

In the case of Deuteronomy 7:1–3, it is difficult to see why it would be necessary to ban treaties or intermarriage with the prior inhabitants of Canaan if these people were meant to be completely exterminated. Presumably, one could only be tempted into treaties and marriages with people who were alive. On the other hand, Deuteronomy 20:16–18 sees the ideal conquest as implying death for 'everything that breaths'. Such tensions raise significant questions of interpretation, and it is not surprising that in later Jewish tradition *herem* came to mean 'shunning' and the regulation in Deuteronomy 20:16–18 was suspended on the grounds that it was no longer possible to identify descendants of the prior inhabitants of Canaan (Weinfeld, pp. 91–92).

There are a number of inconsistencies in the conquest narratives that correspond to the inconsistencies in the law, and the genocidal language of Deuteronomy is not to be found in the earlier traditions. For example, the narrative describing the destruction of Jericho presumes a comprehensive version of *herem* that includes the slaughter of *livestock* along with the mass killing of men, women and children (Joshua 6:21), and this accords with the requirement of Deuteronomy 20:16–18 regarding the conquest of the promised land. Whereas in the narrative about Ai, it is said that 'the livestock and plunder of that city Israel took for themselves, as Yhwh had instructed Joshua' (Joshua 8:24–27). It is very unlikely that the authors of the earlier narrative in Joshua 8 knew the extant version of the Jericho narrative; any conflict between Yhwh's command to Joshua and Yhwh's command to Moses regarding the proper conduct of the *herem* would have required some explanation.

Differences such as these reflect the historical development of ideas about conquest. Similarly, the legislation in Deuteronomy is different from what we find in the older legal tradition in Exodus 23:20–33, which mentions no *herem* against persons but only the destruction of cultic objects: 'you shall not bow down to their gods, or worship them, or follow their practices, but you shall ban them completely (*hrm*) and break their pillars in pieces' (Exodus 23:24). According to the Exodus vision of the conquest, the prior inhabitants of Canaan would be driven out gradually by God alone and not killed by Israelites at all. Deuteronomy reinterprets the *herem* against cultic objects in the Promised Land as implying also the death of all the prior inhabitants, including their animals, an innovation that accords with Deuteronomy's own theological imagination in the seventh century rather than with historical events in previous centuries.

It has often been argued that the demand for ritual slaughter in the *herem* texts conflicts with a key moral principle in Deuteronomy: love for *strangers*, who are regularly linked with widows and orphans as people in need of protection. 'Love the stranger', Deuteronomy 10:19 requires, 'because you were strangers (*gerim*) in Egypt'. It must be recognised, however, that Deuteronomy does not propose protection for all strangers in the same way. The care for 'refugees' or 'sojourners' (*gerim*) depends upon their relative openness to cultural assimilation, whereas unassimilated foreigners are not protected. As Richard Nelson puts it, 'Deuteronomy insists on benevolence and consideration for resident aliens and other needy and marginalised groups, but does so only on the basis of a recognition of some level of community membership and of obligations creation by shared experience' (Nelson, p. 49). Other strangers who have not entered into stable relationships with citizens are called 'foreigners' (*nokri / ben nekar*), and they are not to receive the same consideration. During the seventh century, the time of Deuteronomy's composition, many of the *gerim* would have been Israelites from other tribes in the north who had been displaced from their traditional country by the Assyrian invasion to the north of Judah.

While it may be possible to explain Deuteronomy's conceptual consistency in regard to the love of strangers and the *herem* laws, at least two narratives in Joshua suggest that Israel's theologians may still have perceived a moral problem with the idea of genocide. As already noted, the Jericho narrative provides the paradigm case in which the full extent of the *herem* is enacted (the killing of men, women, children and animals), yet it is precisely the Jericho story which breaks the law in one other respect. An Indigenous prostitute, Rahab, is exempted from the *herem* because she demonstrates loyalty to Yhwh and to Israel (Joshua 6:21–25). In this case, a covenant was made with Rahab to save her family in return for hiding Israelite spies. There was no ambiguity about her being Indigenous, yet a covenant was made anyway, contrary to the requirement in Deuteronomy 7:2 that no covenant or treay (*berit*) be made with the prior inhabitants of the Promised Land. Rahab's clan, the narrator tells us, 'has lived in Israel until this day' (6:25), indicating that the narrator tells the story from the perspective of later times. We can presume then that the narrator knows the genocide law and needs to explain why an Indigenous group lives safely amongst the Israelites, even though Deuteronomy's vision of the future precludes this possibility.

Joshua 9 provides another case where a treaty was made with a local group, the Gibeonites, whose proximity with the sacred country should have earned them death. The Gibeonites, however, claimed that they came from a 'far country', and Joshua makes a treaty/covenant (*berit*) with them without being aware of their Indigenous status (Deuteronomy 20:15 permits treaties with 'distant cities'). When the Gibeonite ruse is discovered, the story puts Joshua into a quandary: should he keep to the treaty, or should he rather keep the law of Moses and kill them all? Joshua keeps his word, against a good deal of pressure from other Israelites, and the Gibeonites therefore are spared 'until this day' (Joshua 9:27). Once again, the narrator is viewing events in the distant past and trying to explain a puzzling aspect of contemporary reality. In this case, however, the issue is not just that Indigenous people continue to live amongst the Israelites on sacred country, but the fact that these people are 'hewers of wood and drawers of water' (9:27). The answer lies in the representation of Gibeonite deception: since they lied, it seems that they bear an ongoing punishment as slaves.

Narratives such as these betray a contradiction between the social realities of seventh century Judah and the theological ideals being proposed by the writers of Deuteronomy. There is a particular concern in the book that Israelites may be led astray by 'mimetic desire':

> When you come to the land Yhwh your God is giving you, do not learn to *imitate*, the detestable ways of those nations (Deuteronomy 18:9).
>
> You shall commit them to the ban—the Hittites and the Amorites, the Canaanites and the Perizzites, the Hivites and the Jebusites—as Yhwh your God has commanded, that they may not teach you to *imitate*, all their detestable practices (Deuteronomy 20:17–18).

Following Rene Girard's theory of mimetic desire, Norbert Lohfink has argued that this fear of religious imitation in Deuteronomy suggests that we look also for a scapegoating process—the exclusion of near rivals—suggested by Girard's theory (Lohfink, pp. 259–60).

This aspect of Girard's theory suggests that mimetic desire produces victims who are seen to be 'outside' the community, when in practice they are usually on an ambiguous margin between 'outside' and 'inside'. And in one permutation of this marginalised position, the victim must be made to appear 'more foreign' than they actually are, in order to reconstitute the community's boundaries (Girard, pp. 271–72). It seems to me that the dynamics of mimetic desire in Deuteronomy can be understood in Girardian terms: the legal discourse excluding the Indigenous peoples arises precisely from a need—perceived by the Deuteronomic authors—to inscribe new boundaries of exclusive loyalty to Yhwh within an Israelite society which over the previous centuries had commonly worshipped other gods alongside Yhwh. Thus, Girard comments that 'there is reason to believe that the wars described as 'foreign wars' in the mythic narratives were in fact formerly civil strifes' (Girard, p. 249). One of the functions of the scapegoating process, then, is to obscure such civil conflicts behind sacred texts and ritual.

What kind of 'civil strifes' does Deuteronomy want to obscure? As already indicated, there is now a consensus amongst archaeologists that early Israel was in fact Indigenous to Canaan. Deuteronomy's reformation of Israelite ethnic identity—centring it on a radically exclusive loyalty to Yhwh—excluded not so much 'Indigenous' peoples but intimate kin who held to different and older religious views and practices. This is the social context of the seventh century which explains the link between the *herem* being declared on Israelite towns in Deuteronomy 13 and the same unusual *herem* being declared in Deuteronomy 20:16–18 against the prior inhabitants of Canaan. What appears on the surface of Deuteronomy 20 as a program for genocide is actually part of an internal social and religious paradigm shift in the seventh century BCE.

The theology of Deuteronomy thus emerges as markedly ironic, since the quest to formulate an exclusivist worship of Yhwh was itself shaped, it seems, by a mimetic logic which is both borrowing from Assyrian culture while resisting foreign influence, appropriating the imperial discourses of loyalty, violence and punishment. And all this is justified by love for a God whose character is revealed in an exodus narrative of liberation from Egyptian imperialism.

Of particular relevance here is Benedict Anderson's (1991) account of how nationalist ideologies create an 'imagined community', an *idea* of 'a deep, horizontal comradeship', usually by selectively forgetting the past, or at times, forcefully rejecting minorities. Deuteronomy's nationalist vision, it seems, which generated a picture of each Israelite being a 'brother' before Yhwh, worked at times positively to urge greater solidarity with the marginalised stranger and with the poor, and at times negatively, to reject those who did not conform to the new homogeneity. This kind of ambivalence can be seen as characteristic of national visions, including those made in Australia.

THE REPRESSION OF SACRED COUNTRY IN AUSTRALIAN SOVEREIGNTY

It would be tempting simply to condemn Deuteronomy as an ancient barbaric artifact that has no bearing on the current Australian situation. But I am suggesting this text is worth examining—even down to its genocidal 'heart of darkness'—as a heuristic tool for opening up a number of questions about the possibilities of envisioning sacred country.

Unlike other jurisdictions within the legal environment of the Common Law, Australian Governments have so far adopted a curiously 'Deuteronomic' position in refusing to make a treaty with the prior inhabitants of our land base. On the contrary, our Governments have up until recent decades attempted to make these people disappear—by forcibly moving them from their traditional countries, by undermining their kinship systems and laws, by denying them citizenship, by withholding a portion of their wages, and by refusing to acknowledge them in national census data. These actions were smuggled firstly under the banner of 'Protection' and then under the policy of 'Assimilation'. Either way, the older and different forms of Australian identity before the assertion of British sovereignty were declared too foreign for the new national standards. *Terra nullius* may be a more subtle form of genocide, but it has been no less deadly than the *herem* regulations in Deuteronomy.

The national ideals of 'mateship' and the 'fair go' also seem to have had a curiously inconsistent application; it seems to have been much easier to deal with strangers and refugees (*gerim*) who are descendants of European tribes and displaced from those traditional countries than to recognise Indigenous people who have been displaced from their traditional countries.

Prime Minister John Howard repeatedly asserted that a nation 'does not make a treaty with itself'. But any presumption that Australia is undivided in its sovereignty—and therefore cannot make treaties with itself—would obscure the complex realities of our 'self'-government (Brennan et al., p. 71). There are different genres of sovereignty, not least because the authority of the Crown in Australian history has shifted from a British monarch to the will of a people whose national identity is now to be distinguished from its British roots.

When, for example, the colony of Victoria first took steps in the 1880s to exclude Chinese immigrants from Hong Kong—even when they carried

British identity papers—this began a complex legal separation from British sovereignty that continues until today (Lake 2008). Federation gave birth to multiple levels of Commonwealth and State Governments that collectively represent the mysterious genealogy of the British/Australian Crown. Apart from a federal Constitution that shares sovereign powers between the Commonwealth and the States', sovereign powers are also divided between the parliament, the executive and the judiciary. In short, our multiply layered self-government is formed by a system of agreements between separate jurisdictions, and there is no reason in principle why Indigenous jurisdictions cannot be added to the federated mix (Bourke & Brett; Atkinson & Brett). Such a move would entail coming to terms with the sacred Indigenous sovereignties that lie within the nation, rather than capitulating to the mimetic desire that finds it necessary to sacrifice the proximate Other.

A treaty is not the only instrument that could be used to establish the legal recognition and rights due to Indigenous people, but it is perhaps the most appropriate way of reconciling the competing sovereignties that beset our national imagination. In 1992, the *Mabo* judgement of the High Court belatedly recognised that traditional Indigenous groups exercise an internal jurisdiction in defining traditional 'laws and customs'—as our jurisprudence tends to reshape claims to sacred country. In this landmark decision, native title rights and interests were importantly identified as 'inherent'—they were recognised rather than 'granted' by the Crown. But instead of seeing the inherent system of traditional rights as implying a sovereign system of law (as in North America), the *Native Title Act* 1993 raised a whole new set of questions about the ways in which Indigenous polities could be recognised in Australia.

In the case of the Yorta Yorta native title claim, the High Court adopted a strangely 'Deuteronomic' fundamentalism by arguing that unless a traditional nation can demonstrate a substantial continuity of law and custom then, according to native title jurisprudence, it is no longer the same nation. The 'authentic' representatives of that nation have been judged by the coloniser's law to be extinguished.

Accordingly, the High Court's decision against the *Yorta Yorta* in 2002 asserted that any developments in Aboriginal law over the last two centuries are not relevant to native title, since the Court recognised 'no parallel law-making system' in territories over which the British Crown had asserted its sovereignty. This legal logic meant that Yorta Yorta traditional owners would only have been recognised as native title holders if they had maintained their legal system, substantially snap-frozen, from 1788. This sets a standard of continuity in law and custom, and connection to country, that the biblical traditions would certainly fail (cf. Weiner).

As the Australian Aboriginal lawyer Louise Taylor has put it, 'Our identity is an issue that should be adjudicated by us, not for us'. Her insistence on this point flows from the accumulated experience of government bias of 'white over black, or etic over emic, standpoints' in successive phases of legislation (Taylor, p. 90).[5] Even when native land title was recognised in Australian law after 1992, white courts retained the power to define which groups were 'authentically' Aboriginal and therefore justified in asserting their connection with traditional lands. Professor Mick Dodson has rightly criticised the persistent tendency in the Australian law and media to distinguish between 'authentic' and 'hybrid' Indigenous people. The right to self-definition, Dodson writes, 'must include the right to inherit the collective right of one's people, and to transform that identity creatively according to the self-defined aspirations of one's people and one's own generation' (Dodson, p. 5).

Indigenous Australians might still take some inspiration from the fact that even Deuteronomy was conceived in resistance to a foreign empire and as a denial of that imperial sovereignty. Postcolonial critics have often been skeptical of the view that the Mosaic traditions might be turned by Indigenous people against their colonisers. But we have already noted the example that Maori biblical interpreters in Aotearoa New Zealand deliberately identified themselves as 'Jews' precisely because they wanted to oppose the dominant reading of the Bible proposed to them by Christian missionaries and colonial administrators. Such are the ironies of biblical hermeneutics. A coloniser's view of sacred county does not constitute the final word.

WORKS CITED

Anderson, Benedict, *Imagined Communities: Reflections on the Origin and Spread of Nationalism*. London: Verso, 2nd edn 1991.

Atkinson, Graham and Brett, Mark G, 'The Making of Treaties.' *Arena Magazine* 98 (Dec–Jan 2008/9): 37-39.

[5] 'Emic' refers here to insider points of view, while 'etic' refers to outsiders' views—whether academic or legislative.

Attwood, Bain and Markus, Andrew, *Thinking Black: William Cooper and the Australia Aborigines' League*. Canberra: Aboriginal Studies Press, 2004.

Barnes, James A, 'Anthropology in Britain before and after Darwin.' *Mankind* 5/9 (1960): 37–74.

Beilharz, Peter, *Imagining the Antipodes: Culture, Theory and the Visual in the Work of Bernard Smith.* Cambridge: Cambridge University Press, 1997.

Bhabha, Homi K, 'Signs taken for Wonders: Questions of Ambivalence and Authority under a Tree outside Delhi, May 1817.' *Critical Inquiry* 12 (1985): 144–65.

Binney, Judith, *Redemption Songs: A Life of the Nineteenth-century Maori LeaderTe Kooti Arikirangi Te Turuki.* Melbourne: Melbourne University Press, 1997.

Berndt, R and C, *End of an Era: Aboriginal Labour in the Northern Territory.* Canberra: Australian Institute of Aboriginal Studies, 1987.

Boer, Roland, *Last Stop to Antarctica: The Bible and Postcolonialism in Australia.* Sheffield: Sheffield Academic Press, 2001.

Bourke, Eleanor and Mark Brett, 'Victoria: Groundwork for a Treaty?' available at www.ntsv.com.au.

Brennan, Sean, Larissa Behrendt, Lisa Strelein, George Williams, *Treaty.* Sydney: The Federation Press, 2005.

Brett, Mark G, 'Israel's Indigenous Origins: Cultural Hybridity and the Formation of Israelite Ethnicity.' *Biblical Interpretation* 11 (2003): 400–412.

—— 'Genocide in Deuteronomy: Postcolonial Variations on Mimetic Desire.' M O'Brien and H Wallace (eds), *Seeing Signals, Reading Signs.* London: Continuum, 2004, pp. 76–90.

—— *Decolonizing God: The Bible in the Tides of Empire.* Sheffield: Sheffield Phoenix, 2008.

Carter, Paul, *The Lie of the Land.* London: Faber & Faber, 1996.

Dodson, Michael, 'The End in the Beginning: Re(de)fining Aboriginality.' *Australian Aboriginal Studies* 1(1994): 2–13.

Evans, WM, 'From the Land of Canaan to the Land of Guinea: the Strange Odyssey of the 'Sons of Ham'.' *American Historical Review* 85/1 (1980), 15–43.

Evans R, K Saunders and K Cronin, *Race Relations in Colonial Queensland: A History of Exclusion, Exploitation and Extermination.* St Lucia: University of Queensland Press, 2nd edn. 1988.

Findlay, Merrill, 'Eddie Mabo comes Home.' *The Age*, 1 June 1996.

Finkelstein, Israel and Neil A Silberman, 'Temple and Dynasty: Hezekiah, the Remaking of Judah and the Rise of Pan-Israelite Ideology.' *Journal for the Study of the Old Testament* 30/3 (2006): 259–85.

Girard, René, *Violence and the Sacred*. Baltimore: Johns Hopkins University Press, 1977.

Harris, Marvin, *The Rise of Anthropological Theory*. London: Routledge & Kegan Paul, 1968.

Harris, John, *One Blood: 200 Years of Aboriginal Encounter with Christianity*. Sutherland: Albatross, 2nd edn 1994.

Hobsbawm, Eric, *Nations and Nationalism since 1780*. Cambridge: Cambridge University Press, 1990.

Hunt Jackson, Helen, *A Century of Dishonour*. Cambridge: Cambridge University Press, 1885.

Kenny, Robert, *The Lamb enters the Dreaming: Nathanael Pepper and the Ruptured World*. Melbourne: Scribe, 2007.

Kent, James, *Commentaries on American Law*. Boston: Little, Brown, 11th edn 1867.

Lake, Marilyn, 'White Australia as the Declaration of Australian Sovereignty: An Investigation of the gendered and racial Subjectivities of the self-governing Male Subject'. Paper read at *New Worlds, New Sovereignties* conference, University of Melbourne, 6–9 June 2008.

Levinson, Bernard, 'Textual Criticism, Assyriology, and the History of Interpretation: Deuteronomy 13:7 as a Test Case in Method.' *Journal of Biblical Literature* 120 (2001): 238–41.

Lohfink, Norbert, 'Opferzentralisation, Säkularisierungthese und mimetische Theorie' in Lohfink, *Studien zum Deuteronomium und zur deuteronomistischen Literatur III*. Stuttgart: Katholisches Bibelwerk, 1995.

Neale, Margo, *Urban Dingo: The Art and Life of Lin Onus 1948–1996*. Brisbane: Queensland Art Gallery, 2000.

Nelson, Richard, '*Herem* and the Deuteronomic Social Conscience' in M Vervenne and J Lust (eds), *Deuteronomy and Deuteronomic Literature*. Leuven: Leuven University Press, 1997.

Niditch, Susan. *War in the Hebrew Bible*. Oxford: Oxford University Press, 1993.

Otto, Eckart, 'Human Rights: the Influence of the Hebrew Bible.' *Journal of NorthwestSemitic Languages* 25 (1999a): 1–20.

—— *Das Deuteronomium: Politische Theologie und Rechtsreform in Juda und Assyrian*. Berlin: de Gruyter, 1999.

—— 'Political Theology in Judah and Assyria' *Svensk Exegetische Arsbok* 65 (2000), pp. 59–76.

Rainbow Spirit Elders, *Rainbow Spirit Theology* (Melbourne: Harper Collins Religious, 1997).

Ranger, Terence, 'Christianity and the First Peoples: Some Second Thoughts', in P Brock (ed.), *Indigenous Peoples and Religious Change* (Leiden: EJ Brill, 2005), pp. 15–32.

Reynolds, Henry, *The Law of the Land.* Melbourne: Penguin, 2nd edn 1992.

Rose, Deborah Bird, 'Rupture and the Ethics of Care in Colonized Space.' In T Bonyhady and T Griffiths eds., *Prehistory to Politics.* Melbourne: Melbourne University Press, 1996.

Said, Edward, 'Michael Walzer's *Exodus and Revolution*: A Canaanite Reading' in E Said and C Hitchens (eds), *Blaming the Victims: Spurious Scholarship and the Palestine Question.* London: Verso, 1988.

Sanders, Paul, *The Provenance of Deuteronomy 32.* Leiden: Brill, 1996.

Smith, Mark, *The Origins of Biblical Monotheism.* Oxford: Oxford University Press, 2001.

Stager, Lawrence, 'Forging an Identity: the emergence of Ancient Israel.' In MD Coogan ed., *The Oxford History of the Biblical World.* New York: Oxford University Press, 1998.

Steymans, Hans Ulrich, *Deuteronomium 28 und die* adê *zur thronfolgeregelung Asarhaddons Segen und Fluch im Alten Orient und in Israel.* Göttingen: Vandenhoeck & Ruprecht, 1995.

Tayler, Louise, 'Who's Your Mob? – The Politics of Aboriginal Identity and the Implications for a Treaty.' In Australian Institute of Aboriginal and Torres Straight Islander Studies, *Treaty: Let's Get it Right.* Canberra: Aboriginal Studies Press, 2003.

Turner, David H, *Life Before Genesis: A Conclusion.* New York: Peter Land, 1987.

—— 'The Incarnation of Nambirrirrma.' In T Swain and DB Rose eds. *Aboriginal Australians and Christian Missions.* Bedford Park: Australian Association for the Study of Religions, 1988.

Weiner, James F, 'Diaspora, Materialism, Tradition: Anthropological Issues in the Recent High Court Appeal of the Yorta Yorta'. *Land, Rights, Laws: Issues of Native Title.* Issues Paper 18: 2002, www.aiatsis.gov.au/rsrch/ntru/ntpapers/IPv2n18/pdf.

Weinfeld, Moshe, *The Promise of the Land: The Inheritance of the Land of Canaan by the Israelites.* Berkeley: University of California, 1993.

THE SARDONIC AND THE SACRED: AUSTRALIAN IDENTITY AND AUSTRALIAN POETIC LANGUAGE

Dennis Haskell

'Australia' and 'sacred' are two words which do not readily come together, except perhaps in relation to sacred sites important to Aboriginal or Torres Strait Island culture. It is well known that traditional Aboriginal and Torres Strait Island cultures enmeshed a sense of the sacred with the events of everyday life, as almost all pre-modern cultures did. Many contemporary urban Indigenous people would argue for a continuing difficult-to-define link with that culture. While it might seem to sceptics that such claims are sentimental and easy to make, my own experience of such people suggests that the link is vague but real, and can be found in the way they talk and think about the land and their ancestors. Non-Indigenous Australians tend to pride themselves on being down-to-earth and having a culture to match, maintaining a degree of scepticism about such large, vague notions as the 'sacred'. In principle, even in a world of Realpolitik, national culture need not inherently be separated from spiritual concerns. A concern with the sacred and with spiritual life might readily be associated with many nations—such as India, Iran, Italy, Spain, Thailand, and the USA—but Australia is not one of them.

This orientation might seem to be embedded in white Australian history, beginning as a penal colony in a climate and landscape which the early settlers found tough and demanding. Of course, late-eighteenth century British society was one which, at least officially, still maintained a strong belief in a Christian God. Sociologist Hans Mol notes that the First Fleet carried a chaplain to the colony, Reverend Richard Johnson. However, 'even at the risk of reduced food rations many skipped church. The hardworking Mr Johnson blamed this on the absence of a building' (1985, p. 51). That this neglect was not confined to the lower classes is evidenced by Johnson's fruitless petitions to Governor Phillip for a building. Mol reports that:

> Finally Johnson took the matter into his own hands and built a church from his own funds. It was opened on 25 August 1793 and could seat as many as 500. However, on Christmas Day that year fewer than 40 people attended ... about 3 per cent of the population (1985, p. 51).

Mol turns from neutral reporting to wry comment: 'Convicts and guards alike spurned religion and certainly did not let it interfere with their gambling, drinking and whoring. In 1798 convicts actually burnt the church' (1985, p. 51). This turn of events is less likely to produce a sense of embarrassment in contemporary Australian hearts than an enjoyment of such larrikin behaviour. Mol's last sentence is like the punchline in a sardonic Australian joke.

Many other sociologists, historians and literary critics have written about Australia in similar terms. Miriam Dixson acknowledges Patrick O'Farrell's argument that the most important historical fact about religion in Australia is 'its weakness ... its tenuous and intermittent hold on the minds and hearts of the Australian people' (1999, p. 82). Veronica Brady, one of the very few literary critics to try to relate Australian literature to religious belief, begins her book on 'Australians and the Question of God' with the declaration, 'Australian society boasts that it has no established religion, and the Constitution forbids any such establishment' (1981, p. 1). Brady further declares that 'our society ... discovered its identity in the shadow of nineteenth century utilitarianism' (1981, p. 1), and that 'the question of God ... gains little or no attention at the level of public discussion' (1981, pp. 1,2). Considering 'our culture and its religious traditions', Tony Kelly argues that 'the extrovert, pragmatic quality of Australian culture has little patience with such non-evident dimensions of life ... Australians are resolutely inarticulate about spiritual issues' (1990, p. 8). The word to particularly note here is 'resolutely', as if the inarticulateness were not just a feature of traditional Australian taciturnity, but wilful. Kelly is a strong Christian and has an explanation for this denial of the sacred: 'The struggle and degradation of our past, to say nothing of the dust and distance and heat, somehow parched our spirits, and made us wary of anything seeming too lush and soulful' (1990, pp. 8–9). Some Australians would see this hard-bitten refusal of pretentiousness in more positive terms. Les Murray (1938–) once wrote that 'At birth, each Australian / receives a stout bullshit gauge' (2002, p. 106). However, for Kelly this sardonic pragmatism is entirely negative: 'There is something about us Australians that prefers to communicate in silences rather than words. Perhaps we are defeated by it all, tongue-tied in the presence of ultimate things' (1990, p. 15).

One poet who would have partially agreed with Kelly is James McAuley. Himself deeply religious, in the mid-twentieth century McAuley characterised Australians as people of 'the doubting heart'. Although 'the air gives you ease',

> There you come home; the magpies call you Jack
> And whistle like larrikins at you from the trees.
> ('Terra Australis', 1971, p. 16)

This sounds playful and slightly larrikin itself, but McAuley's poem turns away from people to the 'demoniac' screams of the cockatoo and the insolence of the emu, to end with the landscape in purgatorial fire. This is the extent of Australian spirituality; in another of his famous poems, 'Envoi', McAuley describes Australian people as 'hard-eyed, kindly, with nothing inside them' (1971, p. 6).

All these are characteristics which white Australians might be seen to have been working towards for a long time. In the same period as McAuley, historian Geoffrey Serle pointed to 'the Christian churches having' no 'political or cultural authority' in Australia (1973, p. 21). Coming from the same historical tradition as Serle, Russel Ward provided what is still the most famous description of the Australian character:

> According to the myth the 'typical Australian' is a practical man, rough and ready in his manners and quick to decry any appearance of affectation in others. He is a great improviser ... he is usually taciturn rather than talkative, one who endures stoically rather than one who acts busily. He is a 'hard case', sceptical about the value of religion and of intellectual and cultural pursuits generally ... He is a fiercely independent person who hates officiousness and authority ... (1966, p. 2)

This is the figure of the Australian Legend, with its roots in the nineteenth century, and particularly in the 1890s, customarily seen as the great decade in the establishment of a distinctively Australian literature in the works of Lawson, Paterson, Furphy and others. Veronica Brady notes that 'the question of God ... is unimportant in the naturalistic tradition of writing, the "Lawson-

Furphy tradition", which critics like AA Phillips have declared to be the Australian tradition' (1981, p. 2).

The most famous works in this tradition—poems such as Paterson's 'Saltbush Bill' and 'The Geebung Polo Club', Lawson's story 'The Drover's Wife', or Furphy's novel *Such is Life*—would suggest that the sardonic looms so large in the Australian tradition as to drive out the sacred. 'The Drover's Wife' is the best-known story in Australian literature, which is extremely strong in the genre. The story presents 'dried-up-looking children' and their stoic mother in a dried-up landscape, and does have a mythic quality in its portrayal of stoicism and courage (1987, p. 110). However, that mythic quality comes through the extremes of deprivation endured without whingeing that the central character exemplifies. She is a battler without compare, and not the least of her deprivations is the absence of any hint of magic, of material for her imagination, or of a spiritual world: 'She thinks of things in her own life, for there is little else to think about' (1987, p. 12). The story portrays heroic endurance of a tough life, but the life is so tough that there is a kind of romanticism to it. With the central enemy a snake with 'an evil pair of small, bright bead-like eyes' (1987, p. 115), a case could be made for reading it as a Garden of Eden story but in inverse terms, with a 'stunted' landscape lacking any horizon and from which the characters are unlikely to be expelled. The story in fact gains much of its power from their containment there.

Paterson's work is much less hard-bitten than Lawson's; Lawson, of course, accused him of romanticising 'burning wastes of barren soil and sand' as 'sunny plains' (Lee 1999, p. 355). Lawson's reference is to Paterson's 'Clancy of the Overflow':

> And he sees the vision splendid of the sunlit plains extended,
> And at night the wond'rous glory of the everlasting stars. (Lee 1999, p. 75)

This couplet does indicate some sense of the sacred, but in a curious way it has less spirit than Lawson's story. Paterson's idea and his phrasing are utterly conventional, and the lines lack any inwardness. They have no glimmer of a Hopkinsian inscape and remain a generalised gesture towards the conventional, even though located in the bush. This sharply diminishes the sense of a spiritual dimension that the lines reach out to claim, and this type of language is characteristic of Paterson's work. While he is a master of galloping rhythms and has a superb sense of humour, his imagery is unexceptional. Interestingly, exactly the same can be said of the rare ventures in the same direction in Henry Lawson's poetry. Lawson's 'In the Days When the World Was Wide' calls for a return to 'the god-like spirit that died / At Eureka Stockade in the Roaring Days' (Lee 1999, p. 30). Despite the phrasing there is little sense of spiritual life here, with 'god-like spirit' coming to seem no more than a Boys' Own spirit of adventure 'ere science controlled the main' (Lee 1999, p. 29).

Paterson's 'Waltzing Matilda', so important to Australians that it has become the unofficial national anthem—and it is a tribute to the contemporary relevance of the Australian Legend that our real national anthem is *not* the official one—does contain a ghost. Although the swagman's ghost may be heard if you pass by the billabong, his character, like that of the whole song, is jokey and folkloric rather than spiritual. Attempts have been made to identify the particular billabong in Queensland that Paterson might have had in mind but they seem beside the point; the billabong has no particularity and is not a sacred site. Again, Paterson's language, while different to that in 'Clancy' and his other ballads, does not have the resonance that we associate with the existence of a spiritual world. The difference is stark if we look at some other poetry written in the same period:

> The cormorants shiver on their rocks;
> I wander on, and shake my heavy locks.
> The grey wolf knows me; by one ear
> I lead along the woodland dear;
> The hares rún by me growing bold.
> *They will not hush, the leaves a-flutter round me, the beech leaves old.*
> (Yeats 1983, p. 17)

Yeats's 'The Madness of King Goll' was written in 1884, early in the period of the 'Celtic Twilight'. It does not state its meanings directly, and uses rhyme, rhythm, assonance and soft vowel sounds to suggest something more than the wind in the rustle of the leaves. These are the words of a man who believed that 'the gross is the shadow of the subtle' and that 'the divine life wars upon our outer life' (Yeats 1961, pp. 155, 158). While the Irish have contributed an enormous, and still insufficiently recognised, amount to Australian culture, the difference between the basic realism of the Australian

Legend and the otherworldliness of the Celtic Twilight could hardly be greater. David Malouf has claimed for the Australian tradition a 'preference for the particular over the general' that has kept our thinking 'close to example and fact, made it pragmatic and wary of abstractions' (1998, p. 27). The language of Lawson and Paterson's writing is, even when telling tall tales, that of a society which values the clear and practical, under what Wallace Stevens called 'the pressure of reality' (Cook 2004, p. 261). Judith Brett has shown how John Howard 'raided the Australian Legend for the Liberal Party' (2003, p. 20), and his many years of success as Prime Minister might be seen to evidence the continuity of the Australian Legend values in characterising Australia. Donald Horne asserted that 'deeply inlaid scepticism is a national style' (1987, p. 27). There are then good reasons for seeing Australian culture as so alien to a perception of the sacred as to be mocking its unprovable and pretentious claims.

POETRY AND THE SACRED

Were there no more to be said this essay would provide a counterweight to others in this book. However, the Australian cultural tradition is more complex than the dominance of the Australian Legend would suggest. Veronica Brady claims that in literature 'the preferred images, human types and situations which keep recurring, raise questions of a spiritual kind' (1981, p. 1) but the works she sets out to evidence her claim are novels, not poems. However, poetry is the literary form in which we might most readily find an approach to the sacred.

There are a number of reasons for this. Poetry, the oldest of the literary genres, has its roots in religious rituals, spells and incantations. Poets as diverse as Virgil, Dante, Milton, and the authors of the *Ramayana* have invoked the idea of divine inspiration. *The New Princeton Encyclopedia of Poetry and Poetics* notes that 'the Indian word for poet is *vishi* ('seer') and the Latin is *vates* ('prophet')' (1993, p. 1023) and scriptures from different traditions employ poetic devices such as symbol, metaphor, extended rhythm and allegory in order to express their meanings. Poetry can provide the most intense use of all the resources of language; it is language used under the greatest pressure. It can make the fullest attempt to unite form and content, to use the rhythms, repetitions and music of language in an effort to say the unsayable. Much of its appeal is to the pre-rational, and perhaps to the post-rational. It is 'as much conducted by metaphors as by definitions and concepts' (Cook 2004, p. 5). Yeats said that poetry attempts to work with an 'element of evocation, of suggestion … symbolism' (1961, p. 155). Poetry may make expressive those silences to which taciturn Australians are given; the silences represent more in Australian culture, I would argue, than the all-too-much-for-us that Tony Kelly perceives. All these features are particularly true of lyric poetry, which is the dominant form in the Australian poetic tradition (as it is in modern and contemporary poetry in English as a whole).

Barbara Hardy notes that 'perhaps most lyrics end in a reverberation of words, but some can move out of vibrant stillness into that familiar silence of strong feeling where words fail us' (1977, p. 17). This is because 'lyric poetry thrives … on exclusions … it leaves out so much of accustomed context and consequences of feeling that it can speak in a pure, lucid, and intense voice' (1977, p. 2). In its attempt to speak through rhythm, music and imagery, lyric poetry seeks a kind of instantaneity, avoiding the sequentiality of reasoning. It prefers sudden revelation to the gradual emergence of answers through reasoning.

These are traditional—which is to say time-honoured—terms, but even a poststructuralist seeking to demystify any metaphysical claims is likely to establish uncertainties which allow for the possibility of other meanings. While that may seem to usher in the possibility of meaninglessness or merely arbitrary claims to meaning, it also allows for an otherworldly guarantee of meaning, since most people's lives, and the statements of poststructuralists, are not characterised by surreal chaos. Once Derrida conceived the idea of a 'supplement' that was always necessary to provide meaning he was opening the way for 'the return of the sacred'. The relatively early modern theorist Roman Jakobson was happy to speak of the 'poetic function' of semiosis, as opposed to the referential function of mimesis (Cook 2004, p. 353). This is the problem with the poetic language of Paterson and Lawson: a lack of subtlety, an excessive reliance on mimesis robs it of richness. Naming is a form of control but Paterson and Lawson are too much in control; quite simply, or quite complexly, our experience of the world is more like Hamlet's 'more things in heaven and earth' than fit their Horatian philosophy. Their clarity is admirable but they have, if anything, an excess of clarity because of the lack of sensory power in their images. C Day Lewis has argued:

> The image cannot, of course, reproduce the soul of things; what it can do is persuade us ... that soul there must be—or if you dislike the word 'soul', to persuade us that there is beneath the appearance of things a life whose quality may not be apprehended in our everyday intercourse nor be gauged by the instruments of science. (1965, p. 107)

Day Lewis is not necessarily appealing to religion but he is appealing to a sense of mystery, in which the sacred might dwell. While couched as an argument, his statement really constitutes an appeal to the reader to test the statement against his or her own experience. Such terms, like many of those above, are imprecise; they do not have the analytical quality of Jakobson or Derrida or even of many less theoretical contemporary professional critics. However, for this very reason they seem preferable terms of argument to me: like the poetry which is their subject, they appeal to emotion as well as intellect; to the senses as well as the conscious, reasoning mind; and to a wholeness of being and experience. It may be a small consolation that they are less vague than the terms 'sacred', 'spiritual' and 'religious', which I have deliberately used almost interchangeably. Tony Kelly has lamented that 'spirituality' is a 'weak word in a world of theories and science and technical know-how. Compared to the taut scientific language, or logical analysis and empirical experiment, it seems as ethereal as the mist around the mountains' (1990, p. 16).

However, it is intrinsic to the concept of spirituality that it is unnameable, that even poetic language might be only a gesture towards its existence, and that it is impossible to *argue* anyone who refuses to admit the concept into accepting it. For those who do admit the possibility of the spiritual, of the sacred, of metaphysics, Kelly's final image may be the most expressive part of his sentence. Day Lewis declares that 'images are elusive things'. (1965, p. 33) but that 'the poetic image is the human mind claiming kinship with everything that lives or has lived' (1965, p. 35).

THE AUSTRALIAN POETIC TRADITION

Traditionally, Australian poetry of any worth has been thought to begin with Charles Harpur (1813–1868), and his most anthologised poem is 'The Creek of the Four Graves'. It is a narrative which presents the landscape in alternately

Miltonic and Wordsworthian terms—mountains 'tented o'er / With canopies of purple and of gold' at sunset and the Hawkesbury bush representing 'all this solemn beauty of the world' (1984, pp. 162, 165). The escape by the lone survivor in the party of five white men attacked by Aborigines has the narrator exclaim, 'O verily our God / Hath those in His peculiar care, for whom / The daily prayers of spotless womanhood / And helpless infancy are offered up!' (1984, p. 169). All these statements are, of course, gestures towards the sacred, but they do not carry a sense of the sacred in their language. Harry Heseltine argues that 'the narrative and the language ... combine to realize a myth of Eden' but 'a secular Eden' (1972, p. 31). Certainly, Harpur's language seems secular, to a large extent because of its conventionality; to cry out for the sacred is not to evoke it, and in that sense, not to take part in it.

The Aborigines in 'The Creek of the Four Graves' are 'painted savages' as 'vengeful as hell's worst fiends'—attitudes which it is easy to feel superior to today. Paradoxically, even Harpur's poem attributes a greater sense of spirituality to them than to the whites—at one point we find them 'standing now in the keen radiance there / So ghostly still as in a solemn trance'—despite his apparent intentions. The poem does usefully highlight the difference between invoking and evoking the sacred; its language is closer to that of Paterson and Lawson than to that of Yeats. Australian poetry has two anthologies of poetry that explicitly concern the sacred, Les Murray's *Anthology of Australian Religious Poetry* (1986, 1991) and Kevin Hart's *The Oxford Book of Australian Religious Verse* (1994). Each includes poems that the editors recognise as contentious. Hart's anthology in particular includes a number of poems about religion that are not religious poems in any other sense, such as four (beautifully constructed) satires and social observations by Geoff Page, in which God is 'hard as a hammer at cattle sales' and 'wipes his feet clean on the mat' (1994, pp. 159, 160). Hart (1954–) notes in his Introduction:

> you can claim, as very different writers have done over the years, that poetry is Orphic: a transfiguration of nature into song that overcomes death and the grave. And so, regardless of its explicit themes, all poetry is at heart sacred. This certainly expands the category of religious poetry, so much so, though, that in effect it abolishes it (1994, p. xx).

In Murray's view 'Art is anciently a part of religious activity, and is surely still at least coterminous with it' (1987, p. 9) and he argues that 'in an age of seemingly hopeless religious fragmentation, poetry itself is one of the few channels of spiritual life all may still have in common. Indeed it may be the only one' (1987, p. 12). Murray believes that 'there is impressive power in what we can imagine, but no transcendence. There is great depth, sometimes, in our perception—but, again, no transcendence'; however, poetry may express 'the true otherness to which we are, as it were, keyed in the depths of our being … the only coin the soul recognises' (1999, pp. 35, 36). In this essay I want to examine Australian poems which approximate this expression, especially poems which do not adopt religion or spiritual belief as explicit subject. This may suggest a dimension of Australian subjectivity and identity that is not well-recognised and that certainly lies outside the Australian Legend, as well as point to the extent to which Australian language can say the unsayable, for the sacred is, almost by definition, that which lies outside normal speech.

Some might find a starting point for this search in the work of Christopher Brennan (1870–1932), a rebel from Catholicism who was intellectually linked to the French Symbolistes and so saw art as a replacement for religion. Brennan sought 'a sphere appeas'd and undistraught' (1979, p. 114) but his diction and phrasing remained somewhat rigidly Victorian. He is a poet of massive intellect whose intellect proved more limiting than enabling, and a sharp contrast to his contemporary John Shaw Neilson (1872–1942). Neilson's delicacy and lyricism, drawn from his Celtic background, are much more given to the expression of the sacred. This is surely the real subject of the much anthologised 'The Orange Tree', with its strange, unexplained perceptions.

In her explanation of an inexplicable light 'not of the sky' but living 'somewhere in the Orange Tree' or falling 'on the Orange Tree', the girl who speaks the poem conjures up a sense of the sacred (1965, pp. 62–63). This light is, perhaps, not even light—it is 'a light, a step, a call' that induces her to attempt a different mode of being so that she ends the poem 'listening like the Orange Tree'. Selective quotation does not do justice to Shaw Neilson's expression, since it misses the linguistic music which does so much to convey the otherworldly fragility and preciousness of her perception and perceptiveness. In a number of poems, such as 'The Poor Can Feed the Birds' and 'The Gentle Water Bird', Shaw Neilson sets such capacity for awareness against formal notions of God. He uses imagery and musicality because the 'Divine' is 'unknowable' in any formal, expository way (1965, p. 165). A bird 'hath his Heaven got' (1965, p. 159) and the 'blue smoke of the mind' (1965,

p. 72) will perceive that Heaven only through the bird's song as it 'sings and sings and sings' (1965, p. 169).

The next great imagistic musician in Australian poetry was Kenneth Slessor (1901–1971). Kevin Hart declares, 'I could not find any trace of religious feeling or thought in his writing' (1994, xxv). Murray includes six Slessor poems, about Pan or landscape or metempsychosis, and one satire on the idea of gods. Slessor was not himself a religious person; in his will he directed that his funeral involve no religious service, which was unusual in 1971. However, his poems frequently appeal to 'religious thought' if that phrase is taken to mean a sense of another realm whose terms are different to those of our world. This is clearest when he writes, as he often did, about time, in poems such as 'Out of Time', 'Sleep' and 'Five Bells'. In the third section of 'Out of Time' Slessor positions his speaker in an experience outside time, employing the shifting, ungraspable imagery of water:

> Leaning against the golden undertow,
> Backward, I saw the birds begin to climb
> With bodies hailstone-clear, and shadows flow,
> Fixed in a sweet meniscus, out of Time ... (1994, p. 130)

At the end of the poem he is 'taken by the suck of the sea' and 'the gulls go down', but for this fleeting period the birds' bodies are clear and shadows can simultaneously 'flow' and be 'fixed'. This imagery, and the following 'lighted beach, the sharp and china sand / Glitters and waters and peninsula', seem to me to offer a glimpse of the transcendent, which is my sense of the sacred, even if Slessor's imagery is more hard-edged than Shaw Neilson's. I would argue this about 'Five Bells' too, even though its expression of the 'Nothing that was neither long nor short' has been seen by some others as nihilistic. There is such richness in the images of waves that 'let their shadows down like shining hair' or 'with diamond quills and combs of light' that I find it impossible not to think of a religious dimension (1994, p. 123).

In general, poems explicitly about the sacred—and there are quite a few in Murray's and Hart's anthologies—do not evoke it but resolutely speak to our world. An exception, included by Hart, is Francis Webb's (1925–1973) most famous poem, 'Five Days Old'. It does both; Webb explicitly declares, 'The tiny, not the immense, / Will teach our groping eyes', and follows immediately with a different kind of statement: 'So the absorbed skies / Bleed stars of innocence' (Hart 1994, p. 22). In structure the statements parallel each other and both seek to be explanatory and instructive. That they are not overbearing is due to their quiet tone and the impression, with every reading, that the poet has discovered these claimed truths only at that moment, and moreover has done so through the simple holding of a baby. It is the shift away from 'ordinary', worldly reference that makes the second claim become a statement of the sacred, although the effect is helped by the quiet tone and steady rhythm common to both statements. While we all know what 'skies', 'bleeding', 'stars' and 'innocence' refer to, combining the words carries us into what our earthly mode might best grasp as metaphor—but that sounds a lame description of what is going on. What are 'absorbed skies'? Absorption is a physical process, which we metaphorically apply to humans whose concentration is entirely taken by one person, thing or event, as Webb's is by holding the baby. Stars do not bleed, and innocence is a human or animal quality, not one ascribed to physical or chemical objects. Of course, 'stars', being literally out of our world, have long had more metaphorical and symbolic meaning than literal, and continue to do so outside the realm of astrophysics. Thus, the lines 'So the absorbed skies / Bleed stars of innocence' do not have any literal meaning but have immense poetic meaning, and it is in this gap that the sacred may be seen—or heard—to inhere. Holding the baby is for Webb symbolic—more than symbolic to him because he experiences the process—of holding the whole mystery of creation. After all, whatever our beliefs, and whatever our knowledge of medicine or biology, every birth of a child is a kind of miracle, more extraordinary than seeing Lazarus come back or a cripple tossing away his crutches. The power of this thought and the power of these lines lie behind the beautiful Franciscan ending of the poem. In the penultimate stanza Webb rhymes 'truth' and 'death'—a half-rhyme of course—and in the last stanza 'danger' and 'manger', 'inn' and 'sin', but one of each of these last rhyme words counters the other. Then the poem ends in a simple, but poetically intricate, and internally-rhymed couplet:

> In the sleeping, weeping weather
> We shall all kneel down together.

It is an ending that technically is almost old-fashioned, but that is part of its power: it seems to take away such matters as fashion in its absorbed breathlessness.

Les Murray opens his essay 'Some Religious Stuff I Know about Australia' with the claim, 'Most people would agree … that something like a religious dimension exists in every being' (1999, p. 19), and he also agrees with the novelist George Johnston that 'nothing human has yet happened in Australia which stands out above the continent itself' (1999, p. 30). I am not sure what this second claim actually means but there is no doubt about the dominance of 'the continent itself' in Australian intellectual consciousness. Given the size and nature of the land and the size of the Australian population—approximately twenty million in an often threatening landscape roughly the size of the USA—this is hardly surprising. A number of people die in that landscape every year. Australian art as a whole—I mean all the arts together—is overwhelmingly an art of landscape. Murray's first claim is correct, I believe, and given the irreligious nature of Australian society, apart from traditional Indigenous society, it was perhaps inevitable that the religious impulse would be transposed onto the land, presented in almost mystical, although often malevolent, terms in Arthur Streeton's paintings, Patrick White's *Voss*, Peter Sculthorpe's music, Peter Weir's film of *Picnic at Hanging Rock*, and even to some extent in 'The Drover's Wife'. In Australia we don't have church, we have landscape. Landscape in Australia means vast space; Murray notes that out there 'the solitary ego could be at once as vast as the horizon and unimportant as a straw of windblown grass' (1999, p. 30).

The Australian poet in whose work these thoughts are most readily apparent is Randolph Stow (1935–), whose first novel was titled *A Haunted Land*. His poem 'The Singing Bones' has as epigraph the famous phrase from Barcroft Boake, 'Out where the dead men lie' (1969, p. 52). Stow, who grew up on a property outside Geraldton, Western Australia, is acutely aware of that 'Drover's Wife' past. His poem identifies the dead explorers Leichhardt and Gibson as 'sand-enshrined lay saints', and he mentions 'Lawson's tramps' as well as Gordon's and Boake's suicides. 'My country's heart', he notes, 'is aftermath of martyrdom.' To 'the scrub-dark flat horizon' that the Drover's Wife experienced he adds the singing of the dead men's bones, 'whose sound / netted my childhood round, and even here still blows'. The death-sites are seen in a hard-bitten Australian way as holy sites of sorts, but 'unreachable' and 'unmapped' so that they exist 'mainly in the mind'. They lie in a landscape that 'their heirs', sheltered in the coastal cities, 'Heed not nor draw near'. But Stow and the crows hear it, a tough voice of the sacred utterly different to Webb's, 'embracing pain'.

A roughly contemporary poet who listened to a different wind in a different landscape, living in Tasmania, was Gwen Harwood (1920–1996). Harwood, a religiously minded person, frequently describes a littoral, a space where land and water meet that might seem conducive to conjuring the transcendent. Indeed, a poem titled 'Threshold' ends with 'the seawind breathing / a prayer of peace and healing / in the pure, authentic speech / that earth alone can teach' (1990, p. 208). A concern with 'authentic speech' and with the power and limitations of language, is strong in Harwood's work. Her poems are also shot through with visits from the dead, rising 'in the mind's image / to walk again with the sharpness of life' (1990, p. 67). Another strong theme is music, which has a power beyond words to 'contain … the unsayable / grace that cannot be defined / yet leaps like light from mind to mind' (1990, p. 61). Yet Harwood in the end is not a poet to evoke the sacred. These statements all talk about it, and Harwood will tell us about the power of music or philosophers' thought; she tells us that her dreams of the dead *are* dreams. 'How shall the heart's true shape be known, / spirit made manifest?' she asks (1990, p. 70), and she is too honest a poet ever to pretend to any vision she did not actually feel. She recounts, in response to this question, how 'Once in / a bare room, shaken by the wind / … / heart leapt beyond music … / to affirm *what is*' (1990, p. 71) but she does not attempt to evoke that experience. Always in Harwood's work there is a controlling self; unlike Webb or Stow, she never lets go, and this seems to be a necessary condition for evocation of the sacred. Harwood's poems are full of images but also of an authorial, controlling presence.

A poet with a less strong presence in poems and who is religious—in fact, a convert to Catholicism—but whose poems mostly remain earth-bound is Bruce Dawe (1930–). Like Harwood, Dawe does refer to the numinous and can present ghosts, such as the dead soldiers on Anzac Day in 'Returned Men' (2006, p. 157), but their poem is a social one. I have argued elsewhere that as a religious poet he remains remarkably social (2002, pp. 211–225). Interestingly, both Harwood and Dawe are powerful satirists.

It is not for nothing that Murray and Hart are the two Australian poets who were commissioned to edit anthologies of religious verse. Both are converts to Catholicism, but it is Murray who has written about his beliefs most, in both poetry and essay. Murray, whose books are all dedicated 'To the Glory of God', includes in his anthology eighteen of his own poems, and some of the choices—such as 'The Euchre Game', about luck and justice, 'The

Mitchells', about ritual Australian male laconicism, and 'Kiss of the Whip', about whip culture from stockyard to porn shop—are surprising choices. Also included are the early poems, 'The Burning Truck', in which a truck that has caught fire becomes a mobile burning bush, and 'The Powerline Incarnation', in which an electrocuted man sees visions. These are instances of the ordinary suddenly made transcendent, and this is always likely to be Murray's stance. However, the teacher is a large part of Murray's temperament, and the poem 'Poetry and Religion' begins with the blunt statement, 'Religions are poems' (1989). This is because both bring the conscious and unconscious, or dreaming, minds together to create 'an experience of wholeness' (1987, p. 14). 'Poetry and Religion' presents this idea and the idea that 'God' is a quality of being, but does not attempt to evoke that quality except, briefly, in its closing image of birds' wings beating. The birds have what Murray calls in his poem 'Equanimity'—a poem central to his oeuvre—an 'unceasing on-off/ grace', but this is pointed out rather than evoked, despite the wonderful (but earthly) images with which the poem begins. There is no doubting Murray's belief in the sacred, or his ability to write about it, but he is, like Dawe, a writer about the sacred rather than a writer of sacred poems.

Of the five poems of his own that Hart includes in his anthology, two are in fact prayers, one by a stone—'The Stone's Prayer', which runs the risk of pretentiousness—and one by an Everyman. The latter, 'Master of energy and silence', is in fact the first of 'Three Prayers' in Hart's *New and Selected Poems*. The poem as prayer is a difficult genre in the contemporary world; each must attempt to be both poetic prayer and prayerful poem. The God who is 'Master of energy and silence' is also the 'Embracer of contradictions' and the poem becomes a series of variations of that first line through paradoxes. The second of the prayers, not included in the anthology, gets closer than the first to both paradoxical definition and evocation of 'my God', who 'glows within each thing / Beyond reach of language / And deeper than silence' (1995, p. 34). These are traditional ideas of God, but stronger as ideas for that, and Hart's hushed tone moves his lines towards embodiment of God-liness. This is the tone of so much of Hart's work and it can seem, perhaps paradoxically, ostentatious away from religious subjects. He is a reflective poet whose language sometimes seems directed to keeping experience at bay. When in the last poem in *New and Selected Poems*, 'L'intelligence avec l'ange', he speaks of 'an angel living deep inside / That speaks the highest silence that there is', he seems to be describing what all his poetry is reaching towards. His work often seems poised between the attempt to define or address and the attempt to evoke, speaking to 'A silence undressing words, a nameless love' (1995, p. 91).

Les Murray's concept of 'wholespeak' as the language of religion and poetry, uniting both our reason and our imagination, seems identical with WB Yeats's concept of Unity of Being (1961, p. 518). Both are protesting against a world dominated by reason and by science as the paradigm of knowledge. It is a battle that poets have been waging, and losing, since the late-nineteenth century. It is no accident that when widespread belief in the soul went, so did the widespread interest in poetry. Because poetry uses the indefinable, mysterious elements of language it is in its nature to speak to more than reason, including perhaps the unreasonable concept of the sacred. Murray says that 'discourses based on the supposed primacy or indeed exclusive sovereignty of daylight reason I call Narrowspeak ... narrowspeak prose doesn't answer to our own inner nature, and cannot describe the cosmos adequately' (1987, p. 18). Unlike prose, narrow or not, poetry can have a kind of immediate epiphany—a meaning generated in image or rhythm that denies the generally sequential nature of language. Thus, at its best, poetry often evokes meanings rather than states them, and this makes it the 'natural' form of language in which to touch the sacred. Murray declares, 'I would certainly never trust anything I could fully understand' (1987, p. 22), a statement that many in modern Australian society could not fully understand. But the poets, secular and religious, would: Robert Adamson has written that 'hope's dead hearted in the name of science' (Kinsella 1999, p. 29). 'We only have our words', wrote RA Simpson (Porter 1996, p. 86). Australian poets come from a largely irreligious society with a tough, hard-bitten tradition, and their work displays none of the easy association with the sacred found in, say, the Irish tradition. Nevertheless, when a poet such as Robert Gray ends his 'Flames and Dangling Wire' with observation of an old radio at the tip, and 'its dangling wire' prompts thought of 'the voices it received / ... still travelling, / ... around the arc of the universe' together with 'the Chopin / which was the sound of the curtains lifting, / one time, to a coast of light' (1995, p. 70), we are on the edge of the mystical, even while 'the muted happenstance of day-to-day' (Dawe 2006, p. 27) and the wrecked stuff of the physical are kept in sight.

WORKS CITED

Brady, Veronica 1981, *A Crucible of Prophets: Australians and the Question of God,* Sydney, Theological Explorations.

Brennan, Christopher 1979, *Selected Poems*, ed. GA Wilkes, Sydney, Angus & Robertson.

Brett, Judith 2003, 'John Howard and the Australian Legend', *Arena Magazine*, vol. 65, June–July 2003.

Cook, Jon (ed.) 2004, *Poetry in Theory*, Malden, Oxford & Carlton, Blackwell.

Dawe, Bruce 2006, *Sometimes Gladness: Collected Poems 1954-2005*, 6th edn, Melbourne, Longman.

Dixson, Miriam 1999, *The Imaginary Australian: Anglo-Celts and Identity–1788 to the Present*, Sydney, UNSWP.

Gray, Robert 1995, *New and Selected Poems*, Melbourne, Heinemann.

Hardy, Barbara 1977, *The Advantage of Lyric*, Bloomington & London, Indiana UP.

Harpur, Charles 1984, *The Poetical Works of Charles Harpur*, ed. Elizabeth Perkins, Sydney, Angus & Robertson.

Hart, Kevin (ed.) 1994, *The Oxford Book of Australian Religious Verse*, Melbourne, OUP.

—— 1995, *New and Selected Poems*, Sydney, Angus & Robertson.

Harwood, Gwen 1990, *Selected Poems*, Sydney, Angus & Robertson.

Haskell, Dennis 2002, *Attuned to Alien Moonlight: The Poetry of Bruce Dawe,* St Lucia, UQP.

Heseltine, Harry (ed.) 1972, *The Penguin Book of Australian Verse*, Ringwood Vic, Penguin.

Horne, Donald 1987, *The Lucky Country Revisited*, Melbourne, Dent.

Kelly, Tony 1990, *A New Imagining: Towards an Australian Spirituality*, Melbourne, Collins Dove.

Kinsella, John (ed.) 1999, *Landbridge: Contemporary Australian Poetry*, Fremantle, Fremantle Arts Centre Press.

Lawson, Henry 1987, *'The Drover's Wife', Collected Stories of Henry Lawson*, Ringwood, Vic., Viking O'Neil.

Lee, Christopher (ed.) 1999, *Turning the Century: Writing of the 1890s*, St Lucia, UQP.

Lewis, C Day 1965, *The Poetic Image*, 2nd edn, London, Jonathan Cape.

Malouf, David 1998, *A Spirit of Play: The Making of Australian Consciousness*, Sydney, ABC.

McAuley, James 1971, *Collected Poems*, Sydney, Angus & Robertson.

Mol, Hans 1985, *The Faith of Australians*, Sydney, Allen & Unwin.

Murray, Les 1987, *Embodiment and Incarnation: Notes on Preparing an Anthology of Australian Religious Verse*, Brisbane, Aquinas Library.

—— (ed.) 1986, rev. ed 1989. *Anthology of Australian Religious Poetry*, Melbourne, Collins Dove.

—— 1999, *'Some Religious Stuff I Know about Australia', The Quality of Sprawl: Thoughts about Australia*, Sydney, Duffy & Snellgrove.

—— 2002, *Collected Poems 1961–2002*, Sydney, Duffy & Snellgrove.

Neilson, John Shaw 1965, *The Poems of Shaw Neilson*, ed. AR Chisholm, Sydney, Sirius.

Preminger, Alex & Brogan, TVF (eds.) 1993, *The New Princeton Encyclopedia of Poetry and Poetics*, Princeton, Princeton UP.

Serle, Geoffrey 1973, *From Deserts the Prophets Come: The Creative Spirit in Australia 1788–1972*, Melbourne, Heinemann.

Simpson, RA 1996, 'All Friends Together', in Peter Porter (ed), *The Oxford Book of Modern Australian Verse*, Melbourne, OUP.

Slessor, Kenneth 1994, *Collected Poems*, ed. Dennis Haskell & Geoffrey Dutton, Sydney, Angus & Robertson.

Stow, Randolph 1969, *A Counterfeit Silence: Selected Poems*, Sydney, Angus & Robertson.

Ward, Russel 1966, *The Australian Legend*, Melbourne, OUP.

Yeats, WB 1961, *Essays and Introductions*, London, Macmillan.

—— 1983, *The Poems: A New Edition*, ed. Richard J Finneran, London, Macmillan.

RETHINKING THE SACRED—POETRY AS *SATYAGRAHA* : A GANDHIAN READING OF LES MURRAY'S 'WALKING TO THE CATTLE PLACE'

Sudhir Kumar

INTRODUCTION

The present essay is an attempt to read Les Murray's poem 'Walking to the Cattle Place' through Gandhi's vision of art, action and aesthetics. At the very outset it is important to note that, in the Gandhian worldview, human life as well as art, if it has to meaningfully contribute to the greatest good of all, should represent or address truth (*satyam*), the universal good (*shivam*) and the beautiful (*sundaram*), which are inseparable values, existing in a creative continuum. Similarly, *satyagraha* as holding on to truth-force, in the Gandhian worldview, enables an individual (a political activist or a writer/artist alike) to non-violently resist injustice, exploitation, inequality and violence prevailing in a society at a particular time. To a writer, her/his text becomes the means or the site where the quest for truth, *swaraj* (self-rule—both political, meaning freedom, and spiritual, meaning self-knowledge) and concerns for universal welfare are aesthetically represented leading to the aesthetic experience of the beautiful and blissful. It is in this sense that the very process of writing is a *satyagrah* or an embodiment of truth-force, which enables a writer not only to represent her/his protest against the prevailing injustice and infliction of violence but also to aesthetically reconstruct an alternative space or reality where the writer as well as the reader become one—sharing an indescribable aesthetic experience or *rasa*. According to Gandhi *Satyagrah* is literally holding on to Truth, and it means, therefore Truth-force. Truth is soul or spirit. It is, therefore known as soul-force. It excludes the use of violence, because man is not capable of knowing the absolute Truth, and therefore, not competent to punish. (*Young India,* March 23, 1921).

Similarly, poetry or art which aesthetically foregrounds and holds on to any aspect of truth is said to resonate with the poetic truth. Writing, in itself (poetry), is a non-violent activity, and therefore, the works of art or literature that are generally considered great or important do not reconstruct the realities in order to advocate or support violence, injustice and untruth. This is what is meant by the term 'poetics of satyagraha' as used in the Gandhian sense in the title of the essay. Gandhi wants art and artist both to be an embodiment of the truth-force, which is best displayed when an artist or writer is confronted with the forces of untruth, injustice, exploitation and violence. A writer, who is committed to the cause of universal good and justice, becomes, in the Gandhian sense, a *satyagrahi*—one who holds on to truth with all his soul-force. Like Gandhi, Les Murray also underlines the significance of 'soul-force' in the act of creation of art or literature:

> What I create, really, is a new body made of words and the potent arrangements of words, in which my soul, as it was, at a particular moment will go on existing ... This I suggest is the essential model and structure of all human creation and the reason we never stop creating. (From the Les Murray Lecture delivered in 1998 for the Rotterdam Poetry International Festival.)

Les Murray's poetry is also a perpetual quest for truth or *satyagraha* in the context of increasing injustice, materialism, spiritual emptiness, violence and exploitation in contemporary Australia and the world at large. Some of the titles of his works easily tempt a careful reader to read his poetry through Gandhi. For example, such terms as 'against economics', 'vernacular republic', 'the people's otherworld' and 'translations from the natural world' have an unmistakable Gandhian resonance of truth and non-violence. Translated into the Gandhian aesthetics, Murray's 'vernacular republic' could be compared with Gandhi's idea of *gram-swaraj* (eco-friendly-village-republic), his 'against economics' would resemble *swadeshi* and *swaraj*, and his 'people's otherworld' would become *sarvodaya* (universal welfare), all embedded in the spiritual values of truth and non-violence.

In order to attempt a Gandhian reading of Les Murray's poetry, let us begin by analysing his two recent statements about his poetry. 'Poetry is the best means to make clear what we mean by sacred. Each of us lives inside a poem which is sacred to us. We enjoy its myths and legends. Poetry celebrates experience. It is visceral and immediate. It is like dreaming and thinking and dancing all in the same instance ... I encounter a lot of open ridicule in the west about religion. But it is not easy to dismiss the existence of God in the light of human experience. I do believe in God. Religion is all about taking us closer to salvation. But when we forget this fundamental fact, we start cutting each other's throats in the name of our gods' (Murray, 'Interview', p. 6).

Gandhi relates art to the sacred or the spiritual in its widest sense that subsumes the so-called secular space also. 'Productions of man's art have their value only insofar as they help the soul towards self-realisation' (Gandhi 1924). Murray also, in a way, seems to connect the outward as reflected in a poem (the text) to its internal context (the articulation of the spiritual or the sacred) like Gandhi. According to Gandhi the external and the internal domains of art are complementary. 'There are two aspects of things—the outward and the inward. The outward has no meaning except insofar as it helps the inward. All true art is thus an expression of the soul. The outward forms have value only insofar as they are the expression of the inner spirit of man' (Gandhi 1924). In his poem, 'Poetry and Religion' (Collected Poems (hereafter CP) p. 267), Murray like Gandhi connects poetry to religion or spirituality:

> Religions are poems. They concert
> our daylight and dreaming mind, our
> emotions, instinct, breath and native gesture
> into the only whole thinking: poetry. (CP, p. 267)

Further still he clarifies his position:

> God is the poetry caught in any religion,
> caught, not imprisoned ...
> There'll always be religion around while there is poetry. (CP p. 267)

Moreover, on the issue of the centrality of religion or the spiritual and the significance of civilisational values endangered by the crassly consumerist logic of late capitalism, Gandhi and Les Murray are aligned:

> The word 'religion' requires some explanation. It is not the Hindu religion but the religion which transcends Hinduism, which changes one's very

nature, which binds one indissolubly to the truth within and which ever purifies' (Gandhi 1920).

Truth, to Gandhi, is the primary *dharma* (moral duty) of a citizen who is also a poet. Gandhi's firm faith in truth as God is also echoed in Les Murray's poems. As Gandhi says, 'To me, God is Truth and Love; God is ethics and morality; God is fearlessness. God is the source of light and life and yet He is above and beyond all these' (Gandhi 1925). And Gandhi aptly says that 'All true art is thus the expression of soul' (*Young India*, 13 Nov 1924). Les Murray also condemns the damning impact of modernity that has surely marginalised poetry in human life, but he reaffirms the spiritual significance of poetry:

> Pop music is a billion-dollar industry ... but verse poetry is marginal, listened to by modest number of people at readings, read on the page by fewer still. There is still an atavistic reluctance to pay poets anything like an ordinary wage, but few realise that this comes from an ancient sense that we like priests and mothers, are sacred folk not to be polluted with money. (The Rotterdam address)

Both Gandhi and Murray, as will be discussed in the essay, show their concerns for the rural poor and environment; they protest against godless, valueless western modernity and emphasise the preservation of civilisational moral/ethical values. The present essay is an attempt to read Les Murray's poems as a *satyagraha* (holding on to truth or soul force in the Gandhian sense) against injustice, violence, exploitation and untruth. I would like to argue that Murray's poetry is a *satyagraha* or non-violent crusade for establishing a society where moral duty, self-realisation/salvation, truth and non-violence are considered the cardinal virtues.

POETRY AS *SATYAGRAHA* AGAINST VALUELESS MODERNITY

While writing the manifesto of the Australian Commonwealth Party ('A Focus of Vision'), Murray critiques modern civilisation based on the abuse of technology and its dehumanising impact on contemporary culture and society. He proposed that the Australian Commonwealth Party would make '[...] a start on the work of eliminating all exploitative and exhaustive techniques from the Australian economy. No Luddite reversion to the past advocated here; bad greed-motivated, typically violent technology must be replaced in great part, by the development of good ecologically responsible technology. We cannot and should not destroy the Machine—we must civilise it' (Bourke 1992, p. 82). Like Murray, Gandhi also wanted to civilise modern science and technology by making it a means of creating an eco-friendly and non-violent society free from hunger and want. In a way, Gandhi's project was to 'civilise' or 'spiritualise' science and modernity both.

That's why Murray asks us in his poem 'SMLE' to 'evade the modernities' (Murray, 1982). Murray criticises the destructive impact of modern civilisation on millions of people: 'The onrush of modern technological development has unseated millions of people from their older centredness in religious faith' (Murray 1978, p. 52). Similarly, Gandhi, in his *Hind Swaraj* (first published serially in *The Indian Opinion* in 1908), critiqued modern western civilisation because of its emphasis on the multiplication of desires and its amoral nature as 'satanic':

> This civilization is irreligion, and it has taken such a hold on the people in Europe that those who are in it appear to be half mad. They lack real physical strength or courage. They keep up their energy by intoxication. They can hardly be happy in solitude. This civilisation is such that one has only to be patient and it will be self-destroyed. According to the teachings of Mahommed this would be considered a satanic civilisation. Hinduism calls it the Black Age. (*Hind Swaraj*, 33–34)

Like, Murray, Gandhi, too, decried the dehumanising and destructive use of machines in modern civilisation: 'Machinery is the chief symbol of modern civilisation; it represents a great sin' (Gandhi 1995, p. 83). And, furthermore, Gandhi warned against the impact of the predominance of machines in a country like India: 'How can a country with crores of living machines afford to have a machine which will displace the labour of crores of living machines? It would spell their unemployment and their ruin' (Gandhi 1935). But even he is not a Luddite in his condemnation of machinery. In *Young India* (13 Nov 1924), Gandhi criticised the use of machinery to serve human greed:

> What I object to is the craze for machinery, not machinery as such. The craze is for what they call labour-saving machinery. Men go on 'saving labour' till thousands are without work and thrown on the open streets of

> die of starvation ... Scientific truths and discoveries should first of all cease to be mere instruments of greed. (*Young India* 13 Nov 1924)

Throughout his life, Gandhi emphasised the difference between the Western (modern) civilisation and the spiritually oriented Indian civilisation:

> Modern civilisation is chiefly materialistic as ours is chiefly spiritual. Modern civilisation occupies itself in the investigation of the laws of the matter and employs the human ingenuity in inventing or discovering means of production of weapons of destruction, ours is chiefly occupied in exploring spiritual laws. (Gandhi 1934, p. 329)

While reading Les Murray's poetry, one cannot miss his aesthetic crusade (poetic *satyagraha*) against the growing tentacles of modernity and the withering of spiritual resources in our life.

Murray's early collections of poetry, *The Ilex Tree* (1965), *The Weatherboard Cathedral* (1969) and *Poems Against Economics* (1972) symbolise an alternative rural cultural space that offers hope to the people who are struggling against the aftermath of a misplaced and valueless modernity in Australia and elsewhere. Similarly, his intertextual 'Walking to the Cattle Place' (Murray 1994, pp. 55–57) included in his collections *The Weatherboard Cathedral* and *Poems Against Economics*, is based on the re-working of the Indic mythical metaphors of Prithu, the king and the civilisationally loaded signifier '*go*' or 'cow'. This poem, which resonates with many significant references to the Indian archetypes, is structured into fifteen sections. The first one is titled 'Sanskrit' and the fifteenth is named 'Goloka' (the Earth); other sections such as 'The Names of the People', 'Death Words', 'The Commonwealth of Manu' and 'The Boeotian Count' are also replete with value-loaded terms central to the spiritual semiotics of Hindu philosophy, which was also used by Gandhi in his political movements.

Murray refers to Gandhi in his parodically subversive poem 'The Dream of Wearing Shorts Forever':

> They are never Robes
> as other bareleg outfits have been:
> the toga, the kilt, the lava-lava
> the Mahatma's cotton *dhoti*. (CP, p. 234)

He wants to subvert the dominant craze for a hollow and hypocritical modernity that decries the wearing of shorts. Murray candidly refers to Gandhi's self-conscious choice to counter western modernity and imperialism by wearing a 'cotton *dhoti*' as 'half-naked *fakir*' (to borrow Winston Churchill's remark). Murray's 'shorts' (though existing in a dream state) and Gandhi's 'cotton *dhoti*' become the objective correlatives of their non-violent struggle (*satyagrah*) for truth and freedom. Les Murray longs to wear 'shorts' to identify with those who exist on the margins of modernity whereas Gandhi himself self-consciously wore 'cotton *dhoti*' and '*khadi*' in order to identify with the so-called subaltern or the deprived in the Indian society and also to resist the temptations of western civilisation. Apart from his 'Walking To The Cattle Place', Murray's other poems such as 'The Dream of Wearing Shorts Forever', 'At Thunderbolt's Grave in Uralla' and 'Poetry and Religion' also articulate his growing unease with modernity and its impact on the rural, aboriginal life in Australia and foreground his faith in the grounding of poetry in the spiritual/religious context.

'Walking to the Cattle Place': Murray's Politics of *Satyagraha*

Murray takes up the Indo-European etymology of the word 'Cow/*go*' which is pregnant with profound symbolic meanings, to explain the genesis of the poem, 'It is really an etymological sequence as much as anything else. It was sparked off by realising from linguistic studies that the oldest root we can trace in Indo-European languages is 'Cow'' (Crawford 1986, p. 27). Interestingly in Sanskrit, the cattle place (or shelter for cattle) is called *gotra* (Williams, p. 364) which also means 'family, race, lineage, the family name, caste, class, group' (Williams p. 364; Apte 1997, p. 353). In this way, by making an aesthetic choice to entitle the poem 'Walking to the Cattle Place', Murray uses 'cattle place', that is *gotra*, metonymically—as *gotra* refers not only to the place where cattle are kept, it also signifies the dynamics of the culture and society that follows a particular way of life, in which cattle and humans live symbiotically. Humans and 'Cattle' are properly placed in an alternative modernity in which the former does not destroy the latter. The word '*go*' in Sanskrit is a loaded signifier, the significations of which connote a whole worldview that was based on the pastoral, simple, Boeotian way of life. '*Go*', which stands for a cow as well as cattle or a herd of cattle, is a polyphonic word symbol in Sanskrit that implies the following:

a. to set out for a battle
b. milk
c. flesh
d. sky
e. stars
f. moon
g. horse
h. water
i. the earth
j. a mother
k. speech (*Saraswati*) (Williams pp. 363–369)

Murray himself aptly comments on the semiotic significance of '*go*/cow': 'I set out to follow a cow and I found a whole world, a specious, town-despising grassland where Celt and Zulu and Vedic Aryan were one in their concerns' (Wilde *et al.* 2000, p. 560). Incidentally, the English word 'cow' also comes from Indo-European '*go*'. That is why Murray names the first section of the poem 'Sanskrit', which begins with an evocative, vivid picture of the non-modern, pastoral world:

> *Upasara*, the heifer after first mating,
> *adyasvina*, the cow about to calve, *strivatsa*,
> the cow who has borne a heifer calf (*atrinada*
> the calf newly born). I will smuggle this sutra (CP, p. 55).

In the Vedic/Indian way of life, *upasara* stands for the first calf from first mating as well as a bull's longing for a cow (Apte, p. 212). *Upasaranam*, another derivative, means 'to go towards somebody/something'. *Adyasvina* implies a woman about to give birth to a child (Apte, p. 23), whereas *Strivatsa* implies the infant she-calf or girl-child which comes from *vatsa* (calf, child, Apte, p. 893). From *vatsa* comes *Vatsala* (Apte, p. 893) meaning one who loves children or affectionate or loving. *Sutra*, in Sanskrit, means 'aphoristic sentence/definition' (Apte, p. 1119), whereas *sutrika* (Apte, p. 1119) denotes the coir used to tie cattle. In the very opening lines, Murray weaves a list or litany of signifiers foregrounding a new civilisation that characteristically suggests a pastoral-rural world full of compassion (*karuna*), love, non-violence (*ahimsa*). The self-conscious use of the verb 'smuggle' in the preceding lines underlines the urgency to re-build this predatory, greed and violence-oriented society on the basis of the ethical values of the cattle place.

Interestingly, the poet wants to smuggle this *sutra* or talisman or mantra to create an alternative rural, simple way of life, so well epitomised by Gandhi in his notion of *Swaraj*, in the midst of mind-boggling materialism. Murray, in the very first lines of the poem, strikes the key-note of his poetic *satyagrah*—his quest for a non-violent society marked by simplicity and eco-friendly existence. The poet-narrator, by identifying himself with this god-centric, spiritual and pastoral early Vedic world, longs for its preservation: 'I will wake up in a world that hooves have led to' (CP, p. 55). Murray in 'Walking to the Cattle Place' also suggests a common (the so-called ancient) cultural heritage of Europe and Asia (including Australia) as it is evident from the dissemination of the linguistic legacy:

> To be of Europe also is a horn-dance
> cattle-knowledge. Even here, where Europa
> dumped rusty in her disgrace, gathered childhood afresh
> by the dray wheel's mercy, on creeks of the far selections. (CP, p. 56)

But the poet is conscious of the disruption of this simple, god-centric 'way of life' or 'alternative culture', which is based on the symbiotic existence with nature, because:

> Today for no sin much, neither killing a *brahmin*
> nor directly a cow, I will follow cattle. (CP, p. 56)

Apparently enough, the so-called civilised, progressive society sanctions violence against cows as well as Brahmins, who were considered sacred in the Vedic society. It was a non-hierarchical, non-violent division of human society grounded in the inevitable differences of aptitudes, approaches, abilities, qualities and professions that was suggested in the *Purush Sukta* in the *Rigveda* or the eighteenth chapter of the *Gita* as the *varna* system. Murray in his poem laments the absence from our society of true Brahmins who are committed to the production and dissemination of knowledge. Murray, in accordance with the *Gita* and Manu, does not confuse *varna* system with its latter-day corrupt form called *caste* or *jati* system.

Similarly, Murray's poem may also be read as an ode to cow-protection, in which a cow metonymically stands for all innocent beings and our fragile eco-system already under a grave threat from the growing consumerist culture of our day. Gandhi like Murray also considers the cow as a 'poem of pity' and a symbol of the lower order of creation: 'The cow is a poem of pity. One reads pity in the gentle animal. She is the mother to millions of Indian mankind. Protection of the cow means the protection of the whole dumb creation of God. The appeal of the lower order of creation is all the more forcible because it is speechless' (*Young India*, 6 Oct 1921). In this imagined cattle republic or *goloka*, the humans as well as the cattle were not to be subjected to exploitation and violence. There was punishment reserved for those who inflicted violence on humans or animals: 'The king should impose a fine in direct proportion to the amount of pain caused when someone strikes men or animals to give them pain' (LM, p. 183).

The poet's imaginary *goloka* is destroyed by the 'wall street tremor', the red-shift on 'the flesh-eating graphs' and by the ghastly spectacle of 'how ghostly cows must be crowding the factory floors now' (CP, p. 56). The *Vyanjana* or suggestion effected by the poet is that the vice of human greed and lust for immorally-earned profit and power are responsible for the depletion of our sustainable environment and the destruction of our symbiotic co-existence with nature including the animal world. It is this Vedic worldview which does not admit of such divisions/partitions of the world as are connoted by the asymmetrical power blocks, the 'rural' and the 'global'; as Murray writes: 'there is no life more global than a village' (CP, p. 57).

Interestingly, in the famous *Prithvisukta* or *Bhoomi Sukta* (the earth mantra) of the *Atharvaveda* (Ch. 12 verse 1–63), the Vedic seers, like Les Murray, imagined a nation not as a politico-economic community but as the civilisational space which was not divided into the politically and economically expedient units of the local, the natural and the animal world. Here, the human beings are supposed to live in complete harmony with the animal and the natural world according to the *Prithvisukta*. The Vedic seer has used the 'Cow/*go*' metaphor about ten times in this *sukta* to refer to mutually interdependent, symbiotic relationship between the resources of the earth and its people. The seer, therefore, imagines this 'cow/earth/*go*' to be his 'mother': 'our mother is the earth; we are the offsprings of the earth' (*Atharvaveda, Prithvisukta* 12.12). In his poem, 'Migratory' (CP, p. 395), Murray's poet-persona identifies with the 'nest', 'the egg', 'the beach', 'the food', 'the shade', 'the right feeling', 'the wrongness of here', 'the crying heads to fill', 'the sand' and all other forms of nature showing the oneness or *advaita* of being—a state in which 'I' becomes all and all 'I'. 'Walking to the Cattle Place' is an ode to this Vedic vision of the good society. The Vedic word '*go*' when it means cattle is in plural number as it connotes a sense of property, 'Cattle is chattel, is owned' (CP, p. 58). The Sanskrit derivative *gotra* also means 'property' (Apte, p. 364). Murray invokes the Prithu myth (Apte, p. 633) of Hinduism in order to foreground the dependence of humankind on the optimum and the ethical use of the earth-resources and sets it against an exploitative modern civilisation 'the seed-eater towns' that go on plundering our natural resources:

> but we could still find common knowledge, verb roots
> and noun bark, enough for an evening fire of sharing,
> Cattle-wisdom
> though it is a great year yet
> till Prithu will milk from the goddess ...
> and down through his fingers into the rimmed vessel earth
> grain and food gardens.
> We are entirely before
> the seed-eater towns. (CP, p. 58–59)

Hence '*go*' or 'cow' serves as metonymy suggesting an alternative world free from the taint of greed and violence as suggested by Gandhi and Murray. Gandhi says, 'Cow-protection, to me, is one of the most wonderful phenomena in human evolution. It takes the human being beyond his species. The cow to me means the entire sub-human world. Man, through the cow, is enjoined to realise his identity with all that lives' (Gandhi 1921). Thus, there is hope for humanity for sustainable, environment-friendly growth so long as we continue to value our 'verb roots', 'noun barks' and 'evening fire of sharing' and 'cattle-wisdom', which create an inseparable union of all beings in an ethical and integrated existence.

The Prithu myth (as narrated in the *Bhagavadapurana*) used by Les Murray in the poem is significant for enlarging the scope and appeal of the poem, semiotically suggesting the need to create a sustainable world that presupposes a true *sahitya* (or 'harmony') between the elemental, the human, the animal and the vegetal worlds. In this sense, Murray, therefore, in his *sahitya* (that is, 'literary text'—another meaning of the word *sahitya*) creates a harmony between the word and the world.

In Indian mythology Prithu was the first king of the earth (Apte, p. 633) and Prithvi, or the earth, was so named after him. When his own people were dying of famine, he forced the earth to yield fruits and vegetables for sustenance. The earth took the form of a cow and started running away from Prithu who kept on following it. The cow (the earth) surrendered and promised to yield the necessary fruits, grains and vegetables for the people only if he provided it with a heifer in order to make it yield milk. Prithu made Manu the heifer and milked the cow (the earth). The Prithu myth in the modern context, as suggested and re-contextualised by Les Murray in his poem, is of crucial significance to all our development and welfare economists who, through their empirical graphs and theories, wish to peddle their logic of sustainable and environment-friendly development from the air-conditioned and insulated cabins of the Planning Commission. But this longed-for pastoral world of 'verb roots', 'noun bark' and 'cattle wisdom' is on the brink of extinction, thanks to the rapid growth of industries and consumerist culture.

The cows are now being led to slaughter to satisfy man's greed for cash and profit:

> They are going to the plains of cash and the captive bolt ...
> ... they are chilled from dripping
> and marbled in their fat they are pillars of the city
> till out of cool rooms they crowd into our view. (CP, p. 60)

In other words, these lines signify Murray's concern about the exploitation of the earth-resources and destruction of nature to pander to human greed in the context of the so-called economic globalisation. The sixth section of the poem entitled 'The Commonwealth of Manu' deals with the four-fold division of human (also Australian) society on the basis of professional/occupational qualities (and not on the basis of heredity or birth as it happens in the caste system). The poet deftly uses the Hindu/Indian *varna*-framework to designate the composition of Australian society:

> just for moment
> it seemed true of our country equally.
> Brahmin, Kshatriya Vaishya, Shudra

the four castes in our country, too plus such as myself
and the black man. (CP, p. 62)

Contrary to the hugely mistaken belief, the ancient Vedic (Hindu) society was divided into four *varnas* (not castes) on the basis of human qualities or *gunas,* and not on the basis of heredity or birth (*The Laws of Manu*, pp. 232–233, 243). Like Murray, Gandhi also visualises the *varna*-system as a strategy for the management of different duties, obligations, and functions on the basis of people's qualities, occupations, and aptitudes, without connoting untouchability or gradation of social prestige or power. He says, 'Varnashrama is not a vertical line, but that it is a horizontal plan on which all the children of God occupy absolutely the same states, though they may be engaged in different pursuits of life and though they may have different qualities and different tastes' (*Harijan,* 18 Feb 1933). The degeneration of *varna* into the so-called hereditary 'caste system', fraught with power-relations and infliction of violence and inequality, is a later story consequent upon the socio-cultural decline of the early Vedic society. Les Murray uses the *varna*-division to characterise the sinister dominance of the Vaishyas (the modern-day capitalists or business tycoons, the controllers of trade and commerce, the big agriculturalists) in the modern civilisation:

Vaishya, though merchant, lowest of the twice-born,
consider his dominance:
the whole nation turning on him
the government his the laws, his the profits
his system the System.
All his, the glory of goods,
to make silent the rivers, to level the untidy hills
a dispensation not found in the laws of Manu. (CP, p. 62)

Thus, the greedy merchant or the late capitalist class is termed the debased *vaishya* by Murray. In these lines, Murray underlines his critique of the unethical economisation of the human existence, which is the sole guiding force behind the so-called 'globalisation' in the world today. Murray and Gandhi both fear the rapid transformation of the desired good society into a goods society propelled by greed and consumerism.

Both Murray and Gandhi find fault with the unethical techno-modernity that destroys the moral health of society and endangers the whole eco-system. But the modern-day *vaishya* instead of believing in the glory of good(ness) works only for the glory of goods—which is not enjoined upon him by Manu:

> When a commoner (*vaishya*) has undergone the transformative rituals and married a wife, he should constantly dedicate himself to making a living and tending livestock. He should know the high or low value of gems, pearls. He should know how to sow seeds, and the worth or worthlessness of merchandise, the good or bad qualities of countries, the profit and loss from trades and he should know the various languages of men, the way to preserve goods and buying and selling. He should make the utmost efforts to increase his goods by means in keeping with the duty and take pains to give food to all creatures (LM, pp. 326–333, 232).

The dominance of the valueless or unethical (*adharmik*), greed-driven Vaishya community (the late capitalists) is the cause of so many undesirable social, economic and political changes in the history of the modern world. Slavery, racism, colonialism, imperialism, indenture-system, *pax* Britannica, *pax* Americana, are the dark chapters of human history which expose what unbridled human greed can do to humanity. Murray also takes a dig at the popularity of Ganesha among the Vaishyas, as Ganesha 'the greedy one' is an 'overcomer of obstacles' (CP, p. 62).

The tenth section, 'The Boeotian Count', presents the image of an alternative rural society to a reader where even the pretense to academic learning is abandoned in order to emphasise the centrality of action or Karma which is a form of *lila* (bliss, play or sport, Apte, p. 880):

> I pray that Hughie.
> will send you
> safe home
> where ploughing is playing
> where karma is *Lila*. (CP, p. 67)

It is this vision of an alternative society and culture, firmly grounded in the notion of the sacred (that is, all the forms of creation are sacred) so ably informed by the notions of *karma* (right actions) and *lila* that remain at the core of Murray's imagined Boeotian society, which reminds us of Gandhi's *Swaraj* (or self-rule, both spiritual and political). According to *The Gita*, it is only through actions or works (*karma*) that the welfare of all on the earth can be realised: 'Janaka and others achieved perfection through works alone. At least, to promote the welfare of the world, you ought to do works' (*The Gita*, p. 116). But, as Murray suggested, Karma or action can only be '*lila*' or sport when performed with detachment as has also been outlined in *The Gita*. Gandhi also believed in the theory of detached action or *nishkama* karma:

> I firmly believe in the Law of karma, but I believe too in human endeavor. I regard as the *summum bonum* of life the attainment of salvation through Karma by annihilating its effects by detachment' (Gandhi 1928). He understood that only detached action can become *lila* or play which is the real meaning of freedom: 'That person who works without attachment is free, that is, he is not bound by the effects of karma. (Gandhi quoted in Hingorani 1985)

In the twelfth section 'Hall's Cattle', Murray again attacks the inhumane modern civilisation and the hegemony of American consumerist culture:

> They will sentence me next time
> they have sentenced our sort
> and all I know is this life
> I know nothing of America. (CP, p. 69)

In the section 'Boopis', Murray makes the poet-narrator reject this non-sacred modern civilisation and self-consciously juxtaposes 'the earth' with 'cow' as the two signifiers become one in the Sanskrit word *go*, which is not only a word but also a world:

> Coming out of reflections
> I find myself in the earth
> My cow going on. (CP, p. 70)

Thus, his reflections on a '*go*/cow'-centric world signify his continuing *satyagrah* for an eco-friendly, non-violent world in which humans, animals and the vegetal world all exist in an existential and ethical harmony. And the continuous nurturance of this 'connection' between the animal, the vegetal and the elemental world is vital for the survival of humankind on this planet. 'Walking to the Cattle Place' re-affirms Murray's faith in Gandhian *Swaraj* in which the human and the natural forms of creation are in harmony with each other, and at peace.

The last section of the poem, 'Goloka', is also the largest section of the poem in which the poet reiterates his commitment to the moral duty to transform this materialistic, consumerist world into a *goloka* (Murray's vision of the good society or *swaraj*). The rural people of peasants/aborigines use their 'speech' (yet another meaning of 'go') to rename their places in accordance with their tradition. Though the maddening march of modern civilisation has numbed the finer human instincts and destroyed the integrated existence, the poet re-asserts his commitment to *satyagrah* (holding on to truth) amidst confusion and chaos:

> The ancient tune is faint (fainter still, the kings in her)
> but it keeps me farming
> rather than raping, or embalming the land.
> The other's the New World. We won't be peasants again. (CP, p. 74)

Even when surrounded by all sorts of materialistic shares, a *satyagrahi* citizen (who has truth-force or soul-force) of Murray's 'Goloka', who practises some sort of *swaraj* or self-restraint, will continue to 'farm' the land in order to connect with the mother earth ('*go*')—living in harmony with her/his ecology. But the other citizens of this brave new economically 'globalised' civilisation will only 'rape' this land—'embalming' it with all sorts of chemicals and fertilisers in order to gratify their vaulting greed and lust for profit—resulting in the destruction of all life on earth. In other words, if Murray's peasants or Gandhi's *satyagrahis* (people with truth or soul- force) opt for this consumerist world, they 'won't be peasants again'—to borrow Murray's words again. This is Murray's *satyagrah* as a poet in the Gandhian sense. Gandhi also said, 'Our civilisation, our culture, our *swaraj* depend not upon multiplying our wants—self indulgence—but upon restricting our wants' (*Young India*, 23 Feb 1921). But the peasants or the rural people who live in harmony with environment will not 'be peasants again' in the 'New World' (CP, p. 74), which is based on the principles of greed and unethical profit. Murray defines his 'good society' in a telling way which readily reminds an Indian reader of Gandhi's vision of *swaraj* based on the spiritual values of Indian civilisation: 'I am looking at equality where it seeks no victories' (CP, p. 76). Or where 'The king of justice (human) would not enter paradise without the lost, or his dog/living and work are one thing' (CP, p. 76).

By referring to an event associated with Yudhistihir, the Pandava king (in the *Mahabharata*) who was also called the incarnation of the moral law and who refused to enter heaven without his dog, Murray has tried to show the centrality of the moral law or duty in his *swaraj* (or *goloka*). When he seeks an equality that does not need victories or wars, he is, in fact, very close to Gandhi's vision of *swaraj* based on truth and non-violence, which harmonises the sacred and the secular into an inseparable civilisation space. 'Under *swaraj* based on non-violence, nobody is any body's enemy, everyday contributes his or her due quota to the common goal' (Gandhi 1939). He, like Murray, situates his good society or *swaraj* in the reign of truth and non-violence: 'My conception of *swaraj* is not mere political independence. I want to see Dhama Raj—establishment of the kingdom of heaven on earth, the reign of Truth and Non-violence in every walk of life. That alone is independence to the starved masses of this vast country' (Gandhi 1945).

'Walking to the Cattle Place' is a form of poetic *satyagraha* in the Gandhian sense for the establishment of a good society in which the humans, the hills, the woods, the cattle, the birds, the insects and all beings and non-beings alike, live in a symbiotic existence with the sun, the moon the stars and the elements. But his seeming utopian vision of *goloka (*or a new self-sustainable world) demands a *satyagraha* against the destructive impact of modern civilisation in order to sufficiently spiritualise it. Murray aptly says:

> It would be something indeed, to break with western culture by not asking, even now, the characteristic second step into alienation, into elitism and the relegation of all places except one or two urban centres to the sterile status of provincial no-man's land largely deprived of any art or any creative self-confidence. This is what is at stake. (Murray cited in Wilde *et al.* 2000, p. 560)

It is only in Murray's imaginary *goloka* or Gandhi's *swaraj* that there would be no gap between 'religion', 'art' and 'action'. Murray affirms that religions are 'poems' and that:

> God is the poetry caught in any religion … a law against its closure
> There'll always be religion around while there is poetry. (CP, p. 267)

Thus, to make an attempt to read Les Murray's idea of the 'sacred', which includes the secular as well, as manifest in his poetry, through Gandhi's poetics/politics of *satyagraha* (truth or soul force) as practiced by him in real life, is to experience a new bliss or *ananda* of aesthetic and cultural *swaraj* (self-rule or freedom—both political and spiritual), which considers all aspects / forms of this vast existence and *srishti* (or creation) 'sacred' and all our actions, including writing, a form of 'sacrifice' (which means, 'making sacred'). To Gandhi, the worth of art or literature does not solely depend on the outward expression of the realities or feelings; it is contingent upon its grounding in the inward, or the 'sacred' space:

> There are two aspects of things—the outward and the inward. The outward has no meaning except insofar as it helps the inward. All true art is thus the expression of the soul. The outward forms have value insofar as they are the expression of the inner spirit of man (*Young India*, Nov.13, 1924).

This is also what Murray suggests when he underlines the significance of writing (poetry) as a 'sacred act', through which a writer endeavours to connect with the 'inner or sacred space'—which is the space of *satya* (truth) and *ahimsa* (non-violence). Les Murray's writings, broadly speaking, make a case for our upholding *dharma* (or moral or ethical duty-consciousness) in all situations of life. The celebration of the so-called 'Sacred Australia' in Murray's poetry represents the poet's *satyagraha* for a new world order based on truth, compassion, love and non-violence—the ideals that Gandhi practiced in real life.

WORKS CITED

Apte, VS, *Sanskrit-Hindi Kosh,* Delhi, Motilal Banarasi Das, 1997, further cited as Apte with page numbers in parentheses.

Bourke, Lawrence, *A Vivid Steady State*, Les Murray and Australian Poetry, Kensingon, NSW Press, 1992.

Crawford, Robert. 'Interview with Les Murray' *Verse*, No. 5, 1986, pp. 21–33.

Gandhi, MK *Hind Swaraj*, Ahmedabad, Navjivan, 1995, first published in 1938, pp. 33–34.

Speeches and Writings of Mahatma Gandhi, Madras, GA Natesan, 1934.

Harijan, 25 March 1939.

Young India, 18 Oct 1928.

Young India, 6 Oct 1921.

Young India, 13 Nov, 1924.

Young India, 8 May, 1920.

Young India, 5 March 1925.

Harijan, 1 March 1935.

The Hindustan Times, 20 June 1945.

Hingorani, AT and GA Hingorani. *The Encyclopaedia of Gandhian Thought*, New Delhi, All India Congress Committee, 1985.

Manu *The Laws of Manu* (Tr. by Wendy Doniger with BK Smith), New Delhi, Penguin, 1991, further cited as LM with page numbers in parentheses

Murray, Les *The peasant mandarin: prose pieces,* St Lucia, University of Queensland Press, 1978.

—— *The vernacular republic: poems 1961–1981,* Sydney, Angus & Robertson, 1982.

—— 'Walking To The Cattle Place' in *Collected Poems*, Port Melbourne, William Heinemann, 1994. Further cited as CP with page numbers in parentheses.

—— 'Interview with Vineetha Mokkil' in *The Times of India*, January 15, 2006, p. 6.

Wilde, W, Hooton J & Andrews B, *The Oxford Companion to Australian Literature,* Melbourne, Oxford University Press, 2000 (first published in 1985).

Williams, M, *A Sanskrit–English Dictionary*, Delhi, Motilal Banarasidass, 2000 (first published in 1899).

BEING JOB—IN THREE PARTS

Peter Boyle

I

Let us suppose a people for whom it is common knowledge that God exists. For them it would make no more sense to say 'Is there a God?' than 'Is there a sky?' or 'Does water exist?' They walk around, they live, they see God, he talks to them, they answer back, he comes up one hour, goes down another, they go to a pond and scoop up a mouthful of God because they need to drink. And though it seems to them God only entered their world quite recently, it also seems that God was there stretching back to the time when landscapes were made. Coming from outside strangers would ask, 'I see the water and the sky and the earth of your land, but what is this God you keep having conversations with?'

Over the course of long stays strangers observed that the conversations with God always became more intense, of greater duration, when things went wrong. When lightning destroyed cattle, when flood washed away part of a village, when a plague broke out, or a child died, the conversations became ferociously sharper or vanished altogether. What was this presence, harsh as the blighting sun, when all water sinks far into the land, what was this being that arose above all at the centre of tragedy?

Suppose God was a synonym for Life, but Life understood and experienced in a very specific way, with extraordinary intensity, with a dazzling inability to do anything but surrender before its power. And, when understood as God, Life became a person, a voice speaking to us. It located itself in the depths of the ocean. It whispered as a breeze opening doors.

Within this world to say God does not exist would be like saying Life does not exist, a perfectly intelligible proposition but difficult to live with. Pinned down by the inexplicable wave of suffering that descends on him, Job faces a choice—to curse Life and die, or to continue praising Life. Job clings to the belief that Life is good, and Life allows Job to come close and talk with him. From the depths of pain Job speaks to Life and asks what this suffering means. (The transition between God and Life is perhaps most of all a matter of gender. In any language I know of, the word for 'life' is feminine.)

Job must speak to God in some language and God must answer back in some language—but which language? It seems reasonable to suppose that God has no intrinsic preference for English over Urdu, Pashtun over Aramaic, Sanskrit over Pitjantjatjara. The language spoken by the aboriginal inhabitants of the Canary Islands would seem as close to his heart as Homeric Greek or old Slavonic. It would be difficult not to assert that God would be equally at home in the elaborate grammar of turtles as in the speech of finches, that the soaring discourse of the eagle carries no more and no less charm than the meditative vibration of hornets.

More importantly, God must exist just as comfortably in languages where there is no word for God, where the possibility of God cannot arise even as the remotest object of thought.

Perhaps those are the languages closest to God's heart, the languages he casts spells in when he speaks from inside a whirlwind.

*

At those times when I exist in an altered realm, a white softness enfolds me. For those moments nothing can touch or disturb that enfolding, and perhaps each thing that is beautiful enough we hold within us, in a way that no anger or violence altogether destroys.

What was it that Job touched that gave him such freedom from inner destruction?

To be Job is not only to suffer unthinkable cruelties. It is also to be connected in some indestructible way to one's own inner heaven, the only one that matters, the one that is here and now and outside of time all at once.

For those of us who don't know how to say the word 'God' but who also intuit that Job addressed a reality that spoke from whirlwinds, what is that reality?

*

It is one thing to write about Job from the outside, but Job was clearly a poet and the poets that follow him, like all good poets, want to write from the inside. For a poet to write about Job is like inviting all the forces that bring death and tragedy to enter one's life. Knowingly even to begin a mere two line poem on Job is to ask plague, schizophrenia, death from collision on an icy freeway, a bomb landing on a village school, a parasitic invasion of the capillaries behind the eyes, to enter one's life, to snap the hinges of the front door and take possession of one's house. For it is not possible to write a poem about Job from other people's sufferings. And it is also not enough to take on the suffering that comes to oneself alone, the lonely man's pain, the transient one who has had many years to get used to being cursed. It is necessary that death seize one's children and that the pustules of blighting erupt along the skin and in the eyes of those you love. For these good reasons no poet should wilfully try to write about Job.

II. Poets who became Job

In the 20th Century two great poets, in my opinion, stand out as having written from the space of Job: Paul Celan and César Vallejo. Like Job, Celan and Vallejo move into a primary innocence. They stand alone before God, confident that suffering can and must be spoken of apart from any complex personal history. They do not want biography to cloud the issue. God stands accused.

For several reasons—partly because he is so well known, partly because he writes from a very specific reality as a Jew and a holocaust survivor, a reality it would be presumptuous of me to speak on behalf of—I will not talk of Celan in this paper. Much less well-known is the Peruvian César Vallejo. Born in 1892 in an Andean village, the son of a local priest and an Indian woman, Vallejo lived all his life in great poverty. He was a Marxist but kept his independence from the Communist party and used Christian symbolism in his poetry, in a way that prefigures Liberation Theology. He died from unknown causes, largely it's thought from malnutrition, on Good Friday 1938, despite the fact that in one of his most famous poems 'Black stone on a white stone' he predicted he would die on a Thursday: (the translations are my own)

> I will die in Paris in a sudden downpour,
> on a day I can already remember.

I will die in Paris - and I don't run away from this -
maybe a Thursday, like today is, in autumn.

A Thursday it will be because today, Thursday,
as I prose these verses, I've put on my humeri
with much ill will, and never like today have I turned,
with all my road before me, to see myself alone.

César Vallejo has died. They beat him,
everyone of them, though he does nothing to them.
They gave it to him hard with a stick

and hard with a rope. Witnesses are
the Thursdays, the humeri bones,
the loneliness, the rain, the roads ...

Vallejo's life in its drama and tragedy speaks to many other lives—the death in childhood of his brother Miguel, the death of his mother, his time in prison, his sense of loss and abandonment, the hardship of his Paris years. Interestingly for a Marxist, in 'I am going to speak of hope' Vallejo describes pain as lying too deep for any cause and says we suffer not as Catholic, Mohammedan or atheist but are simply in pain. Another poem 'The Nine monsters' speaks of pain's centrality to all existence:

... as a result
of pain, there are some
who are born, others grow, others die,
and others are born and don't die, others
are never born but still die, and for others (the majority)
neither are they born nor do they die.

The poem concludes:

How, my human brothers,
not say I can't anymore
and I can't anymore with so much coffin,
so much minute, so much

lizard, and so much
reversal, so much far away and so much thirst for thirst.
Honourable minister of health, what to do?
Ah, unfortunately, human men,
brothers, there is much, all too much
to do.

As a last reflection on Vallejo I include a shortened version of a poem from the book *The Blue Cloud of Crying*—I hope it captures something of the paradoxes of suffering, its unique way of being momentous and banal, appallingly empty and also intensely filled with life:

César Vallejo

I meet you in the hospital
where polishers whirr
enormous circles on the moonlit floor.
The X-rays tacked up on the wall,
their dark scrawl
threading the pain of the earth to the pain of the stars.
A white bird drops by saying 'Open this door.'
The curtain of your sickbed waits to move
like the sail of a ship.
In Peru the horse of your childhood
still chews its grass, tosses its mane
in the last dryness of summer.
A poem or a life
ripples between such trivial and such portentous matter,
incorporates derision,
dispenses its own handshakes.

And if after so many words
not one word
And if among so many breaths
not one sigh
crosses the vacuum

In a dream you woke to find the windowsill opposite your bed
lined with money,
little gold and silver coins that shone at you.
In the next room the same
and at the front door
a row of coins the same.

Such embarrassing gifts among bandaged heads.
Bloom of putrefaction on the skin
of the one who guards twilight.
Graced always with the wealth of the air,
César Vallejo,
under Paris rain
seeking the correct and final gesture,
giving these aesthetic otherworldly objects
their human name.

III. THE TEMPTATION TO BE JOB

At heart every poet would like to claim the mantle of Job, to be the spokesperson for suffering humanity, even if at the price of a sizeable dose of personal unhappiness. But that seems to me to risk indulging in a half truth. Though the Bible states that Job was innocent, Job was a wealthy pastoralist—so who did he steal his land from? Or maybe Job's inherited wealth came from careful alliances, meaning forcibly marrying off thirteen and fourteen year old girls to bring more cattle into the family.

More generally, one has to be true to a double inheritance. We are, it seems to me, both the descendants of the suffering Job and of the destructive vindictive God. If I can't in good faith write as Paul Celan it may be that objectively I resemble more a descendant of the Germans than the Jews—except that while some Germans live in houses stolen from Jews, all non-indigenous Australians live in houses effectively stolen from the aborigines. So I come to the task of writing Job from a double perspective. I have to recognise myself both as belonging to Job the victim, the emblem of innocent inexplicable suffering, and also, through my specific Western colonial fate, as among Job's pragmatic false friends and also as a descendant of a self-righteous vindictive God.

I will conclude with a poem that addresses the second half of that inheritance, the legacy of God the dispossessor, the destroyer. This poem comes from an unpublished work in progress, *The Apocrypha*—fictive translations of imaginary classical texts.

Dawn Ritual of Purification for families and descendants of those who participate in slaughter, to be used by all visitors who enter the Holy City of Kitezh

To the north
bow low
scatter the beads of water
gently scoop tufts of wheat
let the wind trickle
through emptiness

To the east
bow low
scatter the grains of dawn
may your hands be open
kneel
let where the sun is
know you
Speak
'Shame on my head
on my eyes
Shame on my lips and tongue
Shame on my hands
on my walking
Shame of the seed
and of destiny.'
Again dip slowly your hand
into the grain sack
scatter grain
scatter what lives
what will live
Speak

'Grain of grains
dew of sea
fire that rises from mist
accept our shame'
bow again
lightly sprinkle the water

To the south
stand firm that the realms
of the Four Heavens
may see you
bow low
scatter the grains
let the ghosts
know of your presence
scatter the dew of water
let the beads of water
rest on the lips of all people
let the thirst of the living
and the thirst of the dead
be calmed
bow again
wait for the silence
to give you permission
to stand

To the west
eyeing the west as an equal
eyeing the west as a mother
eyeing the west as your child
scatter the grain
scatter the bright joy of water
kneel
kneel do not speak
wait for the light that rises and sets
to touch you
wait for the winds that come

from the lands of all the dead
to filter around your ears
wait for their voices to enter you
wait till their voices speak
wait till the words
are fierce and tender
wait till the words
tear at the sinews of pain
till the words slice
through forehead and skull
till the heart is open to all words
the earth is struggling to say

Kneel longer
wait till their voices
cease
wait till the silence steadies you
speak
'Brothers'
speak
'Sisters'
speak
'I give back
I give back
I give back'

APPENDIX: CÉSAR VALLEJO AND/OR PAUL CELAN

Vallejo seems to ground his poems more openly in the quotidiana of his life—all the references to his family, his brothers and sisters, his mother, the names of his girlfriends in *Trilce*; in later poems continued references to 'blind Santiago', the bell ringer of his childhood village, to the rainless heat of Lima, to specific hospitals, hotels and people from the Paris years, like Alfonso, Georgette, the Hotel des Écoles. The strangest, the most eccentric experimentation is still working for the most part with material gathered from his life. Paradoxically, whilst *avante-garde* in his techniques, there is essentially a continuity of romanticism in the project: to tell his own story, to speak the truth of one's life, to convey one's own life for the sake of its illumination to others. Vallejo's life in its drama and tragedy does speak deeply to many other lives—the poverty and marginalisation, the death in childhood of his brother Miguel, the death of his mother, his time in prison, his sense of loss and abandonment, the extreme poverty of his Paris years. But perhaps there is also the ghost of a certain Romantic idea—that if one is a great poet, if one has been granted unusual artistic, literary abilities, one's own life will be granted a similar exalted status, making it the ultimate subject matter.

Celan, in contrast, has far less material, almost none, from his day-to-day life, or from the details of his past. The material used, the raw material of his poems, is more likely to be intellectual and linguistic. And the focus is not finally one of telling his life. The Romantic quest is gone, abolished in advance. To speak of oneself seems suddenly quite pointless. What lies at the core of Celan is a philosophic, religious quest. It is the world, not himself that most puzzles him. It is the world both sacred and absolutely malevolent around which his poems hover.

THE RACIALISED SELF, ECOLOGY AND THE SACRED IN XAVIER HERBERT'S *POOR FELLOW MY COUNTRY*

Frances Devlin-Glass

INTRODUCTION

Herbert's *Poor Fellow My Country* (1975) anticipated edgy twenty-first century national conversations about race relations and ecology currently occurring in Australia in the disciplines of history and historiography, anthropology, eco-philosophy, and literature. Set in the remote pastoral frontier of the Northern Territory in the 1930s and 1940s, the novel anatomises the genocidal practices of an encyclopaedic range of Australian institutions (political movements of the left and right, the squattocracy, the church, the law, the education and 'welfare' bureaucracies) and satirises the 'Aboriginal industry's' systematic ignorance and denigration of Aboriginal culture. The novel promotes a new kind of nationalism which incorporates Indigenous citizenry as active players. Despite its manifest flaws, its ideological hyperbole and intense pessimism, and perhaps because of its extraordinarily expansive canvas (it is longer than *War and Peace*) and its formal experimentation, the novelist's level of familiarity with Aboriginal culture, and his humanity are remarkable and prescient, especially in the light of current dysfunctionality in Aboriginal communities that have been systematically robbed of cultural pride. This paper looks behind Herbert's satire (tub-thumpery?) to his radical views on what Aboriginal culture and in particular its mythological understandings of land have to offer to the 'common-wealth'. The novel will be read in the light of contemporary post-colonially-inflected and Indigenous-centred oral history, mythology, and Australian eco-philosophy.

The moment of Herbert's *Poor Fellow My Country* (hereafter *PFMC*), published with fanfare in 1975 was hyper-nationalist and Whitlamite, though Gorton as Minister for Arts/Prime Minister had created the conditions for its publication and reception in the previous half decade, and before him the Commonwealth Literary Fund (Macdonnell 1992, pp. 10–11). The novel had had an immensely long gestation over almost three decades since 1937, according to De Groen and Pierce (Herbert, De Groen & Pierce 1992). From the 1930s when Herbert began to be published, symbols of Australia based on the pastoral industry (which had made it rich) and the outback, although not representative of lived realities for the majority of Australians, were the trade currency, and legitimised as iconic in the academy. The subject matter of *PFMC* constituted a response to the changing prominence of Indigenous affairs: the foundation of One People Australia League (OPAL) in 1961 which brought educational opportunities to Aboriginal people, the Gurindji strike at Wave Hill for equal pay in 1966, the enthusiasm for Aboriginal full citizenship expressed in the referendum in 1967, and Charles Rowley's important books exposing colonialist Indigenous policies and history (Rowley 1971, 1972) were all preconditions for its enthusiastic uptake. In retrospect, 1974 was a watershed moment which, though it may have secured the novel in the public imagination, also ensured its subsequent unfashionableness: the iconic symbols of bush nationalism—rough-as-guts bushmen which *Crocodile Dundee* capitalised on—were being replaced by a new confidence in urban cosmopolitanism. As De Groen makes clear, Whitlamism, and before it Gorton's ministry, with their exuberant support for the Arts made Herbert's *magnum opus* possible, indeed a *cause célèbre.* Its theatrical offensiveness, its (admittedly qualified) left-wing politics and feisty pro-Aboriginalism, and canny marketing pitched at lower-than-middlebrow and nationalistic readers (ironic in view of Herbert's capitulation to an English publisher whom he courted assiduously) (De Groen 1998, pp. 244–5) no doubt also contributed to its almost instant status as a classic. Its prodigious length (at 850,000 words, one third longer than *War and Peace* (Clancy 1981, p. 109) and its *longueurs* (it invites a blue pencil), though, probably put it in that select class of books people know a lot about, and avoid reading. However, I propose to argue it is remarkably of our moment even more than of its own, and in particular to read it as an astute proto-post-colonial text (though it is not repeatable and certainly not politically correct), with a subversive version of the nation, and one which offers a radical take on the sacred in Australian lived realities in linking ecological concerns and the sacred in powerfully unexpected ways, in the process challenging atomistic western paradigms.

This is not a novel which is amenable to aesthetic readings. It sharply divides critics (Monahan 2003, p. 3), as easy to fault on aesthetic grounds (Daniel 1978; Clancy 1981; McLaren & Herbert 1981), especially for its crankiness, preachiness and polemics (it is a talk-fest) as to marvel at its epic scope and ambitious canvas. While I admire Sean Monahan's excellent recuperation of *PFMC* as a text which properly belongs, according to Northrop Frye's taxonomy, in the generic categories of Anatomy and Romance, my project is a less formalist and a more politically inflected one, and one that is designed to tease out the links between politics, the sacred and Indigenous-influenced understandings of land. In this section, I aim to locate the text at the beginnings of an important new discursive formation in which bush nationalism is redefined to take cognisance of the reality of Aboriginal contact history, and in particular Aboriginal participation (on their terms, to some extent) in the pastoral industry. I shall argue that the text marks a moment in which European intellectual curiosity about the Indigenous sacred and cosmology moves into dialogic mode and productively emerges from exclusively anthropological discourses. In Herbert, this curiosity and his political passion find expression in a sense of poetic wonder that is simultaneously fired, and grounded in a materialist politics, by the tragic injustices of the whole gamut of colonialist bureaucracies in which Indigenous interests were imbricated. In retrospect, and especially in the light of new eco-philosophical discourses and subsequent Indigenous oral histories and testimonii, *PFMC* recommends itself as extraordinarily visionary for its time, despite its many absurd postures, rigidities and manoeuvres, and can be read as offering a radically new formation of the sacred in Australian literature.

THE REFERENTIALITY OF HERBERT'S NOVEL AND SOURCE MATERIAL

Without wanting to romanticise or hagiograph-ise Herbert, or to claim for him more vision than he possessed (De Groen's biography offers many cautions about his racism and misogyny), the novel was revolutionary on a number of fronts—on race and race policies, and on ecological matters. It also has a great deal to offer contemporary debates about the possibility of Indigenous-influenced European understandings of the earthed sacred.

Herbert's radical views on race derived from a variety of sources, and from lived experience. He occupied a marginal and ambivalent place in the colonialist Northern Territory in the 1920s, 30s and 40s. His inability to secure continuing work within the Indigenous industries was literature's gain, giving him access to an extraordinary gamut of colonial institutions and insider knowledge of their contact policies and history, which he metamorphosed into satire and polemics, and more importantly anatomy (Monahan 2003). He had first-hand experience of a range of settler/indigenous lived realities[1]: he engaged in a variety of labouring jobs including mining alongside Indigenous men, worked as a pharmacist in the hospital treating Aboriginal patients, was superintendent for a short time of the Kahlin compound in Darwin, the Aboriginal reservation to which mixed-descent children were brought. He was close to the McGinness family, a Kungarakan family whose mixed-race children were taken into custody by the Aboriginal Protection Society and one of whose children, Val, became the real-life counterpart for Norman and Prindy. He also befriended professional Territorian Bill Harney whose first-hand knowledge of traditional Aboriginal culture was extensive, if of the red-neck variety (he had an Aboriginal wife, and lived a liminal white/black life). He was also involved with Percy Tresize in locating long lost Aboriginal rock art, and through Percy came to know Dick Roughsey, a Lardil artist and writer. Herbert was also a soldier in the North Australia Observer Unit in the Roper Bar area during the second war alongside anthropologist WE Stanner whose brainchild it was, and in the company of Indigenous soldiers whose local knowledge many times saved the unit. It was also a period in which Stanner was collecting his great work on Aboriginal Religion (Stanner & University of Sydney 1966). Although Herbert pillories Stanner's Britishness and lack of soldierly skills in the figure of Fabian Coote, in the period he was writing *PFMC* he nonetheless consumed as much as possible of his and other anthropologists' writings, including runs of *Oceania*, the Berndts' work, and AP Elkin's. This rich variety of sources, and his fortunate failure to become a member of the Indigenous bureaucracy, transformed him into a proto-post-colonialist promulgating reform of the Aboriginal welfare system and ideas about the Aboriginal sacred and its uses for white Australia. He belongs to that class of cultural relativist who was prepared to acknowledge the limitations of his own culture (and aware that Aboriginal people shared this view) and the

[1] I am indebted to Peter Simon, a journalist who met and wrote several articles about Xavier and Sadie, for information about Herbert's links with Indigenous and other informants (personal communication, 30th January 2006).

complexity of Aboriginal culture (p. 117) in an era when the latter was rarely appreciated.

HERBERT ON MIXED DESCENT

PFMC grew out of a fiction manuscript entitled *Yellow Fellow*, and the title points to one of Herbert's most radical manoeuvres—to contest the normative mainstream prejudices about mixed-descent liaisons that pertained in the 1930s and 40s in Australia. The 'problem of the half-caste' as it was routinely referred to (McGregor pp. 134–41), was imbricated in now-outdated nineteenth century race theory. Government policy in the period (1920s to 1940s) which Herbert was documenting was highly contradictory about the 'half-caste problem'. While there were differences in legislated definitions of Aboriginality between the states, in practice Aboriginality was defined as conservatively as possible, and denied to those with one black parent (or less). Paradoxically, such people, theoretically deemed to be white, were increasingly brought into the ambit of Aboriginal legislation because of fear of the rate at which the 'half-caste' population was expanding (McGregor 1997, p. 135). They were, however, treated as not fully white, unless they could obscure their parentage and pass as white, evading the intrusive law and welfare systems.

Herbert, refusing the problematics of 'miscegenation', argued passionately for a proudly Creole nation. The contemporary mainstream European view was of an abject creole: someone who had the advantages of neither 'race' and the 'defects' of each, and who was not acceptable to either. To resist dysgenic views of interracial liaisons and to have grasped the positive potential of intermarriage in the tropical zone are to imagine a very different de-racialised engagement between the European mainstream and Indigenous Australia. It is also to think in ways that more closely resemble how his Indigenous peers thought about mixed-race sexual relations—scenarios whereby 'a blackfella can be a whitefella or a blackfella; a whitefella and a yellafella [i.e. mixed descent] can likewise be a blackfella, but a yellafella can never really become a full whitefella' (personal oral communication with Yanyuwa elder, Annie Karrakayn, December 2002). My Aboriginal informant uses the terms *yellafella* and *halfcaste* not as terms of abuse nor does she construct them as less than herself. Herbert's reinscription of the mixed-descent type begins clumsily in the discourse of eugenics. Refusing the designation of a mixed-descent person as 'physically evil', ugly and uncivilisable (Daisy Bates's view and that of many of Herbert's contemporaries) (Bates 2004, pp. 68, 72, 163; McGregor 1997, pp. 128–31), Herbert argued that physically beautiful people are rare in any race, but that children of Aboriginal/European alliances are particularly so:

> the perfect symmetry of the Aboriginal face makes up for the lack of it in the average white face (Herbert p. 110).

This distasteful eugenics discourse is, however, accompanied by a rather more penetrating analysis of the mutually demeaning conditions under which such liaisons were conducted:

> In my opinion a beautiful breed of people could have been created if only our forefathers'd had the courage to breed with the Aborigines like men, instead of like dirty little boys ... and one that would have loved the land because they truly belonged to it (Herbert p. 110).

Herbert's views on sexuality owed a great deal to the new sexology and to an ill-digested Freudianism (and perhaps scientism) which disdained moral framings of sexual practice. He risked offence by realistically representing and naming, for example, transmission of STDs as genocidal (Herbert 1975, pp. 491–2). And he interestingly challenged what was difficult for Europeans to acknowledge: that white men might find Aboriginal women sexually attractive (and the attendant implication of the low moral standards of white men), and that Aboriginal women affirm their own personal and sexual power (understood in magical/ritual terms within their own cultural frameworks as the operation of *charada*, 'love magic,' specifically women's love/power songs, p. 1293) by seducing white men. Such notions challenge sexual, gender identity, perceived class differentials, and cultural norms simultaneously. Further, the point about the possibilities of creating a proudly hybrid Australian goes to the heart of the despair and shame which still surround discussions of the Stolen Generation, most of whom were the unclaimed offspring of settler European men.

> 'Have you ever thought what the Australian nation would have been like if the pioneers had succoured their hybrid offspring, had given even a little of the care they gave their stock ... stead of letting them starve to death on the withered breasts of mothers starving because that very stock had

> destroyed the hunting grounds, or else were murdered in the camps when seen as pale-skinned monstrosities visited on them by devils. [...] We'd have been a Creole Nation [...] we'd've had that uniqueness to contribute to the world, in music, literature, politics ... instead of being just lousy copies of the stock we came from. [...]
>
> I do declare that all of us bushmen would have mated frankly with Aboriginal women, but for those prudish harridans, our Irish, Scotch, Welsh, and English mothers, sisters, aunts, cousins ... all of them. They only have to see you treating an Aboriginal woman like a human being to raise the cry *Gin Jockey* ... and we bolt like bandicoots at the howl of a dingo.' (pp. 53–4)

Although Herbert is not reflective about the misogyny of these comments, the action of the novel reinscribes a counter-orthodox dynamic of race relations. It entails a grandfather, Jeremy Delacy, acting *in loco parentis*, precisely because the real father, his own son, will not acknowledge his progeny and cannot recognise his beauty of soul and potential as a human being. Further, Jeremy is represented as being in a mutually respectful, eroticised relationship with an Aboriginal wife, Nanago. The boy Prindy is constructed as a preternaturally gifted child, competent beyond his years in a variety of cultures, as handsome in a suit as in the buff, and as competent in western learning as in Aboriginal learning. It is significant that Prindy is competent in both domains, but Herbert's more insistent point is that whitefellas have a responsibility to learn Aboriginal ways of thinking about land, or be defeated by the special conditions of the Top End and unworthy of land ownership, a case I will argue in detail below.

Herbert's race politics, though old-fashioned in their essentialism and focus on blood, are nonetheless suggestive of a path not taken in the Australian imaginary, until manifested recently in some groundbreaking fiction and life-writing (Miller 2003; Mahood 2000) and more commonly in the new history/historiography of the pastoral and missionary industries. Prof. WEH Stanner in his Boyer Lectures for the ABC in 1967 had identified pastoralism as the 'great wrecker' of tribal life with its legacy not only of dispersal of Indigenous people but also its sexual and welfare fallout, in the way it dispossessed and dispersed Indigenous people. He noted that talk about the sexual legacy of pastoralism, and in particular that acknowledgment of the

Stolen Generation, was taboo because of the iconic place of bush nationalism in Australian culture (Stanner 1991). This silence was maintained until the 'Stolen Generation' report was published in 1997 (National Inquiry into the Separation of Aboriginal and Torres Strait Islander Children from their Families (Australia), Wilson and Australia. Human Rights and Equal Opportunity Commission). After a long period of invisibility in historical discourses, what Stanner refers to as 'the great silence' (Stanner pp. 22–9), the new historiography charting the dynamics of the pastoral industry's impact began in the 1970s and gathered momentum from the 80s onwards (Baker; Crawford and Walsh; Evans; Foster; Foster, Attwood & National Museum of Australia; Giblett; Goodall; Griffiths; Huggins, McGrath & Saunders; Jebb; Rosalind Kidd, *The Way We Civilise: Aboriginal Affairs—the Untold Story;* Rosalind Kidd, *Black Lives, Government Lies;* Ros Kidd; Loos; Marshall & Lawford; May; McGrath; Nicholson; Pedersen & Woorunmurra; Read & Coppin; Read, Read & Institute for Aboriginal Development (Alice Springs NT); Reynolds, *Frontier: Aborigines, Settlers and Land;* Reynolds, *Dispossession: Black Australians and White Invaders;* Reynolds & James Cook University of North Queensland History Dept; Riddett; Roberts; DB Rose, *Reports from a Wild Country: Ethics for Decolonisation;* Rosser; Rowley, *Outcasts in White Australia;* Rowley, *The Destruction of Aboriginal Society*; Strang; Watson). These works, however, offer a more nuanced account than Stanner would have expected. They document both the cruelty and genocidal activities of the pastoralists. More significantly, they also argue Aboriginal collaboration, even complicity, with the pastoral industry on their own terms, especially in relation to the preservation and enactment of culture. It is undoubtedly true, though, that these debates may not have penetrated far beyond academe, except of course in that dangerous formation referred to in the mainstream media as the 'history wars', or the 'black armband' version of colonial history, which again work to absolve hegemonic males of responsibility. Herbert's novel presciently anticipates the more Indigenous-centric new post-colonial histories, and one wonders why his novel was not more potent than it was in changing the direction of the debate. His satire may have a great deal to answer for, and this paper aims to refocus what Monahan identifies as the Romance elements of the text (Monahan 2003, pp. 141–52), in particular Herbert's representation of mixed-race identity and his grasp of how Indigenous mythological narratives could animate westerners' understanding of Australian land itself.

Although Herbert was certainly practising a discourse of race that essentialised and fetishised blood, in line with those of the period in which *PFMC* is set, he nonetheless represented a new direction in thinking about it. Instead of thinking of mixed descent as a liability and a diminishment, he promoted the future of Australia as in fact dependent on it, and indeed on multiculturalism, though that is not a direction I can take in this paper. Deploring the accepted Government policy of Detribalisation (p. 31), he advocated Land Rights, but also, and more confrontingly, a 'Guilt Tax' designed to 'square' the 'primary guilt' of land theft (p. 1035).

Further, Herbert's democratic take on the realities of mixed race in the remote Northern regions partakes in a utopian discourse of multiculturalism. In pursuit of his multicultural agendas, the novelist takes a violently anti-British, even anti-nationalist stance. Prindy, the golden boy, the Aboriginal son of an Australian pastoralist-settler, enacts the utopic possibilities of the re-inscription of the mixed-race person. Herbert represents his education as being conducted, properly, via multiple mentors, and his training in each case is essentially in sacred realities. The most significant of these educators is Bobwirridirridi the traditional Elder and Law Man, but there are many others, all of whom teach him how to be: Ah Loy (his Chinese stepfather), Esther a Jewish refugee and earth-mother figure, Ram Barbu an Afghan hawker and would be father-in-law, Monsignor Maryzic, a Polish missionary, and subsequently Fr Glascock, by any definition a liberal Catholic priest, and finally Jeremy Delacy, the aggressively nationalist grandfather of the child whose final well-meaning but tragically ill-judged intervention costs the child his life. This mixed-race 'parentage' / mentoring committee is no accident as Herbert's vision of Australia was multicultural before the term had common currency, and the syncretic layers of culture these more or less saintly mentors demonstrate are precisely what Herbert valued about his renovated Australia. There are many points in the novel where the golden-skinned boy Prindy is made to bear the hope of the entire nation, none more memorable perhaps than the moment he is lured into Ali Baba's golden-finch-net by the power of music, and thought to be an Indian god, 'all shiny gold of skin and towselled [sic] hair, so luminous of eye, so calm' (Herbert p. 472). This novel abounds in such idylls, moments of transformation where mundane realities (e.g. the fish served at Rivkah's *shabos*) acquire enlarged significance, usually of a sacred character, but also and simultaneously a politically inflected one.

HERBERT'S CRITIQUE OF SETTLER CULTURE

'Wonder', in Herbert's lexicon (Herbert p. 24), the sense of enchantment, is the faculty which he claimed was underdeveloped in the European settlers in Australia, and Herbert's analysis is thought-provoking. He claims that rootedness-in-place and the sense of wonder that comes with it failed to migrate from its many haunts in Europe, Africa and Asia Minor in the emotional baggage of the émigrés who settled Australia:

> 'Have you ever been to Germany?'
>
> 'Not yet. I hope to go.'
>
> 'Well, you must know something of its legends … of the nymphs of the Rhine and the giants of the Alps, and all the rest. Even as a stranger there … I spent a bit of time with the Army of Occupation … I couldn't help but feel the wonder of the place, because of its legends and history. It's the same everywhere … Britain, France, Egypt, Asia Minor … everywhere but here, where we live in a land the wonder of which, as damned and doomed Colonials, we've been unable to see. What wonder is in our lives is taken at second-hand, moth-eaten, only half-comprehended, from our origins.'
>
> 'Well, we've got no real history yet.'
>
> 'I didn't say history alone … but legend, tradition … which this land's packed with.'
>
> 'Aboriginal legend …'
>
> 'What's wrong with that? Are the legends of the Ancient Druids any the less satisfying to the English because based on culture long ante-dating the coming of the people who became the English … or the legends of Germany because dating from the Visigoths or someone?'
>
> […]
>
> '… I don't want to feel alien in … my own native land. According to the blackfellow there's magic in everything … every rock, tree, waterhole … even in the things he makes … his spears, dilly-bags. In fact, if you take the trouble, you yourself can find wonder in everything. We do in scientific things … what we see through a microscope, what takes place in chemical reaction. As geologists we'd find it in the rocks through rationalism. As zoologists in the pools, botanists in the trees. The blackfellow's reverence for things strikes me as much more intelligent than

> the blank disregard of the mass of our own people ... who'd still be simple-minded enough to believe in the divinity of Christ and the sanctity of the Virgin Mary, the Holy Ghost, and all the rest of it.' (Herbert pp. 24–5)

It became Herbert's ambitious project to attempt to recreate and communicate just such wonder as he found in Indigenous cosmology, and in particular its mythological narratives, and bring them to a wider readership of Australians, and to argue that the knowledge they enact is essential to being at-home in country. To name it as baldly as this, though, is to simplify the project immensely.

DRAMATISING THE INDIGENOUS ECO-CENTRIC SELF

For Herbert race issues are intimately linked in his thinking with ecological principles and with what ecosopher, Freya Mathews would call an eco-centric view of self (Mathews 1991, p. 118). Struggling to articulate a philosophy of land that seems more congruent with certain strands of environmentalism of our times, Herbert argues the sophistication of Indigenous eco-centrism and its potential for teaching whitefellas about the uniquely fragile and demanding qualities of the land they have settled. His argument proceeds in stages: first, he satirises European land-abuse; secondly, he identifies how Aboriginal mythological narratives embody very specific forms of ecological knowledge and affect; and thirdly, he attempts to dramatise that by systematically teaching his white readers how to understand eco-centric nature of Dreamtime logic. This multi-stage process is best understood through the theoretical frame of ecophilosophy as practised by Val Plumwood (Plumwood, *Feminism and the Mastery of Nature;* Plumwood, *The Struggle for Environmental Philosophy in Australia*) and more particularly, Freya Mathews (1991). They question anthropocentric philosophies which put human beings at the centre of existence, though they write two decades after Herbert and with a fuller consciousness of the responsibilities of post-colonialism, and tread more cautiously in Indigenous ecocosmology than Herbert does. Satire is the mode Herbert uses to lambast the exploitative degradation of land by European settlers. He identifies such land-use as a pathology stemming from 'Europocentricity' (p. 112), what Plumwood would call 'denying the agency of place' (Plumwood, 1999, p. 158), and images it as akin to a blighted sexual relationship:

> It's a wide silent land … a brooding land … and full of spirit things, even if you don't believe in them. Unless you can come to love it, you come to hate it … […] like either loving or hating a woman. Most Australians … bush Australians … the others aren't really Australians at all, just transplanted Pommies or something equally alien … hate it. They live in it only because they have to. The shooting is hate … hate of your mate, hate of the boss, hate of the blacks … on the surface … but deep down, hate of the land, because it's for ever strange to you, and you need it, as every creature needs earth of its own, and you're left frustrated. Again, it's like a woman to you … like loving an unresponsive woman … (p. 110).

Leaving aside the outmoded and questionable sectional bush-identity politics, Herbert's narrator, Jeremy Delacy, enacts his sensuous and rapturous apprehension of the beauty of the landscape (p. 141) and is critical of destructive land-use practices. Plumwood, drawing on Mathews, theorises the destructive process in terms with which Herbert might concur:

> The movement towards a universalising relationship to place is one of the hallmarks of western modernity. Its economic and epistemic systems are geared to denying the agency of place, bringing place within the medium of rationalist exchange as 'real estate' through the market, through science via assumptions of the neutrality of place and impersonality of knowledge, and through culture via the marginalisation of nonhuman meanings. As place loses agency along with salience, places themselves can become interchangeable, irrelevant and instrumentalisable, neutral surfaces upon which 'rational' human projects can be inscribed. (Plumwood 1999, p. 158)

Herbert, ever the story-teller, makes a case for deep ecological knowledge being embedded in what, to whitefellas, are incomprehensibly magic-saturated mythological narratives. His reinscription of these in forms more closely aligned with western-style narratives construct the earth as a sentient being, responsive to humans. Herbert's notion of the land as a female lover is graphically demonstrated in the image he creates of the luxuriance of the wet season:

> So Wet Season passed, leaving the land languishing in that Edenesque tranquillity and fruitfulness its creator, the Ol'Goomun-Ol'Goomun, had intended for it always. (p. 275)

The context suggests a time for *tchinekin* (specifically sexual mischief, coded in this text as a pleasurable good) as well as for gathering cocky-apples, bush plums, risking ticks (shell-backs) and hookworm, and drinking beer. His inclusion of the sharply observed realistic detail differentiates his writing from landscape utopianism or romanticism. It aims for the pragmatism of Aboriginal acceptance that even the hookworm also acts according to its nature, and that victims of the hunt can be sung to accept their fate (p. 591). Wet season is represented as the time that Country, constructed always as sentient and as having agency in Herbert, basks in the well-being of the cooperation between Tchamala, the rainbow serpent, and in the top-end associated with the cyclonic wet and Ol'Goomun, the West Arnhem Land name for Kunapipi, the fertility principle.

Herbert reserves his most ferocious satire for what happens when whitefellas and stock despoil the billabongs: their traces make the pig seem a 'cleanly animal' (pp. 428–9):

> They made camp that evening on the biggest billabong they had yet come to, where there were no pigs at all, but what was worse, the remains of several piles of guts that were still being pulled about by kites and crows, and stinking to clean blue heaven. Also there were no water-birds, except half a dozen or so lying as little islands of bright blown-up feathers each with its cloud of bluebottles, out amongst the lilies [...] That the despoilers weren't black was evident from the tracks of motor vehicles, scattered beer bottles, a couple broken, newspaper in sheets and scraps, some of the scraps lying with a couple of heaps of what looked like squirming heaps of irridescent metal, so thick were they with happy bluebottles, but were in fact what their owners would have called *coprus*—because according to the knowledgeable Queeny, airing her knowledge in response to the little-literate Prindy's puzzling over the odd lettering on other bits of the paper, they were Greeks. [...]

> They went on next morning into open forest. Everywhere now were signs of His Lordship's, the absent landlord's stock: countless hoof-torn pads criss-crossing through the cropped clumps of rusty kangaroo grass and broken spear-grass; new pads, little rivers of dust, old ones, scoured out by Wet Season rains, miniature gullies exposing the conglomerate beneath the skin of grey talc. No more knee-deep Flinder's grass growing on the little flats that wound between the hummocks of raised ground as when only the kangaroo as herbivore roamed the land. The little flats were bare white patches. Every shady spot was now a dung heap.
>
> The calling of the cattle was now the music of the land. [...]
>
> What had been done to the country ... by pigs and cattle was nothing compared with what the gold miners of forty or fifty years before had done [...]. It was hereabouts that Civilization of the land had begun in force where the process known as Opening Up The Country had really begun. Quite literally had this country been Opened up. *Disembowelled* would be an apter term. (pp. 428–30, current writer's emphasis)

The genealogy of mismanagement runs in a degenerative line from an absent Lord Vaisey (modelled on the British absentee cattle king Vestey), through two lower orders, the Old Australians (descendants of pioneers like the Duracks and Costellos), and the New Australians (who sport monikers like Dago, Hun, Wop, Balt, Pom) (p. 428).

One of the most striking aspects of Herbert's representation of Aboriginal cosmology is the collaborative dialogue in which human beings and nature engage. After the death of King George and Queeny, respectively his traditional uncle and aunt, Prindy has to negotiate huge tracts of country, normally considered unnavigable wilderness by whitefellas, in order to return to his own country, Lily Lagoons. He is represented as an unusual traditional man in being 'solitary' rather than communal in his habits (p. 464), but he is far from being alone. His matrix constitutes a 'plenum metaphysic'(Mathews p. 142): creatures and country dialogue with him; a lone dingo and a plenitude of birds drawn to him by his musical abilities direct him, feed him, cheer him. The discourse can be read as neo-romantic, utopian, but is more powerfully read through the lens of *plenism* (Mathews p. 142)—the dynamic process (which owes more to Einsteinian cosmology than to Newtonian atomism) whereby the self/other distinction collapses in an unfolding process in which the individual perceives himself and becomes part of a wider biodiverse field:

At last he was free to follow his *Rown Road.* That could be in no direction but his own choosing, or rather the choice of the forces primarily dominating such a life as his—those of Nature. The seasonal wind was from the south-east, bringing the sounds and scents on which as a creature of the wilderness now his well-being would depend, as well as advantage over other creatures to windward of him. The Ol'Goomun-Ol'Goomun made her first beckoning appearance in the south-east. Even Igulgul, by the angle of his sinking, would be making his rising for this season South of East. The very birds seemed to be heading that way.

Indeed the heading of the birds his way may have been more in the way of collaboration than coincidence, the way they came to take a look at him, in flocks, in pairs, in families, or alone, according to their natures, surely struck by the sight of the small long figure whose hairless skin glowed in the sunlight and wind-blown topknot glinted, and who could speak their language, joining them in the carolling, twittering, chattering, cawing, whistling, croaking to each other about him. Where was he going? How could he find succour in that blasted land? Someone must show him. The parrots showed him the kapok trees he would otherwise have had to hunt for. The crested bell-birds showed him where the grasshoppers were lurking, ringing their tiny bells of voices. Crested wedgebills, delighting in his mimicry of their sweet song, and especially when they tried to trick him with a bit of ventriloquism and found he could do the same, showed him pods opening to shed seeds that made good nutty munching. Red quandong cherries were the spotted bower-birds' offering. The red-breasted babblers only wanted to talk about him, flying from bush to bush ahead and hanging upside down to get a different aspect of him to babble about. He got even when a prindi came scuttling along to take a look, nodded when given the sign that they were Mates, and led him to a clump of bushes where the babblers had a community of nests, and while those sitting the eggs chased him away, gave his young two-legged mate the chance to do a nice bit of thieving. Night parrots led him to water in the gecko-holes while he was still in the rocky wastes of the devastated land of the Frog Men. When he came out of that into the grey gijia, the finches, in their multitudinous breeds and multifarious hues, and the budgerigars in their singing myriads, took him to their little gilgais. Once when he hadn't been doing so well through the generosity of his new-found friends because of a bit of unbountiful

> country, he was about to commit the unforgivable by sneaking with his boomerang on a bower-bird he heard going through its repertoire in its bower, to be saved getting the reputation of Wanjin the Dingo by a black-breasted buzzard, who circling above, gave the warning, then called the would-be treacherous one away to show him a much more honest and satisfying meal in the shape of a clutch of emu's eggs in a patch of trampled grass with no one in attendance. There were a baker's dozen of them.
>
> [...]
>
> Now dingoes like to attach themselves to solitary humans, and apparently without ulterior motive, since it has never been recorded that one has broken such a truce. It is always in the nature of a truce, because the dog's approach is very wary; and no doubt about it, he can read people's minds. He stayed with Prindy for quite a while, actually up to Igulgul's reaching his fullness; that is he stayed within sight of him, just out of the range the clever pink-eyed fellow reckoned those short skinny arms were capable of hurling one of those small weapons; while yet they were truly together. They shared the bustards and wallabies that one or the other brought down, this being better country. They shared their watering, which White Wanjin found. They camped together. At night Prindy would see the red eyes glowing like coals, reflecting the light of his fire. He would talk to him sing to him. Wanjin [the albino dingo] never answered. Perhaps he expected Prindy to read his mind, too. Legend had it that the original Wanjin learnt to read others' minds from the Ol'Goomun, whose dog he was, of course. (pp. 465–6)

The discourses in action here point to human and non-human selves that are at the same time autonomous (self-maintaining, potentially at the expense of other creatures) but also interconnected, dependent on other selves, whether bird or gecko or dingo. Herbert dramatises one of the major tenets of Deep Ecology (which of course long postdated his writing, and which Mathews draws on and critiques), 'biocentric egalitarianism':

> The intuition of biocentric equality is that all things in the biosphere have an equal right to live and blossom and to reach their own individual forms of unfolding and self-realization within the larger Self-realization. This basic intuition is that all organisms and entities in the ecosphere, as parts

> of the interrelated whole, are equal in intrinsic worth. (Devall & Sessions 1985, p. 67)

Herbert's representation of Indigenous cosmology/physics/metaphysics enacts a sense of land itself and the living selves (human and non-human) as a web of interconnections which valorises the diversity of life-forms. It is precisely this ethical stance, that biodiversity is a gift born of the interconnectedness of Ol'Goomun-Ol'Goomun and Tchamala (the Rainbow Serpent) which makes so offensive and morally urgent to Herbert the destruction described above by pigs (p. 1121) and cattle and miners of the delicate Top End soils and lagoons which are critical to the sustenance of biodiversity (human and non-human). For Herbert, the matter is simultaneously scientific and sacred: the environmental abuse is both indefensible in terms of sustainability, but also an affront to the sense of wonder in the earth's plenitude itself. Contemporary ecological science argues a similar case: Rose cites the ecologist EO Wilson as noting that 'the more species that inhabit an ecosystem … the more productive and stable is the ecosystem' (Rose 2005, p. 301).

THE VITAL, THE SUPERVITAL AND THE SACRED

Further, the phenomenon that Bradley & Tamisari (2005) call the interdependence of the vital and the supervital, whereby the literal object is substance, and self, and also sacred self depending on its representational mode, underpins the whole novel but is also enacted in this passage. The novel is saturated with the doings of two dynamic spirit beings, Ol'Goomun-Ol'Goomun (the Kunapipi fertility principle) and Tchamala (the Rainbow Serpent whose activities are cyclical and monsoonal), and Herbert works hard to ensure they are larger-than-life narrative subjects and fellow agents of Prindy, though they do not appear in the extensive *dramatis personae*. The uses to which he puts what in European tradition is thought of as mythological material is beyond the scope of this paper.

Herbert's counter-hegemonic sense of earthed, topography-specific metaphysical principles contests nature/culture and also physical/sacred binarisms. It also helps to explain his sense of how western culture, so unshackled from the sense of place, inappropriately displaces ecological consciousness with its own oppressive scientism, though Herbert continually underscores the uses of scientific paradigms in land and animal and human management and well-being. What Prindy's encounter with the 'wilderness' (here problematised because nature is culture in Indigenous understandings) demonstrates is a self-realising individual in no way separable or discretely related to the sentient ecosystem in which he finds himself and which itself constitutes a plenum of non-human selves (the moon, the winds, the birds, the dingo, the minute gecko rockholes, the eggs, and so on). This passage challenges the notion that selves could be constructed separable from this plenum. Prindy's personal ego is 'grounded in a recognition of the metaphysical fact of connectedness'(Mathews 1991, p. 148) and expands as he moves into wider and wider dimensions of the ecocosm. This is more than the journey of the hero of romance for some external prize, but a growth in understanding specifically of his ecocosmology, of the continuity of nature and human as categories, of interspecies ethics, and one that is insistently both sacralised and politicised by Herbert. Deborah Bird Rose, whose writing about Aboriginal cosmology postdates Herbert's writing by over a decade, explains the localised and interdependent nature of Aboriginal understandings of region in terms that are congruent with and amplify Herbert's research:

> The living world can be divided up into portions or countries, each of which is a unit or living system. Each country is independent; this means that it is its own boss. But no country is self-sufficient. Each one is surrounded by other countries, so that across the continent and on into the sea, there is a network of countries. No country is ruled by any other, and no country can live without others. It follows that no country is the centre toward which other countries must orient themselves, and, equally, that each is its own centre. (Rose 2006)

The notion of land as having agency, being its own 'boss', being capable of relationship, expanding from the point where a human being finds him or herself, is critical to both Herbert and Rose. What Herbert points to in his representation of Prindy's journey is the principle that the 'Country tells you', a proposition which in Rose's terms 'prioritises country's communication, and positions human responsibility as knowledgeable action in response to country'(Rose 2005, p. 300). Human knowledge directs action in response to other-than-human communication by way of sounds, smells, actions, brightness, beauty: 'Within the communicative matrix of country, people respond to the patterns of connection and benefit, nurturing their own lives and the lives of others' (Rose, p. 300). Prindy survives his extraordinary journey because he is alive to the connectivities, the synergies of mutual benefit that entangle species and enrich them, and because, rather than imposing his agency and subjectivity onto his environment, he is called into action by the other-than-human world, taught by it, nourished by it. There is a serious playfulness in Herbert's dramatisation of the other-than-human hawk educating Prindy in the ethics of preferring unguarded emu eggs to disrupting the bowerbird.

Without romanticising either Indigenous or European races (see p. 117), Herbert argues the need for two kinds of exchange: sexual equality on the one hand, and knowledge-exchange that is based on the possibility of a dialogue with the 'more-than-human world' (Plumwood 1999). One metaphor he proffers, which is simplicity itself but gains salience from ecocentric philosophy, is that of the black and white ibis who act according to their individual 'selves', but are 'equally proud of their breed' (Herbert 1975, p. 215). To lack a sense of the agency of selves, whether of land itself or human selves of whatever colour, is in Herbert's economy to squander the common wealth.

In conclusion, then, for its time, *PFMC* was unusual in its inclusiveness, especially of mixed-descent persons, in insisting that Indigenous perspectives and culture had to be embraced if Europeans were to even begin to understand the specificities of the new physical conditions and especially its economy of ecological mutual benefit. It is unique, I suggest, in apprehending the links between science, culture and the sacred, and celebrating it.

WORKS CITED

Baker, Richard Munro. *Land Is Life : From Bush to Town : The Story of the Yanyuwa People.* St Leonards, NSW: Allen & Unwin, 1999.

Bates, Daisy, ed. *My Natives and I,* Victoria Park (WA): Hesperian Press, 2004.

Bradley, John and Franca Tamisari. 'Place and Event', in *Animal Names,*ed. G Ortalli A Minelli, G Sanga. Venice: Instituto Veneto Di Scienze Lettere Ed Arti, Plazzo Loredan, Campo Santo Stefano, 2005.

Clancy, Laurie. *Xavier Herbert.* Boston, Mass: Twayne Publishers, 1981.

Crawford, Evelyn & Chris Walsh. *Over My Tracks.* Ringwood, Vic; New York: Penguin Books, 1993.

Daniel, Helen. "Outsiders and Society: 'Poor Fellow My Country'." Westerly no. 4 (1978): pp. 37–47.

De Groen, Frances. *Xavier Herbert : A Biography.* St Lucia, Qld.: University of Queensland Press, 1998.

Devall, Bill & George Sessions. *Deep Ecology.* Salt Lake City, Utah: GM Smith, 1985.

Evans, Raymond, Kay Saunders & Kathryn Cronin. *Race Relations in Colonial Queensland: A History of Exclusion, Exploitation and Extermination.* Brisbane: University of Queensland Press, (2nd edn), 1988.

Foster, Robert. 'Rations, Coexistence, and the Colonisation of Aboriginal Labour in the South Australian Pastoral Industry, 1660–1911.' *Aboriginal History, vol.* 24 (2004): pp. 2–26.

Foster, SG, Bain Attwood, and National Museum of Australia. *Frontier Conflict: The Australian Experience.* Canberra: National Museum of Australia, 2003.

Giblett, Rod. 'Kings in Kimberley Watercourses: Sadism and Pastoralism.' *SPAN Journal of the South Pacific Association for Commonwealth Literature and Language Studies, vol.* 36, 1993.

Goodall, Heather. *Invasion to Embassy : Land in Aboriginal Politics in New South Wales, 1770–1972.* St. Leonards, NSW: Allen & Unwin in assoc. with Black Books, 1996.

Griffiths, Tom. *Hunters and Collectors : The Antiquarian Imagination in Australia. Studies in Australian History.* Cambridge; Melbourne: Cambridge University Press, 1996.

Herbert, Xavier. *Poor Fellow My Country.* Sydney: Collins, 1975.

Herbert, Xavier, Frances De Groen & Peter Pierce. *Xavier Herbert : Episodes from Capricornia, Poor Fellow My Country and Other Fiction, Nonfiction and Letters.* UQP Australian Authors, St Lucia, Qld: University of Queensland Press, 1992.

Huggins, Jackie, Ann McGrath & Kay Saunders. *Aboriginal Workers.* Sydney: Australian Society for the Study of Labour History, 1995.

Jebb, Mary Anne. Blood, Sweat and Welfare: *A History of White Bosses and Aboriginal Pastoral Workers.* Nedlands, WA: University of Western Australia Press, 2002.

Kidd, Ros. 'Australia's Debt: Unpaid Wages to Indigenous Pastoral Workers.' *Australian Prospect* (Easter 2004): pp. 1–17.

Kidd, Rosalind. *Black Lives, Government Lies,* Frontlines. Sydney: UNSW Press, 2000.

—— *The Way We Civilise: Aboriginal Affairs–the Untold Story.* St Lucia: University of Queensland Press, 1997.

Loos, Noel. *Invasion and Resistance: Aboriginal–European Relations on the North Queensland Frontier, 1861–1897.* Canberra: Australian National University Press, 1982.

Macdonnell, Justin. *Arts, Minister?: Government Policy and the Arts.* Sydney: Currency Press, 1992.

Mahood, Kim. *Craft for a Dry Lake.* Sydney: Anchor, 2000.

Marshall, Paul & Eric Lawford. *Raparapa Kularr Martuwarra: All Right, Now We Go 'Side the River, Along That Sundown Way, Stories.* Broome, WA: Magabala Books, 1988.

Mathews, Freya. *The Ecological Self.* Savage, Md.: Barnes & Noble Books, 1991.

May, Dawn. *Aboriginal Labour and the Cattle Industry: Queensland from White Settlement to the Present. Studies in Australian History.* Cambridge; Melbourne: Cambridge University Press, 1994.

McGrath, Ann. *Born in the Cattle: Aborigines in Cattle Country.* Sydney: Allen & Unwin, 1987.

McGregor, Russell. *Imagined Destinies: Aboriginal Australians and the Doomed Race Theory, 1880–1939.* Carlton, Vic.: Melbourne University Press, 1997.

McLaren, John & Xavier Herbert. *Xavier Herbert's Capricornia and Poor Fellow My Country.* Essays in Australian Literature. Melbourne: Shillington House, 1981.

Miller, Alex. *Journey to the Stone Country.* Crow's Nest (NSW): Allen & Unwin, 2003.

Monahan, Sean. *A Long and Winding Road : Xavier Herbert's Literary Journey.* Nedlands, WA: University of Western Australia Press, 2003.

National Inquiry into the Separation of Aboriginal and Torres Strait Islander Children from their Families (Australia), Ronald Darling Wilson, and Australia. Human Rights and Equal Opportunity Commission. *Bringing Them Home: Report of the National Inquiry into the Separation of Aboriginal and Torres Strait Islander Children from Their Families.* Sydney: Human Rights and Equal Opportunity Commission, 1997.

Nicholson, John. *Kimberley Warrior: The Story of Jandamarra.* St Leonards, NSW: Allen & Unwin, 1997.

Pedersen, Howard, and Banjo Woorunmurra. *Jandamarra and the Bunuba Resistance.* Broome, WA: Magabala Books, 1995.

Plumwood, Val. *Feminism and the Mastery of Nature.* Opening Out. London: Routledge, 1993.

—— 'The Struggle for Environmental Philosophy in Australia'. *Worldviews: Environment Culture Religion,* vol. 3, no. 2 (1999): pp. 157–78.

Read, Jolly, and Peter Coppin. *Kangkushot: The Life of Nyamal Lawman Peter Coppin.* Canberra: Aboriginal Studies Press, 1999.

Read, Peter, Jay Read, and Institute for Aboriginal Development (Alice Springs NT). *Long Time, Olden Time: Aboriginal Accounts of Northern Territory History.* Institute for Aboriginal Development Publications, Alice Springs, NT, 1991.

Reynolds, Henry. *Dispossession: Black Australians and White Invaders.* Australian Experience. Sydney: Allen & Unwin, 1989.

—— *Frontier: Aborigines, Settlers and Land. Sydney*: Allen & Unwin, 1987.

Reynolds, Henry, and James Cook University of North Queensland. History Dept. *The Other Side of the Frontier: An Interpretation of the Aboriginal Response to the Invasion and Settlement of Australia.* Townsville, Qld: History Dept. James Cook University, 1981.

Riddett, LA, *Kine, Kin and Country: The Victoria River District of the Northern Territory 1911–1966.* Darwin: Australian National University North Australia Research Unit, 1990.

Roberts, Tony. *Frontier Justice: A History of the Gulf Country to 1900.* St Lucia: University of Queensland Press, 2005.

Rose, Deborah. 'An Indigenous Philosophical Ecology: Situating the Human. *Australian Journal of Anthropology* vol. 16, no. 3 (2005): pp. 294–305.

Rose, Deborah Bird. 'Nourishing Terrains: Australian Aboriginal View of Landscape and Wilderness.' 1996. Commonwealth of Australia. Available: http://www.ahc.gov.au/publications/generalpubs/nourishing/index.html. 7 March 2006.

—— *Reports from a Wild Country: Ethics for Decolonisation.* University of New South Wales Press, 2004.

Rosser, Bill. *Dreamtime Nightmares.* Ringwood (Victoria): Penguin Books, 1987.

Rowley, CD, *The Destruction of Aboriginal Society.* Aborigines in Australian Society; 4. Ringwood, Vic.: Penguin Books Australia, 1972.

—— *Outcasts in White Australia. Aboriginal Policy and Practice; vol. 2.* Canberra: Australian National University Press, 1971.

Stanner, WEH, *After the Dreaming.* Crows Nest, NSW: ABC Enterprises for the Australian Broadcasting Corporation, 1991.

Stanner, WEH and University of Sydney. *On Aboriginal Religion.* Sydney, NSW: University of Sydney, 1966.

Strang, Veronica. 'Of Human Bondage: The Breaking in of Stockmen in Northern Australia.' *Oceania,* vol. 72, no. 1, 2001.

Watson, Pamela. *Frontier Lands and Pioneer Legends: How Pastoralists Gained Karuwali Land.* St Leonards, NSW: Allen & Unwin, 1998.

SACREDNESS AND UNCARING FOR THE OTHER: LEVINAS AND PATRICK WHITE[1]

John Docker

> The word of the LORD came expressly unto Ezekiel the priest, the son of Buzi, in the land of the Chaldeans by the river Chebar; and the hand of the LORD was upon him. And I looked, and, behold, a whirlwind came out of the north, a great cloud, and a fire infolding itself, and a brightness *was* about it, and out of the midst thereof as the colour of amber, out of the midst of the fire. Also out of the midst thereof *came* the likeness of four living creatures. And this *was* their appearance; they had the likeness of a man. And everyone had four faces, and every one had four wings. (Ezekiel 1: 3–6)

> They call themselves Palestinians. (Levinas 1979)[2]

In this essay I confess to a certain perplexity. I am baffled by, and seek to challenge, a received reverence for two major twentieth century intellectual and cultural figures. One is the philosopher Emmanuel Levinas, the other is the novelist Patrick White. I'd like both to question the reverence each enjoys and also to create a conversation between their writings. In so doing I will suggest that their apparent achievement in exploring spirituality and the sacred—sensitively, imaginatively, profoundly, and subtly—is illusory. On the contrary, what we should contemplate is that their explorations of the sacred are imbricated with monologic and totalising critiques of Western thought and the

[1] Earlier versions of this essay were given as a seminar paper at the Menzies Centre for Australian Studies, King's College, London, 3 May 2006, and in John Docker, 'An Early Holocaust Novel: Patrick White's *Riders in the Chariot*, a Critique', *Holocaust Studies: A Journal of Culture and History*, vol.13, numbers 2-3, 2007, pp.87–108.

[2] Emmanuel Levinas, 'Politics After!' in Seán Hand (ed.), *The Levinas Reader* 1989; Blackwell, Oxford, 2003, p. 278. All Levinas references will be to this text.

Enlightenment, and the violence of essentialising, ethnicising, and racialising. A further question then suggests itself: is the 'sacred' ever a pure category? The very grain of the 'sacred', I will argue, is marked and edged, figured and disfigured, by the multiple conflicts, tragedies, and delusions of history. If world history, as I contend in my *The Origins of Violence: Religion, History and Genocide*, features intergroup violence evident in genocide, conquest, massacre, colonisation and empire, the 'sacred' also is engrained by such phenomena even if or while proclaiming its opposition to, removal from, or transcendence of them.[3]

Levinas is the central and acclaimed figure in the turn to ethics that is held to have occurred in the 1990s, establishing ethics as attentiveness to and responsibility for the other; concern for the other should be seen as the primary human condition, the basis of an ethical philosophy that can be an alternative to conventional Western philosophy, which he saw as attempting an illusory complete knowledge of reality. Levinas was born in Lithuania in 1906 of Jewish parents; in 1923 he went to Strasbourg, the closest French city, in order to study philosophy; in Germany in 1928–29 he attended a series of lectures by Husserl on phenomenology, and also became interested in Heidegger; in the 1930s he took French nationality; at the outbreak of World War Two he was made a prisoner of war, where, between periods of forced labour, he read Hegel. After the war, Levinas returned to Paris and became director of the Ecole Normale Israélite Orientale; from 1973 he taught at the Sorbonne, and died in 1995.[4] Levinas is appreciated for his critical spirit, his interest in yet independence from major philosophical movements like phenomenology; but I wish to question his status of being free from conventionality.

Levinas has become a saintly figure, a prophet of a new way, and his ideas are apparently now so well known that the adjective 'Levinasian', as in a 'Levinasian concern for care of the other', has become almost common currency and obligatory in philosophy, and cultural theory more generally, including postcolonial theory, concerned with identity.

Patrick White (1912–1990) is Australia's Nobel Prize winning author, whose novels frequently offer, in the spirit of twentieth-century high literary modernism, portraits of Australian society as signifying a Western modernity

---

[3] John Docker, *The Origins of Violence: Religion, History and Genocide*, Pluto Press, London and Ann Arbor, MI, 2008.

[4] Sean Hand (ed.), *The Levinas Reader*, Introduction, pp. 1–2.

that is relentlessly superficial, spiritually deadening, conformist, and dangerous in its desire to crush or punish outsider figures. White's reputation remains high in the world of Australian Studies, though it is perhaps otherwise receding.[5]

I want to query the justice of both reputations, and it is what these two unlikely figures share that is the target of my critique. In the first part of the essay, I explore some key essays of Levinas that discuss monotheism, Judaism, and Zionism, with a framing question in mind. Who, for Levinas, in religious, ethnic, racial and civilisational terms, qualifies as the other? Or, to rephrase that question, who and what for Levinas constitute history and humanity? Asking this question will involve some reflections on modernism, phenomenology, and European-Ashkenazi notions of Jewishness. Such reflections will then set the stage for moving on to White, focusing on his 1961 novel *Riders in the Chariot* and in particular its portrait of Jewishness in the character of Mordecai Himmelfarb. *Riders in the Chariot* is notable as an early evocation of the Holocaust.[6] While Levinas's essays and White's *Riders in the Chariot* emerge from and work with very different traditions, I detect convergences that arise from shared twentieth-century contexts of modernist opposition to modernity. Both seek to meet modernity with redemptive visions of salvation and perhaps utopia; and it is that interplay of negation and positive values that may have proved so appealing in a century and now a new millennium that appear relentlessly to bespeak disaster and catastrophe.

Visions of salvation, redemption, utopia, are always dangerous, even more dangerous when apparently of universal allure. What overall I will reflect on is the disagreeable thought that Levinas and White betray the notion of care for the other. I will conclude by wondering what such betrayal implies more generally for the intellectual and cultural history of the twentieth century that we inherit in the twenty first. My fear is that most attempts at cosmopolitanism, or care for the other and the stranger, continually threaten to

---

[5] See Hu Wenzhong, 'The Myth and the Facts: A Reconsideration of Australia's Critical Reception of Patrick White', *Australian Literary Studies*, Vol.16, no.3, 1994, p. 335.

[6] I owe this point to Dan Stone. In the beginning of *The Rise of the West and the Coming of Genocide* (I.B. Taurus, London, 2005), Mark Levene uses a quote from *Riders in the Chariot* as an epigraph. See Docker, 'An Early Holocaust Novel: Patrick White's *Riders in the Chariot*, a Critique', p. 87. See also David Ritter, 'Distant Reverberations: Australian Responses to the Trial of Adolf Eichmann', *Holocaust Studies: A Journal of Culture and History*, vol.13, numbers 2–3, 2007, pp. 72–3.

turn into their opposite. For both Levinas and White, this means repudiating anything or anyone that threatens their desired sacred histories.

LEVINAS

It mystifies me that Emmanuel Levinas is admired as the great ethical philosopher of responsibility for the other. What stands out for me in his writings are his egregious Eurocentrism, his European-Ashkenazi sequestering and essentialising of Jewish identity, his inhuman support based on the Bible for settler-colonialism in antiquity and the present, his univocal reading of the Bible as centred on universal concern for humanity, and his outlandish racism towards non-Europeans. Let's start with Levinas at his very worst. Indeed, any discussion of Levinas now has to begin with an essay, published in *Radical Philosophy* in 2000 by Howard Caygill, entitled 'Levinas's Political Judgement: The *Esprit* Articles 1934–1983', Caygill contending that the political dimension is of central importance to Levinas's life and work.[7]

Esprit, a Catholic journal, asked its contributors to combine ethical and political judgement in response to concrete political issues, and Levinas, Caygill tells us, wrote essays for it over a number of decades. Caygill, an admirer of Levinas, is nonetheless dismayed by one particular contribution of 1960, 'The Russo–Chinese Debate and the Dialectic', prompted by reports of growing Sino–Soviet tension. As Caygill puts it, Levinas responds to this historical situation with reflections which are tormented, mysterious, strange, and shocking. Levinas oddly, says Caygill, keeps referring throughout the essay to the Soviet Union as Russia, and he assumes for Russia an essential national and cultural identity. Levinas urgently suggests that Russia has to stay away from China, Russia has to realise that for almost a thousand years it has belonged to Europe. Russia, Levinas avers, has to understand that to form an 'exclusive community' with 'the Asiatic world', that is to say, in abandoning the West, it would 'drown itself in an Asiatic civilization', would join peoples who have always been 'strangers to European history', Europe as the 'Graeco, Judaic, Christian West'. Instead, Levinas urges, Russia should form an alliance with Europe against Asia.[8]

---

[7] Howard Caygill, 'Levinas's political judgement: The *Esprit* articles 1934–1983', *Radical Philosophy* 104, November/December 2000, pp. 6–15, here p. 11.
[8] Caygill, p. 11.

One would have thought, Caygill points out, that, given Levinas's concern for the other and the stranger, he would be open to the Asian other. On the contrary. Caygill then quotes what he refers to as a 'shocking passage' where Levinas approvingly uses the term 'yellow peril'.

> The yellow peril! It is not racial, it is spiritual. It does not involve inferior values; it involves a radical strangeness, a stranger to the weight of its past, from which there does not filter any familiar voice or inflection, a lunar or Martian past.[9]

As Caygill comments, it is difficult to believe that the phrase 'the yellow peril' can ever *not* be racist, and equally disturbing is the image of the Asiatic past as belonging to the history of another planet. Levinas, Caygill is puzzled to observe, is repudiating the stranger for being too strange.[10]

In his closing remarks, Caygill reflects that this 1960s *Esprit* contribution is an 'uncharacteristic essay that must be reckoned with in any responsible interpretation of Levinas'.[11] I'll take up that challenge. I will argue that Levinas's notion of the other, far from being universal, is extremely restrictive, characteristically so.

In perhaps his most well-known and influential essay, 'Ethics as First Philosophy' (1984), Levinas contended, in totalising spirit, that openness to the other is not part of conventional Western philosophy. The 'whole history of Western philosophy', Levinas writes, from Aristotle through Descartes and Hegel to Husserl, features a dominating consciousness (the *cogito*) that 'appropriates and grasps' reality. Western philosophy creates a 'regal' sovereign consciousness concerned only with itself (the problem of phenomenology in its focus on self-consciousness) and its obsessive intention to know, where knowledge and reality (being) coincide in a kind of closed circle, and where such sovereign consciousness with its claims to wisdom always feels free. The labour of thought in Western philosophy, says Levinas, 'wins out over the otherness of things and men'. Inheriting Hegel's optimism about history as progress, 'modern man' unfortunately exists, Levinas feels, in a kind of happy

[9] Caygill, p. 11.
[10] Caygill, p. 11.
[11] Caygill, p. 12.

consciousness (*bonne conscience*), concerned only to maintain his own powers of sovereignty.[12]

In this key essay Levinas now proposes for 'modern man' an alternative vision, an ethics that dislodges Western philosophy. He creates a primal scene where humanity, in a primordial act, is always open to the other. How does this primal scene occur? It will be everything that conventional Western philosophy is not; indeed, the self of the primal scene knows that the usual sovereign consciousness of Western philosophy, one's usual external conscious intentional self, is 'hateful'. For Levinas, the self that comes to be attentive to the other is in a state of 'pre-reflective consciousness', it is 'non-intentional', and it persists in a kind of 'immemorial' time or duration; the kind of suspension of consciousness, of will and ego, that, Levinas recognises, phenomenology has evoked in the term *epochè*. In the primal scene, the self exists in a state of unhappy consciousness (*mauvaise conscience*), knowing itself as a sojourner on earth in a state of 'pure passivity', of 'timidity', yet also 'spontaneous' and ready to 'respond'. One knows that one's very existence in the world has been an act of usurpation of someone else's life, the 'usurpation', Levinas feels, 'of spaces belonging to the other man whom I have already oppressed or starved, or driven out into a third world'. In this state of unhappy consciousness and responsible conscience, in my extreme exposure, defencelessness, and vulnerability, where I belong to no-place, to 'utopia', I must bring the face of the other near to me and respond to that face. It is as if, Levinas ventures in a disturbingly violent metaphor, my usual conscious self has been shot at point blank range by the Other, creating a proximity and neighbourliness that was not there before for the lonely passive interior self.[13]

I'll quote Levinas here concerning the face of the Other, 'the face' that 'before me summons me, calls for me, begs for me, and in so doing recalls my responsibility, and calls me into question'.[14] Levinas then explains:

> Responsibility for the Other, for the naked face of the first individual to come along. A responsibility that goes beyond what I may or may not have done to the Other or whatever acts I may or may not have

[12] Levinas, 'Ethics as First Philosophy', pp. 76–8.
[13] Levinas, 'Ethics as First Philosophy', pp. 80–85.
[14] Levinas, 'Ethics as First Philosophy', p. 83.

> committed, as if I were devoted to the other man before being devoted to myself.[15]

In a kind of utopian epiphany, Levinas tells us that the self responding to the other establishes a kind of 'fraternity' that can exist in 'extreme separation'. In this utopian pre-reflective state, an 'interiority' which cannot be represented in terms of sovereign consciousness, I experience a 'responsibility for my neighbour, for the other man, for the stranger or sojourner'. Furthermore, claims Levinas, such responsibility is a return to being 'human' as such.[16]

'Ethics as First Philosophy' would appear to be admirable as a self-questioning and generous ethics. Yet I remain very uneasy about, very suspicious of, this essay. In particular, I dislike the implications of the theatrical scene Levinas creates here, of the self saying, and it is twice repeated as if in an incantation, that the face of the other 'before me summons me, calls for me, begs for me'. I find repugnant here the image of cravenness, a lack of dignity, for if I too am an other to another self, then I too must envisage myself as craven, as begging, yet also as violent, as shooting someone's outer self at point blank range, a rather demotic image, one might have thought, more at home in Hollywood gangster movies.

I'm pleased to note that one of Levinas's fellow philosophers, Judith Butler, also remains skeptical, in her irreverent 2000 essay 'Ethical Ambivalence'. Butler here reports her suspicion that the return to ethics figured in Levinas's writings has led to a heightening of moralism that reminds her of Nietzsche crying out about Hegel, 'bad air, bad air!'. Butler particularly finds worrying the combination in Levinas of an urging of both passivity and violence, and she asks why 'violence' should be a mode for ethics, wondering 'what becomes of an ethics of non-violence'.[17] Strangely, in these formulations, Butler does not invoke Gandhi as relevant to contemporary ethics.[18]

In an essay on Levinas in her 2004 book *Precarious Life*, Butler again records her puzzlement at Levinas's notions of a necessary violence in relations between self and other. Butler calls attention to a passage where Levinas writes

---

[15] Levinas, 'Ethics as First Philosophy', p. 83.

[16] Levinas, 'Ethics as First Philosophy', pp. 84–85.

[17] Judith Butler, 'Ethical Ambivalences', in Marjorie Garber, Beatrice Hanssen, and Rebecca L Walkowitz (eds), *The Turn to Ethics* (Routledge, New York and London, 2000), pp. 15, 24–27.

[18] Cf. Debjani Ganguly and John Docker (eds), *Rethinking Gandhi in a New World Order: Global Perspectives* (Routledge, London, 2007).

that the very precariousness of the other is at once the temptation to kill and a call to peace. Why, asks Butler, should the very precariousness of the other produce a temptation to kill?[19]

In the essay 'Ethical Ambivalence' Butler makes another objection, that Levinas suggests we must acquiesce to the demand to be responsible for the other before any critical evaluation of the demand can be made; we have to acquiesce uncritically and unthinkingly. How, Butler asks, can we distinguish between a fascist or non-fascist demand?[20] Butler is making an excellent point and asking an interesting question, but, as we saw in Caygill's article, Levinas very much does *not* feel responsible to the naked face of the first individual who comes along or to strangers and sojourners, or those separated from oneself—or, for that matter, to many people, peoples, religions, and civilisations at all. He *does* distinguish between various others and their demands. Who or what qualifies as the other? We have already seen his views on Asians, and he also refers to Muslims as an enemy, Caygill telling us that in an essay in *Esprit* in 1968 on the Six-Day War between Israel and the Arab States, Levinas refers to 'my Muslim friend, my unhated enemy in the Six-Day War'.[21] Such is a highly curious religious designation in a war where the Arab states were secular.

Then there is the dramatic revelation of Levinas's attitudes to Palestinians, again made under the pressure of events, during a radio discussion in Paris soon after the 1982 massacre of Palestinians in the Sabra and Chatila refugee camps in Beirut, a massacre conducted by the Phalangists under the supervision of the Israeli invading forces (and for which Sharon was held by a later Israeli inquiry to be responsible). In the interview, Levinas repeats ideas and phrases from 'Ethics as First Philosophy'. He refers to 'an original

[19] Judith Butler, *Precarious Life: The Powers of Mourning and Violence* (Verso, London and New York, 2004), ch.5, 'Precarious Life', pp. 134–36, 139–140. In the last part of the chapter (pp.140–151), Butler attempts to operationalise Levinas's concept of the face in order to construct an 'ethic of Jewish non-violence', discussing issues of representation, media, and state power involved in the United States war in Iraq. This attempt to use Levinas productively is strained and unconvincing.

[20] Butler, 'Ethical Ambivalences', p. 18.

[21] Caygill, p.14. In *Precarious Life*, pp. 135–6, Butler is worried by Levinas's possible Eurocentrism, Levinas, she feels, positing a 'Europe in which Hebraism has taken the place of Hellenism, and Islam remains unspeakable'. In talks, Butler has also objected to Levinas's attitudes towards the Asian Other and Muslims: see Nicholas Boston, 'Tackling the West Bank Issue', *Gay City*, Vol.3, issue 310, March 4–10, 2004, and Samantha Henig, 'Butler Asks for Mideast Dialogue', *The Cornell Daily Sun*, posted 11.11.05.

responsibility of man for the other person', a responsibility which the Bible teaches us, which 'constitutes every man's responsibility towards all others' and which has 'nothing to do with any acts one may really have committed': 'Prior to any act, I am concerned with the Other, and I can never be absolved from this responsibility.' The interviewer then asks Levinas, given what has just happened, isn't the other for the Israeli above all the Palestinian? Levinas remarkably replies, no, the Palestinian is not an other. 'My definition of the other', Levinas confides to his listeners, 'is completely different. The other is the neighbour, who is not necessarily kin, but who can be. And in that sense, if you're for the other, you're for the neighbour.' Then Levinas says that in 'alterity we can find an enemy, or at least then we are faced with the problem of knowing who is right and who is wrong, who is just and who is unjust. There are people who are wrong.'[22]

It is almost as if Levinas were anticipating Judith Butler's later worry about an unthinking and uncritical assessment of the demands of the other. For Levinas, this problem does not arise, because, it turns out, the other is not anyone, any other, any stranger, any sojourner, any individual, any people, the other is my own neighbour, perhaps even my own kin, with whom, clearly, I share a core of values; an other, it would very much appear, not very different from oneself. Levinas's concern for the oppression and suffering of the other, the stranger, the different, is revealed to be a mirage, a proclamation now manifest as bad faith.

It is interesting to note that where Levinas reacted to Sabra and Chatila by suggesting that the Palestinians as a whole people were wrong, Primo Levi responded very differently. Butler, in an online essay entitled 'Jews and the Bi-National Vision', calls attention to Levi saying that after Sabra and Chatila the Israeli state had become morally unacceptable to anyone who survived the Nazi genocide; Levi signed a petition, with other survivors, to demand the recognition of all peoples of the region.[23]

It's clear from Levinas's now notorious post Sabra and Chatila interview, and from references elsewhere in his essays, that Levinas excludes from his notion of the other not only Asians, Muslims, Palestinians, but also a long list

[22] Levinas, 'Ethics and Politics', pp. 290, 294.

[23] Butler's article was originally given as a talk at The 2nd International Conference on An End to Occupation, A Just Peace in Israel–Palestine: Towards an Active International Network in East Jerusalem January 4th–5th, 2004.

of other categories. Women would not appear to figure at all—Levinas's language is insistently androcentric and in some essays he poses an admired virility of thought ('the muscles of the mind') against the bewitching idolatry of art and images.[24] Polytheistic pagans cannot qualify, that is, only monotheists can be considered as constituting history and indeed humanity itself.[25] The history of humanity is the history of monotheism. Monotheism constitutes history's true past and its ideal future, embodied in the modern state of Zionist Israel; since the Jewish people are the creators of monotheism in its sacred form, as care for the other, a land, a nation, is required because that is where justice, care for the other, can be ideally practised.[26]

We must to some degree distinguish, however, Levinas argues, between the political and the sacred. The political history of the modern state of Israel reveals that Israel sometimes has to act like other nation-states, though we are, Levinas makes clear, to be proud of its post-1948 achievements. But Israel the political state must also answer to a sacred history, where, as Levinas writes in his essays on Judaism and Zionism, the Jewish people are indeed unique, are chosen, because their Bible teaches an original and universal generosity towards others. Levinas's hope is that the political state of Israel can messianically answer to biblical Israel's prophetic promise and save humanity by establishing care for the other as history's transcendental meaning.[27]

Curiously, while Levinas rejected Hegel's historical optimism, his own view of the progress of a true spirit in history appears very Hegelian indeed, as does Levinas's exclusion of so many peoples and continents from the passage of this spirit. And in spiritualising the Israeli state, that it should answer to Israel's prophetic promise, Levinas's thought can be compared not only to Hegel but to the German historicist tradition descending from Ranke early in the nineteenth century.[28]

---

[24] Levinas, 'Reality and Its Shadow', pp. 142–43. Cf. Luce Irigaray, 'The Fecundity of the Caress', in Richard A Cohen (ed.), *Face to Face with Levinas* (State University of New York Press, Albany, 1986), pp.231–56.

[25] Levinas, 'Reality and Its Shadow', p. 141; 'Difficult Freedom', pp. 250–251, 257, 264; 'Beyond the State', pp. 274, 277.

[26] Levinas, 'The State of Israel and the Religion of Israel', p. 261.

[27] Levinas, 'Politics After!', pp. 282–3.

[28] Pieter Geyl, in his post World War Two essay 'Ranke in the Light of the Catastrophe', felt that Ranke's spiritualising of the state was particularly disturbing. See Geyl, *Debates with Historians* (BT Batsford, London, 1955), pp. 4–12, 18; Ann Curthoys and John Docker, *Is History Fiction?* (UNSW Press, Sydney, 2005), p. 117.

It's worth noting that for Levinas the Indigenous have no rights in terms of regarding the earth they inhabit as their native soil. Levinas implies that the biblical Israelites entered the land of Canaan, of the Canaanites, because it was promised to them by their sacred texts, and that promise overrides any former possession by any other people.[29] The Palestinians, Levinas advises, should join their fellow Arabs in the vast Arab land mass—'Land, land, land, as far as the eye can see'—that adjoins Israel, a nation which should be, Levinas here referring to Herzl the founding figure of Zionism, a Jewish-only state.[30] Levinas is directly enjoining the genocidal concept of population transfer, irresistibly bringing to mind the powerful work by Ilan Pappé, *The Ethnic Cleansing of Palestine* (2006), exposing and evoking the extreme colonial violence, epistemological as well as military, that the Zionists visited upon the Indigenous inhabitants of Palestine in 1948; ethnic cleansing carried out in terms of massacre, urbanicide, and memoricide.[31] By contrast, Levinas appears now in history as a kind of philosopher-ideologue for Israel as a genocidal settler-colonial state.[32]

One other thing that I very much object to: Levinas creates the historical figure of the Jew as always one of persecution and victimhood.[33] In so doing, he essentialises, totalises, and universalises a European Ashkenazi worldview and understanding, and ignores other kinds of Jewish historical experience, in medieval Moorish Spain, and in North Africa, the Mediterranean, and the Levant before the coming of modern Zionism and the 1948 state of Israel, a history of Jews living with Christians and Muslims for many centuries; a history, as Ammiel Alcalay argues in his *After Jews and Arabs*, where the Jew was not a stranger but an absolute inhabitant of time and space.[34] Levinas also excludes the non-Jewish Jew, its inaugurating figure Spinoza. Levinas criticises Spinoza's philology, his detached study of the biblical texts as texts, for

[29] Levinas, 'Difficult Freedom', p. 261: 'The subordination of the State to its social promises articulates the significance of the resurrection of Israel as, in ancient times, the execution of justice justified one's presence on the land'.
[30] Levinas, 'Politics After!', pp. 278, 282.
[31] Ilan Pappé, *The Ethnic Cleansing of Palestine* (One World, Oxford, 2006).
[32] See Docker, *The Origins of Violence*, ch.5, 'Victimology and genocide: the Bible's Exodus, Virgil's *Aeneid*, pp. 124–8.
[33] Levinas, 'The State of Caesar and the State of David', pp. 276–77. Cf. Butler, 'Ethical Ambivalences', p. 24.
[34] Ammiel Alcalay, *After Jews and Arabs: Remaking Levantine Culture* (University of Minnesota Press, Minneapolis, 1993), pp. 1, 64–5, 67–71.

ignoring Revelation, the Revelation that ensures Israel's sacred history, in the ancient past and now in the post-1948 present; a sacred history that is more important than any profane history, even of political Israel, for it constitutes the essence of humanity's being.[35]

Patrick White

I'll move on now to Patrick White's *Riders in the Chariot*, one of the novels White wrote when he returned to Australia after World War Two. White was shaped by, and shaped himself in, the modernist literary movement while residing (chiefly) in England between the First and Second World Wars. He was also influenced by the prophetic and pantheistic traditions of English Romanticism, indeed he crossed romanticism's optimism about the nearness of plenitude, of unity of spirit with nature, with modernism's hard edges, its apocalyptic sense of history as the nearness of disaster. The White we observe in David Marr's massive biography *Patrick White: A Life* (1991) is a writer who saw himself as a permanent outcast to mainstream Anglo-Australian society. That society was in a state of wilderness, but such was occasion for opportunity as well as bleakness and bitterness. He would attempt to use his art to raise the spiritual level of the Great Australian Emptiness he found around him. Especially after his postwar return to this 'immense void of Australia', he felt driven to 'fill the Australian vacuum'.[36]

In his biography Marr tells us that White spent the early 1930s almost untouched by European politics, unworried by fascism, and hardly aware of the fate of the Jews. Later, however, Marr observes, White wished to make amends, particularly when living back in Australia. He now felt Jews were his fellows in exile, bringing European culture, sophistication and intensity to Spiritually Empty Australia. In the Castle Hill district on the edge of Sydney in the 1950s he and his partner Manoly Lascaris got to know various Central Europeans and together they formed an outpost of Europe. Preparing to create the key character of Mordecai Himmelfarb for *Riders in the Chariot*, White

---

[35] Levinas, 'Difficult Freedom', p. 251, Levinas here referring scathingly to 'Western Jews' like Spinoza in *Tractatus Theologico-Politicus*; 'Politics After!', p. 282. Concerning Spinoza, see John Docker, *1492: The Poetics of Diaspora* (Continuum, London and New York, 2001), ch.5.

[36] David Marr, *Patrick White: A Life* (Random House Australia, Sydney, 1991), pp. 312, 337. Cf. my review in *Australian Historical Studies* 99, October 1992.

began to study Judaism and the history of European Jews, and he was 'particularly keen to meet Jews'.[37]

Riders in the Chariot, much of its action set in the philistine world of postwar suburban Sydney, is insistently structured in terms of a binary contrast: the unredeemed and the saved. On one side we observe with distaste the appalling surburbans. In a dangerous chain of false being, the suburban host includes Mrs Flack and Mrs Jolley and indeed conventional respectability-seeking ladies of lower middle, middle, and upper middle class pretension generally; the chain extends to the mass of the hornyhanded, female as well as male. When Himmelfarb, working at Harry Rosetree's bicycle lamp factory, is assaulted and crucified by his colleagues, a group of drunken hands who had been celebrating a lottery win, they are eagerly encouraged by the women who work there in the office. Blue, the crucifixion party's leader, is somehow being controlled by the spirit of his mother Mrs Flack and her friend Mrs Jolley, the same Mrs Jolley who, as housekeeper for the ageing Miss Hare, tries to destroy Xanadu's resident visionary. In romantic and modernist terms, such characters belong to an external, practical, utilitarian world of superficial instrumental reason, using words as weapons, and they envy and wish to destroy those they feel are different, those they suspect possess a secret centre of true being, those who make them register their own corelessness: 'To some it is always unendurable to watch the antithesis of themselves.'[38]

The suburban host also, alas, includes Harry Rosetree and Shirl Rosetree, once Haïm and Shulamith, as they attempt to conform to what they think are the norms of respectable conventional Australians. Once Jews, they chose to become Christians. But assimilation is hard if not impossible; they can never quite get it right, bringing their children up as Catholic in a largely non-Catholic area. Himmelfarb's face reminds Harry of 'the one great archetypal face' of his Jewish fathers. The factory owner thinks of his childhood, when he was young Haïm and cherished religious tradition, knew the 'wisdom of the Torah and the teaching of the Talmud'.[39]

Just before his crucifixion Himmelfarb crosses Sydney Harbour by train and enters uninvited the house of Harry and Shirl, the house in the wealthier suburbs where the Rosetrees try to become part of a life of 'ruthless

[37] Marr, *Patrick White*, pp. 225, 227, 332, 491, 523, 612.

[38] Patrick White, *Riders in the Chariot* (1961; Penguin, Harmondsworth, 1964), p. 402.

[39] *Riders*, pp. 202–4, 376–77.

materialism', of 'plastic ladies' and watering the lawn. Himmelfarb's sudden appearance is traumatic for Harry. Torn between his superficial social identity and his lost authentic Jewish essence, knowing always a 'latent misery', he breaks down, cries, and hangs himself. Shirl Rosetree is not, however, similarly moved. Shirl has lost her essence, that which she had been, Shulamith 'the black, matted girl' of her European past. She had never really loved Harry ('Mrs Rosetree had a secret longing for hard, blond men') and dedicates the rest of her life to trying ever harder to conform: 'She had a kind of gift for assimilation'. What was most important to her was the texture-brick home, the streamlined car, the advanced shrubs, the grandfather clock, the walnut-veneer radiogram, the washing-machine, and the mixmaster.[40] Women, the reader of *Riders in the Chariot* soon realises, represent the worst and the best of earthly creatures.

On the other side, there is the struggle and pain of a visionary élite, indifferent to material reward and social conventions and status, they who will eventually ride in the chariot of illumination, but who meantime are trapped amongst the unworthy. There is eccentric Miss Hare, mistress of decaying Xanadu, daily reborn in the womb and birth canals of nature, nature as dark secret busy organic activity, as growth, decay, death and new growth. Not far away in a humble shed lives her friend Mrs Godbold, earth mother[41], ever bountiful with children and lovingkindness. Nearby as well in an unpretentious house lives Himmelfarb, their leader, messiah, saviour, prophet, an Elijah. The ascension of this elite of spirit will be painted by the Aboriginal artist Alf Dubbo just before he dies, his life's work arriving at its fruition as it performs this act of homage.

How does Mordecai Himmelfarb manage to avoid becoming another Harry Rosetree, lapsed Jew, Christian convert, superficial suburban?

The prehistory of Himmelfarb as a European Jew is evoked at some length in *Riders in the Chariot*. It is 'dark' female presence and wisdom which saves Himmelfarb as he grows up in Germany. *Riders*' narrator tells us that Mordecai was born in a north German town sometime in the 1880s. His father, Moshe, was a dealer in furs, and though the family had many kin connections with Jews from Eastern Europe and Russia, Moshe himself chose to identify with

---

[40] *Riders*, pp. 382, 386–7, 402–3, 447, 450, 483.

[41] Cf. James Joyce, *Ulysses* (1922), intro. and notes by Declan Kiberd (Penguin, London, 1992), p. 870, where Bloom, in his final moments of sleep, refers to Molly as a Gea-Tellus.

Germany and Western Europe, where Jews had been emancipated in the new age of Enlightenment and universal brotherhood. Moshe still went to synagogue, but regarded himself as a 'worldly Jew of liberal tastes', as 'the reasonable man'. Mordecai's father, then, has allowed himself to be seduced by an attachment to an 'outside world', a false Germany of apparent acceptance, culture ('the beauties of Goethe'), and prosperity. By contrast, Mordecai's mother felt that it was only in 'certain dark medieval streets' that she could escape from the oppressive material existence that so pleased her husband. The mother welcomed to their home cousins fleeing the pogroms back east, cousins 'orthodox' and 'dark' who embarrassed the father. The father will later convert to Christianity and leave the mother, his life declining into indifferent death as all around him, Christians and Jews, regard him with contempt.[42]

The son fortunately becomes increasingly drawn to his mother and her traditional values. Such was not clear at first or for many years, because Mordecai grew up a brilliant scholar, going to Oxford and returning to become a university teacher of English literature. But Mordecai as student and then academic increasingly senses the emptiness of the life of the mind, realises that 'reason is far too imperfect a weapon'. Living the life of reason means for Mordecai a 'shrivelling of the spirit in himself', that he had 'dried up'. He has to recover 'his faith' and the 'oil and spices of tradition' despite 'his rational self', and he effects this by studying mystical Kabbalistic texts and by drawing closer to the spirit of his mother. It finally becomes evident that his mother had 'given him her character', that he had been created out of the 'mother's silence and solitude of soul'. He rejects the spirit of his 'self-congratulating father', absorbing his mother's spirit by non-rational means, 'through the tips of her fingers or subtler colloquy of souls'. A distant cousin the mother had once welcomed to their home when he was a child, the 'Galician rabbi' whose hands were 'almost womanly', comes to supplant Mordecai's father as spiritual guide. The woman Mordecai marries, Reha, is like his mother reborn, devout, uninterested in scholarly knowledge, 'homely', even myopic like his mother, and similarly disliking 'worldly practices'. Reha is an 'initiate' of 'mysteries' chiefly because of her very 'simplicity'. She is devoted to Mordecai; every night while he does his academic preparation she keeps him company, sewing or knitting for poorer Jews. She is sure that he will become a saviour of his 'race' and of humanity, those Reha thinks of, including herself, as 'the ordinary

[42] *Riders*, pp. 96–99, 104, 115–16, 205.

ones'. She is privileged to keep him company on this part of his life's journey—'with humility, conscious of the minor part she would be given to play'.[43]

Once Mordecai Himmelfarb has realised that he must go the way of his mother and Reha, of non-reason, he can strive for the simplicity and humility that accompany his fatedness as a saviour, a *zaddik*. It is a difficult and tragic journey that the narrator now has to trace for us in the midst of the Holocaust. Himmelfarb will lose Reha to the concentration camps; he himself will survive because of an uprising at the camp he is sent to, which allows him to drift with partisans in the forests and make his way to Palestine and eventually to Australia. It was expected by his conventional sponsors and advisers that as a former university professor he would apply for a post equal to his intellectual gifts. But Himmelfarb declares: 'The intellect has failed us'. He makes his way to the outskirts of suburban Sydney, 'the fringes of the city', away from any Jewish community or urban intellectual life, choosing to do routine factory work. Here as if ordained he makes contact with Miss Hare and Mrs Godbold. After talking to Miss Hare and evoking his life's narrative, Himmelfarb tells her that she too is a redeemer, a 'hidden *zaddik*', one of those who in each generation go secretly about the world 'healing, interpreting, doing their good deeds'. Himmelfarb and Miss Hare realise that they along with Mrs Godbold will become riders in the 'Chariot of God', *zaddikhim* not confined to Jews but redeemers of humanity. Miss Hare and Mrs Godbold are riders because, like Reha, such women possess an 'extreme simplicity of soul' existing at a deep level below 'words'.[44]

Throughout the elect desire to share a communion of silence, since words are the instrument of repressive reason; each enjoys or strives for unity with nature, that which reason cannot understand or reach, and each possesses a secret core, an essence, of true being.

Himmelfarb is constructed in *Riders in the Chariot* as embodying 'certain inherited truths'. He becomes a walking 'archetype', who would have 'shamed his apostate father'. In Australia, talking to Miss Hare, he presents himself as the essential Jew, the conscience of his people, wanderers who can only live in houses that are 'fragile and ephemeral': 'I am a Jew, you see.' He assumes that Jews are European. To Miss Hare he refers to himself as 'the Jew'. When he

[43] *Riders*, pp. 96–7, 99, 103–4, 110, 113, 116, 123, 125–6, 129–130, 136, 140–42, 427.

[44] *Riders*, pp. 97, 154–55, 198–99, 308, 427.

enters the Rosetrees' house, Shirl Rosetree sees Himmelfarb as representing the 'one Jew' of history.[45]

In this conception, identity has little to do with the 'outer man' that ordinary humans perceive. In his fragile house Himmelfarb humbly cherishes religious texts, and in such humility, unreachable by the arrogance of intellect, he comes ever closer to the 'centre of his being'.[46] This 'centre' of true Jewishness is in continuity with medieval Jewry (as was his mother) and with Eastern European and Russian Jewish experience. But it is not realisable by those Jews like his German-Jewish father who identify with the Enlightenment of Western Europe, and indeed Himmelfarb's own intellectual productions, as dutiful academic author of some literary critical analyses of mostly minor English literature, are derided in the novel.

Himmelfarb, having chosen not to go the way of Enlightenment Jewry, emerges as unified in his being, authentic, coherent, and certain of Jewish identity as religious, mystical, redemptive, messianic, traditional, organised around the 'certain inherited truths' that are apparently originary and should be telos for all Jews.[47] Yet we can have our doubts about this unitary identity, doubts inspired by certain textual stresses in the novel, excesses of meaning that undo the Himmelfarb-friendly narrator's attempts to present Himmelfarb as archetypal. In particular, there are tensions in the novel between Himmelfarb as ideal Jew where Jewish identity, especially after Himmelfarb reaches Australia, is increasingly *assimilated* to certain inherited English Romantic ideals.

Himmelfarb is follower as well as leader. In Europe he learnt from his mother and wife how to be a proper Jew, to observe the single true way. In Australia he learns from Miss Hare certain other originary truths. When Himmelfarb meets Miss Hare he tells her, under a canopy of tree branches, that Jews, confined within ghettoes, were excluded from contact with trees and flowers, the natural world. With the example of Miss Hare before him, he learns the reward of humble attention to nature, his core becoming, as he sits on his veranda at dusk, like 'some darker, greener flame'. While walking beside the 'green river' next to the factory, the water, in an epiphanic exchange, glistens for him, so that now a 'green effulgence … emanated from, as much as

[45] *Riders*, pp. 91, 144, 301, 307, 383–4, 387.
[46] *Riders*, pp. 194, 198–99.
[47] *Riders*, p. 387.

it enveloped, him'.[48] In terms of romantic neo-platonism, Himmelfarb's inner core harmonises with a universal order of Nature.

In Himmelfarb's journey towards true knowledge *Riders in the Chariot* is romantic *Bildungsroman.* His opposition to Jews being attracted to Enlightenment reason blends with a romantic opposition to the Enlightenment and instrumental reason. Himmelfarb's learning to listen to the inner self formed by religious tradition and throw off his outer self of reason and intellect joins a romantic binary, of social surface as against true inner being: the romantic core constituted in exchanges with natural processes, the green world. When, in a moment of negative epiphany, Himmelfarb crossed by train the city and the Harbour Bridge and registered Sydney as life denying and distorting, as inferno, as the grotesque garish future unless humanity can be redeemed by those who know, his mood of millenarial anti-urbanism inherits not only early twentieth-century modernism but canonical English Romanticism as in Blake and Wordsworth, not least those long anti-urban passages *The Prelude* stages in London. As with Wordsworth, there is in *Riders* a romance of the margins, valorising idiosyncratic characters—Miss Hare is a kind of Wordsworthian idiot woman or leechgatherer, an *Erdgeist* or earth spirit[49]—existing apart from conventional superficial society.

What happens when English Romantic concepts are transposed to a colonial-settler society like Australia? In a colonising way, *Riders in the Chariot* suggests that—for the elect, those blessed by God and journeying towards God—the passage can be smooth, direct and untroubled. Those touched with truth can, like Miss Hare and Himmelfarb, strive for a oneness with the antipodean natural world, a unity of whites with Aboriginal nature, whites who are the descendants of those who conquered, who dispossessed the Indigenous, whites who continue to be advantaged by that brutal dispossession. Indeed, in this romancing of the margins, the white heroes of the narrative are themselves insistently evoked as 'dark', from the right kind of Jew in the old world to the chariot riders of the new.[50]

In *Riders* the margins are unified, so unified that their romantic possession of the natural world in Australia is accepted, sanctioned, and celebrated by the novel's Aboriginal character. In one of his culminatory paintings Alf Dubbo,

---

[48] *Riders*, pp. 89, 197, 205.

[49] See David Marr, *Patrick White: Letters* (Jonathan Cape, London, 1994), pp. 153, 196.

[50] *Riders*, pp. 99, 131.

the 'solitary blackfellow', evokes Himmelfarb as 'the Jew-Christ', portraying Christ 'darker' than is usual in convention. When Dubbo paints Miss Hare as the Second Mary, he evokes her as like a 'ring-tail possum' in a 'dreamtime womb of transparent skin'. *Riders* happily permits an Aboriginal character to enfold certain white characters into his own land and mythology, his own 'dreamtime', his own chronotopes. Here is romantic desire grounded indeed in white mythology. It is, however, an interesting textual trace of a different history that Alf Dubbo should regard Miss Hare as not only like the indigenous possum but as 'fox-coloured', an image that whispers of contradictory signification, of invasion and predation.[51]

In *Problems of Dostoevsky's Poetics* Bakhtin, contrasting Tolstoy and Dostoevsky, argues that in Tolstoy's fiction the author dominates his texts in a monologic way, is all-knowing and all-controlling.[52] In these terms, *Riders* offers the panoptic perspectives of a single all-seeing narrator, whose knowledge of every character is exhaustive and complete, and whose language is one of endless evaluation and judgement. In *Riders* we're told that suburbia as in Mrs Flack and Mrs Jolley 'took for granted its right to pass judgement on the human soul, and indulge in a fretfulness of condemnation'.[53] Yet if the narrator, masculinist and aggressive, omnipresent and omniscient, omnipotent and omnivorous, doesn't like this or that character, those who fall on the wrong side of the binary divide, he will pursue and pursue them until revenge is enacted.

Throughout *Riders* the narrator bludgeons and harasses, himself fretfully intolerant of difference and multiplicity, inducing a cumulative crudity of aesthetic effects. In particular, the narrator is unable to resist a dismissive condemnatory mode, as in the continuous references to 'plastic ladies', accompanied by endless physical disparagement.[54]

So judging and bludgeoning is the narrator that, in relation to Jewish characters he despises for not being truly Jewish, for not being graven in the image of Himmelfarb, he also cannot resist physical disparagement. When Nazi soldiers guard Himmelfarb's group of Jews before they enter the train,

---

[51] *Riders*, pp. 434, 454–6.

[52] Mikhail Bakhtin, *Problems of Dostoevsky's Poetics* (Manchester University Press, Manchester, 1984), pp. 47–75.

[53] *Riders*, p. 211.

[54] *Riders*, p. 382. In this aspect *Riders*' narrator reminds me of the egregious narrator of Peter Carey's *Oscar and Lucinda* (1988).

one guard 'inserted the blade between the great buttocks of a fat Jew'. We're to understand this as the Nazi guard's brutal perception, yet how different is this formulation from the narrator's notation of Himmelfarb's brother-in-law Ari in Palestine 'trying to rid himself of phlegm' as he 'fidgeted about on his broad behind'? On the train to the concentration camp, when Himmelfarb talks to a formerly wealthy Jewish woman, the Lady from Czernowitz, we learn of 'her floury breasts', though a little later we see that she has 'one dug', that 'hung down beside the ancient scar which represented the second'. On Himmelfarb's way to Palestine, there is a 'Jewess' supervising distribution of clothing, who 'wore a moustache', where 'little points of perspiration were clearly visible on the hairs'.[55] Such language is, I think, perilously close to the anti-Semitic, to Judeophobia.

CONCLUSIONS

I will hazard some comparative observations of Levinas and *Riders in the Chariot.*

Levinas's texts and *Riders* share an essentialising of Jewish identity as European, indeed Eastern European, contemptuous of Western European Enlightenment Jewry.

They share a structuring binary opposition to a notion of reason as dominating consciousness, and they prefer, in a recognisably modernist way, to seek as true authentic being what is below consciousness, what is dark rather than light.[56] Levinas in some essays refers to a desired state of 'insomnia'.[57] *Riders* refers to the communion with nature to be achieved in silence. In terms of a modernist aesthetic, such states can't be represented in realism, which refers only to the surface of an alienating society and consciousness.

They share a similarity in narrative tone, a kind of discourse of certainty, the presence everywhere of an authoritarian narrator: the very kind of narrator they despise in Western Reason.

---

[55] *Riders*, pp. 175, 184, 189–90, 192.

[56] Levinas, 'Ethics as First Philosophy', pp. 79–80; 'God and Philosophy', p. 167, where Levinas attacks Western philosophy for its hubris of wishing for oneself 'to be illuminated'. For wider context see *Martin Jay, Downcast Eyes: The Denigration of Vision in Twentieth-Century French Though*t (University of California Press, Berkeley, 1993).

[57] Levinas, 'God and Philosophy', pp. 169–170.

They share a common romantic heritage. Levinas draws on the phenomenological notion of *epochè*, a suspension of all conditioned knowledge, all definitive orientations towards the world, in order to re-establish some form of pure experience and pure perception, an idea that recalls notions of pre-critical or naïve poetry in Herder and Schiller.[58]

They share an acceptance, indeed a welcoming of violence. For Levinas, this means the other violently intruding into the self, splitting it.[59] Himmelfarb, insisting on representing himself as archetypal, is authoritarian in his relations with Harry Rosetree, in his eyes an apostate like Himmelfarb's father. Himmelfarb refuses to accept Harry Rosetree's new identity ('We are Australians now'). In the factory Himmelfarb had already felt called upon to address Rosetree as Rosenbaum, and tried to get him to talk German with him and to admit he was Jewish—'Surely you are one of us.' For all that Himmelfarb submits almost with 'contentment' to the crucifixion in the factory, and that he desires humility and simplicity, we see him hunting Harry Rosetree to his home, and, in a kind of stalking epistemic violence, refusing to Rosetree the dignity of choice, that Rosetree or anyone else's identity could be fragmented and contradictory, multiple and unknowable.

They share a common Zionism. *Riders*' narrator is not only Eastern-European-centric about Jewish identity, but also Orientalist in relation to Palestine and the Levant. The narrator does not question the right of European Jews to colonise the 'stony soil' of Palestine, 'the Land', the right of Jews who 'resisted the elements because there, at last, it was natural to do so': 'For the Jews were at last returning home. They would recognize the stones they had never seen, and the least stone would be theirs.' Ari and his *sabra* wife Rahel on their kibbutz 'belonged to their surroundings, like the stones, or the olive tree beneath which they were sitting'. The Arabs of Palestine are, however, barely visible to the narrator, except for a 'couple of Arabs' who 'laughed' at Himmelfarb in Jerusalem: the Indigenous people of the land of Palestine are not evoked as belonging to its stones and olive trees; rather they are dismissed in a single contemptuous phrase.[60] In such images, *Riders* intersects with a long tradition of Zionist thought and writing descending from the nineteenth

[58] I owe this point to Ned Curthoys.

[59] Cf. Judith Butler, 'Ethical Ambivalences', p. 24.

[60] *Riders*, pp. 143, 187, 189, 191–2.

century, for example, in the speechifying of the *zaddik* figure Mordecai in George Eliot's *Daniel Deronda* (1876).[61]

Nevertheless, Himmelfarb refuses to stay in Palestine and join with Ari and the other Zionists in bringing apparently indispensable European skills, energy and vision to make a Middle Eastern land bloom, a tired Zionist and favourite colonialist metaphor that Levinas also deploys.[62] Himmelfarb perceives Ari as 'dangerously arrogant'. He feels that the Zionist focus on the 'National Home', on 'force', and 'work' as 'the panacea', ignores soul and spirit. Rahel the *sabra* already strikes Himmelfarb as merely 'practical'.[63] Yet here too the novel shares a similarity with Levinas, for whom quotidian political Israel has to answer to Israel's sacred history and ethics.

They share an ethnicising and racialising of culture, identity and history, drawn attention to most strikingly by Caygill in the case of Levinas, but also egregiously present in White's 1981 autobiography *Flaws in the Glass: A Self-Portrait*, which relishes a language of ethnic and racial insult, particularly towards those—Turks, Orientals generally, Slavs, Germans—he sees as threatening the true and essential character and traditions of the peoples he admires.[64]

Theoretical reflection would do well to cease the uncritical celebration that continues to attend consideration of both Levinas and White, and subject their writings—as Judith Butler has courageously done in the case of Levinas—to searching critique.[65]

What we might then contemplate is the disturbing thought that Levinas and White's writings reveal and exhibit how much in world history the sacred is indeed associated with various kinds of violence.

---

[61] George Eliot, *Daniel Deronda* (1876; Penguin, London, 1995), p. 541. I'm not suggesting a direct connection between *Riders* and *Daniel Deronda*, which, according to a letter, White didn't read until 1972; see David Marr (ed.), *Patrick White: Letters*, p. 398, letter to Elizabeth Harrower dated 1.vi.72.

[62] Levinas, 'Politics After!', p. 278, refers to the 'small piece of arid land which had belonged to the children of Israel more than thirty centuries before'; since the beginning of the twentieth century the 'labours' of Jewish communities 'have made it flower again'.

[63] *Riders*, pp. 191, 193.

[64] Cf. John Docker, 'Romanticism, Modernism, Exoticism: Patrick White in Biography and Autobiography', *Southern Review*, vol.26, no.3, 1993, pp. 358–76.

[65] Cf. my critique of the 'Levinasian' late-Derrida in John Docker, 'The Question of Europe: Said and Derrida', in Ned Curthoys and Debjani Ganguly (eds), *Edward Said: The Legacy of a Public Intellectual* (Melbourne University Press, Melbourne, 2007), pp. 273–282.

ANZAC: THE SACRED IN THE SECULAR[1]

Graham Seal

The sacred is commonsensically defined as that which is held by many to be inviolable, sacrosanct through reverence for a particular imputed significance. But as a recent consideration of the subject suggested (Burns Coleman & White 2006), it is still an often-vague concept, applied by all sorts of people to all sorts of places, states, experiences and concepts. In Australia, the conceptual complex of history, folklore, commemoration and place known as 'Anzac' is a talismanic mythology powerfully associated with dominant concepts of nation and cultural identity. Anzac is routinely referred to in the media, by politicians and public servants, in the tourism business and on the World Wide Web as 'sacred'. But despite this sacralisation Anzac is, in contrast with the rendering of national commemorative ideals in other countries, light with signifiers of standard religious rhetoric, observance and dogma. Instead, this characteristically Australian mode of public observance and the considerable state and military apparatus and popular sentiment that surrounds it has been invested with the sacred through the concept of nation rather than through religion. While we embrace the notion and the power of the sacred in Anzac, we mostly refuse its religious dimensions. This ambivalent situation is characteristic of Australian mythologising. It can be seen in both the tangible and intangible representations and expressions of Anzac, in the history of the term and its uses, in the folklore, rhetoric and rituals associated with Anzac and Anzac Day, and in memorials that commemorate and focus these many meanings.

The historian Ken Inglis drew attention many years ago to the sacralisation of the secular that has taken place as an important aspect of Anzac (Inglis 1965, 1970). He has continued this approach, most notably in a well-

[1] This paper appeared in a slightly different form as 'ANZAC: The Sacred in the Secular', *Journal of Australian Studies* 91, 2007.

known study of war memorials and their significance, *Sacred Places* (Inglis 1998). Inglis initially began researching and writing at a time when Anzac and its observance was subject to widespread disinterest and at times trenchant criticism from a generation brought up on the notion 'make love not war'. But since then, and particularly over the last fifteen years or so, there has been a strong swing back towards the popular observance of Anzac Day, not only in Australia but also in such originary locations as Gallipoli and the Western Front, on the Kokoda Track and at Long Tan. The Australian War Memorial regularly attracts the largest number of visitors of any tourist attraction in the country and the numbers of Australians and New Zealanders, especially the young, cramming the restricted area of the Gallipoli landings has become a major concern of both the Australian and Turkish governments (Scates 2006). This recrudescence of interest has only served to emphasise the strongly secular nature of Anzac and its centrality to widespread notions of Australian nationalism.

THE SACRED AND MYTHOLOGISATION

The sacralisation of the secular is one important element of the larger mythologisation of Anzac, which also involves the folkloric stereotype of the digger and the political-military imperatives of successive national governments. Like all cultural constructs, Anzac is a conflation of history and myth. The history is that of Australia at war from 1914 and over subsequent conflicts. The myth involves more complex and older processes of the romanticised pioneering experience of the mainly nineteenth century, political and military imperatives, popular notions of national identity and the central role of the larrikin digger.

The general shape of the mythologisation process is a familiar one that can be briefly outlined. An event, or events, occurs which is invested with unusual, in this case national, significance. The event and its aftermath are the subject of not only historical scrutiny and discussion but also of politicisation, romanticisation and folklorisation, drawing both on pre-existing cultural elements and perceptions as well as the real or imagined aspects of the originary event. As the confluence of history and myth endures it is further strengthened—in this case by its observance each Anzac Day; and by iteration of its establishing circumstances—in this case in a subsequent world war and a number of other conflicts including Korea, Malaya and, most notably it now turns out, Vietnam. Because of its growing power, this mythologisation also draws into itself disparate, sometimes antagonistic elements and players in the cultural script produced. In the case of Anzac, these players include children, women and even old enemies.

The ability of a mythology to continually renew itself in this way is an infallible sign of its health—that is, its propensity to retain significance (not necessarily the same significance) for large numbers of groups and individuals within the community that originates and maintains it. There are early indications that Anzac is absorbing, if controversially, the commemoration of the civilian victims of the Bali bombings through the adoption of the Dawn Service observance for the annual remembrance activities. Whatever the ultimate role of such latter elements in Anzac, the mythology has rarely been stronger in the Australian community, except perhaps during and immediately after the two World Wars.

This mythological sacralisation of the secular involves a number of rhetorical, iconographic, ritual and textual elements interacting with the motivating imperatives of national identity to create 'Anzac' as we currently understand it.

ANZAC—FROM ACRONYM TO ICON

The term 'Anzac' was originally the acronym 'ANZAC'[2] derived from the telegraphic code for 'Australian and New Zealand Army Corps'. As with the origins of most significant terms, and in keeping with its mythologisation, the term—like 'digger', another iconic element of Anzac—has a contested etymology. What is certain, though, is that the word was sufficiently deployed in the vernacular of the First AIF to be applied to the area of the Turkish coast where Australian and New Zealand forces landed on 25 April 1915. It was immediately taken up at Gallipoli and the neologism quickly became a widely used term, at first in the speech of the 'Anzacs' themselves, and then in the broader Australian population. So rapidly did the word diffuse and so quickly did it attain its powerful charge of nation that the Australian government moved rapidly to enshrine its usage in law and so protect it from everyday use, effectively imbuing it with a special status that further impelled its ascent to the

[2] Properly, the acronym of the telegraphic address should be 'ANZAC' and other uses of the term as simply 'Anzac'. This is how the terms are used here, though usage elsewhere is extremely varied.

sacred. From 1 July 1916, a regulation was enacted that forbade the use of the term 'Anzac', or anything resembling it, 'in connection with any trade, business, calling or profession …' (Gammage 1990, p. 3). The 28 July edition of the *Anzac Bulletin* for the same year noted that a Senator Lynch had recently proposed changing the name of the nation's proposed capital to 'Anzac' (*Anzac Bulletin, N*o.9, 1916, p. 2). On 20 October 1916, the War Precautions Act was proclaimed. Part of the Act forbade the use of ANZAC, or any words resembling ANZAC, as the name, or part-name, of any private residence, boat, vehicle, or charitable or other institution. The penalty for so doing was a fine of one hundred pounds or six months imprisonment (*Anzac Bulletin*, No. 62, 1916). The decidedly secular processes of parliamentary government were employed to protect and sanctify the word and the powerful notions of sacrifice, commemoration and nation that it denoted and connoted. As early as December 1915 the Melbourne *Argus* quoted an army officer referring to Gallipoli and Anzac as 'sacred' and the term was being routinely applied by 1916 (Ziino 2006, pp. 1,161). Thus the word and its significations were given sacred status at both the folkloric and the formal levels of Australian society at a very early moment in the history of 'Anzac'.

The rhetoric that came very quickly to be the standard evocation of Anzac—and continues to be so—also contributed to the sacred status of the term. The 'Anzac spirit' or 'the Anzac legend' (a word originally meaning a story of a saint's life) were and are commonly used intensifiers that connote the sacred through privileging of the secular qualities associated with Anzac and the broader concepts of national identity, while avoiding or marginalising the explicitly religious. Other terms that were early applied to and continue to be deployed in relation to Gallipoli and Anzac include 'pilgrimage', 'spirit', 'legend' and, at a slightly further level of connotation, 'ritual' and (controversially outside academia) 'myth'. It is also common to read or hear the word 'sacrilege' used when an individual or group feels that some aspect of Anzac has been misused or abused.

However, there is a significant gap between the rhetoric and the main public honouring of Anzac, the observation of Anzac Day itself. The following extract from the program of the 2006 National Anzac Day ceremony at the Australian War Memorial is characteristic:

> ANZAC Day—25 April—is the day Australians remember the original landing on Gallipoli in 1915. The spirit of ANZAC, with its human

qualities of courage, mateship, and sacrifice, continues to have meaning and relevance for our sense of national identity.[3]

While such statements are infused with the sacred ambience long conveyed in Anzac rhetoric, the observation of which it was a part was almost completely secular in character. No religious representatives were officially present at this event, which included the Prime Minister, representatives of the Commonwealth, the defence forces, the RSL, Legacy and so on. Although two hymns were sung, the robustly militaristic 'Oh, Valiant Hearts' and the sombre 'Abide With Me', these were the only religious components of the ceremony, apart from a mention of the Salvation Army and a Right Reverend member of the Council of the Australian War Memorial in the Acknowledgments section. Notes were included on the significance of the Last Post/Silence/Rouse bugle calls, the laying of wreaths and the floral symbolism of various plants, including red poppies. Likewise the fourth verse of Binyon's poem 'For the Fallen', referred to as an 'Ode', the flying of flags at half-mast, and the catafalque party. None of these explanations alluded to any religious significance, dwelling instead on mourning, commemoration and duty. The meaning of the Unknown Soldier was also explained in the process of describing the Australian Unknown Soldier, first placed in the Memorial's Hall of Remembrance in 1993. While the British Unknown Soldier lies in the consecrated precincts of London's Westminster Abbey, the Australian equivalent lay firstly in state at King's Hall in Parliament House and then, finally, in the secular shrine of the Australian War Memorial.

Another indication of the means by which Anzac became infused with the sacred was the considerable public and political controversy over the appropriate way to observe Anzac Day. This proceeded intensely through the 1920s in particular and has been revisited sporadically ever since. During the debate, Anzac Day itself came to be called, significantly, 'the 53rd Sunday'.

THE 53RD SUNDAY

Even before the war ended, official war correspondent Charles Bean, soon to be editor of the *Official History of Australia in the war of 1914–1918*, was thinking about appropriate ways of commemorating the great sacrifices that

[3] http://www.awm.gov.au/commemoration/anzac/program2006.pdf. Accessed December 2006.

had been made and the great gallantry displayed by Australian troops. Nor was he alone. Politicians and the diggers themselves were soon to turn their minds to the same problem and it was not long before the lines of conflict were drawn up. On the one hand were those represented most powerfully by the Returned Sailors' and Soldiers' Imperial League of Australia (RSSILA) who wanted 25 April to be seen as a national day and to be a 'close' holiday, meaning one during which all activities not related to commemoration would be suspended. A variety of commercial and some political interests opposed this. The 1920s featured the playing out of these differences in state and federal parliaments as the apparently conflicting impulses to commemoration of the dead and celebration of the birth of the nation were resolved.

The first state to officially declare Anzac Day a public holiday was Western Australia. In 1919 the briefly reigning National Party Premier, Hal Colebatch, declared that returned soldiers in the employ of the state should be given the day off work with full pay. Anzac Day was made a statutory Public Service and Bank Holiday later that same year by the James Mitchell National–Country Party coalition government, though exactly which day it was to fall on and how it was to be observed was not stated. In 1921 Prime Minister William 'Billy' Hughes had suggested at the Premiers' Conference for the year that the numerous and various observances of 25 April taking place in venues large and small around the country might be regularised in some way (Wilson 1974, p. 203). At the 1923 Premiers' Conference, in Melbourne, it was recommended that Anzac Day should be Australia's National Day, that it be celebrated on 25 April, that each state would take whatever steps were necessary to implement the day's observance, and that the morning would be religious and commemorative, while the afternoon would be devoted to various appropriate addresses and the inculcation of Anzac into children (Sekuless & Reece 1986, p. 48).[4]

These recommendations were in line with the general opinions of the returned soldiers' organisations and most of the digger periodicals. As early as 1920, for example, the peacetime continuation of the diggers' newspaper *Aussie* had suggested that Anzac Day be called 'Australia Day'.[5] In 1924, as it had in previous years, Anzac Day again received considerable attention at the State Conference of the RSSILA, and *The Listening Post* wrote of the need to make

[4] See also AWM Research Note No 546 (2nd series), 2 April 1952.

[5] *Aussie*, 2:15, 15 May 1920, p.12.

representations to the Premier regarding Anzac Day being made a 'sacred day'.[6] By 1925 the ninth annual federal Congress wanted Anzac Day to be treated as a Sunday.

By the decade's end Anzac Day was gazetted as 'the 53rd Sunday', not only in the west but in all states and territories of the Commonwealth. The states of Victoria, New South Wales, Tasmania and Queensland enacted legislation in accordance with the League's objectives: by 1925 in New South Wales under JT Lang's Labor government; by 1927 in Tasmania; by 1928 in Victoria under John Allan's National–Country Party coalition (though not instituted until 1930); and by 1930 in Queensland under AE Moore's National–Country Party coalition.[7] Although there were some differences of detail between these states, the effect of each one's legislation was to turn 25 April into a uniform or 'close' public holiday comparable to the Christian religious days of Good Friday and Christmas Day.

Since then Anzac Day has continued as an event that is at once a celebration and a commemoration. It is a celebration of the ideals and aspirations of the Australian people and nation and also a commemoration of those who have given their lives for those ideals and aspirations. The nation state is a secular entity, while the need to commemorate the fallen demands the discourses of the sacred. In the context of the strong popular Australian reluctance for public displays and strong avowals of religious adherence, the religious aspects are minimised and marginalised. But commemoration requires sacralisation and if it is not available through the usual formal religious modes and rhetoric it can still be achieved through other cultural processes that elevate the secular 'Anzac' to an almost holy term.

This occurs through many of the ritual aspects of Anzac Day. The pre-dawn meal and drink that is a semi-private observance at a number of veterans' associations is symbolic of the original Anzacs' last meal before landing at dawn on 25 April 1915. It is a ritual that also resonates inevitably with Christian beliefs regarding transubstantiation. A folk custom on Anzac Day in Perth involves participants at the dawn service climbing the hill, Mt Eliza, on which the State War Memorial stands in a deliberate folk re-enactment of the original

[6] *The Listening Post*, 24 Oct 1924, p.14? (inside back cover).

[7] See AWM Research note No 546 (second series), 2 April 1952. Also Hills, op. cit., pp. 56-8; *League Post*, 1 Oct 1932, p. 23, discussing Anzac Day celebrations in Queensland from 1930. South Australia had instituted the Anzac Day holiday in 1922, by accident, it seems. See Robertson J, *Anzac and Empire*, p.251.

landings on the hilly beaches of Gallipoli. However, the most widely observed element of Anzac Day is the ceremony at dawn itself.

THE CEREMONY AT DAWN

In 2004 the commemoration for the Australian victims of the 2002 Bali bombings took the form of a 'dawn service'. This characteristically minimalist Australian ceremony has its origins in and after World War 1 as the nation sought to find commemorative modes appropriate to memorialise the sacrifice of its soldiers and the emotional sense of nationhood the Gallipoli campaign had engendered. Since then the ceremony at dawn has been both an important discrete element of Anzac Day as well as a vital component of the other activities that take place each 25 April. The ceremony is therefore crucial to any understanding of Australia's most powerful and, so far, enduring mythology of nation.

Despite its centrality to the Anzac tradition and popular constructions of nationhood, the origins of the ceremony at dawn are unclear and the subject of ongoing controversy, yet it is the one element of Anzac Day that has continually attracted significant numbers, even at those periods when the Anzac Day march itself has been in apparent decline as a national spectacle. In some of the earliest reports of the event—and associated claims for originary status—the compelling character of the ceremony at dawn is already clear:

> ... It needs the pen of a master to portray the strange wonderment of scene and the deep impression created [by the dawn laying of wreaths]. One had to be there to understand. It was expected that a few representative war veterans only would be present to lay wreaths, but diggers and the public turned up in their thousands. The ceremony at dawn has not only come to stay, but it is our opinion that next year it will be extended throughout the country...[8]

The ceremony at dawn has demonstrated an ability to adapt to changed circumstances, as evidenced by its adoption for the Bali commemoration and the importance of the ceremony in the increasingly popular 'pilgrimages' being

[8] *The Listening Post* (WA RSSILA) 24 May 1929, p.7.

made by Australians to Gallipoli, the Western Front, the Kokoda Track and Hellfire Pass.

As with other aspects of Anzac, the dawn service downplays the religious in favour of a sombre marking of the dawn landings of 1915. The term 'dawn service' itself implies religion even though there may be little or no formal religious observance or utterance at these events. It is a 'service' that is not a service, yet is replete with observances that resonate of religious commemorative forms, including wreath-laying, the playing of the 'Last Post', and the one or two minutes silence, a prayer-like moment in which no prayer is uttered, though Laurence Binyon's widely used dedication 'For the Fallen' is effectively a secular credo:

> They shall grow not old, as we that are left grow old:
> Age shall not weary them, nor the years condemn.
> At the going down of the sun and in the morning
> We will remember them.
> Lest we forget.

Memorials

The nation's most significant war memorial was designed both as a shrine and as a museum.[9] It is a place of remembrance and of commemoration but not of religious display. The man who played the greatest single role in the creation of the national mythology, Charles Bean, also referred to Anzac's tangible locus, the Australian War Memorial, as 'sacred'.

The Hall of Remembrance in the Australian War Memorial is spiritual but without religious symbolism. While intended to recreate the atmosphere of a cathedral and utilising a domed cruciform layout, there is nothing explicitly or even implicitly religious in Napier Waller's mosaics, which instead refer to classical and even art deco mythological and architectural traditions rather than to Christian symbology. The fighting men and women are honoured 'with the west window embodying the social qualities of Australian service men and women—'comradeship', 'ancestry', 'patriotism', 'chivalry' (to the defeated) and 'loyalty'. The east window represents AIF fighting qualities—'coolness' (in

[9] http://www.deh.gov.au/heritage/national/sites/war-memorial.html.

action), 'control' (of self and others), 'audacity' and 'decision'. (AWM 1961, 1984) As a historian of the Memorial has noted:

> Bean's notion that the relics were 'sacred', that they required a 'final resting place', that the men of the AIF needed to be 'worshipped', and that the names of the fallen should be recorded on the walls of the building imbued the Memorial with the same quasi-religious sentiment. Irrevocably linked with the Anzac mythology, these ideas became firmly embedded not only within the precincts of the Memorial, but also within Australia's national consciousness.[10]

Less exalted local memorials also partake of the secular sacred. In a study of the Canning war memorial in Western Australian John Stephens discovered that the families of deceased ex-servicemen were having their ashes interred in the gardens that formed part of the memorial precinct. As Stephens notes, 'this enhances the idea of sacredness'. His investigations revealed that the practice was being carried out at other memorials in metropolitan Perth.

Stephens's research also uncovered a developing example of the Anzac mythologisation process investing war memorials with the secular sacred. Among those interviewed for the research project, a number claimed that the practice of interring ashes at memorial sites was further stimulated by the rise to prominence of Aboriginal land rights, and the understanding of Aboriginal claims to the land as sacred through the interred presence of their ancestors. 'In this context the Canning memorial takes on the added role and meaning of a war cemetery—a landscape that could be considered twice sacred and a landscape that morphs from a memorial into a shrine.' (Stephens 2006).

Here, further layers of complexity are being added to the sacred significance of such memorials as Anzac continues to be mythologised at formal and folkloric levels and at national and local sites. These layers are commemorative of wartime sacrifice for the nation; they represent the Anzac spirit; they are tangible markers of national identity, reinforced and reaffirmed each year through the dawn service (and cognate events, such as Remembrance Day); they are war graves; and they are sacred sites, both in terms of their

---

[10] Millar A, 'Gallipoli to Melbourne: The Australian War Memorial, 1915–19', *Journal of the Australian War Memorial*, no. 10, April 1987, p.41. See also Inglis K, 'A sacred place: the making of the Australian War Memorial', *War & Society*, 3:2, 1985.

relationship to Anzac and, whatever the overtones of cultural appropriation, to the absorption into Anzac of indigenous concepts of the sacred (Gelder & Jacobs 1998).

FOLKLORE, FILM AND LITERATURE

Other folkloric customs and traditions associated with Anzac are not religious but have sacralised status, such as the placing of poppies next to the names of fallen ancestors in the Wall of Remembrance at the Memorial. The wearing of a sprig of rosemary on Anzac Day, primarily derived from the presence of this plant around Anzac Cove, is also usually said to relate to ancient Greek funerary traditions. In keeping with the processes of mythologisation, this effectively draws the hallowed heroic past into the mythic complex in the same way that the language of Homeric epic was almost immediately deployed in describing the Gallipoli experience (Ely 1985).

More elaborated traditions include the legend of the Lone Pine seedlings. As with all folkloric narratives there are a number of variations on this story that need not concern us here. But the wide availability and planting of seedlings said to be descended from those brought back to Australia by survivors of the Lone Pine action, or their comrades, is another indication of the significance we place on what can be accurately referred to as the 'relics' of Gallipoli.

Trivial though some may consider such discourses of our underculture, they could not exist without the participation of significant numbers in diffusing and maintaining such traditions. They need to be taken seriously, both as authentic vernacular expressions and perceptions and as significant elements within the mythological structure of Anzac. When such discourses interact with the more formal and official imperatives of politics and military exigency, the resulting amalgam is a potent one, as demonstrated through the institutional legend of Simpson and the Donkey.

In this story the colourful 'Simpson' is redeemed through heroic self-sacrifice. Although barely acknowledged by the Anzacs themselves in a situation where such selfless gallantry was commonplace (Cochrane 1992), Simpson and his donkey's selfless actions were glorified by the media of the day and have subsequently been portrayed to generations of schoolchildren as acts in support of the greater good of the secular state and the sacred bonds of mateship. They inevitably resonate with the story of Jesus' flight from Herod and the subsequent Christian folk belief that donkeys are especially blessed. In this, as in so many other ways, the Anzac myth manages to invoke the religious even without acknowledging it, let alone embracing it.

The collusion of the formal and the folkloric, the informal and the institutional in the creation and perpetuation of Anzac and its many meanings was well displayed in Peter Weir and David Williamson's celebrated film *Gallipoli* (1981). The narrative accurately crystallises and depicts these aspects of Anzac in its canonical retelling. As well as artfully weaving fact and folklore together in a visual representation of the Anzac mythology, *Gallipoli* steadfastly resists religiosity other than in a brief shot of soldiers at prayer and a few silhouetted crosses on Anzac graves as the film approaches its climactic moments. The last of these has the finest flower of Australian youth transfixed in almost-death in the final frame of frozen time. This everybloke becomes a secular martyr to the military ineptitude of the British 'brass', another favoured theme of the Australian version of Gallipoli and, more generally, as part of the anti-authoritarianism inherent in our broader notions of cultural identity.

Gallipoli well represents and reinforces the relationship of Anzac to other sacralised secularities of Australian mythology. These include the notion of mateship, as already mentioned, as well as the veneration of the bush and concomitant demonisation of the city. These are also fundamental elements of Anzac, particularly as mediated and represented by the stereotypical figure of the 'digger', a stereotype that includes a strong antipathy to clericalism and other formalised expressions and observances of religion. In this matter, as in many others, the digger is the twentieth-century heir to the nineteenth-century bushman.

The bush hero was romanticised positively by Paterson and negatively but just as effectively by Lawson, aided by hosts of other known and anonymous bush balladists and singers. From this literary and folkloric fusion came the image of a strong, bold nomad who lived life on his own terms, brooked no nonsense from bosses and was an independent and endlessly inventive improviser and survivor, skills that translated well into the requirements for a World War 1 soldier. The idealised bushman was also fiercely democratic, the origins of the continuing notion of 'a fair go', a brawler, a drinker and a gambler. His guiding lights were the collective solidarity of the union and unquestioning loyalty to his mates. It hardly needs saying that there was little room for more than any perfunctory observance of religiosity in this secular creed, as depicted so well in Lawson's sparse short story 'The Union buries its dead', in which the presiding minister is referred to as 'the devil'.

These characteristics, together with the usually laconic humour of the bush, were drawn directly into the image of the digger that evolved so early in the war simply because it only required the swapping of billycan, swag and bush hat for the rifle, pack and turned-up slouch hat. The bushman's gambling became the diggers' game of two-up, his fighting became the diggers' legendary battle skills and his drinking transmuted into the larrikinism of the digger. The dislike of the boss became the diggers' reluctance to salute officers, and his unionised loyalty to his mates became the holiest of all digger attributes, loyalty to your mates. Just as his predecessor had little time for religion, so the digger relegated its representatives to 'sky pilots' and 'padres', the latter being given only grudging respect if they helped out with the fighting, as some did, or simply being tolerated if they performed their necessary duties discreetly and efficiently. As the essential hero at the centre of the non-religious Anzac mythology, the a-religious digger could only be represented in secular terms. It is one of the sustaining strengths of the Anzac mythology that it manages to negotiate the culturally necessary balance between the sacred and the secular in its powerful and monopolistic representation of Australianness.

In folklore, though not in fact, Gallipoli was also the locus of the term 'digger', a necessary mis-belief that connects the digger directly with the sacralised site of Anzac's birth. The term 'digger' as a descriptor for the Australian foot soldier was not used at Gallipoli. It probably evolved among Australian troops in Britain in late 1916 and did not become widely used until early 1917, long after the Anzacs and their allies had triumphantly retreated from the defeat of the Dardanelles (Seal 2004). Yet most Australians—certainly all those working in the media—believe that the Gallipoli campaign was conducted by soldiers who called themselves 'diggers'.

Conclusion

The overall effect of all these colluding, colliding and continuing traditions is to sacralise the secular in minimalist terms of Christian belief and observance. Anzac therefore becomes another, yet the single most powerful, manifestation of our ambivalence, an ambivalence that lies at the heart of our sense of national identity. This ability to hold jumbled, even contradictory perceptions together is an aspect of Australian culture that can be seen in national icon

Ned Kelly's simultaneous status as hero and villain (Seal 1980, 2002). It is also seen in our sense of kinship with Britain and the accompanying rivalry evident especially in cricket through 'the Ashes' tradition, as well as other international sporting competitions.

Australia has been referred to as the first post-Christian country, a misreading based on the extremely low-key nature of religious expression. With the partial exception of Manning Clark's Old Testament approach, Australian historians have often ignored religion as a significant aspect of our experience and attitudes. But as recent census results consistently show, around 75% of adult Australians describe themselves as religious, with most of the remainder being atheists, agnostics or simply not bothered. The high level of voluntarism that is characteristic of Australia, including volunteer bushfire fighting, surf lifesaving, charities and so forth, can be interpreted as another indication that the Christian value of good works is alive and well, even if rarely articulated in religious terms. As Kevin Rudd has argued, the Australian ideals of helping less fortunate others and the 'fair go' are a social gospel to which, whether they would use this term or not, many Australians relate (Rudd 2006). While Rudd was writing in the context of a developing political strategy over the issue of religion, the popular preference for any religious belief to be demonstrated through selfless acts rather than through conventional observations and expressions of piety is at the root of the sacred secular ambivalence of our central myth of nation.

The Anzac mythology is a balance of oppositions, a mediation of apparent contradictions. The tension produced by this interaction provides the energy that drives the cultural script it produces and which powers the values, attitudes and beliefs of the very large numbers of Australians who follow the ambivalent complexities of its plots and sub-plots. The invocation of the sacred through the doggedly secular is a characteristically Australian mode of observance.

WORKS CITED

Anzac Bulletin No. 9, July 28, 1916, No 62, Dec 1, 1916.

Australian War Memorial, *The Hall of Memory*, Canberra (1961), 1984.

Bouma, G, *Australian Soul: Religion and Spirituality in the 21st Century*, Cambridge University Press, Melbourne, 2006.

Burns Coleman, E and White, W (Editors), *Negotiating the Sacred: Blasphemy and Sacrilege in a Multicultural Society*, Sections 1 and 2. ANU E Press, 2006.

Cochrane, P, *Simpson and the Donkey: The Making of a Legend,* Melbourne University Press, Melbourne, 1992.

Ely, R, 'The First Anzac Day: Invented or Discovered?', *Journal of Australian Studies* 17, 1985.

Gammage, W, 'Anzac's Influence on Turkey and Australia', unpublished paper presented at Australian War Memorial History Conference, July, 1990.

Gelder, K & Jacobs, J, *Uncanny Australia. Sacredness and Identity in a Postcolonial Nation*, Melbourne University Press, Melbourne, 1998.

Inglis, KS, 'The Anzac Tradition', *Journal of Australian Studies*, 17, 1965.

Inglis, KS, 'The Australians at Gallipoli'. Parts 1 and 2, *Historical Studies* 14:54, 55, 1970.

Inglis, K, 'A Sacred Place: The Making of the Australian War Memorial', *War & Society* 3:2, 1985.

Inglis, K, *Sacred Places: War Memorials in the Australian Landscape*, Miegunyah Press, Melbourne, 1988.

McKernan, M, *Here is Their Spirit: A History of the Australian War Memorial, 1917–1990*, UQP, St Lucia, Qld., 1991.

Rudd, K, 'Faith in Politics', *The Monthly*, October 2006.

Scates, B, *Return to Gallipoli: Walking the Battlefields of the Great War*, Cambridge University Press, 2006.

Seal, G, *Inventing Anzac: The Digger and National Mythology*, University of Queensland Press, St Lucia, 2004.

Seal, G, *The Legend of Ned* Kelly, Hyland House, Melbourne, 2nd edn. 2004 (1980).

Sekuless P & and Reece, J, *The History of the Returned Services League, 1916–1986*, Sydney, 1986.

Stephens, J (2006) 'Commemoration, Meaning and Heritage of Western Australian War Memorials' in Miller, CL and Roche, MM (eds), *Past Matters: Heritage, History and the Built Environment. 8th Australasian Urban History/ Planning History Conference*, Massey University, Wellington, New Zealand.

The Listening Post (WA RSSILA) May 24, 1929.

Wilson, M, 'The Making of Melbourne's Anzac day', *Australian Journal of Politics and History*, vol. 20, no. 2, pp. 197–209, 1974.

Ziino, B, 'Who Owns Gallipoli? Australia's Gallipoli Anxieties 1915-2005', *Journal of Australian Studies* 88, 2006.

A WORLD OF THE INVISIBLE

Claudia Terstappen

This essay refers to my personal observations and experiences of aspects of religious belief in contemporary life in Europe, the US, Japan and Australia. It will address how people deal with uncertainty, fear, illness, death, sorrow, fertility and the desire to predict their future and gain stability in a life that is characterised by unforeseeable changes.

Pictures, objects, rituals and places are intertwined in building a symbolical network that withdraws from logical argument. It is a world of materials that represent a world of the invisible. Altars, whether man made or natural, memorials for the dead, objects and rituals that connect us with the past and address the future; all of these are as contemporary as ever. It is uncertainty and emotion that drive people to believe, have faith and act in certain ways.

My observations evolve from my personal practice as an artist that explores a diverse range of contemporary expressions of religious beliefs.

The essay is accompanied by images of my artwork as well as photographs from my archive that have inspired my research[1]. I will address the following four areas:

- Altars and sacred places
- Memorials for the dead
- Objects and desires
- Sacrifice and gratefulness

[1] The photographs and images in this essay can be found at Claudia Terstappen's webpage: http://artdes.monash.edu.au/terstappen/gallery/sacredaustralia; or at http://www.cloudsofmagellan.net/terstappen.html.

ALTARS AND SACRED PLACES

Image: Chapel interiors, Cruz del Romero —Andalucia, Spain 1994

In Catholicism the altar represents the closest proximity to God. This is comparable to the majority of other religions. In most cases the altar is elevated and separates itself from the surrounding area. Usually the altar consists of a selection of objects that inherit a symbolical function or that are used in rituals. Each of these elements plays a role within the overall construct and is essential for the ritual to work. The French author Philipe Peltier remarks:

> To create an altar means to build a network, a symbolical system of meaning, that withdraws itself from any logic, thus becoming open for lively conjuration.[2]

The image that is created of a real place is here directly linked to the counter image of the imagined place, in which everything is different. The invisible world is constructed through the objects that instigate images in the viewer's mind. The Priest, Shaman, Voodoo or Macumba person plays a central role in this set-up. Only they understand which objects are consecrated, where and how they should be placed and what rituals are necessary to connect with the invisible powers. They claim to be the social and spiritual leader of the people and are accepted as such. In most cases they have not been chosen by the people but by self promotion. The people accept their powers, believing that the spirits speak through them and their actions only and therefore their knowledge and performance is essential to benefit them. This secures their role and respectability.

The German artist Joseph Beuys (1921–1986) used these powers in performative works that he called '*actions*'. In *I Like America and America Likes Me* (1974), Beuys wrapped himself in felt and walked around with a crook, confined in a room with a coyote for several days (René Block Gallery, New York). Beuys took the role of a Shaman, whose knowledge would enable him to communicate with a primordial world, thus drawing the connection

---

[2] Peltier, Philipe, 'Altäre - Versuch einer Einführung' in Martin, Jean Hubert, *Altäre, Kunst zum Niederknien*, (Altars, Art to kneel down for); Museum Kunst Palast Düsseldorf 2001 Hantje Catz, p 17.

between the spiritual world and contemporary society. The coyote was representative of a Native American God, with the power to move between the physical and the spiritual world. Beuys saw the near extinction of the coyote brought on by European settlers as a symbol of the damage done by white men to America's indigenous peoples.

Beuys' action was an attempt to heal some of those wounds. He spoke about the healing powers of art, thereby fusing art, magic, science, philosophy, politics and religion.

Image. Car altar—Victoria, Australia 2007

Altars can appear in any form or shape and in both private and public spaces. Their place signifies the focussing point of the spiritual power. Their location can be indicated through specific objects, materials and rituals, or marked by colours on the ground, lines of stones, or fences etc. These markings define the boundaries of the sacred area within which communication can take place. They should be respected and in some cases even feared.

Image. Roadside memorial surrounded by stones—South Australia 2008

The objects themselves define the boundaries and the altar itself. They are the instruments that anticipate animation but it is the ritual that empowers the altar. Philipe Peltier continues:

> 'The altar doesn't exist without objects and without rituals it cannot live.' (ibid.)

There are altars that have been created by nature itself and that man called sacred, such as mountains, specific trees or other sites. Many of these natural altars are also elevated and thus are closer to the spiritual world. Some mountains are believed to be the home of the God's or spirits. They should be respected in order to maintain a good and healthy relationship with the spiritual world.

Image. Holy mountain, da'diilzhish, *(Navajo Indian:* let us dance*) —USA 1990*

The American writer Robert McPherson writes in *Sacred Land-Sacred View* about Navajo Indians:

> Sacred mountains should not be climbed unless it is done in a proper way through prayer and song and they should be returned to by medicine men every 12 years to renew their Blessingway prayer. Failure to follow correct procedures leads to either individual harm or the loss of powers of a sacred site. Treating sacred places on a mountain in sacrilegious ways, including mining, road construction, logging, ranching, and recreation causes the holy beings to flee and their power to be lost. [3]

MEMORIALS FOR THE DEAD

Roadside memorials are common in various countries. They communicate sorrow to a wider public than a conventional grave as they appear along public roads rather than being accommodated within the boundaries of a cemetery. They have the advantage of being free from any religious constraints. The memorials are often created by parents who do not want to give up the responsibility of care for their child that died in an accident. The actual place at which the accident happened contains a strong spiritual connection to the person. This connection is made visible through the altar that they create.

It seems that the institutionalised place that is defined by society does not fulfil the expectations of the aggrieved. The grave at the communal cemetery signifies the decline of the unique. For many people it does not meet the characteristics of a place for sorrow.

With roadside memorials, relatives or friends create the aura around the dead person with objects and images. The memorial mediates between the inner and outer world. The person who passed away is symbolised through handwritten notes, photographs and personal belongings, objects that are unusual at a public cemetery. In addition a personal shrine can be created spontaneously at a personally chosen place and in an unconventional way.

These shrines can be overwhelmingly powerful when we think of the transformation of Kensington Gardens, London into a sea of bouquets, notes and candles following the death of Princess Diana on the 31st August 1997.

---

[3] McPherson, Robert , *Sacred Land-Sacred View* ,1992 Brigham Young University, USA

Image. Roadside memorial with handwritten notes, photographs and personal belongings—Melbourne 2007

These objects are charged and placed with emotional values. They connect the living with the dead. It is unimportant if the objects are pretty, ugly or trivial; they describe the deceased and bring them closer to us. They give evidence to their existence and make them one of us. The deceased has a name, is such and such age, and died here at this place under such and such circumstances.

Since the terrorist attacks on the Twin Towers on 11th September 2001 in New York and the Bali bombings on 12th October 2002 another aspect entered the reading of temporary shrines. In her essay *Postmodern Rituals: Contemporary Australia, Responds to Bali,* Lyn McCredden refers to the temporary shrine people created at Parliament House in Melbourne after the Bali bombing. She described something going beyond the expression of loss. Several highly personalised notes drew a revealing connection between a religious ritual and an ideological response. McCredden refers to two notes that she saw. One said '*Christ will win in the end*' and the other '*The Rosary will strangle al Qaeda*'. In her essay McCredden discusses the shrine as a public demonstration of grief, anger, revenge, forgiveness and bewilderment, drawing attention to the connection between ritual and ideology in postmodern society.[4]

The objects not only describe the deceased to us but also communicate and visualise the pain of loss, the frustration, anger and sometimes the wish for revenge. Memory is coagulated and preserved in the attributes, writings and images that refer to moments, places, hobbies, professions and ideologies.

The memorial becomes a place for safekeeping.

In many cases the roadside memorials show a photograph of the deceased. This picture plays a crucial role: it makes the deceased a non-interchangable character and brings them back to life by showing us their face. Absence is reversed to presence.

Image. Roadside memorial with photographs of the deceased and his family and objects—South Australia 2008

---

[4] McCredden, Lyn, *Postmodern Rituals: Contemporary Australia Responds to Bali,* Antipodes, vol 17, American Association of Australian Literary Studies, Brooklyn, New York 2003.

Susan Sonntag writes:

A photograph is both a pseudo-presence and a token of absence.[5]

The private photograph becomes a public one. The photograph of the deceased person, who was still alive when it was taken, suggests their true existence. It lets us participate in their life, even if we can only grasp a fragment of it in the picture.

It is interesting to see that relatives often choose pictures that show the deceased person in a 'full of life' situation, often showing images that are taken years before the accident happened. The images idealise the deceased, as they show them as an active, happy person who had a long life in front of them, thus underlining the absurdity of death.

Photographs, objects such as toys, car and motorbike parts, are composed in such a way that they help to create the character of the deceased and preserve them for the living.

Image. Roadside memorial 'Budgie', with truck parts, mobile phone, walky-talkies—Victoria 2007

These objects do not only belong to the present but also describe a time that cannot be repeated. Together they build a force that works against the decay of memory. We do not question if the person really lived, because the selection of objects and images enable us to participate in both the deceased's life and also their death.

In his essay 'About the work on Memory / the search for the perfect moment' Barry King calls this a fetishised recording that seeks to overcome the loss. It also pictures the deceased as a hero.[6] We see this as well in commemorative plaques and stamps, souvenirs, medals and postcards of celebrities.

The location of the roadside memorial does not represent the reality exclusively for the relatives but also for the passengers of passing cars. The

[5] Sonntag, Susan, *On Photography*, Canada 1977, Penguin Books, p 16.

[6] King, Berry, *Uber die Arbeit des Erinnerns/Die Suche nach dem perfekten Moment,* (About the work on Memory / the search for the perfect moment), in Diskurs der Fotografie, Band II, Suhrkamp 2003, p. 174).

experience can be disturbing or stressful for drivers, especially if they knew the person whose memorial they pass. The place for memory becomes a warning memorial for drivers, a black spot. This is not surprising: the memorial is reminiscent of death. While the drivers are passing they are suddenly reminded of their own mortality or of someone else's painful loss. Their thinking space has unexpectedly been interrupted and invaded.

Image. Crash Markers—South Australia 2008

In Australia personal roadside memorials are being removed and replaced by black crosses for fatal accidents and red angled stripes for people seriously injured in traffic accidents. It is an attempt to standardise and functionalise the sign for death/accident. However it seems that this does not satisfy many who have experienced the death of someone close to them.

This attempt at standardisation seeks to take the individual expression and emotion out of the memorial. It makes the deceased person anonymous and reduces their death to a standardised warning sign for drivers. Thus people are now finding ways to personalise the crash markers. This might involve installing a roadside memorial close to the crash marker, decorating the marker itself or finding other ways to bypass the standardisation and subsequent stripping of emotion.

Regardless of any other adornments, the black cross on the crash marker is still reminiscent of death and can still be a disturbing reminder to those that pass it.

Image. Crash Markers—South Australia 2008

The significance of a photographic image in recording and memorising a person who had died was already important about 160 years ago in Australia.

Image. Found photograph of parents with their dead daughter, who has been staged as if she was alive, private collection Gene Bawden, Australia

Recently I saw a photograph showing a dead girl that had been staged as if she was alive for the photographer. A construction had been built to support the body of the teenaged girl and her eyes had been painted onto her eyelids to make her look alive and appear to be looking towards the viewer. Similar pictures can be found that show mothers and fathers with their dead babies. At first sight the images look like typical family shots in which case one would expect the parents to look happy holding the child. However, at closer inspection they look distressed. Only the parents' faces indicate that the child is not asleep but dead.

The mental image is directly linked to the physical image. Hans Belting claims that in his theory of perception Plato says about memory: the only perception that one can have of a human being, is through his physical appearance.[7]

These photographs were the only possible answer for keeping a picture of the person and memorising them. Not only did they testify that the parents had a child but the photograph was also the answer to a pure but imageless memory of their daughter. The photograph is here given the power to act instead of the deceased. The picture symbolises life, by showing us a dead girl as if she was alive. Death is denied and neglected.

In this context it is interesting to look at the French artist Christian Boltanski. In his oeuvre he tested both photographs and objects as a medium of collective memory.

In his series *The Dead Swiss* (Kemper Museum of Contemporary Art, Kansas City, 1990) and *The Reserve of the Dead Swiss* (Tate Gallery, London,

[7] Belting, Hans, *Bildanthropologie, Entwürfe fuer eine Bilderwelt,* Wilhelm Finck Verlag, Munich 2001, p. 175.

1990), Boltanski used photographs of anonymous dead people from obituary notices in Swiss newspapers. While the photographs do not show any personal traces, the scale of death suggested by the title and the repetitive presentation give us an overwhelming appearance of loss.[8]

In his installations and so-called artists books 'inventories', Boltanski uses objects such as cloths, furniture, kitchen wear and books that confront the viewer with the complete set of personal belongings of a household. The second-hand look of the objects takes them out of their neutral context. The human trace inscribed into the object captures and testifies to the reality of its owner.

Boltanski's images and installations do not communicate any specific detail of the people themselves but act as stimuli that activate the viewers' own personal history, thus questioning a collective experience of loss and absence. The roadside memorials and photographs of dead children already discussed work in the same way for outsiders, except for the families and friends, where they signify pain.

This underlines Roland Barthes' statement about the subjectivity of photography. In his book *La Chambre Claire*, he uses the example of a childhood photograph of his mother. Most viewers of the image will only reflect on fashion, history and the attractiveness of the portrayed, but for Barthes the image is personally hurtful.[9]

OBJECTS AND DESIRES

Apart from 'non-conformist' shrines helping to connect the living and dead, there are objects that function as a channel for desires and hopes.

In 1995 and 1996 I interviewed people in the French countryside (Dordogne) about their beliefs. The wish for marriage and children was addressed in various ways.

If I wanted to get married within the next year I was told that I needed to find a small chapel near Perigueux, a small town in the Dordogne. This chapel would host a Madonna. I was told that if I put a safety pin into her garment I would be getting married within the next 12 months. I searched for this small

[8] see also: Gumpert, Lynn, *Christian Boltanski, Lessons of Darkness*, Flammarion, Paris 1994, pp. 132–136.

[9] Barthes, Roland, *La Chambre Claire*, Paris 1980, p. 43.

chapel and found it. It looked dusty and in need of repair. It didn't look as if anybody had been in there for years, but when I stepped inside I immediately saw the small Madonna with a bright blue garment. It looked shiny and new and it was covered in safety pins.

Image. Small Madonna with blue garment—France 1996

In a neighbouring town a different ritual was advocated: one should take 3 metal pins and throw them into a nearby well. If two would settle on the bottom of the well forming a cross, then one would soon be married.

In Brantome (also in the Dordogne) women who wanted to become pregnant were supposed to move the huge door bolt of the local church forwards and backwards several times, this ensuring that they would soon become pregnant.

In Japan people write their wishes onto a piece of paper and tie it to a particular tree. The spirits, they say, live in the tree and take care of the wishes and make them come true.

Image. Wishes written on small pieces of paper, fixed to the tree—Japan 2004

The creation of a picture of a spirit or God is often quite flexible in regard to specificity as one deals with the invisible and not with something that has been confirmed in its appearance. Any possible clarity is excluded.

In Spain people use Ex-fotos to address their wishes. Ex-fotos are objects and images that are related to a specific person (like the roadside memorials). The objects usually describe a condition, such as an illness, pain or a desire of some sort. The object that embodies the wish can be hand crafted or mass produced and bought in a shop.

Image. Wax limbs fixed to the chapels ceiling—Spain 1995

Replica limbs of the human body are used to alleviate pain in the corresponding areas on the body. For example, if I have pain in my arm I will craft or buy a wax arm and deposit it in the chapel. Wax children can symbolise the wish for marriage and fertility or are used to heal/protect an ill child.

The object connects the person with the spiritual world and expresses an intention, for example to heal or to prevent danger, thus accepting that there is some danger that is real.

Again, the immaterial world is described with materials. The objects define the vocabulary that is used for communicating and connecting with the invisible world, thus making it accessible. Here no priest is necessary to act on behalf of the believer. The believer himself animates the object that communicates to the spiritual world. Unlike the 'used objects' in Christian Boltanski's installations most of the wax limbs are bought in a religious shop. They do not show any human trace but are human through their own shape. (We should remember here too the difference between a museum and a chapel)

Some objects may be repulsive and unhygienic such as blood stained clothes etc. As we know from roadside memorials these attributes inherit an incredible power of persuasion, bringing the mystical, wonderful and supernatural into existence. It is the power of stillness where stationary attributes become mediators between the visible and invisible world. They lead us to the world of the believer and let us participate in the act.

The location (church, chapel) is accepted and respected as the place of power, diversity and significance.

Image. Wax limbs fixed to the chapels ceiling, frames with texts and objects on the walls—Spain 1995

SACRIFICE AND GRATEFULNESS

Once the healing has taken place or the wish is fulfilled, the believer has to sacrifice something. This can be done in various ways.

Image. Woman's hair plat in a frame with text—South of Spain 1994

In the South of Spain I saw a frame that contained a hair plait. It was installed in a small chapel amongst other objects. A woman had cut her hair plait in order to thank the saints for a moment she had with her father. The text said: *'Por la conversion de mi padre a la hora de morir'* (signed: *M Jesus Garcia) (For the conversion of my father in the hour of his death.)*

In Spain people either produce their own sacrifice or buy something they sacrifice; alternatively they also donate money or light a candle etc.

In 1912 the French sociologist Emile Durkheim argued that all religions, whether simple or complex, tend to divide the world into two mutually opposite categories. Existing quite apart from the familiar and profane order of everyday life, the sacred represents a transcendent realm—the uncanny and magical as well as the sublime and rapturous—that can only be made accessible through a designated set of rites and rituals.[10]

In conclusion, the images I have taken throughout my journeys are witness to emotions that struggle to fit into a world that is dominated by science, technology, rational thinking and logic.

I feel that it is important to show that these sites, shrines and altars are places for contemplation, reflection and experience. Innovation, imagination and visual thinking bring these creations into existence. They are constructions of reality that withdraw themselves from any mass product.

Altars can adopt any form and change over time and with the needs of individuals and their societies in different cultures. Museums organise their objects around scientific or historical concepts. This order makes the collection accessible and understandable for the viewer, perhaps like a dictionary explains the meaning of words. We should understand objects in personal and temporary shrines in the same way.

Here people have found a way to break boundaries and voice their emotions in an active and creative way that can be seen and experienced outside the commonplace.

If we accept the museum as a place for cultural memory, we need to look at these religious installations as a medium for spiritual memory. They are aesthetic and autonomous constructions that visualise artistic principles. Their language speaks to us about what we are and how we deal with our inner world.

These are also the basic rules of art and the emotions that originate from art and through art.[11]

---

[10] Kaufmann, Suzanne, *Consuming Visions–Mass Culture and the Lourdes Shrine*, Cornell Univ. Press, Ithaca and London, 2005, p. 6.

[11] see: Martin, Jean Hubert; *Altäre*, in: *Altäre, Kunst zum Niederknien, (Altars, Art to kneel down for)*, Museum Kunst Palast Düsseldorf 2001 Hantje Catz, p. 8–15.

SPORTS LOVING AUSTRALIANS: A SACRED OBSESSION

Geoff Cheong

A NATION OBSESSED

The extraordinarily elevated place that sport holds in the Australian way of life is reflected in comments by two former Prime Ministers. Prime Minister John Howard (1996–2007) was known to speak of the most honoured position in Australia as that of captain of the Australian cricket team. Prime Minister Bob Hawke (1983–1991) colourfully declared that all employers should not hesitate to give their employees a holiday following *Australia II's* historic win in the 1983 Americas Cup regatta. One might well ask how such eminent leaders, generally so careful about every word or message they convey, could confidently express such opinions. The answer is simply found in understanding the depth of passion Australians have for their sport. It could be said that Australians regard sport as *sacred* to their way of life. If this statement seems to be an overstatement, then it is well worth asking, 'How many countries would have their most famous deceased racehorse displayed in the state museum?' Sport and culture are here seen to be intricately interwoven.

So significant is sport to Australians that an evaluation of their life without an understanding of their attitude towards sport would lead to an incomplete result. Australia's sporting prowess influences people's sense of well being. Success in any international sporting event is so important that it is greeted with great acclaim. To compound this mentality Melbournians lead the way by proclaiming their city as the 'sporting capital' of the world. Its iconic Melbourne Cricket Ground seats one hundred thousand people and, in addition to its own popular sports events, it has hosted many other international functions. In addition Melbourne treasures its status as the home of the Australian Tennis Open, its place as one of the hosts of the International

Formula One motor racing circuit and its annual Melbourne Cup horse race, now of international status and which has the reputation of being 'the race that stops the nation'. This obsessive devotion to sport reflects just how sacred sport is to Australians.

UNDERSTANDING THE SACRED

As Australians seek to make meaning out of their lives they regularly turn to sport as one of the essential components that contribute to their story. Each thread which shapes the great tapestry of its national identity is sacred to its people and sport is certainly one important thread.

The sacred has been understood to indicate *things of ultimate meaning and value.* Often such things go so far as to have a quality which surpasses the common, yet these sacred realities are the very things that expand and intensify the meaning of our daily existence.

In our postmodern era contemporary perceptions suggest that the thought of separation between the spiritual and the common is inaccurate. All things are interrelated. Nothing can be truly isolated or broken away from other things. Scholars such as Sri Aurobindo, Laszlo, Wilber, Gebser and Beck are a few of the leading minds to have elaborated upon this integral understanding of life. Their approach encourages us to respect all things as expressions of the sacred and recognise them as being means by which we can understand the sacred meaning of our lives. Ken Wilber builds his integral theory around a model which describes all experience under the categories of physical science, sociology, culture and psychology (Wilber, 2006, p. 18f). Each of these categories is integrated with the other. He proceeds to describe these categories as the manifestation of the three 'faces' of the spirit of God, the good, the true and the beautiful (Moore 2008, p. 161).

In searching for the sacred in Australia, then, it is natural to turn to sport for its contribution. I believe we can gain great insight into its sacredness to Australian people by reflecting upon it in conjunction with Australia's national history. Through this history we will see the intermingling of Ken Wilber's four categories of life, the physical, the sociological, the cultural and the psychological. Each of these categories plays a part in revealing the sacredness of Australia's story.

THE IMPACT OF AUSTRALIA'S EARLY HISTORY ON THE FIRST SETTLERS PSYCHE

To understand why sport has taken such a primary place in the Australian psyche we begin by reflecting upon both Australia's history and geography. While there are some records of sport or games played by indigenous Australians there is little evidence to suggest that such activity contributed to the present state of sport in Australia (Moore 2008, p. 283). Essentially it's preoccupation with sport is a characteristic of the European era of its history, which covers the relatively short period of just over two hundred years. Its European history began with its discovery in 1770 (Clark 1982, p. 14) and its settlement began in the following decades with the great southern island continent being used as a penal colony for the British in the 18th and early 19th centuries. This created a very harsh foundation for this latest era of its history. Convicts were expatriated for relatively minor offences to solve poor living conditions in England. This punishment by exile was harsh, yet it was imposed for even relatively small offences such as stealing bread. Sentences were passed as seven, fourteen or twenty-one years for crimes of increasing degrees of seriousness. Imprisonment was usually most unpleasant, and further punishment for troublesome prisoners often brutal. Thus disdain for authority grew amongst prisoners, while simultaneously support amongst fellow sufferers became commonplace. The relaxed, yet loyal camaraderie which now exists amongst fellow Australians—regularly referred to as *mateship*—is acknowledged as central to the Australian character and can possibly be traced back to its earliest white settlement years.

If the early events of its penal history were harsh, then when freedom did come there was a very harsh land waiting to be conquered. Theirs was a very physical way of life. Only those who embraced this extraordinary challenge with determination and a willingness to persist were the ones who could hope to survive. Thus from the beginning Australians learnt to be physical and determined, and loyal amongst their own as they faced their adversaries.

Geography made its own particular contribution. Ship travel from England to Australia might take three to five months without sight of land before travellers disembarked in what seemed to them to be the most distant land on the planet, a land which had been discovered only a few years before. Isolation was a primary characteristic of early settlement in Australia. Although it was possible for some, few dared dream of the chance to return to a homeland which had offered them little opportunity in the past. The early Australians had to learn to live in a land far from the rest of the world.

THREE EVENTS WHICH ENABLED AUSTRALIANS TO RECLAIM SOME PRIDE

Three events over the following century helped the new Australians to reclaim a relationship with their formerly known world. In each case it is reasonable to argue that the life conditions in the new land actually shaped the behavior of the Australians in these endeavours.

The first event was simply the opportunity to play cricket against their rivals, a team from England. From its earliest years the common pastime for the new colonial settlement was cricket, a popular sport played in the motherland. Not only did it provide a distraction from the harsh way of life but it provided an opportunity for a pleasant social forum. It was one real opportunity to reestablish some pride in relation to those who had treated them so badly either as convicts, or as inferior if they had come freely looking for new opportunities. The first English team to tour Australia was in 1861 (Headon 2001, 58). In 1863 George Pan led a side to tour Australia. In 1868 a touring team of Aborigines became the first team to visit England from overseas. In 1873 WG Grace led an English team to Australia. And in 1878 a team of white Australians toured England. The great heritage of Australian and English cricketing rivalry had begun. Far from being the inhabitants of a forgotten, neglected or isolated land, Australians became worthy competitors—and thus a competitive relationship was forged (Green 1988, p. 88).

The second event was not so much one event but rather two over several decades. Neither was it a sporting event—but nevertheless it called for physical attributes similar to those apparent in the Australian sporting psyche. It was Australia's willingness to enter the two World Wars. In both wars the Australians developed a substantial reputation for their abilities to fight, cope with the harsh conditions and display great loyalty. Most importantly Australia was very much involved in the events of the wider world and thus Australians regained their pride and sense of self respect. By the mid-twentieth century improved transportation made more realistic the possibility of regular travel between Australia and the wider world. Australians were ready to take their place on the world stage.

The third great event that stands significantly in the history of Australia's sporting development was the 1956 Olympic Games, held primarily at the

Melbourne Cricket Ground (Gordon 1994, p. 203). This surely was the symbolic statement which declared that Australia was part of the world community. These have been well remembered as the *friendly games* for this was the first time that the Games had concluded with the athletes entering the stadium for the final ceremony as one great mass of participants and not in national groupings. The Australian camaraderie had spilled over to all others whom it respected, whether friend or opponent. If this event became an iconic statement about Australia's standing in the world, it also consolidated the iconic standing that Australia's sporting heroes would hold within its own culture. The success in swimming and athletics of Australians, both men and women, proved beyond doubt that Australians could match the rest of the world. Cuthbert, Strickland, Jackson, Landy, Fraser, (Gordon 1994, p. 212) Crapp, Henricks and Rose became heroes in the minds of Australians (Atkinson 1999). They stand beside other great Australian sports people who had reached the pinnacle of international sport during these years. Within the tennis world Sedgeman, Hoad, Laver and Fraser amongst the men and Smith amongst the women—along with Thompson (Smith 1982) on the golf circuit—had become Australian heroes.

THE EMERGENCE OF SPORTING 'ICONS'

The emergence of such an array of Australian sports heroes inevitably created a measure against which other similarly successful sports people could be evaluated. Donald Bradman stood alone, and became immortalised in Australian history for his achievements (Headon 2001, p. 168) which far exceed those of any other cricketer from any other nation. Such was his exceptional status he became an icon of not only cricket, but even sport itself. Clearly he stands on the very pinnacle of Australia's sporting mountain. Strangely the second great sporting icon for Australians is the legendary race horse, Phar Lap (Headon 2001, p. 228). Racing in the time of the Great Depression he brought hope and success to a struggling and depressed people. The fact that following his untimely death he was mounted and displayed in the Melbourne museum indicates just how significantly he entered the hearts and minds of a people always eager to embrace their champions.

It is through these great figures of sporting achievement that we can reflect upon and gain an insight into the psyche of Australian sports lovers. For a people so wounded as convicts and isolated on this distant land these iconic sports heroes provided the necessary message to proclaim our value, worth and ability. The short European history had not provided deep enough foundations for broad excellence in other fields. The physically harsh way of life shared by all meant that Australia's iconic heroes would most likely emerge in the physically orientated world. The *mateship* prevalent across the nation meant that one person's success was shared and claimed by all. The identity of Australian's was being formed through its physicality and, most importantly, sport.

These icons have been elevated to such a level that, rising out of the struggle of Australia's history, they shine as beacons of inspiration and are so perceived as sacred. They are both inspirational for others to follow and symbolic of who we all are. The Australian culture was being strongly flavoured by its devotion to sport and its iconic heroes.

A TIME OF TRANSITION

It could be said that the 1956 Olympic Games formed a transitional signpost for Australian sporting history (Gordon 1994, p. 203). They took place at a time in Australia's history when sport was changing from being an amateur activity to a professional one. This transition was well assisted by the emergence of the country as a truly prosperous land providing all people with great opportunity to pursue the lifestyle of their dreams. Australia is sometimes referred to as the *Lucky Country*. To further develop an understanding of this latest era of Australian sporting history and see why it is so sacred to its people we need to consider several factors. Geography, wealth, expanding immigration, the variety of opportunities, the strength of both body and character necessary to survive—especially in the early days—attitude to work and recreation, all played some part in shaping this development over the second half of the twentieth century.

To begin our reflection upon Australia's extraordinary development we need to cast our mind back to 1856 when by legislation what was known as the '*eight hour day*' was implemented. Its advocates maintained that, of the twenty four hours of a day, eight hours should be allocated for work, eight hours for rest and eight hours for recreation. This was the first occasion on which such a pattern of time use was established anywhere across the world. It was a clear indication of the enormously high regard the Australian population held for the importance of recreation and sport in their lifestyle. It was this mentality that would ensure that 'when the time was right' for the massive growth in sport and recreation the opportunity could be grasped wholeheartedly. I believe that such a state of mind was well and truly entrenched in the Australian psyche by the middle of the twentieth century.

Australian geography, land, surrounding coastal waters and climate were all important conditions that made the country so conducive to many different types of sport and recreational activities. The climate is such that sport is played throughout the entire year. The abundance of land meant that there was never a shortage of facilities. It is also worth emphasising that the expansion of activities was aided by the influx of migrants from Europe following the World Wars and, toward the end of the century, from Asia and Africa. It would be difficult to compile a complete list outlining the variety of such activities that appeared in this country throughout this prosperous half century, but a sample of significantly supported sports include football, cricket, tennis, golf, squash, basketball, netball, lawn bowls, hockey, baseball, softball, surfing, life saving, water skiing, scuba diving, hiking, snow skiing, track and field athletics, archery and rifle shooting. A complete list would reveal that the number is enormous. There are opportunities for people of all ages, from the youngest to the most senior of citizens, from all levels of ability—including those with disabilities—to participate in some form of sporting activity.

The social dimension of sporting life stands central to many of these activities. Whether through churches in the middle of the twentieth century, suburban teams, country townships, or gatherings of people with common interest, sport provided a healthy activity for those who simply enjoyed being together with others. We can again note the importance of these groupings in consolidating a person's or group's identity.

It is well worth noting two fundamentally different motivational streams for why people are involved in sport. The first is the professional sports person. Extraordinary amounts of money are paid to the elite sportsperson, for it is now expected that s/he will pursue his/her goal on a full time basis. Following the poor performance of Australian athletes in the 1980 Olympic Games in Moscow the Government established its Australian Institute of Sport. Government has poured money into the training of its elite athletes in so many different areas of sport. Numerous other variations of such institutes were established to ensure that Australians can achieve the highest standards and status on the world stage. The best coaches are sought from across all countries. For different reasons, but equally important for the development of the professional, is the corporate sponsorship dollar. So highly are successful sports people regarded that to have a product endorsed by them is worth extraordinary amounts of money to business organisations. The Australian sporting world is clearly now a professional one. This is readily accepted by a large proportion of the population because sporting success is so important to the Australian identity. In fact it is unquestioningly expected.

The amount of money committed to its sport is an indication of just how deeply the nation embraces it. It is one of the very concrete ways in which Australians indicate the sacredness of sport to their way of life.

To gain a more comprehensive understanding of Australian sport it is necessary to recognise that the professional sport scene is really built upon the contributions of social, health and fitness-seeking citizens. Sport, to Australians, means both a healthy body and a healthy mind. People look forward to their eight hours per day of free time, their weekends and four weeks' annual holiday for the enjoyment of their favorite sport or recreational activity. It is the strength of this relaxed approach to one's recreational life style that undergirds the Australian's appreciation of his/her elite sports hero. During a recent discussion on Melbourne radio listeners were invited to telephone and discuss what their involvement in a sporting club meant to them. The many passionate replies were perhaps best summed up by one well known media commentator. He claimed that while achievement and other 'trimmings' were part of any club involvement, the central issue was *people.* People could be themselves and build long-term relationships. We are again reminded that sport, for Australians, stands at the heart of both their personal and social identities, and also motivates their pursuit of health and fitness. Such health and fitness are so treasured that they stand for life itself—a further declaration of the sacred.

The two extremes of approaches to sport, being on the one hand the professional, and on the other the volunteer, come together to illustrate the passionate nature of the Australian sporting mentality. The general populace is devoted as spectators to its most popular 'bread and butter' sports. Here I speak of its national cricket team in the summer and the football codes in the winter. From the latter decades of the nineteenth century these sports captured the hearts and minds of the local population. Week in and week out throughout the winter month's, massive crowds follow their favourite football teams and built countless rivalries. Voluntary support became compulsive devotion to their super heroes. Throughout the summer the less frequent occasions, but eagerly-awaited opportunities, to see the world elite cricketers battle it out captivates Australians. It is the place these two great sports hold in the hearts of the Australian sporting public that reveals the depth of the Australians' love of sport. The rhythms of time, from weekly patterns to the seasons of the year and special annual events shape people's calendar. Sport becomes deeply entrenched in the fabric of people's lives.

In recent years the extent of media coverage has grown to dominate their programming. The appetite of the Australian for sport coverage seems insatiable. It is worth noting that the sports radio station that recently went to air in Melbourne to provide twenty-four hour discussion of all sport has proved to be a great success. The popularity of *sports nights* with champion sports people providing the entertainment and the prolific availability of sports books indicate the extent to which sport consumes people's lives.

SOME LASTING DIVISIONS

The strength of interest in sport of its citizens has generally served to unite the people of Australia, yet it would be wrong to assume that this is a comprehensive evaluation. Throughout Australia's history sport has been a male-dominated activity. Restrictions have always limited the opportunities for women. While recent decades have seen significant changes to this great divide, generally women are not afforded the same adulation as men, even though female participation in sport is strong. Netball, basketball, tennis, track and field athletics, swimming, gymnastics and field hockey are examples of well-supported female sports activities. Participation by the young females of the country is as strong as that of young males. Women's National teams have reached pinnacles on the international stage similar to those reached by the men's teams, yet the financial remuneration offered to successful women athletes or women's sporting teams is a very small portion of that offered to men and their teams. Commercial television coverage is determined by the advertising dollar so that there is a significant lack of coverage of women's sport by the media.

As an increasingly developing multicultural country, sport in Australia is only on the fringes of providing unity amongst sports people from all its cultures. From the earliest years of its history the elite level of sport was dominated by white English or Australian-born and English-speaking men. Their more robust forms of football were seen as proof of physical superiority over European soccer. It took many years for this to change (Tatz 2000, 140–142). By the end of the twentieth century it was common for different codes of football to name 'Teams of the century'. In Australian Rules football, of the numerous teams named, versions of the Teams of the century consisting of players with Greek or Italian heritage were proudly named and honoured. Finally it was clearly being acknowledged that in Australia a sportsperson of any national background could display the level of excellence and mentality respected by all Australians. The multicultural nature of modern Australian society is increasingly being witnessed in the sports arena.

A multicultural example of particular importance concerns that of the indigenous Australian. The generally divided nature of white and black Australian society was grounded in a strongly prejudiced attitude. Such an attitude was, in fact, enshrined in law known as the White Australia Policy. Its roots go back to the middle of the 19th century with the general dislike of Asian people who had flocked to Australia for the gold rush period. Immigration was restricted from 1901 by law to white people. Gradually these restrictions were reduced until finally, in 1975, the passing of the *Racial Discrimination Act* by Parliament brought a legislative end to the prejudice. Attitudes to indigenous Australians were caught up in such a policy with voting rights really not granted to all adult Aborigines until 1965. During the 20th century the occasional Aborigine was able to succeed at the highest level of international sport. Evonne Goolagong in tennis (Goolagong 1975) and Lionel Rose in boxing are fondly remembered national sporting heroes. The most recent example is that of Cathy Freeman, who won a gold medal at the Sydney Olympic Games of 2000. Another area of significant development with regard to this cultural issue has been the involvement of Aboriginals in the uniquely Australian Rules brand of football. This is the sport which the Aboriginal community has most strongly embraced. Its free-flowing character, with multiple skills of both foot and hand, combined with speed and spontaneous and intuitive team work, captures most readily the freedom-loving nature of the Aboriginal. The elite teams of this football code have increasingly welcomed numbers of Aboriginals. They bring some envied qualities hard to find in people of other racial backgrounds. However, the increasingly high status accorded to successful Aboriginals in football should not blind us to the fact that much still remains to be accomplished in improving the place of indigenous Australians in society.

Sport continues to reflect the state of life across the entire breadth of Australian culture; racial relationships are still being worked out. But just as the nation at large addresses this issue so do the organisers of sport continue to work toward harmonious resolutions. The image of gold medalist Cathy Freeman lighting the Olympic flame remains an iconic symbol of the place of indigenous Australians as equal fellow sports people. Even further it focuses the Australian mind on the belief that all citizens of this country are equal. Its message is characteristic of the Australian bywords of *mateship* and *a fair go for all.* Such concepts born out of its earliest commitment to supporting one another in the harshness of the penal days declare very clearly ideals sacred to Australians.

Sport is not a utopian escape from life; rather for Australians it is a fundamental expression of life, where success and failure meet and where problem and solution are sought.

MONUMENTAL ICONS

Sport is a wonderful expression of the life of a people. It covers such a broad range of admirable human qualities: discipline, intuition, free spirit, skill, courage, to name a few. If certain humans so excel that they are elevated to 'iconic' status by the general populace, then the arenas within which they accomplish such feats become parts of the ongoing story of their accomplishments. Australia is blessed with thousands of miles of golden sand-rimmed coastline so conducive to surfing and swimming. Yet it is Bells Beach which has become its iconic location as the symbol of board surfing, or Bondi for bodysurfing. While other beaches may be preferred by many, Bells is the location for the Australian event of the annual world championship series, while Bondi is the 'iconic' location of the recreational sun-worshipping beach-lover. Both have become monuments to their sport or recreation because of the long history of their popularity. Numerous other sports have developed similar such physical monuments as symbols of their histories, yet the grandest of all such sporting locations is the famous Melbourne Cricket Ground (Dunstan 2000). Located in the heart of Melbourne, the self-proclaimed sporting capital of the world, devotees of this ground take pride in their belief that it is the benchmark for the 'world's best practices' for such venues. Known as the *people's* ground for its convenience to spectators who have witnessed over the years its unfolding story of epic sporting battles, it has a highly prized membership of one hundred thousand people, with another one hundred and seventy five thousand on the waiting list. The arena itself is regarded as sacred ground and is generally protected from any intruders other than participants. Within the massive grandstand structure the Long Room is fondly referred to as the 'Holy of Holies'. The 'G' as it is also affectionately known, is the pinnacle of the iconic sporting locations of the country. Such venues become highly regarded as sacred space.

Planning the future

As one looks to the future of the Australian nation, an evaluation of its sport will need to be part of the agenda. Sport will, no doubt, remain significant in contributing to the formation of the identity of Australians. The 'temples' of sports heroes, now referred to as 'halls of fame' will continue to occupy a prime place in the Australian story. Many of these heroes will be upheld as icons of accomplishment. They will continue to provide images to which young people will aspire to accomplish their own dreams. What will need to be kept in mind is the way the world is changing. The global nature of the modern human society means that greater knowledge of the plight of so many people in the Third World and other countries increases the responsibility which the fortunate few have toward all other humans. Just how much money should be directed toward accomplishing sporting dreams? With just how much money can individuals be rewarded? At what point does the sum become immoral? Are all stakeholders being equally valued? Money in itself is not the problem. It is the psyche of the people that influences the way people manage their lives. The pursuit of excellence by elite athletes can remain inspirational to all people simply seeking health and fitness. Sport can be sacred to a people without it becoming its God. Questions of balance will need to be addressed.

When sport holds such an elevated place in the life of the nation it has great opportunities to formulate policies and shape the attitudes of its citizens. It would be a great sadness if its only role is as an outlet or escape from the remainder of life. Clearly, in Australia it is much more than this. It is so deeply entrenched in the psyche of the people and the culture of the populace that it has become a sacred part of Australian life. Its central standing in society allows it to provide great opportunity for leadership. Already sport has provided a forum for addressing issues such as religious discrimination, racial prejudice, gambling, drugs and environmental concerns. It can continue to be a major player in addressing these and other issues as well as continuing to shape both the general health of its citizens and the social well-being of the nation as a whole.

If the 1956 Olympic Games mark a time of transition from an amateur to a professional approach to sport, then the global nature of the 21st century will mark another time of transition. Rather than being an arena solely for individual glory and reward it will be the era of greater social responsibility. The sacred messages of its sport will be redefined accordingly.

CONCLUSION

In my own case I recognise how two great stories have been instrumental in shaping my own life and search for the sacred. The two great stories are sport and religion. My family tree reveals a connection with HCA Harrison one of the leading sportsmen of his era and T Wills, joint founders of Australian Rules Football (Hibbins 1987). My own father was an elite baseball player of the 1930s, representing both Melbourne Cricket Club, baseball division, and Victoria. Following my own modest sporting career I have been a Member of the Melbourne Cricket Club for forty years. In addition to this sporting background I was also brought up in the Anglican Church of Australia. I was ordained as a Minister of the church in 1973. Our family ate, slept and breathed a life shaped by these two great stories.

Now as an Anglican priest of 35 years and a lifelong sports lover reflecting upon life in the 21st century I am mindful of the changes taking place not only in Australia but right across the world. Our 'global village' has confronted all with new perspectives, opportunities and responsibilities. The sacred stories that have bound people together and shaped the meaning and purpose of their lives have become far more interwoven in our multicultural societies. Many stories representing different traditions live side by side. In the Western world Christianity is not now as dominant as it was in the past; therefore its story is not as readily turned to or respected. The Administrators of the main sporting codes are regularly discussing whether the once sacred holy day of Good Friday should be preserved for religious purposes only. Asian traditions are entertained and embraced by increasing numbers. The rationally dominated scientific philosophies still abound, while the economic rationalists demand their say. This melting pot of philosophies shapes not only Australian society but societies across the world. A new era of history is emerging and an understanding of the sacred is being reassessed. Many of the great stories of each different philosophy will help shape new perspectives. Sport in Australia will continue to be considered as one contributor to the search for the sacred. Far from a philosophy of life, to Australians it is a vital component through which its life is both expressed and celebrated. It continues to be one expression of life through which Australians find meaning, value and a sense of belonging.

In this new integral era, the various stories that bring meaning to people's lives will intermingle and speak to one another. From a Christian perspective Australian sport could be said to carry the marks of the great Crucifixion/Resurrection story. White Australian history began with death to England and its ways, and the pain and suffering of rejection. Today Australians regularly celebrate their sport as an expression of their triumph in life. Relatively small in number, nothing deters them from ever tackling the Goliaths of international sport. They continue to count each and every victory as an affirmation of their own valued identity. Their sporting life is one of their declarations of resurrection. Just as this example illustrates how the stories of two traditions can come together we are entering an era of history where this will happen even more so. An integral perspective cannot separate one great story from the other. Each story contributes at least something to the whole. Sport is one way of viewing Australian life. If it sees itself as separate from the rest of life, it becomes an obsession. If it is seen as integral to all life then it shares in the sacredness of life.

WORKS CITED

Atkinson, Graeme. *100 Great Australian Olympians.* Noble Park: The Five Mile Press, 1999.

Clark, Manning. *A Short History of Australia.* South Melbourne and Crows Nest: The Macmillan Company of Australia Pty Ltd, 1982.

Dunstan, Keith. *The Peoples Ground. The MCG.* Kew, Melbourne: Arcadia/Australian Scholarly Publishing Pty Ltd, 2000.

Goolagong, Evonne & Bud Collins. *Evonne.* London: Hart Davis MacGibbon, 1975

Gordon, Harry. *Australia and the Olympic Games.* St Lucia: University of Queensland Press, 1994.

Green, Benny. *A History of Cricket.* London: Barrie and Jenkins, 1988.

Headon, David. *The Best Ever Australia Sports Writing A 200 Year Collection.* Melbourne: Black Inc., 2001.

Hibbins, Anne & Gillian Mancini. *Running with the Ball.* Melbourne: Lynedoch Publications, 1987.

Moore, Greg de. *Tom Wills His Spectacular Rise and Fall.* Crows Nest : Allen and Unwin, 2008.

Smith, Terry. *Australian Golf The First 100 Years.* Sydney: Lester - Trownsend Publishing, 1982.

Tatz, Douglas & Colin Booth. *One - Eyed A View of Australian Sport.* St. Leonards, NSW: Allen and Unwin, 2000.

Wilber, Ken. *Integral Spirituality.* Boston: Integral Books, An imprint of Shambhala Publications inc., 2006.

BIBLIOGRAPHY

Armstrong, Peter & Geoff Thompson. *Phar Lap.* Crows Nest: Allen and Unwin, 2005

Australian Sports Almanac. Hardie Grant Books, Annual Series.

FitzSimons, Peter. *Everyone but Phar Lap. Face to Face with the best of Australian Sport.* Sydney: Harper Collins, 1997.

Kirkwood, Lyn & Rhett Kirkwood. *The Phar Lap Collection.* Melbourne: BAS Publishing and Glen Iris: Equus Marketing, 2005.

Metzler, Paul. *Great Players of Australian Tennis.* Artarmon: Harper Row, 1979.

Page, Michael. *Bradman. The Illustrated Biography.* South Melbourne and Crows Nest: The Macmillan Company of Australia Pty Ltd., 1983.

Perry, Roland. *The Don, A Biography.* Sydney: MacMillan, 2001.

Quist, Jack & Adrian Egan. *Tennis the Greats 1920–1960.* Sydney: ABC Enterprises and William Collins, 1984.

Rosenwater, Irving. *Sir Donald Bradman, A Biography.* London: BT Batsford Ltd, 1978.

Wilber, Ken. *Eye to Eye. The Quest for the New Paradigm.* Boston, Shambhala Publications Inc., 2001.

Wilber, Ken. *Sex, Ecology, Spirituality.* Boston, Shambhala Publications Inc., 1995.

Womack, Mari. *Sport as Symbol.* Jefferson, North Carolina: McFarland and Company Inc. Publishers, 2003.

ONTOPOETICS IN AUSTRALIA[1]

Freya Mathews

PRELUDE

For many years I taught feminism in addition to ecological philosophy. There was one figure who towered above the other feminist theorists. This was Simone de Beauvoir. The existentialism of *The Second Sex* was a philosophical vehicle more profound, I felt, than any other available to feminists. However, although it was compelling in its profundity and its sheer intellectual force, de Beauvoir's philosophical vision was not, to my mind, particularly sympathetic. I would even go so far as to say I found it chilling. It was a vision pervaded by the ideal of 'transcendence'. De Beauvoir's intense scorn for the merely given, for the encumbrances of materiality, for the apparently mindless repetitiveness of nature, provided the energy which fuelled her call to women to shake off the coils of immanence and join men in their ascent into the realm of the possible, the freely chosen, the as-yet-undetermined. Such transcendence was, from her point of view, the very *telos* of human subjectivity, the condition for the realisation of the sovereignty of the human self.

It struck me, whenever I re-travelled this familiar philosophical road in the course of my teaching, that such a fantasy of human supremacism could only have originated in that crucible of urban modernity, Europe, where nature has been thoroughly and finally routed by civilisation. (It is especially inevitable that it should have originated in Paris, the world—if not the galactic—capital of human narcissism!) Such a view could never, I mused, have emanated from Australia. Here in Australia, 'nature' is still bigger than 'culture', and on a

[1] An earlier version of part of this paper appeared under the title, 'An Invitation to Ontopoetics: the Poetic Structure of Being' *Australian Humanities Review* 43, 2007; several passages are also adapted from my Introduction to a Special Issue on Australian Perspectives of the journal, *Worldviews: Environment Culture Religion* 3, 2, 1999. Thanks to the publishers for permission to reproduce this material.

subconscious level we Australians accordingly have no choice but to defer to it, however reluctantly. A settler society, like ours, set down arbitrarily in country bigger than itself, under the mute but appraising gaze of an indigenous people who did not share Western fantasies of transcendence, could never have become as deeply and unselfconsciously anthropocentric as the society which expressed itself through de Beauvoir's Existentialism. This is not to say that Australian culture is not anthropocentric, nor that settler society has not imprinted itself everywhere and in every way on the face of this continent, but only that we have not yet succeeded in dwarfing the huge expansiveness of our country; here we have not yet walled in the sky and thoroughly domesticated the land, as has occurred in western Europe.

Our anthropocentrism is accordingly ambivalent. Loud and brash as our national persona is, insistently masculinist as our posturings to the wider world are, there is a vulnerable underside to this culture, an introspective and self-doubting subconscious that is manifest in our habit of understatement, self-deprecation, irony and reticence. We are split between 'transcendence', a conscious commitment to modernity, to the certainties of our European heritage, on the one hand, and a subconscious surrender to the authority of a landscape that patently exceeds us, on the other.

Although this split between an attitude of bravado-and-dominance and one of tristesse-and-surrender creates a certain unease in the settler psyche, the undercurrent of surrender works to defuse the characteristic anxieties of modernity, giving rise to that distinctively Australian equanimity expressed in the signature sayings, 'no worries' and 'she'll be right, mate'. 'She'll be right, mate' represents a tacit relinquishment of control that is even faintly Daoist in flavour—and one that would have appalled de Beauvoir.

In light of this ambivalence between culture and nature, transcendence and immanence, control and surrender, it is not surprising that, in addition to the chest-beating, more-reductionist-than-thou masculinism of its post-war philosophy[2], Australia should also have thrown up some of the earliest critiques of anthropocentrism or human supremacism.[3] It was such critiques that marked the beginnings of the current international wave of radical

[2] See, for instance Val Plumwood, 'The Struggle for Environmental Philosophy in Australia', *Worldviews: Environment Culture Religion* 3, 2, 1999, pp. 157–176.

[3] See Richard and Val Routley, 'Human Chauvinism and Environmental Ethics' in Don Mannison, Michael McRobbie and Richard Routley (eds), *Environmental Philosophy*, Australian National University, Canberra, 1982.

ecophilosophy. Positioned as it was on the very periphery of Western civilisation, with an environment that refused to be 'transcended', Australia, like Norway, the other major cradle of ecological philosophy, was an inevitable site for the re-valorisation of nature.

Indeed, as the most ancient of continents, immersed since time immemorial in a distinctive meditative entrancement, known as the Dreaming, Australia seems to many to this day still to be pervaded by a spirit of wholeness which the hierarchies of civilisation have fractured and divided in other parts of the globe. With its spare soils unstained till historically recent times by large-scale war or predation, this country emanates a deep sense of peace that has largely disappeared elsewhere. Still in the grip of a preoccupation of its own, it communicates a presence so powerful it is palpable even in city blocks. Add to this the fact that the terrain is richly inscribed by one of the oldest, most spiritually-minded yet at the same time most thoroughly earthed of peoples—a people uniquely resistant both to the blandishments and to the shackles of the modern cultures of materialism—and it is perhaps not too much to hope that Australia might, to the extent that it can free itself from the blinkers of colonialism, have a special role to play in the current world-wide renegotiation of the human relationship with nature.

In this paper I would like to explore this prospective role by considering not only the influence of Europeans and indigenous Australians but also the influence of another party who was a major player in the early scenario of settlement: that of the Chinese. All three of these influences have been powerfully active in the Australian subconscious since the beginnings of colonialism. I propose merely to play with these influences here, intuitively and hermeneutically, rather than seeking to track them in a strictly analytical and historical manner. My aim is to see whether a distinctively Australian experience of nature takes shape through this lens of their intermingling.

A STORY

I would like to start with a story that perhaps provides an instance of such a distinctively Australian experience of 'nature'. The story is of an event that occurred some years ago in outback Central Australia at an old cattle station named Hamilton Downs about 80 km to the northwest of Alice Springs. The event was a gathering, one in a series of 'sense of place' colloquia that were held in various interesting venues over a number of years. The principal organiser and animateur that year was Craig San Roque, a Jungian analyst then resident in Alice Springs. Described as a 'coming into country', the gathering was intended to introduce the Hamilton Downs country to various scholars and academics interested in the idea of place. Participants had written and circulated their papers on place beforehand, so there was no need for formal presentations at the event. This left people in a prepared and receptive state of mind but free to engage with one another and with the place itself.

The site was utterly beautiful. There was an old stone homestead set way out in the rangelands, with a windmill at the gate, a palm tree, a dry riverbed lined with large rocks and ancient white gums. The house looked over the riverbed to a range of arid pink cliffs in the distance.

The event was to last five days, and Craig San Roque had invited many local identities—artists and musicians and environmentalists, and, most importantly, Aboriginal custodians—to be with us for the first couple of days.

Those first few days were spent basically just milling around, with talking circles, dream circles, walks into country, an excursion to a numinous local site called Fish Hole. Stories were told: these included Dreaming stories for that country, offered by one of the indigenous custodians, and a walking tour of the area's ecology led by a local ethnobotanist, who spoke intimately of each plant he pointed out, as if it had a personal story to tell. Amidst all this creative ferment, people bonded, wondered what they were doing there, felt disoriented, argued, sorted themselves out, and gradually woke up to the huge and majestic presence of country all around them.

It wasn't until the second last day that the real work of the colloquium was ready to begin. We broke up into separate male and female groups and each group spent the day working out a 'story of place' that expressed their own responses, and their address, to this shimmering country. In the evening the two groups came together in a series of explosive performances in the dry riverbed by the light of a monumental bonfire.

Overall, what was most astonishing, to my mind, about this colloquium was that it seemed to unfold via a logic of synchronicities. A set of initial conditions had been put in place to provide the framework or container for the event, but the event was, within that container, largely self-determining. What happened at one moment suggested what should happen at the next, and the structure of the entire event was highly recursive: each happening or offering fed back into, and inflected, everything else that was happening. On account of this extreme open-ness, skilfully preserved by Craig as animateur, there was plenty of opportunity—plenty of gaps in the 'script'—for serendipity.

The upshot was that a complex and elaborate poetic invocation took shape organically in the course of the five days, and this seemed to elicit a complex and elaborate poetic response from the world. Many of the participants found themselves called into, or caught up in, incidents or circumstances that symbolically played out central themes of their lives, or challenged them to take steps they had not till then been able to take. Different individuals, acting independently, found their activities meshing to form poetic scenarios or narratives that they could not have imagined, yet which were perfectly apposite for the circumstances. Each time we came to a gap in the proceedings, it was as if the land, or the world, stepped in, and offered poetic comments or denouements that exceeded anything we could have devised. There was a breathtaking display of lightning, for instance, just at a particular 'flat spot' in the women's final performance of place; multitudes of actual frogs gathered on the slope leading down to the river bed just after the men had performed a frog dance; crucial conversations were punctuated, at just the right moments, with expressive bird calls; three participants who had become lost temporarily at Fish Hole were about to sit on a strange rock when a loud report mysteriously emanated from it; indeed, seat-shaped rocks seemed to offer themselves in the riverbed whenever one turned, tired, looking for a place to rest …

The response of this country to our call consisted of different but cross-referenced responses to different individuals, together with common responses for the collective. It felt like a coming alive of the world, a flow of configurations of circumstances along axes of meaning.

At the end of the event one was left wondering how to make sense of it. The logic of its unfolding was so different from the tenor of everyday life—in modern societies, at any rate—in which events occur as a result of human intentions intersecting with causal conditions, but without any kind of internal thread of meaning supplied by the world itself. How then to explain this inner thread of meaning that was so much in evidence at Hamilton Downs, this responsiveness of the world to our call?

MAKING SENSE OF THE STORY

In my own mind at the time, the experience presented itself as one of Dao, an experience of the ceaseless flow of energy into meaningful but ever-unfolding patterns: 'it felt to me as if one were riding something alive out there, a dragon, a great serpent, a current of energy. It would not necessarily carry one to where one wanted to go, but with a little steering, a little reining in, it would keep one moving, in process, evolving. To my mind it was the Dao. Out in that archaic world, the Dao was a bucking, plunging presence, wild but trustworthy, as real as a desert river in full flood…'[4]

Daoism had long been seeping into my consciousness as a philosophical perspective that was very helpful in articulating the way I had experienced the Australian landscape since childhood. How it first entered my consciousness I have no idea. It simply seemed, when I did discover it, to provide a perfect fit with my experience, which perhaps suggests that it had been an active, if subconscious, influence in the culture that had shaped my thinking. But we might wonder how useful really can Daoism be as a point of entry into the mystery that a Hamilton-Downs-like event represents for modern sensibilities. How tenable, we might ask, are the terms of Daoism today?

We know that the world in which the first texts of Daoism were written down—by Laozi and Zhuangzi—was a world of magic. We know too that this magic was largely a matter of superstition, of magicians or sorcerers or Daoist practitioners importuning the supernatural on behalf of themselves or their clients, seeking to manipulate reality by means of symbolic instruments. Most people today no longer take this aspect of Daoism seriously. With the vast apparatus of modern science now at our disposal, we have no need of instrumental magic, and even less belief in it.

But although this old world—this world of enchantment—was undoubtedly in part a figment of superstitious imagination, it may not have been entirely so. Daoism identified a movement in things, a directedness in their unfolding. The elements of nature (the 'Ten Thousand Things') are really, according to Laozi and Zhuangzi, patterns in an underlying flow. These patterns form and re-form under the influence of the patterns forming and re-forming around them. This is, in other words, an order of mutual arising, a symbiosis in which no particular form or pattern can emerge independently of

---

[4] The event at Hamilton Downs has been discussed in Craig San Roque and John Cameron, 'Coming into Country: Catalyzing the Process of Social Ecology', *PAN Philosophy Activism Nature* 2, 2002. I also included a chapter on Hamilton Downs in my book, *Reinhabiting Reality: towards a Recovery of Culture*, University of NSW Press, Sydney, 2005. The reflections I offer there however are very different from those I am about to offer here, though Daoism is a strong influence in the book, as it is—more explicitly—here.

the forms or patterns resolving and dissolving all around it. Moreover, when the Ten Thousand Things are left to arise spontaneously in this way, under the mutual influences of one another, the universe assumes *its* own proper pattern or form—it follows *its* proper course.

This movement in things, or directedness in their unfolding, was presumably not merely imaginary, because Daoist practitioners who had received appropriate training—through various Daoist arts—could reliably detect it and adapt their activity to it. But nor was this movement in things, this directedness, merely the working of the laws of physics. Yes, it was a kind of energy (*qi*, in Chinese), but this was not the energy of $E=mc^2$. There were external indicators of it—pulses in the human body, for instance, and 'dragon veins' (detectable pathways of energy flow) in the landscape.[5] But it was not a purely external energy.[6] This was because it emanated from a cosmology that did not distinguish, in an absolute way, between an internal and external aspect of things. According to this cosmology, reality was irreducibly psychophysical in character, a forever changing and unfolding pattern of movement that was as much psychic as physical. The external appearances could be described by physics, but the psychic interiority was the province of Dao.

What was it then to experience the world under this interior, psychic aspect? The classical Daoist texts are of course not explicit about this. But I would try to spell out the kind of experiences to which these texts are (rather cryptically) alluding as follows: if one somehow managed to slip under the psychic skin of the world, and 'enter' its subjectivity, one would experience the 'outside' as 'inside'. If one stepped inside the world, in this sense, the trees and grass and rivers would no longer appear as external to oneself. They—along with oneself—would now be experienced as internal to the psyche of the world. One would be experiencing them, and oneself, from inside the world, rather than from outside it, from whence they appear as an object-manifold. As soon as one slips under the subject-object membrane in this way, one feels the

[5] See Stephen L Field, 'In Search of Dragons: the Folk Ecology of Fengshui' in NJGirardot, James Miller, Liu Xiaogan (eds), *Daoism and Ecology: Ways within a Cosmic Landscape*, Harvard divinity School, distributed by Harvard University Press, Cambridge MA, 2001, pp. 185–200.

[6] Wing-Tsit Chan defines *ch'i* as 'material force', meaning both energy and matter, but also as psychophysical power, associated with blood and breath. As such it is translated as 'vital force' or 'vital power'. See Wing-Tsit Chan, *A Sourcebook in Chinese Philosophy*, Princeton University Press, Princeton NJ, 11963, p. 784.

psychic streaming with which things, as emanations of psychic process, are charged. One feels the directed energy of psychic arising that belongs to all psychic process. Viewed from within the subjectivity of the world, the Ten Thousand Things are charged with this psychic streaming. But when they are viewed from the outside in the normal way, as objects, this psychic streaming is non-manifest.

This streaming that animates things when they are viewed under the world's psychic aspect might correspond, I want to suggest, to the directed movement in things that Laozi and Zhuangzi called Dao. Once one slips inside the world and begins to experience things from within its psychic interior, one can be drawn into this interior. One has only to surrender one's subject/object mind-set—where this encompasses all discursive thinking—and relinquish one's discursive goals and ends, in order to be borne along on its fast current. When this occurs, a path begins to open up in the midst of the phenomena. Although the phenomena, under their external aspect, are, as I've said, describable by physics, the path that opens up when the phenomena are perceived under their internal aspect is not plotted by the laws of physics. It is plotted by this inner principle of psychic process. Being psychic, this process is not only energic but essentially imbued with *meaning*. The path, in fact, is plotted by meaning. That is to say, the path that opens for me amongst the phenomena is a path appointed by meaning, meaning which is uniquely apposite for me; it is a meaning uniquely referenced to the key significances of my own life.

If the world is indeed a psychophysical reality, and if things, viewed from within its psychic dimension, are indeed charged with a psychic streaming, then we would expect to find intimations of this inner aspect of things in a range of traditions—not only Daoism. We would expect that Daoism would be only one of various possible points of entry into the mystery of events like Hamilton Downs. In particular we might expect that Aboriginal thought in Australia might shed light on such events. And this is indeed the case. I have found in an Australian Aboriginal context another account of the kind of 'path' phenomenon that I have just described. This account emanates from the Kimberley region, and revolves around the notion of *liyan* or *le-an*, the inner spirit of both persons and land. Karajarri spokesman, Mervyn Mulardy Jnr, speaks of elders looking at people and feeling them not from the outside but from the inside. He speaks of *liyan* as the spirit or feeling within a person that connects them to the inside of country. 'They [the elders] look and feel you from the inside, what they want that person to become. So, basically trying to get their *liyan* [feeling, spirit] back to what they bin brought up, what they liyan bin bring them, and their spiritual connection to the country.'[7] Frans Hoogland, a Dutch-born initiate into Aboriginal Law from the Kimberley, provides a vivid account of the actual experience of *le-an*. (Hoogland has lived for decades amongst Aboriginal families to the north of Broome, and is a trusted Law man in the region.) The experience that he describes as *le-an* is, I want to suggest, exactly what we might expect from a psychophysical reality once we have ceased perceiving it from the outside, under its object aspect, and have begun to experience it from the inside, under its subjectival aspect. I shall quote Hoogland's account at some length here because it provides a precise and detailed phenomenology of the experience.

> 'In order to experience [this feeling], we have to walk the land. At a certain time for everybody, the land will take over. The land will take that person. You think you're following something, but the land is actually pulling you. When the land start pulling you, you're not even aware you're walking—you're off, you're gone. When you experience this, it's like a shift in your reality. You start seeing things you never seen before … all of a sudden [the training process you have acquired through your upbringing] doesn't fit anything. Then something comes out of the land, guides you. It can be a tree, a rock, a face in the sand, or a bird.
>
> 'You might follow the eagle flying, and the eagle might go somewhere. Through the eagle you can see the red cliffs. Then another thing might grab your attention, and before you know it there's a path created that is connected to you. It belongs to you, and that is the way you start to communicate with the land, through your path experiences. And that path brings you right back to yourself. You become very aware about yourself. You start to tune finer and finer. Then you become aware that when you're walking the path, it's coming out of you—you are connected to it …'[8]

---

[7] Monique La Fontaine (compiler), *New Legend, a Story of Law and Culture and the Fight for Self-Determination in the Kimberley*, published by Kimberley Aboriginal Law and Culture Centre, 2006, p. 175.
[8] Frans Hoogland in Jim Sinatra and Phin Murphy, *Listen to the People, Listen to the Land*, Melbourne University Press, Melbourne, 1999, p. 19.

Hoogland goes on to explain that although the responsiveness of country is ever-present, those of us who have stepped straight out of the materialist context of modern civilisation can't feel it or see it. We bring all the clutter of our possessions with us into country, and what we see around us is mediated by the meanings of these, and all our other, internalised, possessions. So we pass through the landscape not noticing, not feeling, caught up in our own thoughts rather than being open to the intricately activated presence around us. However, as we begin truly to *walk the land*, becoming more fully present to it, a shift in mind occurs, a shift in mind that drops down to a feeling. When this shift does occur,

> 'we wake up to feeling, what we call *le-an* here, and we become more alive, we start feeling, we become more sensitive. You start to read the country. Then all of a sudden there's an opening down there. Before there was only a wall, but now that tree has meaning, now that rock has meaning and all of a sudden that thing takes you. You just follow. Then you wake up, and you see a lot of things and the country starts living for you. Everything is based on that feeling *le-an*, seeing through that feeling.'[9]

Hoogland proceeds to offer an illustration of *le-an*. He tells a story of waking up in his camp one morning near the sea at Coconut Wells and being aware of the feeling and, without even waiting for his usual cup of tea, taking off. Without knowing why, he heads straight for the reef. The reef cuts his bare feet but he walks right out onto it. There he finds a large turtle wedged in a rock pool, unable to regain the sea. The turtle is unafraid of him and seems to be summoning him. Hoogland struggles to help the turtle out of the pool and eventually, after much flailing and heaving, succeeds. Before it swims away, the turtle lifts its head out of the water and turns to look at him one last time. Then it's gone. Seemingly in a single step, the pain in his feet vanished, Frans finds himself back in his camp, having a cup of tea. And that, as he says, is *le-an*.[10]

Le-an, as Hoogland describes it, is the experience of being called by world into world, but into world as we have never experienced it before, because we have been viewing it from the outside, as a manifold of objects. To experience

[9] Ibid.
[10] Ibid p. 21–22.

the world from within, as Frans explains, is to experience it as a field of communicative meaning, meaning that draws us from one encounter to another. This seems to match the 'world hidden within the world', that Zhuangzi cryptically indicates:

> 'A boat may be hidden in a creek, or in a bog, safe enough. But at midnight a strong man may come and carry away the boat on his back. The dull of vision do not perceive that however you conceal things, small ones in larger ones, there will always be a chance of losing them. But if you conceal the whole universe in the whole universe, there will be no place left wherein it may be lost.'[11]

The only thing of true worth, Zhuangzi seems to be saying—the only thing worth trying to hold onto—is the world itself, under its 'hidden' aspect, which is to say, its inner aspect, the psychic aspect of our psychophysical universe. This is the only thing of true worth because it is the thing that brings us to life, that ushers us into a state of numinous streaming and meaning. And this is a thing that, once found, cannot be lost. It is there under everyone's nose, but no-one can take it from me once I have found it, because this 'hidden' world, as revealed to me or my community, belongs exclusively to us and can't belong to anyone else: its meaning is referenced to meanings that are uniquely salient to us. In other words, to find the world hidden within the world is to experience an opening of the ordinary world into poetic significance.

Dao then, from this point of view, emanates from the unmanifest dimension of the ordinary, manifest world. It is not an occult force, like forces posited in sorcery, that exist in addition to the forces posited by physics, and that are, like them, discovered from the outside. Rather, Dao indicates a way that opens up within the landscape,[12] like the famous portals that opened up, for Daoist initiates and immortals, into the interior of the sacred mountains.[13] In Daoist lore, according to initiate Kristofer Schipper, mountains harboured

[11] Herbert A Giles 1889 translation Ch 6, par 6, available online.

[12] The centrality of this image of ways opening up in the midst of the appearances is evident in the very title of NJ Girardot, James Miller, Liu Xiaogan (eds), *Daoism and Ecology: Ways Within a Cosmic Landscape*.

[13] See, for instance, Kristofer Schipper, *Taoist Body*, translated by Karen Duval, University of California Press, Berkeley, 1993.

vast inner labyrinths, residences for gods and spirits. There were times, known as 'Hidden Periods', when a given mountain was open or closed. Without knowledge of these Hidden Periods, an adept would not be able to overcome the resistance of the mountain and this inner world would remain closed to him forever. With knowledge of the Hidden Periods however, the adept would be able to find the 'opening' in the mountain's shield, slip inside, and be totally absorbed into the landscape.[14] Although the portals and pathways indicated in Daoism are revealed through ritual protocols, they might nevertheless be understood in terms of *le-an*, as a kind of opening into the psychic interiority of world. When such paths open—which is to say, as Frans puts it, when the path starts to come out of oneself—one must follow it unquestioningly, even hurrying to do so, lest it should close up again.

What I am suggesting then is that experiences such as those that occurred to many of us at Hamilton Downs—experiences of the world's poetic responsiveness—make sense if the world is viewed not merely as a physical manifold but as a psychophysical reality.

I have tried elsewhere to make sense, in Western rather than Daoist or Aboriginal terms, of the idea of reality as fundamentally psychophysical rather than purely physical in nature. In my book, *For Love of Matter,* I seek to show how reality can be psychoactive, and in that sense potentially communicative and responsive to us, while also conforming externally to the laws of physics.[15] I call such a view of reality 'panpsychist': 'pan' meaning everything, 'psyche' meaning soul or subjectivity or mentality. 'Panpsychism' is an old philosophical term denoting the view that there is a psychic or mentalistic dimension to everything; that mentality—whether in the form of spirit, subjectivity, soul, purpose, agency, conativity or intentionality—is as primitive an aspect of reality as materiality is. Although panpsychism has been very much a minority tradition in the history of Western philosophy, serious accounts of it have been advanced from time to time.[16] My own variant of this

[14] Kristofer Schipper, *Taoist Body,* translated by Karen Duval, University of California Press, Berkeley, 1993, p 173.

[15] *For Love of Matter: a Contemporary Panpsychism,* SUNY Press, Albany NY, 2003.

[16] Exponents of panpsychism in the Western tradition have included Spinoza; some of the Romantics, especially Schelling and to some extent Goethe; the process philosophers, most notably Whitehead; and a variety of contemporaries, such as Timothy Sprigge, Christian de Quincey, and David Skrbina. A number of recent ecophilosophers and ecocosmologists assume viewpoints that might be described as panpsychist, insofar as they attribute agency or intentionality to inorganic

venerable view represents the manifest world, as described by physics, as the outward appearance of an inner field of 'subjectivity', in an expanded sense of subjectivity. Reality is, from this point of view, both a unity and a manifold of differentia, a One and a Many. Viewed from within, it is a field of subjectivity, with a conativity (that is to say, a will to realise itself and increase its own existence) of its own and a capacity for communication. From the viewpoint of its finite modes, or those of them that are capable of acting as observers, it is an order of extension, as represented by physics. As a locus of subjectivity and conativity in its own right, the universe is capable of and actively seeks communicative engagement with its finite modes, the Many, or, again, with those of them that are capable of such engagement. Wherever this communicative engagement is actualised, it is manifest in a *poetic* order—an order of poetic revelation—that unfolds alongside the *causal* order. This poetic order, or order of meaning, exceeds the causal order but in no way contradicts it.

But, we might ask, what activates the poetic order? How can one slip under the skin of the world into that streaming that opens up in the midst of the phenomena and carries one from one poetic conjunction of circumstances to another? There are no doubt various techniques and strategies for entering this state, including Daoist arts such as feng shui, tai chi, calligraphy and ritual dances that induce a suspension of discursive thought and an alignment with the flow of energic streaming; sometimes this shift might even occur spontaneously, or as a result of spontaneous lapses into dreamlike or meditative states. But judging from the experience at Hamilton Downs, and other experiences of a kind that would be familiar to many of us, it seems that the poetic order may also be fairly reliably activated by *invocation*, particularly invocation in narrative form. That is to say, the poetic order seems able to be activated by *story*, told, or better still enacted, with invocational intent. Perhaps this is what happened at Hamilton Downs: out of the stories that were told in the early phases of the event, by indigenous custodians and colloquium

elements of the natural environment, but since they rarely claim the label 'panpsychist', and since they often eschew metaphysical theorising in principle, it would take me too far afield to try to sort the panpsychists from the non-panpsychists here. In any case, few of these thinkers take up the idea that reality is not only, so to speak, sentient, but also communicative in the sense indicated here. In other words, few propose that a poetic order is actively constituted through our engagement with the world.

participants alike, a rich narrative context was created. This then provided the poetic terms of reference for the world's own poetic interjections.

Narrative invocations such as these may be one-off affairs, as at Hamilton Downs. But they might also perhaps be systematically integrated into the daily praxis of an entire community, with the result that members of that community slip routinely between awareness of the world under its external, uncommunicative aspect and awareness of it under its interior, communicative, poetic aspect. In such communities awareness of the world under its poetic aspect might direct individual action and collective affairs as routinely as practical thinking does. Invocational and practical thinking might be so seamlessly intermeshed that there is no tension or contradiction between them. This is the sort of situation in which Frans seems to be dwelling. Whole cultures might be built on a ground of poetic/storied invocation, which serves to 'sing up' the world in which the community dwells and make that world an active participant in communal life.[17]

Indeed, we might ask, is this what *Dreaming* is? Is it the interior, psycho-active aspect of reality, called forth into communicativeness by narrative address which provides it with the poetic elements by means of which it can speak?

If this is so, *why*, we might further ask, is story efficacious? Why is it *story* that activates the poetic order?

In response to the latter question, I'd like to backtrack a bit and start with a different, cosmological question. In the space available here I can offer only the slenderest outline of a reply to this and the former question, but such an outline will suffice to indicate the direction in which I think the present line of inquiry leads.[18] The cosmological question is this: why does the observable

---

[17] Of course, any communicative exchange, whether between person and person or between persons and their world, requires interpretive nous and good judgment: just as we have to refrain from inappropriate assumptions and projections in interpreting the behaviour and speech of other persons, so we have to learn both how to recognise communicative intent and how to interpret intended communiqués in our relations with world. Acknowledging the existence of a poetic order is not an excuse for the kind of narcissistic self-indulgence (not to say psychotic derangement) that interprets the significance of all events in tediously self-mirroring terms. This is why it helps a great deal, in negotiating the poetic order, to have the wisdom and accumulated experience of a society already attuned to the communicative dimension of reality to guide and tutor our intuitions in this connection.

[18] I have explored aspects of the ideas that follow in various other works, in particular *For Love of Matter*, op cit, and *Reinhabiting Reality*, op cit, particularly Chapter 4. These ideas are further

world—the world under its external aspect, as represented by physics—hang together in the way that it does? Why is the universe a *uni*verse, a unity? Why is space—the frame of physics—unbounded yet unbroken, an indivisible wholeness, a fieldlike manifold? Why doesn't it break up, granulate, fragment, and hence cease to be the field that it is, the ground for physical existence?[19] Physics of course has no answer to this question. It cannot explain why there are laws that hold physical structures together and thereby guarantee the overall cohering of things. From the viewpoint of physics, this cohering is *ad hoc*, contingent; there is nothing in the nature of physicality *per se* that appears to underpin it.

If an inner, subjectival dimension is seen as integral to the nature of physicality however, then the necessity of this cohering of physical existence into a unity, a *uni*verse, an indivisible manifold such as that of space-in-time, is explained. Why? Because subjectivity is, by its very nature, fieldlike, holistic, internally interpermeating, indivisible, unbounded.[20] My subjectivity—or call it my psyche—cannot be constituted atomistically, as an aggregate of discrete units of experience, nor even as a continuum of point-like experiences. If psyche is as primal as physicality—if psyche is immanent in physicality *per se*—then it is clear that physicality must participate in the indivisible nature of psyche. But *why* is psyche necessarily indivisible? *Why* must the subjectival aspect of reality be conceived as a field? This field-likeness of psyche is tied up, I would suggest, with the fieldlikeness of *meaning*—the intrinsically interleaving and over-layering and interpermeating nature of meaning—and thereby with the constitution of experience through meaning. The kind of holistic internal indivisibility that confers unity on psyche, in other words, is tied up with the necessary indivisibility of meaning. Subjectivity is the medium for a tissue of meanings that cannot be pulled apart without ceasing to be meanings—and without subjectivity thereby ceasing to exist. In other words,

---

developed in a longer version of the present article entitled 'The World Hidden Within the World: a Conversation on Ontopoetics', *The Trumpeter* 23, 1, 2007, http://trumpeter.athabascau.ca/index.php/trumpet/issue/current.

[19] Of course there are theories in physics which do ascribe a sub-particle foamlike or granular structure to space. But these are not inconsistent with the perfect macro-level cohering of space as the frame for physical process.

[20] Historically speaking, the philosopher Henri Bergson has provided the most detailed phenomenology available demonstrating the necessarily holistic and internally indivisible and interpermeating nature of consciousness.

to the extent that psyche finds meaning in its experience, its structure must cohere into a unity. This is not of course to say that we might not identify or describe individual experiences by abstracting them from the field of experience—as *this* sense datum or *that* itch or *this* moment of elation. It is just that such experiences cannot actually *exist* in isolation from the entire field of the subject's experience, and this field-like structure of subjectivity is a function of meaning.

In speaking of this field-like structure of subjectivity as a function of meaning, I am using the term 'meaning' not in a semantical but in a more fundamental sense, to indicate the basic feeling of things *mattering*—of things having relevance, significance, importance. In other words, I'm using 'meaning' in the sense of meaningfulness, the meaningfulness that we impute to life itself when we ponder 'the meaning of life'. And meaningfulness in this sense is clearly the province of *self*. And by *self*, in turn, I mean not merely the human self but any *self-realising system*—any system that maintains itself in existence by its own intentional efforts.[21] Selves are defined by interests: they have a constitutive interest in self-maintenance and self-increase. It is relative to the interests of selves that things—particular objects, circumstances – assume significance, relevance, importance. If there were no selves in the world, everything would just be what it is—nothing that occurred would matter more or less than anything else, so nothing would have meaning. But selves, we might notice, are intrinsically structured as *story*: a self has a beginning, middle and end. It also has a goal, a purpose—its existence has a point, and a very compelling one, namely to survive, to thrive, to postpone its death for as long as possible. The quest of the self is continually beset with dangers and difficulties. This gives existence for the self the element of urgency and suspense that is essential to story. It is self in fact which furnishes the template for story.

This resonance between story and the structure of self presumably explains why stories are compelling only in the telling—why, in other words, stories crumple like punctured balloons and lose their charge as soon as they are ended. Listeners bring the huge suspense of their own existential uncertainty to

[21] Self in this sense can be defined in terms of autopoietic theory. See the work of Humberto Maturana and Francisco Varela; but this notion of self-realisation as the essence of self goes back at least as far as Spinoza; see my book *The Ecological Self*, Routledge, London, 1991.

a story as long as it is being told and while its outcome is as yet unknown; but this investment is lost as soon as the story is finished.

Meaning then, understood as this basic sense of meaningfulness, is tied at its root to story. And story is the province of self. If *world* is also 'self', in the sense that it is a psychophysical system with a subjectivity of its own and an impulse to realise and increase its own existence,[22] then its inner structure will, like ours, resonate to the structure of story: world will seek to story itself. It may be for this reason that world responds to our narrative address, or that story is efficacious in activating the poetic order.

If it is accepted that a psycho-active dimension is immanent in the manifest world, then our metaphysical task, as humans, may indeed be to *invoke* that psycho-active dimension, to *sing it up*, and allow ourselves to be drawn into story with it. Our invocations will of course have to be phrased in the poetic language of *things* as opposed to the conceptual language of words, since even a psychoactive world presumably does not think, at least in any literal way, in the conceptual language of words. This poetic language is however familiar to us from dreams, where meaning is conveyed predominately through objects and circumstances rather than through abstract discourse. Our narrative address will accordingly best be physically enacted or performed, preferably in situ, at the actual sites that figure in the narratives in question.

Conclusion

In seeking to understand events such as those that occurred at Hamilton Downs in the kind of metaphysical terms that I have suggested here we are entering a field that I would term *ontopoetics*.[23] Ontopoetics rests on the premise that there exists an inner aspect of reality which is expressed via a communicativity that coexists with but does not over-ride physical causality. If physics is the study of the causal order, then *ontopoetics* might be defined as the study of the poetic order, of the meanings that structure the inner aspect of being. I have suggested that in Australia various philosophical influences have fused to open even European psyches to the possibility of ontopoetic experience—in a way that would not have been possible for Simone de Beauvoir, for instance, firmly ensconced as she was in café society at *La Cupole*,

[22] See *The Ecological Self.*

[23] See 'The World Hidden Within the World: a Conversation on Ontopoetics', op cit.

though it might have been possible for some of the German and English Romantics. Ontopoetics is certainly not the exclusive province of Australia, but our unique philosophical heritage may indeed render Australia a kind of bridge for ontopoetics into global consciousness. And such a bridge is, I think, needed, for if ecology has in recent decades defined the first phase of the re-negotiation of the relation of modernity to reality, ontopoetics might be integral to the second phase.

PERFORMANCE ART, RITUAL AND SHAMANISM

Anne Marsh

I imagine grace / though I'm not / versed in scriptures / I hear you calling out names / one after another / saint or sinner / disciple one way or another . . .[1]

This passage from Australian poet Christopher Barnett is a reminder that the call to something beyond the human and the everyday is often found within the arts. Music, poetry, painting and dance often aspire to reach beyond language and conventional codes and create another space, another experience. These aspirations have been criticised in modern and postmodern times as the romantic mutterings of egotistical artists who are wrongly informed about the role of art in society. There are some compelling reasons to resist the role of the artist as seer or shaman, not least of all because the artist can be narcissistic and compelled by a false sense of his or her own importance.[2] But none of these arguments has stopped artists exploring ritual and catharsis, the spiritual and the unknown, the joyous and the bleak dark underside of life. In times of war and depression, in times of change and social upheaval, art has often created a critical pause, a radical intervention and a call for humanity.

The artists I will consider here use ritual and shamanism in various ways. They are all performance artists and they draw on the experimental genesis of this genre as it developed from the late 1960s. Initially this was a radical art practice that sought to challenge the parameters of the white cube of the modernist gallery by presenting events that could not be contained within such an antiseptic space. In Germano Celant's words the artist's 'intent is perhaps to insert a subversive element into the tidy, antispectic and asexual paradise of

---

[1] Christopher Barnett, *The Blue Boat/Bateau Bleu*, Paris: Le Nouveau Commerce, 1994, . 9.

[2] See, for example, Lea Vergine, *Body Art and Performance: The Body as Language*, Milan: Skira, 2000, and, more generally, Christopher Lasch, *The Culture of Narcissism*, London: Abacus, 1980.

art'.[3] Others worked outside the museum structure and presented work in the urban or natural environment. These artists were concerned with the relationship between 'man' and machine, technology and city. Their work focussed on the alienation of the subject in the world, or the disappearance of the subject as we have come to understand it—as a soft, wet, human body. Those artists who made works in the natural environment were often compelled by the devastation of the environment and the collapse of natural eco-systems. All were, in some instance, seeking to close the gap between art and life. To bring art closer to life, to make art which was life: a live art which was based in experience.[4] The experience of the artist's body often manifested as endurance works which tested the physical limits of the body, or the psychological experience of the artist as individual, or the individual as representative of a group—often the metaphorical group of human kind.

In this essay I want to introduce the works of several artists who work in this area and to provide some case studies and analyses of specific performance events. Some of the artists are mature: their work developed in the 1970s against a background of social change which saw art come off the wall and venture into different contexts. Others are emerging artists who represent a resurgence of performance art in the twenty-first century which embraces new technologies so that the performance itself maybe made on video/DVD.

CATHARSIS

Jill Orr has always been a cathartic performance artist. The spectre of the shaman is never far away. Interviewed in 1987, Orr said her performances were like moments or glimpses that she had imagined.[5] In 2007 dressed in a nun's habit she crawled along the main street of Darwin writing messages in chalk—in the form of a prayer—to the stolen generation of Aboriginal Australians. Responding to the Rudd government's 'apology' she wrote meditative and personal statements across the sidewalk in a bustling town. Heckled and cheered, saluted and despised, she continued this act of penance literally writing from one side of the town to the other. In part Orr wrote:

---

[3] Germano Celant, 'Dirty Acconci', *Artforum*, November 1980, p. 79.

[4] RoseLee Goldberg, *Performance Art from Futurism to the Present*, London: Thames & Hudson, 1988.

[5] Taped interview with the artist, June 24th 1987.

I stand on Larrakia land

I pray for the children
All over the world
I pray for women
For men

I pray for forgiveness
We missionaries offered sugar for redemption
This was a bribe

I pray because I am afraid
Elders are not heard
Our government is in raptures with its own power

I pray for the land
She is our home

I pray for wisdom
As we take their land again

I pray for empathy

I pray that we are not deceived again

Don't let them take your land

Did Jesus die for nothing?
We are still bleeding.[6]

This kind of cathartic performance is characteristic of Jill Orr's performance art. Exhibiting since the 1970s, Orr is an artist who speaks from the heart and engages with social issues. She speaks out against discrimination, war, violence and society's tendency to construct the Other as enemy. She has

[6] Edited sections from the poem inscribed on the street, courtesy of Jill Orr—provided to the author 20 November 2008.

consistently put her own body on the line by exposing herself to danger and ridicule in order that people may come to assess their responses to these actions and thus better know themselves.

In 1998 she presented *The Hunger* in Sydney, and later in Quebec and Toronto.[7] In this performance Orr gave birth to the carcass of a bloody lamb. There was a religious undercurrent to the work as the now mature artist appeared as an aged 'virgin' mother who produced a deformed and horrible body from between her legs and then paraded it throughout the audience as if it were a sacred child. The birthing and nurturing action was presented in front of a large luminescent painting of classical arches reminiscent of Renaissance architecture. Framed within these portals the 'virgin' mother gains an iconic status and her child, battered and bleeding, completes the pieta. The artist says that the work was driven by urban horror, the myth of Frankenstein, the Jewish myth of the *golem* and biological disasters. She wanted to ask the question: can we love the Other, even if it is an abhorrent creation of our own making? *The Hunger* was the beginning of a new series of work, a series that would resonate in the viewer's memory after the terrorist attacks of 11 September 2001 and the subsequent wars waged in the name of the free world.[8]

The Sleep of Reason Produces Monsters—Goya (Artspace, Sydney 2002) was Orr's cathartic response to the terrorist attacks in New York. In this performance the artist went back to art history, specifically to the etchings of Goya.[9] *The Sleep of Reason Produces Monsters* was a bloody performance in which tons of carcasses were strewn on the floor of the gallery. This was the raw material that Orr would work with for twelve hours. Dressed in a simple apron, reminiscent of a medieval surgeon or butcher, Orr proceeded to carve the bones and carcasses into human and animal form. This produced a bloody

---

[7] At Ivan Dougherty in Sydney, part of the exhibition *Telling Tales, Trauma and Memory, Cross Cultural Perspectives*, curated by Jace Dunn and Jill Bennett, and in 2000 at Le Lieu art space, Quebec as part of the International Performance Art Festival and at 11a 7d Toronto.

[8] On September 11 2001 (9/11) highjackers associated with al-Qaeda fly domestic airline planes into the Twin Towers of the World Trade Centre in New York City and the Pentagon in Washington. The USA retaliated by waging a War on Terror with the invasion of Afghanistan.

[9] *The Sleep of Reason Produces Monsters* is the title of one of Goya's etchings from the series *Los Caprichos* (first exhibited in 1799). The series presents a bitter critique of the Spanish aristocracy, the clergy and human nature and covers topics such as child sexual abuse, witchcraft and prostitution. See http://www.eeweems.com/goya/sleep_of_reason.html (accessed 27 November 2008).

and smelly abstract narrative of bodies dancing in the dim light of the once clean gallery space. Bodies that had been tortured and maimed: not pretty bodies, but ugly, misshapen forms of life that presented the body as an abject horror.

To contextualise this work historically we need to look at its genesis in the body art of the late 1960s and 1970s. This work often expressed an individual consciousness, but it stressed the psychological, spiritual and/or physical states of the artist, often testing the limits of the artist's body, or creating rituals which were set in the landscape. The spirit of the land was and still is a recurring theme in performance art. Sometimes this is expressed as a concern for the natural environment which is being ravaged by human destruction. Sometimes this takes the form of a quirky humour; at other times artists explore the dark, mysterious and other worldly aspects of nature, presenting it as an arena in which horror erupts.

Kevin Mortensen's performance art is site-specific or situated as part of a sculptural installation. In 1973, with fellow artist, John Davis, he performed as part of a ten day religious ceremony at St Paul's Cathedral in Melbourne. Davis installed 'prayer mats' and animal heads on the columns surrounding the baptismal font at the rear of the Cathedral, and lit the installation with candles and oil lamps. Mortensen, wearing a goat's head, sat on the back pew near the font bathed by the soft light. Interviewed in 1988, Mortensen said that the clergy and the congregation appeared to accept his presence as part of the conventional ceremony but the local press said that his figure represented an 'evil' element.[10]

Shamanism is apparent in the goat head figure as it is in other performances where the artist appears as a kind of bird–man. In *The Seagull Salesman, his Stocks and Visitors, or Figures of Identification* (1971) Mortensen sat for hours wearing an elaborate bird's head surrounded by birds in cages and two sculptural figures which stood to the side as spectators or witnesses. The artist saw this as a statement about the art market and the ways in which artists are required to 'hawk' their merchandise in the gallery system.[11]

---

[10] St Paul's Cathedral in Melbourne has been supporting the arts for decades and regularly showcases art inside the Cathedral.

[11] For further discussion of Mortensen's work see Anne Marsh, *Body and Self: Performance Art in Australia, 1969–1992*, Melbourne: Oxford University Press, 1993, pp. 30–31 and 155.

Ken Unsworth is likewise a sculptor who presents performances within installation contexts. Works in the 1970s were often endurance works which tested the limits of the body in the form of a kind of penance. The series *Five Secular Settings for Sculpture as Ritual* (Institute of Contemporary Art, Sydney 1975) included the artist being precariously suspended by his neck between two heavy wooden beams which created a triangle with Unsworth's head at the apex. *Burial Piece* from the same series saw the artist sitting in a glass case with his heart beat amplified. The case was slowly filled with sand and carefully levelled off by an assistant before the glass was smashed and the artist could breathe again.

Body art and ritual performance often explore alternatives to Western metaphysics by turning away from science, rationality and organised religion. These types of performance art also stress the personal, psychological and mythological. In many respects the meeting of the body and ritual has a particularly nostalgic and romantic resonance. In 1978 Graeme Sturgeon wrote:

> In a society in which the ceremonies of Church and State are dismissed as the hollow symbols of a discredited authority, the performance artists' acts take on increased significance as attempts to recreate mysterious, allegorical rituals which, seemingly intellectual in origin, spring from the subconscious and speak to the tribe (the spectators) in a highly-charged and partly understood, partly felt language of symbols. The artist once more assumes the role of witchdoctor, healing his society through a process of catharsis.[12]

The tone of Sturgeon's writing is impassioned; in ritual performance he sees a renewed role for the artist as romantic seer. Like Robert Lindsay and Daniel Thomas, he embraced this type of performance as part of a new avant-garde nostalgic for pre-modern lifestyles. Expressing a similar sentiment Robert Lindsay said:

> It is the power and simplicity of communication which is inherent in totemic objects, archetypal images and tribal rituals, that the artist hopes

[12] Graeme Sturgeon, *The Development of Australian Sculpture, 1788–1975*, London: Thames & Hudson, 1978, p. 232.

> will cut through the habit of contemporary sophisticated forms of communication. It is a return to fundamentals, the simple realities of life that through magic and mystification may evoke archetypal responses and emotions.[13]

Investigations of physical and psychological stress, inscriptions on the body, and rituals in which the artist appears as shaman, are all activities which probe forms of experience and existence. This attempt to reclaim a lost primitivism or tribalism, which had seduced Western art throughout the twentieth century, was criticised in the 1980s and 1990s because it was seen to underline the colonial tendencies of the West which captured and tamed the exotic Other, turning distant cultures into aesthetic objects.[14]

THE EXISTENTIAL BODY

Mike Parr's obsessive and compulsive investigations of pain and endurance, from 1971 to 1978,[15] drew on the works of Reich, Freud and later Lacan, to provide a kind of auto-psycho-analysis of the self. The artist's attempts to come to terms with his self-image, as a one-armed man, present a compelling analysis of masculinity and the Oedipal triangle as he seeks to carve out a place for himself in the social order. For Parr, coming to terms with the Law of the Father is a torturous experience, most pronounced in the rites of passage works which appear as modern day acts of penance, such as:

- Repeatedly drop a brick on your foot.
- Remove a small portion of flesh from your body.
- Take up fighting. Fight your fellow man … Fight everyone without discrimination.

[13]. Robert Lindsay, 'Relics and Rituals', in Paul Taylor (ed), *Anything Goes: Art in Australia 1970–1980*, Melbourne: Art & Text, 1984, p. 108.
[14] See Hal Foster, 'The Primitive Unconscious in Modern Art', *October*, no. 34, Fall 1985, pp. 45–70; William Rubin (ed.), *Primitivism in 20th-Century Art*, 2 vols., New York: Museum of Modern Art, 1984 and Marianna Torgovnick, *Gone Primitive: Savage Intellects, Modern Lives*, Chicago and London: University of Chicago Press, 1990.
[15] Developed throughout the series *150 Programmes and Investigations* (1971–72), *Idea Demonstrations* (1971–72), and *Rules and Displacement Activities* (parts 1, 2 and 3, 1973–78).

The performance directions for *Repeatedly Drop a Brick on your Foot* underline an Oedipal test of strength and a psychological trauma; but they are equally a super-ego struggle against the Law of the Father (patriarchy, God, law):

> Perform the piece mechanically. Do not allow your leg to quiver as you raise the brick. Do not cry out, or 'act' in any way (a stoical demeanour is important). Look straight ahead as the brick hits your foot. Afterwards sit perfectly still until the visitors leave the room.[16]

Parr's infamous performance *Cathartic Action, Social Gestus 5* (Sculpture Centre, Sydney and the Paris Biennale, both 1977), where he appears before his audience wearing a life-like prosthesis filled with blood and offal and proceeds to chop it off in a violent assault with a meat clever, was described then, and, remains now, a body work designed around autobiography (his disability) and self therapy. Parr talks about it as a cathartic experience, coming to terms with his disability by re-living and re-staging his castration anxiety. This performance was one of the first to clearly underline the psychopathology of the artist and his family. After the 'arm chop' his sister—Julie Rrap—came onto the stage and carefully fitted a knitted prosthetic limb. A soft pink arm replaced the bloody mess wrought my Parr's aggressive action. Rrap acted as a maternal figure who attempted to heal the wound.

Parr is one of Australia's premier body artists although he also produces work across visual media including drawing, painting, photography and installation. Much of the work has been self-reflexive and involves an intense psychological probing, however, much like a shaman his body is often used as a kind of 'everybody', a representative for the traumas of a sick society. This is most apparent in *Close the Concentration Camps* performed at Monash University Museum of Art in 2002 and broadcast over the Internet. This was a powerful political statement which drew attention to the plight of refugees who had entered Australia in leaky boats as 'illegal immigrants' fleeing poverty and terror in other parts of the world. On arrival they were promptly arrested and detained in detention centres where they were isolated from mainstream society for months and sometimes years before the immigration office made

[16] Mike Parr, 'Photo(graphed)', *Nine Contemporary Australians*, Los Angeles: Los Angeles Institute of Contemporary Art, 1984, p. 57.

decisions about their futures. This gave rise to depression, mental instability, self-harming, suicide attempts and hunger strikes. The images of self-harm that resonated most loudly with the Australian public were those which showed people with their mouths sewn shut as part of a hunger strike.

Using his own body as a social site, Parr had his lips and eyelids sewn shut; other sutures were inserted into his ears and nose so that his face became a deformed and wounded portrait. He also had his leg branded with the word 'ALIEN'. The performance occurred over five hours in front of a wall-sized mirror and below a large wall text which read CLOSE THE CONCENTRATION CAMPS. Nikos Papastergiadis wrote that Parr 'temporarily used his body as a metaphor for the disfiguration of civic space'.[17]

Matthew Perkins is a younger artist who begins his performance art career in the twenty-first century. He is aware of an older generation—Mike Parr, Ken Unsworth, Vito Acconci and Hermann Nitsch, among others, are all male protagonists is his field. Perkins enters in the late 1990s and reconsiders the male existential angst of his forefathers. He creates work which situates masculine anxiety on another threshold. His performance *Prick* (2006) is an endurance work but it references the feminine in an attempt to undo masculine heroism. *Prick* is excruciating to watch. There are two pin cushions (a reference to the feminine and craft). One presents an array of sewing needles, the other is barren, empty. Perkins carefully extracts one needle after the other with his mouth. His mouth is soft, the needles are hard and sharp. As the performance continues the artist experiences physical distress. Needles pierce him—he is pricked—it is as if this is a kind of penance. A retribution for being the 'prick' (a derogatory term for a man). Perkins endures his own suffering—he wounds himself over and over—by taking one needle at a time out of the full needle cushion and placing it into the empty cushion. In many ways this is an act of penile penetration: a sexual act which undoes itself in the most profound way. Every time he takes a needle from the full cushion and he has to bear down with his mouth into the other (virgin) cushion he risks injury. In the video of the endurance action the viewer comes to understand that this is more than irony. The man bleeds most often when he penetrates the virgin cushion. In the end the man bleeds from his prick(ing), he bleeds

[17] Nikos Papastergiadis, 'Art in the Age of Siege', *New Glocal Times* http://www.glocaltimes.k3.mah.se/viewarticle.aspx?articleID=36&issueID=4 accessed 19 November 2008.

from his nose (phallus) and his mouth. The soft pink mouth becomes almost synonymous with the vulva. Perkin's performance verges on a masculine feminism. This is an event that could only have been performed by a younger man post-feminism. This is a man/subject that understands his own wounds in relation to the Other. In the language of psychoanalysis it is 'an enunciation that denounces itself … the trace of what must be in order to fall from being'.[18]

TECHNO-HUMANS

Ritual and shamanism also manifests in Sci-Fi futuristic events and narratives which supposedly stress the wonders of technology and machine-made futures. Performance artists who operate on the frontiers of technology often distance themselves from the psychological and ecological concerns of their humanist colleagues, however, the cyborg could well be the shaman of the future.

In Stelarc's projection of a cyborg future, the corporeal body is metaphorically eclipsed by a futuristic narrative which speaks of the obsolescence of the body. But his particular body is still probed and pierced. There was a habitual masochism in the suspension events of the 1970s where the artist's body was suspended by hooks inserted into the skin. Images of ancient rites and shamanism pervade as the artist endures almost intolerable levels of pain to create his art. Although the modern primitivism of the suspension rituals is framed in techno-speak, the social events (the performances) share aspects in common with Parr's 'primal scene' since they too can be read as Oedipal tests of strength or rites of passage. The skin piercing suspension events can also be compared with acts of penance enacted in religious ceremonies where believers go into trance-like states and parade in the streets with heavy objects hanging from their flesh. In the Hindu festival of Thaipusan the Kavadi ritual involves body piercing and some devotees suspend their bodies with meat hooks.[19]

Although the suspension events produced by Stelarc can be clearly aligned to shamanistic ritual, later works which experiment with a techno-

[18] Jacques Lacan, 'The Subversion of the Subject and the Dialectic of Desire in the Freudian Unconscious', in *Ecrits: A Selection*, New York and London: Norton and Company, 1977, p. 300. First published in French in 1966.

[19] See Hans-Günter Heimbrock and Barbara Boudewijnse (eds.), *Current Studies on Rituals: Perspectives for the Psychology of Religion*, Amsterdam: Rodopi, 1990.

biological interface appear to be more scientific. Impelling us to burst from our 'biological, cultural and planetary containment'[20], Stelarc argues that: 'The significance of technology may be that it culminates in an alien awareness—one that is POST-HISTORIC, TRANS-HUMAN and even EXTRATERRESTRIAL'.[21] The idea that this alien, artificial and superior intelligence evolves from man confirms some of Western society's greatest myths as 'man' becomes a kind of techno-god or cyborg-shaman.

Stelarc's project seems to embrace some of the worst aspects of modernity. The omnipotence of mankind and the rationalising codes of Western scientific thought are dominant in this discourse which strives to escape a devastated planet and conquer unknown territories.

The desire for omnipotence and omniscience has a long history stretching back to the very first conceptions of gods upon which 'man' projected his ideals. But as Freud pointed out in the 1930s: 'Man has, as it were, become a kind of prosthetic God. When he puts on all his auxiliary organs he is truly magnificent; but these organs have not grown on him and they still give him much trouble at times'.[22]

Jill Orr, Stelarc, Mike Parr and Matthew Perkins use their bodies as objects in various ways. There are aspects of shamanism, however, there is also an intense physical and psychological testing of the limits the body and its pain threshold.[23] There are obtuse connections between the artists. Stelarc evolves as a cyborg artist in the 1980s and in so doing encapsulates the future of shamanism for many. Parr, like Orr, explores the psycho-social realms of subjecthood. Perkins addresses the existential anxiety of masculinity through a screen of cultural history. He understands his own place in this history and the affect that his masculinity bears. Orr does likewise by realising her position as Other—the woman who will always lack the prick: the woman who, in Irigaray's sense, 'is not one'.[24]

---

[20] Stelarc, 'Enhanced Gesture/Obsolete Desire: Post Evolutionary Strategies', *Remote Stelarc*, exh. cat., Ballarat, 1990, no pagination.

[21] Ibid.

[22] Sigmund Freud, *Civilization and Its Discontents*, trans. James Strachey, New York and London: Norton and Company, 1961, p.39. First published in German and English in 1930.

[23] See my essays 'Techno-bodies: Spectacles, Dreams and Desires', *Binocular*, Sept. 1992, pp. 129–147 and 'Bad Futures: Performing the Obsolete Body', Nicholas Zurbrugg (ed), *Electronic Arts in Australia, Continuum*, vol 8, no. 1, August 1994, pp. 280–292.

[24] See Luce Irigaray, *This Sex which is Not One*, trans. Catherine Porter with Caroline Burke, Ithaca, New York: Cornell University Press, 1985 (first published in French in 1977).

A REMEDIATED PENANCE

The remediation of performance art for video is a recent phenomenon that has created debate amongst artists and scholars. Some believe that the audience has to be there in 'real time' in the presence of the artist to truly experience the performance, others believe that a performance can be reconstructed through its documentation.[25] This argument has been confounded by artists who make performance specifically for the camera.

Debates about medium specificity have resurfaced in the last ten years as a response to interdisciplinary practices in the visual and performing arts. Although some of the literature is compelling, it has created a conservative backlash in some quarters where a return to medium specificity is used to support conventional practices. Too much specificity leads back to formalism and art for art sake which saw the arts distanced from society and enclosed in an elite ivory tower.[26]

Monika Tichacek's video *The Shadowers* (2004) is a powerful and provocative work that stretches the boundaries between body art, ritual and sado-masochism by assaulting the senses and transgressing the social realm. In psychoanalytic terms it tears at the screen of the real and immerses the viewer into the abject world of instinctual response where language has no authority.[27]

Viewing the video, we are lured into an exotic environment. At first the viewer is presented with a relatively safe and alluring visual scan of nature, but all is not well. We are quickly engulfed by a rapid sequence of unforgiving images that present a disjunctive narrative. The narrative is disturbing and verges on the obscene.

Three women make up this narrative, at first one appears to dominate the other but it soon becomes apparent that there is a contract between all three women. Each seems to alternate between oppressor and victim—the role-playing is carefully orchestrated between the characters of shaman, torturer and

---

[25] See Philip Auslander, 'The Performativity of Performance Documentation', *PAJ A Journal of Performance and Art* vol. 28, no. 3, 2006, pp 1–10 and *Liveness: Performance in a Mediated Culture.* Also Rosalind Krauss, 'Video: The Aesthetics of Narcissism', *October* no. 1, 1976, pp. 50–64.

[26] See Clement Greenberg, 'American Style Painting' in *Art & Culture,* Boston: Beacon, 1961.

[27] See Hal Foster, 'The Real Thing' in Karel Schampers and Talitha Schoon (eds.), *Cindy Sherman,* exh. cat., Rotterdam: Museum Boijmans Van Beuningen, 1996, p. 79.

victim with the shaman figure oscillating between good and bad mother. The ritual that unfolds is dramatic and abject.

As viewers we are voyeurs looking into a ritual that is hardly fathomable. Here the social order is defunct. It has been consumed by something other—it is primordial, instinctual, cathartic. Tichacek trespasses into the dangerous zone of the pre-Oedipal, a stage before language where the barbarity of the unconscious holds sway. A realm in which we are all murderers.[28]

In one scene the torturer impales the tongue of her victim on an old tree stump with a hypodermic needle which she produces from her hair. She pierces the organ of speech and renders her subject mute. Harrowing animalistic screams assault the viewer but they appear to be coming from the torturer who wails to the forces of nature as if summoning up demons. The bad mother then nails the long white fingernails of the younger woman to the stump so that she is immobile.

In the next scene, the witch doctor/bad mother figure threads wires from the tacks impaling her victim's fingernails to the mouth of another woman. A horrible tug of war unfolds which wounds both women. The first victim—Tichacek—now appears to be in excruciating pain, her tongue has turned black, her eyes roll in her head, she quivers. But this is a performance for video and if one looks closely it is apparent that Tichacek has already had her tongue pierced so the needle goes through easily and much of this agony is simulated. The second victim engaged in this abject struggle appears to have injured her mouth—this is a self-inflicted wound (on video). At this stage the witch doctor removes the needle from the tongue of the first victim and ungagged she attempts to pull the tacks from her finger nails to release the other woman.

The Shadowers is part of a new wave of performance art work that is mediated through video and presented on screen for the audience. Although some critics have insisted that such remediation forecloses on the real time aspects of performance, *The Shadowers* clearly demonstrates that the visceral elements of body-centred performance can be transposed to the video medium without compromising the body art genre.[29]

[28] Slavoj Zizek, *Looking Awry: An Introduction to Jacques Lacan through Popular Culture*, Cambridge, Mass., MIT Press, 1991, p. 16.
[29] For a discussion of the various critical positions see Philip Auslander, *Liveness: Performance in a Mediated Culture*, London and New York: Routledge, 1999.

Catherine Bell's *Felt is the Past Tense of Feel* (2006) is an endurance event in real time but there is no 'live' audience, just the photographer and the video operator.[30] The performance is designed as a public act of mourning for the artist's recently deceased father.

Dressed in a pink felt suit, Bell sits alone on a stage in a pool of black squid ink and astride a mound of forty squid.[31] Light floods the performer and the squid glisten as if they are still alive. She slowly sucks the black squid ink from the marine creatures and then spits it onto the suit. The sucking and spitting are abject actions which would have been enhanced in the performance venue by sound and smell (the video is silent). Body fluids are exchanged between the molluscs and the human. This trespasses a social taboo, a blurring of bodily boundaries between the species.

After all the squid have delivered their ink, Bell rubs the ink evenly over the suit, her face, hair, feet and hands and stuffs as many squid as will fit into the jacket. The rest she bundles in her arms and between her legs. Remaining in a sitting position she wriggles backwards out of the spotlight so that she fades to black. She says: 'Some shamans will escort the soul to the underworld and so that they won't be recognised … they smear their face with soot'.[32]

The pink felt suit is tailored as a duplicate of a suit that her father wore which she wears beneath the pink skin-coloured costume. The artist's body is covered by two external skins: her father's suit which once covered his living body and on top of this the pink felt double which acts as an absorptive skin which provides a staining surface onto which Bell squirts the black salty ink of the squid.[33] The suit remains pink on the back and in multiple creases where her limbs and body created folds on the material. This pink scarring represents the wounding that occurred during the performance. When exhibited as a

[30] There are two videos: one made by the static (dumb) camera, a real time (52.11 minute duration) and another made with a hand-held camera which records 28.18 minutes of footage. The video operator is Annie Wilson (who is also a performance artist and video maker).

[31] Bell commissioned a commercial fisherman to line catch the squid so that the tentacles, eyes and ink sacs were intact. As she sucked the squid she looked into their eyes.

[32] Catherine Bell, *Liminal Gestures*, p. 133. After the performance the bodies of the squid were consumed at a BBQ. Bell says this was integral to the performance because she did not want to waste the food, however, it is also a ritual offering which is shared.

[33] Art historically, Bell nods in the direction of artist-shaman, Joseph Beuys, who famously used felt in his performance works to symbolise spiritual warmth. He characteristically wore a felt fedora and in 1970 he had a felt suit tailored from one of his own garments as a multiple to be hung on the walls of art galleries (*Felt Suit*).

remnant of the performance, the smell was putrid, a deathly decaying stench that caused some viewers to retch when it was first exhibited.[34]

CONCLUSION

Ritual in performance art is multifarious. Although there are clear links to place and identity in works by Jill Orr and Kevin Mortensen, others use ritual elements as a way of probing psychological states or testing the limits of the body.

In a book about the sacred and Australia performance art creates a rupture. This is because the ritual elements in the work are employed to create debate. This is poetically astute in Kevin Mortensen's work at St Paul's Cathedral and in Jill Orr's prayers for Indigenous Australians. But it is equally as powerful in the acts of abuse and penance evident in works by Mike Parr, Matthew Perkins and Catherine Bell. None of these works are explicitly addressing the sacred. If anything they are sacrilegious—a deliberate attempt to insert an irreverent politics into the sacred yet secular space of the museum.

In the 1970s and 1980s this work was often interpreted as a return to the mysterious, the 'primitive' and the symbolic. This is apparent in the writings of Graeme Sturgeon and Robert Lindsay, however both critics also saw in this work a radical edge that spoke to the world through catharsis. Performance art is certainly linked to the generations of the 1960s and 1970s. Some of the artists discussed here are of those generations, however it would be misleading to suggest that the works are concerned with counter cultural revolt alone. Performance art may take its genesis from aspects of that time, but much of the strongest work concerned with the body has concentrated on the psycho-political. It draws from personal experience, it focuses on trauma (both personal and political), and in doing so it creates a dynamic visual language for our times. The psychology of self and Other is played out in all this work, even in Stelarc's quest with the extraterrestrial body there is a residual fear of the Other which resonates in the violence of our times. Stelarc has pronounced that the body is obsolete and he envisages a merger between human kind and machines where 'wetware' (the body) is redesigned by software. In this essay Stelarc is the maverick, the other artists stand substantially within the field of

[34] Catherine Bell in conversation with the author November 17, 2008.

the psycho-political where a probing psychoanalysis of self and other destabilises the sacred to become a new secular religion.

SACRED ICON: JØRN UTZON'S SYDNEY OPERA HOUSE

Peter Murphy

THE SACRED AND THE SECULAR

Australia is a secular society—in many ways, an emphatically secular society. There are few visible traces of organised religion in the daily life of its people. The process of secularisation has bitten deep in the Australian psyche. Only a small minority of Australians attends church or engages in any form of corporate religious activity. When Australia was settled by Europeans at the end of the eighteenth century, churches were still an important social institution. Today they are marginal. Everyday habits continue to be shaped by the ingrained ethos of Protestantism and Catholicism. But organised religious activity and ritual has shrunk into the social background. It barely rates a mention in conversation.

The big turning point—the one that led to the loss of interest in institutional religion—occurred in the 1960s. This was an era of accelerated, sometimes even pyrotechnic, cultural modernisation. In its midst, large numbers of Australians began to shrug off Christian morality—or else see it as simply irrelevant. As the Australian satirist Norman Lindsay had hoped, prelates and priests became figures of fun—dusty relics of an increasingly bygone age. The wry, skeptical streak in the Australian character found traditional piety difficult to put up with, and so it was abruptly dumped. Attendance at church plummeted, and Australian society became trenchantly secularised. Yet along with cultural modernisation came a counter-movement of re-sacralisation. The more secular Australia became, the more a streak of the sacred persisted—and grew. The collapse of church observance emancipated the sacred from the constraint of traditional religion.

Traditional religion offered redemption in the afterlife and moral codes in this life. As cultural modernity spread, these lost their appeal. Yet as conventional religious observance declined, the influence of the sacred increased. Symbols of the sacred in effect began to replace the power of institutional religion in Australian life.[1] This begs the question, though: what exactly is the sacred, and by what means or media is it expressed? To define it negatively, the sacred is distinct from ordinary or profane life. It is what elevates, expands, and edifies. The sacred has a time and space of its own kind. It does not exist in ordinary time or space, but rather in an enigmatic space-time that is 'mysterious'. 'Mystery' is simply another way of saying that something is 'out of the ordinary'. This 'out of the ordinary' is the realm of the sacred.

One distinguishing mark of the sacred is the way it is communicated. The sense of the sacred is always indirectly communicated. One cannot command the sacred. Thus it is always better expressed by music rather than catechism—or by parable rather than judgment. The sacred takes the sanctimonious out of religious life. It resists and expels, and often satirises, the moralising and morbid dimensions of traditional religion. The English composer Ralph Vaughan Williams illustrates the distinction perfectly. For all of his life he was an atheist or agnostic, and yet he wrote some of the most beautiful sacred music of all time.

When the winds of cultural modernisation hit Australia in the 1960s, traditional religion collapsed like a house of cards. A threshold was crossed—and crossing backwards proved impossible. The shattering of traditional belief happened suddenly. When it did, traditionalists expected moral anarchy and a crisis of meaning to follow. Australia did experience a little of that, but in reality not very much. For nature abhors a vacuum. In spite of plummeting belief in the moral law of the church, Australian society kept chugging along. Because the most fervent advocates of cultural modernity were often empty-headed—and not a little stupid—there was something in the complaints of the traditionalists.[2] Cultural change, innovation and progress frequently had a hollow, shallow ring to it. Despite this, cultural modernisation did not produce widespread anomie. It did produce some idiots—but then all societies have their fools. We suffer them—easily or not—according to our temperament. Still it is notable that cultural modernisation in Australia did not create a

[1] Institutional religion was what the young Hegel had dubbed 'positive religion'.

[2] The intellectuals grouped around the Australian magazine *Quadrant* were among the most influential and interesting of the traditionalists.

generation of lost souls. There was the occasional casualty along the way, and much of the posturing of the 1960s looks embarrassing in retrospect. But Australia did not descend into a mad maelstrom. The predicted worst did not happen—because of the paradox of secularisation.

Secularisation tossed aside the catechisms and law-codes of organised religion. Australian society became more complex and more hazardous as a result, but also more interesting. Australian cultural modernisation, though, did not simply replace certainty with doubt—or faith with questioning. If it had, there would have been more serious problems. Rather secularisation was met with the equal and opposite movement of sacralisation. Sacralisation—it needs be stressed—was not simply the reassertion of faith in place of doubt. Rather the sacred was an ambidextrous condition in which faith and doubt coexisted. Faith and doubt, along with tradition and innovation, were intertwined and folded back into each other.

Traditionally, the sacred was an enigmatic—or quantum—quality that lurked in the heart of religious mystery. Secularisation emancipated that mystery from institutional religion. To do so, it had to brush aside the doctrines, interdictions, and rituals of the churches. At the same time, it had to fill the empty vessel of modernisation with the enigmatic substance of culture. *Cultural modernisation had to overcome tradition and at the same time overcome itself.*[3] It had to retire tired meanings, while avoiding the narcissism and nihilism of self-devouring modernity. It had to indirectly communicate meaning that could no longer be directly communicated—at least in any plausible fashion.

There are numerous forms of indirect communication of religious feeling. Music and architecture are classic examples, long associated with the churches. Everything from cricket pitches to detective novels to philosophy—culture in the wide-ranging sense—played a role during the twentieth century in expressing the sacred tangentially in secular societies. But if the arts stood out, this was not because art was a substitute religion, as some thought, but rather—and more simply—because great art was well suited to conveying the enigmas of the sacred. For what makes great art in practice great is its capacity

[3] This view is most strongly represented today in Australia by the group of thinkers associated with the journal *Thesis Eleven* (Sage Publications) and the Thesis Eleven Centre for Cultural Sociology at La Trobe University in Melbourne.

to internalise and express contrary forces—to be traditional and modern, and both and neither of these, simultaneously.

Australians built beautiful churches in the nineteenth century. The neo-Gothic cathedral of St Patrick's in Melbourne—designed by William Wardell—is a wonderful example of this. Buildings of this kind were artifacts of traditional religion. They were conceived as places of social congregation and spiritual retreat that underscored the moral laws of Christendom. They pointed back to a more unambiguously Christian time—the European gothic age. And yet the restlessness of Gothic architecture had a strong hint of modernity about it. The past, it seemed, contained the future. Even more enticingly, the Christian gospels hinted at an unfathomable mystery—at the 'faith–doubt' enigma and the irresolvable puzzle that there is no faith without doubt, and no doubt without faith.[4] Even though the nineteenth century was the last age of traditional Christian observance, it was also the age of Kierkegaard.

The building of gothic piles in Australia was a comic mystery—hilarious in a way, and yet perfectly right. If they principally did what they were meant to do—which was to sustain traditional belief—the best of them nonetheless hinted at the double overcoming of tradition and modernity. In the 1960s, when the avenging angel of doubt hit with the force of a hurricane, the gothic edifices emptied out. The lesser examples were deconsecrated and sold off as cafés. No one seriously resisted this. Indeed, the epicurean strain in the Australian character relished it. Norman Lindsay smiled naughtily from above. Still, anomie did not rage through the land. For a sacred dimension asserted itself in the moment of disbelief. Ironically, it was the act of disbelief that made this possible. Modernity's angel of doubt turned out to be a paradoxical carrier of faith. How odd! This was a mischievous angel—one who impersonated the person of faith and the person of doubt simultaneously. You never knew quite who you were dealing with. As with all enigmas, you were dealing with both.

[4] The great Australian cultural sociologist, John Carroll, assays the enigmatic nature of the Gospel of St Mark in his book, *The Existential Jesus* (Melbourne: Scribe, 2007). Carroll emphasises both the irrelevance of the church to the story of Jesus and the paradoxical message of the Jesus story: *For whoever wishes to save his soul will lose it, but whoever loses his own soul on account of me and my Story will save it* (p. 67).

THE OLD AND THE NEW

This angel—or was it a daemon?—sat on the shoulder of one of the greatest characters who ever washed up on Australian shores. In the 1960s, the Danish architect Jørn Utzon (1918–2008) came to build Australia a cultural monument. Like most of those buildings, it could have turned out to be an unsightly dud. But it didn't. For Utzon was an enigma. He was filled with the modern spirit—a bearer of cultural modernism to far-flung foreign parts. Yet he was to create a work—the Sydney Opera House—in touch with eternity. This was a work that was an almost perfect example of the double overcoming of tradition and modernity. His mischievous angel–daemon would smile forever on the future. This smile was the impish grin of someone who takes the pretentious clap-trap of tomorrow and the tired arts of yesterday and cancels them out, in the spirit of the uncanny, mythical, sometimes even magical, time and place of the sacred.

I grew up hearing, from time to time, the name Jørn Utzon. It was a name tinged with controversy. As I passed from childhood to adolescence, the Sydney Opera House was under construction (1959–1973). Like all great projects it had its detractors. Many complaints were directed at Utzon. On the surface of things, the cause of complaint was cost overruns, the bugbear of all large works. The criticisms escalated in 1965 when a new state government in New South Wales was elected, under the premiership of Robert Askin.[5] The project costs had been under-estimated by earlier governments for political reasons. Utzon became the scapegoat for what then became inevitable—snowballing expenses.

But, in truth, as politicised as the cost of all large public works are, this was not the only—or even the principal—source of the antagonism towards Utzon. There were deeper, more complex, resentments at play. One argument advanced at the time was that Utzon was a victim of philistinism. He fell foul of a public sentiment that was culturally immature and hence uneasy about modern architecture. There was doubtlessly an element of this at work. But this is also a story that echoes all too closely the self-flagellating but oddly self-promoting narrative of 'no one understands our genius' that the Modern Movement in art and architecture at the time so liked to tell about itself. Out of self interest, it overestimated the public's resistance to Modernism. Indeed,

[5] Australia has a federal system of government modeled on that of the United States.

in a curious way, the legitimacy of architectural Modernism often depended on the idea that there was fierce resistance to its ideas. 'I am right because many people tell me I am wrong' was (more or less) the view. The qualities of virtue and heroism that Modernism rather too easily ascribed to its own self were justified by stories of a philistine world that was frustrating art.

It is not clear, though, that Australian publics of the 1960s were especially philistine or even especially resistant to Modernism in architecture. Since the 1820s, the state of New South Wales had had a long history of constructing architecturally elegant and sophisticated public buildings, including universities, museums and art galleries. The extensive, often exquisite, public architecture that populated Sydney and other Australian cities was traditional in style and spirit—memorably so.

From the days of the colonial governor Lachlan Macquarie, in the early nineteenth century, a large investment in public building was a distinguishing mark of Australian life. Max Dupain, Australia's greatest photographer, spent a large part of his career photographing this brilliant architecture. Much of it, stylistically speaking, until the 1960s, was historicist. Classical, Italianate, and Gothic styles were very popular. But the Modernist proselytising idea that a shocking break with a historicising past had brought forth a revelatory Modernism was an exaggeration. For instance, it was the most natural of things for Max Dupain to go down to the Opera House site every week while it was being constructed to take photographs.[6] There was a natural continuity between that work and Dupain's beautiful images of early colonial Australian late Georgian architecture.[7] In the inter-war period of the twentieth century, Modernism had already made a big and stylish impact on Australian use of classical form in architecture. The stripped classicism of Australia's Provisional Parliament House (1927) is a case in point.

One of the best examples of the fusion of modern ethos with classical form in Australia is the Royal College of Surgeons (1935) building in Spring

[6] 'With hindsight, it seems inevitable, a blindingly obvious conjunction of architect, photographer and building: Jørn Utzon, the Sydney Opera House and the man often cited as the world's greatest architectural photographer, the late Max Dupain. Indeed, as Utzon has recently written: "Max Dupain was the finest architectural photographer I have known. For the past 40 years I have kept his marvellous pictures of Sydney Opera House close at hand. They are a constant reminder of those wonderful years on Bennelong Point, when our dream of creating the Sydney Opera House was turned into reality."' 'Seduced by the sails', *Sydney Morning Herald*, October 4, 2003.

[7] Max Dupain and Morton Herman, *Georgian architecture in Australia* (Sydney: U. Smith, 1963).

Street, Melbourne—designed by Leighton Irwin. In the buildings of the inter-war generation, architects had already accepted Adolph Loos' arguments against ornamentation.[8] Doubtless full-fledged Modernism in architecture in Australia in the 1960s still took some getting used to, yet in retrospect it all seems very tame, even (now) very traditional. As the public became accustomed to the new multi-storied office building type, and as the discomfort that it initially provoked dissipated, the classic form, or classic geometry, of the best of these buildings became easier to recognise and appreciate. Of course there were many bad examples of Modern buildings constructed, but then atrocious building dogs all architectural periods. There seems to be no escaping it.

The continuities are just as apparent as the divergences when we look at the juxtaposition of the 1930s-era Royal College of Surgeons building and Melbourne's first glass curtain-wall skyscraper built across the road from it. Orica (formerly ICI) House was completed in 1958. Designed by the modernist architectural firm Bates Smart and McCutcheon, it was located just outside Melbourne's Central Business District in order to avoid height restrictions, a typical modernist defiance of ordinance. But moving around Melbourne today, one is struck by the chasteness, even modesty, of such buildings. Perhaps, as with all art, it takes time for the meaning of buildings to become clear. First they are loaded with the claims of their own time, many of them ridiculous. Then they have to live with the inevitable repudiation of those claims. Finally, the real judge of things, Time, does its work, and buildings of real virtue, whatever their style, emerge as classics.

THE ENVY OF CREATION

If High Modernism sparked voluble, and at times interesting, debates about architecture in the 1960s, these were also (so far as their practical import was concerned) short-lived. Modernism was already the establishment architecture of Australia by the 1970s. As Max Dupain's photographs of the time illustrate, architectural modernism was the triumphant—and in practice the only coherent—aesthetic of the new generation of tall office buildings that appeared

[8] On Loos' philosophy of architecture, see Peter Murphy and David Roberts, *Dialectic of Romanticism: A Critique of Modernism* (London: Continuum, 2004),

in Sydney in the 1960s.[9] The Sydney Opera House was simultaneous with this. Construction work on the base and pedestal of the Opera House proceeded through 1957–1963, but the signifying geometry of the project—the buildings' great sails—were erected through 1963–1967, a period neatly book-ended by the two monuments of Sydney sixties' modernism: Peddle Thorp & Walker's 1962 AMP Building on Circular Quay and Harry Seidler's 1967 Australia Square Tower in Sydney's Central Business District.

Perceptions of the power and orthodoxy of Modernism in the 1960s have been muddied by the fact that Modern Movement architects were often the last to acknowledge this, relishing as they did their status as radicals and provocateurs. But then all modern establishments behave in exactly the same way, because they derive their legitimacy from claims to reform. Everyone comes to power with a reform agenda. Whether a reform movement has any value, though, and whether it succeeds in generating meaning—or whether it is just a lot of hot air—depends on whether it can create durable classics. It has to turn the promise of change into the reality of continuity, and contemporaneity into immortality. That is exactly what Utzon did.

Interestingly, it took a shorter time than in most cases for this to be generally acknowledged. Thus it is not at all evident that Utzon was vulnerable to removal from the Sydney Opera House project because either the general public or art-supporting elites had traditional aesthetic tastes. Indeed it is far from obvious that this was actually the case. Utzon *was* vulnerable, though, when ministers in government and ambitious figures in the architecture profession undermined him. Their motives were not to rebut his aesthetic but rather to grab control of it.

What drove Utzon's enemies was envy. It was the envy of his peers for his great abilities. The envy of ability is the homage that mediocrity pays to great talent. One should, I suppose, at a great distance, be pleased for it because it is always the first sign we have that something exceptional is afoot. There is never a Mozart without a Salieri.

Utzon's talent was enormous. He designed and oversaw much of the construction of a building that will be the Australian icon forever. It is a building that ranks with the Parthenon and the Pantheon. This is the real reason that Utzon was chided and berated. Not because he was an incompetent

[9] Max Dupain and Rex Dupain, *Inside Sydney* (Frenchs Forest, NSW: New Holland Publishers, 2004).

project manager. In fact, his early work with Ove Arup, the engineer on the Opera House project—to find efficient engineering solutions for Utzon's radical design—appears to have been both effective and ingenious. But Utzon, like the great generally, also played the Sun to the wings of Icarus when it came to less talented engineers. As Arup's partners at the Sydney site assumed greater and greater responsibility for the project, Utzon found himself without friends on the project.

Beware when the second rank deals with the first rank! The result is rancor. Those of first rank are very demanding, and they always make demands that the second rank, the average of a profession, cannot meet. Without intending to do so, those of first rank humiliate the second raters. But those who are humiliated, those who harbour hurt feelings, still want to be like the giant who humbles them. Rancorous feelings of envy and jealousy result. These are paradoxical feelings. The rancorous person dismisses the person of great talent (as an incompetent) and yet wants to be like them (a person of superior talent).

In short, the reason that Utzon got a hard time was the envy of his peers. The most appalling case was the architecture professionals who happily grabbed the direction of the project from Utzon when the state government offered it to them. The strangest case of envy, though, was that of the New South Wales Minister of Works, Davis Hughes, who at times seemed to think he could personally take over the project from Utzon. And we think that architects are egomaniacs! Hughes badgered Utzon not just about costs and the timetable of construction, but about the design itself.[10]

In the end, the minister stopped paying Utzon, who then had no choice but to resign from the project. Utzon left Australia in 1966, and never returned. This was a shameful episode. Yet the irony of it is that Australians love Utzon's creation. They know it is their icon. It represents them to the world and to themselves. They see their own selves reflected in that building. The Sydney Opera House is to Australia what the Parthenon is to Greece. Official amends were eventually made to Utzon for the shoddy treatment of him. He was awarded an Order of Australia, and an agreement was made with him in 2000 to have him work on redesigns of the building. But none of that

[10] Philip Drew astutely observes that 'although Hughes would have vigorously denied it, somewhere inside him lurked a desire to be creative'. *The Masterpiece: Jørn Utzon A Secret Life* Melbourne: Hardie Grant, 1999, p. 384.

official atonement is anything like the simple enduring respect that Australians pay Utzon by visiting, admiring, and musing on this most remarkable of creations.

PORTAL CITY AND PLASTIC SPIRIT

Why is the Sydney Opera House such a great building? The answer, simply, is the form of the building. One of its most notable aspects is the starkness of its form. It is not embellished. It is not decorated, or not in such a manner that detracts in any way from the power of its form.

In conceiving the idea for the design of the Opera House, Utzon took an orange and divided it into segments. That was the essential act of creation. Those segments, transformed into the shells of the building, and arranged artfully with regard to its site on Bennelong Point, are the essence of the Opera House. In some sense, this act of creation was child's play, but child's play of an impossibly high order. An act of creation that will last millennia, and which is not just vogue or fashion, but is elemental. That which is the most difficult is the simplest of all.

The segmented hemisphere on which Utzon based his design echoes the form of the orb or sphere that is found throughout nature—from the glories of planetary systems to, yes, the humble orange. What great architecture does is to mimic the forms of nature. In the architectural act of creation we see the re-creation of the proportions, symmetries, ratios, and shapes of nature. Architecture is pure artifice. But, at its most powerful, it is an artifice that is a second nature. Architecture, thus, is different from nature, but it is also very like nature. From that paradox it draws its power.

No matter how difficult a project is, and in engineering terms the Sydney Opera House does seem to have been quite difficult, the success of architecture rests on something essentially simple. It draws its power from the subtle elegant geometries of nature that all human beings understand intuitively at a glance.

Most architecture, in the end, is a failure. It fails because it cannot outlive the era in which it was built. It cannot do that because it draws its meaning, and thus its power, from the signifiers, the meaningful symbols, the styles, of the day. Most architects cannot resist trends. They are no different from novelists, painters, film makers, journalists, and academics. They are all the same. They love the surge of importance that comes with saying and doing in the dominant style of the times. The illusion is only compounded when the dominant style fancies itself to be subversive or transgressive. But even if every single contemporary says that what has been done is important, style still cannot create works of importance.

There are only ever a handful of such works. They transcend the conventions of their time. Utzon created one of those rare works. That granted him immortality. His work will outlive him. Most works die with their creators. They fade from memory. They become neglected, forgotten, weathered, chipped, and eventually will be torn down or, worse still, stored in some dark archive as an embarrassing relic of the bad taste of the period.

Hundreds of thousands of Australians visit the Sydney Opera House each year. Some come to see productions staged there. Many more come to visit Utzon's creation. It is now one of Australia's most sacred places. It is not a temple or a church. It has none of the trappings of institutional religion. It is not even a work of romantic aesthetic religion. Rather it is an artifact of Australian civil religion. It is one of the places where Australians come to think about who they are. The Australian War Memorials in Canberra, Melbourne and Sydney play a similar role in the national psyche. These are places where Australians can ask themselves the question 'what kind of people are we?'

Of all of Australia's sacred artifices, the greatest is the Opera House. It is the Australian Parthenon. But, significantly, it is *not* located high up on a hill, on an acropolis, but rather on the edge of a great harbour on Australia's east coast. It sits like a white trireme, eternally ready to sail into the distance.

For the most part, the nationality of an architect does not matter much. But in Utzon's case, nationality is significant, for he brought from Denmark to Australia something that Australians understand very well and take very seriously. This is an architecture inspired by the watery margin of a society by the sea. This has a great significance for Australians. To understand what the Opera House means to Australians is also to understand that its architect was a Dane, and that he grew up at the very far west reach of the Baltic—a child with a love of sailing who was raised in a naval architect's home.

Australia is a littoral society. Most of its population is concentrated in large cities on its coastal circumference. Almost from its beginning Australia has been one of the most urbanised societies in the world. While Australians have always enjoyed romantic stories about their thinly populated continental interior, these have had little practical impact on the urbanised maritime Australian form of life. By the 1990s, four out of five Australians lived in cities, one in four of the population lived within fifteen minutes drive of the coast, and population growth was almost entirely confined to urban coastal corridors.

Because Australia always had a strong urban bias, it was also by default a society that heavily invested in science and technology—what today we call a knowledge society. This is a pattern that we find widely repeated among littoral, island, archipelago, and peninsular societies across the world—from the British Isles and Ireland to the Coasts and Great Lakes of America, from maritime East Asia to the Baltic and the Mediterranean. These societies—along with their riverine cousins such as Baden-Würtenberg at the triangular intersection of the Rhine and Danube rivers—have been the world-historic centres for the development of economies based on the arts and sciences.[11]

In part this is because these places become nodes for the regional and global trafficking of goods, persons and information. But, in equal part, this is also because these are places that manage, at the same time, to create strong identities which anchor the flows that occur in and out of them. This is the enigma of portal cities and littoral societies. They combine qualities of flow and fixture, liquidity and plasticity, change and stability, fashion and civilisation in equal measure. They are dynamic and impassive, local and global, open and bounded. Their strength follows from this paradoxical mix of things. Successful portal societies embody powerful incongruities that they effortlessly unite into a seamless whole.

That also explains the success of their arts and sciences. For great arts and sciences are founded on powerful paradoxical enigmas like the unmoved mover, space-time, the wave-particle, learned ignorance. From Aristotle to Eisenstein, Heisenberg to Socrates, this has been true. Knowledge at its deepest vein is structured like a parable of Kierkegaard. It is a brilliant conjunction of opposites, a mesmerising union of contraries.

---

[11] Peter Murphy, 'The Art of Systems: The Cognitive-Aesthetic Culture of Portal Cities and the Development of Meta-Cultural Advanced Knowledge Economies' in David J Pauleen (ed.) *Cross-Cultural Perspectives on Knowledge Management* (Westport, CT: Greenwood, 2007), pp 35–63; 'Social Phusis and the Pattern of Creation', *Budhi: A Journal of Culture and Ideas* IX: 1 (Manila: Ateneo de Manila University, 2005), pp 39–74. On the American case, see Peter Murphy, 'American Civilization', *Thesis Eleven: Critical Theory and Historical Sociology* 81 (London: Sage, 2006), pp. 64–92. The Australian case is examined in Peter Murphy, 'Sealanes' in P Beilharz and T Hogan (eds) *Sociology—Place, Time and Division* (Melbourne: Oxford University Press, 2006), pp. 38–44.

The arts and sciences always concentrate. They cluster in a relatively small handful of places. One of the most common places is the portal city. This is because, being where they are, by the sea, and doing what they do—trading and trafficking—portal cities encourage the kind of boundary crossing and cross fertilising that is one of the conditions of knowledge formation. But, and this is an important qualification, the flow in and out of portal cities is not the only key condition of a knowledge society. For as well as being cities that live from flow, the most successful of these cities embody the very antithesis of this. They are great plastic entities.

Sydney is both. It has powerful flows in and out. But it also has an equally powerful identity embodied in a distinctive plastic form. We see this paradox perfectly captured in the Sydney Opera House. It is sited by the sea. It is the emblematic sailing ship—the signature of movement in and out of the portal. Yet it is also a great impassive plastic creation. Utzon's building is a sculpture. Meditating on Bennelong Point with a genius' eye for potential, Utzon observed that 'this peninsula popping out in a harbour would mean that it would be looked upon from all sides'. Or as ancient Judaism held: *God sees from all sides.*

This is the essence of the portal. Its architecture signifies not just flow, the in and out of global traffic, but also the circular motion of circumnavigating the unmoved mover represented by the divine sculpture, the temple of the gods—that is, the fixed point of flow, the impassive anchor of activity, the sign of a cosmic necessity at the centre of the world of freedom and contingency.[12] This is the necessity that endows human contingency with meaning. It is nature's geometry. This geometry, elevated or translated into architectural sculpture, is what gives the Sydney Opera House—like the Parthenon—its enigmatic iconic power as an inexhaustible source of meaning.

AUSTRALIA'S DREAMING IMAGINATION

Utzon designed his masterpiece using the sparse simplicity of Euclidean geometry. He simply sliced up a sphere. The result was a near perfect Platonic form—resistant to time and fashion. Utzon in the end was hounded out of Australia in a frenzy of political backbiting and devious ambition. But the

[12] For a further discussion of this, see Peter Murphy, 'Marine Reason', *Thesis Eleven* 67 (London: Sage, 2001), pp 11–38.

raucous bunch of politicians and jealous professional peers who caused Utzon to be removed still allowed Utzon's creation to stand. They envied it, they feared it, they wanted to shine in its light, but above all they could not, and did not, destroy it.

Utzon's creation is an example of immortal architecture. There are not many such examples. It is a creation that echoes the design of the cosmos. Utzon's fellow Dane, Kierkegaard, would have understood why this was so. In its absolute fidelity to things, Utzon's creation escapes the deadweight of moralism and the kinds of sentimental hand wringing and dry appeals to duty that so often pass for civics, citizenship, and religion. By the sea, close in spirit to the cosmos, its simple geometry and its graceful sails are a representation of a tremendous Heraclitean necessity—an order beyond law that is by turns pleasing, beautiful, demanding, exacting, buoyant, and terrible. This is an order for which sacrifices are made. It is an order of things beyond calculation, will, or choice. It just *is*. This great order can make us better than we are. It can move us to do more than we would otherwise do. It can lead us up, out of everyday life and care, into the dreaming domain of the imagination.

This dreaming imagination begins its work on the beach—the hospitable strip between the infinity of the ocean and the empty expanses of an island continent. The children playing at the far end of the beach in Max Dupain's classic 1940 photograph *The thin man* are the imagination's apprentices. Some will become masters of making, shaping and creating. Others will grow up simply enjoying the fruits of that creation. A small number will do what Dupain himself does in *The thin man*. They will summon up the abstract forms of a beach civilisation. The same curvilinear geometries that Utzon employs echo through Dupain's image—the curve of the seashore and the contrasting arc of footprints in the sand. This is the social physics of a world where two straight lines on the surface of curved space can enclose an area. In such space, margins converge to make a centre, and the centre is always on the periphery.

In this world, children grow up playing on the beach, speculating about patterns in the sand. These speculations are the first inklings of art and science—and the greater human puzzlement about the pattern of creation. Eventually these children morph into adults like the one in Dupain's *Bondi sand patterns with figure*—a purposeful strider, marching erect across the beach, thoughtful, immersed in creation, surrounded by its larger force, relaxed in its embrace, not cowed by it but also quietly aware that in the lengthening shadows of the late afternoon light a storm may be brewing that will tear up creation's rippled sand pattern only to have tomorrow's placid nature remake it once more.

LIQUID STONE

The beach—the meeting point of the land and the sea—is the most enduring aspect of the Australian demotic sense of the sacred. The beach is a paradox—both earth and water, the place simultaneously of family obligation and hedonistic escape, noisy abandonment and quiet musing. The beach is the everyday sacred place of Australians. It is beloved in a way that only sacred things are—the object of an endless ritual, the eternal return of Australians each year to the same places and the same patterns of behaviour: the building of castles in the sand and letting the sea swallow them up. This is not pantheism or a religion of nature, but enchantment with the enigmatic double—the mysterious thing that embodies its opposite. It is this that human beings find a cause of reverence. In the shadow of such things, human beings find a place to quietly dwell, for a moment, in awe of eternity.

The rituals of the beach begin with the fascination with a paradoxical place. This fascination draws people back. They return eternally. It is paradox, though, that explains the fascination in the first instance. Paradox is the driving force of the sacred, and the sacred is what is left of religion in the aftermath of the tidal wave of modernity. Modernity makes societies secular. Yet in doing so, it does not necessarily diminish their interest in the sacred. It may transform this interest, and reshape it, but it does not obliterate it. Indeed in modernity it is often the most secular societies that retain at their core the greatest sense of the sacred, while traditional religious societies are tempted by sacrilegious acts in the name of religion. That we should find the sacred amidst the secular is merely the zenith of other paradoxes of the sacred that we have already encountered. This reminds us of the centre that is a margin—or the still-point that sets in motion tumultuous flows.

The stillness that abides at the heart of motion—the unmoved mover—is perhaps the most common way in which the sacred is experienced in everyday life. Sacred space is the place where those who are born in time can step, momentarily, out of time. Whether we call this intuition of being 'out of time' eternity, immortality, mystery, transcendence, the uncanny or the enigmatic, it remains an indubitable part of the human experience. The sacred invariably evokes the sense of some kind of sanctuary from time and motion. In modernity, the sacred place is the quiet place of thinking that exists amid the pandemonium of the metropolis. The great sacred building marks out a space of quiet. It is the quiet of sanctuary. This is not just calm *per se* but the calm in the eye of the storm. The person who is on the run from danger finds sanctuary in the place that is sacred. This is the sheltering canopy where the heart no longer has to beat urgently in fear and anxiety. The sacred sanctuary releases us, for a time, from the temporal sense of mortality—a sense that danger always heightens.

In Christian societies, the primal emblem of that sanctuary was the medieval cathedral. The cathedral was surrounded by the market—and yet separate from its urgency and mutability. It was a place of quiet and contemplation amid the human hubbub. As European societies underwent the painful process of modernisation, the primacy of the church as a place of sanctuary diminished. Other more secular symbols of sanctuary emerged. In the eighteenth and nineteenth centuries we see the appearance of the garden retreat in the city square, and later the landscape park in the midst of the great metropolis. The urban pastoral of industrial society—no less than the Norman church set among the green fields of the old English agrarian society—represented the paradoxical desire of mobile and animated human beings for immobility and tranquility.[13]

Religion of a traditional church kind provided a rich palette for describing, representing and embodying sacred calm amid profane agitation. Modern tourists still trek endlessly to old church yards to catch a whiff of this enchanted peace. But those who live in thoroughly modern societies have also invented their own ways of describing, representing and embodying the paradox of the sacred. The work of another of Kierkegaard's countrymen, the great Danish painter Wilhelm Hammershøi (1864–1916), exemplifies this exactly. Hammershøi was a master of portraying the uncanny stillness at the heart of a world in motion. We look at his paintings and recognise scenes of modern urbanity. But these scenes have been translated by the painter into symbols of an almost perfect metaphysical stillness. Giorgio De Chirico did something similar. In Hammershøi's case, a metaphysical light penetrates the windows of the city apartments that he repeatedly depicted. He bathed these

---

[13] The paradox is personified in the character of Stan Parker in Patrick White's 1955 novel *Tree of Man*.

interior scenes in the lucid stillness of light—the universal constant of Einstein and the symbol of the divine of the Neoplatonists. When we look at Hammershøi's paintings we understand Einstein's conclusion that the faster you travel, the more time slows down. In Hammershøi's art, the speed of light begets stillness.

The mystical characters of Patrick White's great novels represent a parallel uncanny quality—in White's case, the rising of silence out of sound.[14] White's Australian characters personify the emergence of mute intuition out of breathless reason. White writes what cannot be written, and makes explicit what can only ever be tacit—which means that his words become something else altogether. As Wittgenstein observed—about those things that are important, we cannot speak. What we do, rather, is to depict them. We use language to paint pictures.[15] White paints pictures, and what he depicts—the intuitive and the mystical—are the characteristic media of the sacred.[16] In White's novels—the speculum of the Australian mind—speech and reason, always in a hurry, tire and turn into the subdued garden of silent metaphysical thought.

Reverence and awe—the feelings of the sacred—quiet us. We speak, if at all, in hushed tones in the presence of sacred things. This rule of silence applies to religious commandments as much as it does to anything else. No institutional religion, no religious law, no codes, no catechism, no interdictions—this is what becomes of religion in modernity. Religion thereby is stripped down to its sacred core. If this does not happen, then religion tends to mutate into violent reaction. This never happened in Australia, the most tranquil of societies. Instead religion simply shed its institutional clothes. This

[14] Mary Hare, Alf Dubbo, Mordecai Himmelfarb, and Ruth Godbold in *Riders in the Chariot* (1961); Arthur Brown in *The Solid Mandala* (1966).

[15] On the nature of Wittgenstein's paradoxical and mystical picture language, see Peter Murphy and David Roberts, *Dialectic of Romanticism: A Critique of Modernism* (London: Continuum, 2004).

[16] White's life-long interest in painting and painters is discussed in Helen Verity Hewitt, *Patrick White, Painter Manque: Painters, Paintings, and Their Influence on His Writing* (Parkville: Melbourne University Press, 2003). If White considered the medium of paint to be more direct, more powerful than words, and if he experimented in his writing with replicating painterly effects, he was also sensitive to the fact that the medium of painting itself was torn between surface and depth. White's life companion Manoly Lascaris described the tension this way: '… At the end of his life he became a Pythagorean! He rejected the Orphic enchantment with surfaces and colours which had earlier fascinated him, and took on the whirlwind of abstract geometries …' Vrasidas Karalis, *Recollections of Mr Manoly Lascaris* (Blackheath: Brandl & Schlesinger, 2008), p. 58.

means that hardly anyone anymore goes to church. The pews are deserted. But this did not represent the end of the sacred—quite the contrary. Patrick White despised the Church of England of his Australian upbringing.[17] Kierkegaard spent his adult life at war with the state church of Denmark. Yet both had an exquisite feeling for the sacred.

Kierkegaard observed how, in modernity, aesthetic life competes with duties sanctioned by the old institutional religion. Bohemians poke fun at the pious bourgeoisie.[18] Yet Kierkegaard rightly resisted the Romantic inference from this that art was somehow a new religion. It wasn't—though great art did prove in practice more able to represent the sacred than the old theologians. Paintings by Mark Rothko or Arthur Boyd convey a much more powerful sense of the sacred than any twentieth-century theology could. This is because great art convincingly depicts the impossible union of a 'full time' or an 'end time', the resurrection of the dead or a humanised god. It convincingly evokes stillness in an unstable world. What, after all, is a classic work of art—like the Parthenon marbles—but a contradiction in terms: liquid stone, sculptural stone that, to the eye, is animated and alive?

The art of the sacred is not the celebration of the ego of the artist—or even of the creativity of the artist. Rather it is a representation of the paradox of creation—of the impossibility that underlies the possibility of the act of creation. Art does not ask us to *believe* in the absurd or the mysterious. Art simply *depicts* what intrigues us: enigmatic images of fixity in flux, constancy in change, and the solidity of a world that melts before our eyes.

As Kierkegaard shrewdly observed, some of the best stories of this impossibility are the parables of Christianity—stories of lambs and lions, lost

---

[17] 'It was begun during the last of our eighteen years at Castle Hill. The painter Lawrence Daws had given me Jung's Psychology and Alchemy, which had a great influence on me. It projected me into my Solid Mandala. Jung's teaching also bolstered me up during a wavering of faith on realising I could not accept the sterility, the vulgarity, in many cases the bigotry of the Christian churches in Australia. Manoly [Lascaris, White's partner] seemed secure inside the structure of Eastern Orthodoxy. I had nothing from my upbringing in a kind of social C. of E. (a visiting card on the pew, clothes outgrown or no longer fashionable sent off to the jumble sale, a grateful rector and his wife calling to express gratitude for patronage.) So I evolved what I think Manoly has always seen as my non-religious or mystic circus.' Patrick White, *Flaws in the Glass: A Self Portrait* (London: Jonathan Cape, 1981), p. 146.

[18] A tireless proponent of Australian bohemia against the purportedly pious and philistine bourgeoisie was the artist Norman Lindsay (1879–1969).

sheep, mustard seeds and fig trees, each with their paradoxical twists.[19] Great artists, like Utzon and White, create works out of paradox. The French Jewish Catholic mystic Simone Weil, a particular favourite of White's, called these paradoxes 'unions of opposites'.[20] Weil drew examples of these from both Christianity and the Greek Presocratics.[21] White also dabbled with the image of the Hindu and Buddhist Mandala—and with allusions to the Jewish Kabbalah.[22]

At the heart of all of these experiments in thought lies the double nature of creation. The characters that Patrick White created spoke of speechless intuitions and possessed hermaphrodite-like identities.[23] Such dazzling two-in-ones—enigmatic unions of oppositions: male and female, colonial and metropolitan, bourgeois and bohemian—animate creation. All creation is an analogy: the representation of one thing by another thing. In mimesis we create one thing in the medium of something else. Thus the interior of the Gothic church represents the primal forest in stone—just as Utzon represented the sea-side shells of his childhood in tiles. To the viewer, these tiled shells look like the sails of a ship billowing in the wind. This is the double nature of creation, the paradox of liquid stone: the sculpture that seems alive—the sacred enigma that elicits eternal fascination.

An earlier version of this article was delivered as a paper at the Royal Academy of Fine Arts, School of Architecture, Copenhagen, in April 2007. Thanks to Henrik Oxvig and Anders Michelsen who extended the invitation.

WORKS CITED

John Carroll, *The Existential Jesus,* Melbourne: Scribe, 2007.

Philip Drew, *The Masterpiece: Jørn Utzon A Secret Life,* Melbourne: Hardie Grant, 1999.

[19] Thomas C Oden (ed.) *Parables of Kierkegaard* (Princeton, NJ: Princeton University Press, 1978).

[20] On the philosophical history of the 'union of opposites', see Peter Murphy, *Civic Justice: From Ancient Greece to the Modern World* (Amherst, NY: Humanity Books, 2001).

[21] Simone Weil, *Intimations of Christianity among the Ancient Greeks* (London: Routledge, 1957); *The Notebooks of Simone Weil* (London: Routledge & Kegan Paul, 1956).

[22] *The Solid Mandala* (1966), *Riders in the Chariot* (1961).

[23] Most memorably, the characters of Mordecai Himmelfarb in *Riders in the Chariot* (1961) and Eudoxia/Eddie/Eadith in *The Twyborn Affair* (1979).

Philip Drew, *Sydney Opera House Jørn Utzon,* London: Phaidon, 1995.

Max Dupain & Morton Herman, *Georgian Architecture in Australia,* Sydney: U. Smith, 1963.

Max Dupain & Rex Dupain, *Inside Sydney,* Frenchs Forest, NSW: New Holland Publishers, 2004.

Max Dupain, *Beaches,* Sydney: Chapter & Verse, 2000.

Helen Verity Hewitt, *Patrick White, Painter Manque: Painters, Paintings, and Their Influence on His Writing,* Parkville: Melbourne University Press, 2003.

Vrasidas Karalis, *Recollections of Mr Manoly Lascaris,* Blackheath: Brandl & Schlesinger, 2008.

Peter Murphy, 'The Art of Systems: The Cognitive-Aesthetic Culture of Portal Cities and the Development of Meta-Cultural Advanced Knowledge Economies' in David J Pauleen (ed.) *Cross-Cultural Perspectives on Knowledge Management,* Westport, CT: Greenwood, 2007.

Peter Murphy, 'American Civilization', *Thesis Eleven: Critical Theory and Historical Sociology* 81, London: Sage, 2006, pp. 64–92.

Peter Murphy, 'Sealanes' in P Beilharz and T Hogan (eds) *Sociology Place, Time and Division,* Melbourne: Oxford University Press, 2006.

Peter Murphy, 'Social Phusis and the Pattern of Creation', *Budhi: A Journal of Culture and Ideas* IX: 1, Manila: Ateneo de Manila University, 2005, pp. 39–74.

Peter Murphy and David Roberts, *Dialectic of Romanticism: A Critique of Modernism,* London: Continuum, 2004.

Peter Murphy, 'Marine Reason', *Thesis Eleven* 67, London: Sage, 2001, pp. 11–38.

Thomas C Oden (ed.) *Parables of Kierkegaard,* Princeton, NJ: Princeton University Press, 1978.

Simone Weil, *Intimations of Christianity among the Ancient Greeks,* London: Routledge, 1957.

Simone Weil, *The Notebooks of Simone Weil,* London: Routledge & Kegan Paul, 1956.

Patrick White, *Tree of Man,* New York: Viking Press, 1955.

Patrick White, *Riders in the chariot,* London: Eyre & Spottiswoode, 1961.

Patrick White, *The solid mandala,* New York: Viking Press, 1966.

Patrick White, *The Twyborn affair,* London: Cape, 1979.

Patrick White, *Flaws in the Glass: A Self Portrait,* London: Jonathan Cape, 1981.

Contributors

BILL ASHCROFT is Professor of English and former Head of School of English, Media and Performing Arts at the University of New South Wales. He is the author and co-author of several books on post-colonial theory, including *The Empire Writes Back* (Routledge, 1989) and *Post-Colonial Transformation* (Routledge, 2000). He was appointed as Chair Professor in English at the University of Hong Kong for a three-year period from 2006.

DEBORAH BIRD ROSE is a Senior Fellow in the newly established Fenner School of Environment and Society at The Australian National University, and a Fellow of the Academy of Social Sciences in Australia. She writes widely in the fields of anthropology, history, philosophy, and religious studies. Her recent book *Reports from a Wild Country: Ethics for Decolonisation* (UNSW Press, 2004) was shortlisted for the NSW Premier's Awards.

PETER BOYLE is one of Australia's leading poets. His first three collections of poetry *Coming Home from the World* (1994), *The Blue Cloud of Crying* (1997), and *What the Painter Saw in Our Faces* (2001) have received several awards including the New South Wales Premier's Award, the South Australian Festival award and the National Book Council Award.

JOHN BRADLEY is a senior lecturer in Anthropology and Deputy Director of the Centre for Australian Indigenous Studies at Monash University. He has worked with the Yanyuwa people of the south west Gulf of Carpentaria for the last three decades. His research interests are in the use of memory and song in creating a sense of belong to place; he is also interested in issues of knowledge production and relationship between western and indigenous forms of knowledge.

MARK BRETT teaches at Whitley College, Melbourne, and his interdisciplinary research traverses Hebrew Bible, social theory and postcolonial studies. He is author of *Biblical Criticism in Crisis* (Cambridge University Press, 1991), *Genesis: Procreation and the Politics of Identity* (Routledge, 2000), *Decolonizing God: The Bible in the Tides of Empire* (Sheffield Phoenix, 2008) and editor of *Ethnicity and the Bible* (EJ Brill, 1996 / 2002). He is also the Policy Officer at Native Title Services Victoria.

FRANCES DEVLIN-GLASS is Honorary Associate Professor in Literary Studies at Deakin University. She has co-edited with Lyn McCredden *A Feminist Poetics of the Sacred: Creative Suspicions* (OUP, New York, 2001) and is the annotator of Joseph Furphy's *Such is Life* and *The Buln-buln and the Brolga* (both published by Halstead Press). She has worked for the last decade with Yanyuwa people (Northern Territory) on issues to do with the preservation of their culture.

JOHN DOCKER is adjunct senior fellow in the Research School of Humanities, Australian National University. Since the publication of *1492: The Poetics of Diaspora* (2001), he has researched and written on monotheism and polytheism, and on genocide in relation to the Enlightenment and to colonialism. With Ann Curthoys, he published *Is History Fiction?* (2005).

GEOFF CHEONG is a priest in the Anglican Parish of Holy Trinity, Balaclava and Elwood, Diocese of Melbourne.

DENNIS HASKELL is Professor at the School of English and Cultural Studies at the University of Western Australia. He has authored 17 books that include *Listening At Night*, a collection of poems (Angus and Robertson, Sydney, 1984); *Kenneth Slessor: Poetry, Essays, War Dispatches, War Diaries, Journalism, Autobiographical Material And Letters* (University of Queensland Press, St Lucia, 1991).

SUDHIR KUMAR is a Professor of English at Panjab University Chandigarh. The author of many academic papers on postcolonial literatures and theories, his forthcoming books include *Nation-in-Katha: A Study of Muslim Writers* and *Mahatma Gandhi* in the Makers of Indian Literature series. Recently Prof. Kumar delivered extension lectures as a Visiting Scholar on 'Gandhi and Literary Theory Today' at the School of Oriental and Asian Studies, University of London.

ANNE MARSH is Professor, Theory of Art & Design and Associate Dean Research in Art & Design at Monash University. Anne's research areas include: photography, performance art, feminism, postmodernism and psychoanalysis. Her book *Body and Self: Performance Art in Australia, 1969–1992* (Oxford University Press, 1993) is a major contribution to the field.

FREYA MATHEWS is Associate Professor in the Philosophy Program at La Trobe University where she teaches ecological philosophy, co-ordinates the Environmental

Enquiry major, and co-edits the journal, *PAN* (Philosophy Activism Nature). Her writing is mainly focused on ecological philosophy but includes questions of metaphysics, epistemology, ethics and politics as well as a variety of themes, such as cosmology, place, identity and indigeneity versus modernity.

PETER MURPHY is Associate Professor of Communications at Monash University. He has authored *Civic Justice: From Ancient Greece to the Modern World* (Humanity Books, Amherst, New York, 2001), and has co-authored *Australian Perspectives on Southeast Asia, Australia and the World* (PASN/Ateneo de Manila University, Manila, 2005) with Joel Kahn and Joseph Camilleri.

MAKARAND PARANJAPE is a critic, poet, fiction writer, and literary columnist with over thirty books, 100 published academic papers, and more than 200 reviews, notes, and popular articles to his credit. He is currently Professor of English at Jawaharlal Nehru University, New Delhi. His latest book is *Another Canon: Indian Texts and Traditions in English* (Anthem Press, forthcoming).

GRAHAM SEAL has published a number a number of works on the cultural history and mythology of Anzac and the digger, including *Inventing Anzac: The Digger and National Mythology* (UQP, 2004) and *Echoes Of Anzac: The Voice of Australians at War* (Lothian, 2005). In recent years he has researched the relationships between commemoration, memorialisation and cultural identity. He holds a personal chair as Professor of Folklore at Curtin University of Technology.

DAVID TACEY is Associate Professor and Reader in Arts at La Trobe University, where he teaches literature, spirituality and Jungian psychology. He is the author of several books on spirituality and culture, including *How to Read Jung* (London: Granta Books and New York: WW Norton, 2006), *The Idea of the Numinous: Contemporary Jungian and Psychoanalytic Perspectives* (edited with Ann Casement) London and New York: Routledge, 2006, and *ReEnchantment: The New Australian Spirituality.*

CLAUDIA TERSTAPPEN is Professor of Fine Arts at Monash University. Claudia studied German Literature and Philosophy at the Heinrich Heine University and Sculpture and Photography at the Art Academy in Düsseldorf, Germany and is now a practicing artist of more than 20 years standing with a string of international exhibitions, awards and publications to her name. Her artistic work focuses on the interrelationship between religion, superstition and science in relation to place, culture and time.